Victor Griffuelhes and French Syndicalism, 1895–1922

VICTOR GRIFFUELHES AND
FRENCH SYNDICALISM
1895–1922

BRUCE VANDERVORT

Louisiana State University Press
Baton Rouge and London

Manufactured in the United States of America
First printing
05 04 03 02 01 00 99 98 97 96   5 4 3 2 1
Designer: Michele Myatt
Typeface: Garamond
Typesetter: Impressions Book and Journal Services, Inc.
Printer and binder: Thomson–Shore, Inc.

Library of Congress Cataloging-in-Publication Data
Vandervort, Bruce.
    Victor Griffuelhes and French syndicalism, 1895–1922 / Bruce
Vandervort.
        p.   cm.
    Includes bibliographical references and index.
    ISBN 0-8071-2045-6 (cl : alk. paper)
    1. Griffuelhes, Victor.   2. Trade-unions—France—Officials and
employees—Biography.   3. Syndicalism—France—History.   I. Title.
HD6685.G75V36   1997
335'.82'092—dc20
[B]   96-16741
                                                                     CIP

Frontispiece courtesy of Institut C. G. T. d'Histoire Sociale,
Montreuil, France

To my parents, Lawrence Carl Vandervort (1915–1984) and
Leone Purdy Vandervort, with deepest gratitude

Contents

Victor Griffuelhes and French Syndicalism, 1895–1922

PREFACE

This book belongs to a venerable but lately much maligned genre, the life-and-times biography. It also betrays a fascination with a subject equally out of favor these days: labor politics. Based largely on French archival sources and printed materials of the time, *Victor Griffuelhes and French Syndicalism* takes another look at the phenomenon of French radical trade unionism in the late nineteenth and early twentieth centuries, using as its vehicle the life and career of Victor Griffuelhes, the artisan shoemaker who served as general secretary of France's largest trade-union center, the General Confederation of Labor (Confédération générale du travail, or CGT), from 1901 to 1909.

Haughty and imperious despite his humble birth, a gifted orator and propagandist, and a born organizer of strikes and demonstrations, Victor Griffuelhes was the first French labor leader of genuine working-class origins to achieve national stature. Griffuelhes' single greatest claim to the attention of his contemporaries (and of posterity) probably lies in his role as the coauthor and mover of the Charter of Amiens, the resolution adopted at the CGT Congress of Amiens in 1906 that made revolutionary syndicalism the official doctrine of the prewar CGT and that has served as the reference point for French organized labor ever since.

I have been sharing my life with the truculent M. Griffuelhes for over twenty-five years. My version of his story began its long odyssey toward print in the 1960s, in the form of a dissertation project launched under the direction of the late Professor Harvey Goldberg at the University of Wisconsin. Although my field of study and the framework within which the dissertation was conceived was called "Modern European Social History," in reality, what I and my fellow graduate students studied was the political history of the French working class, as seen from the vantage point of its representative institutions: trade unions and political movements of the Left. This focus naturally lent itself to producing dissertations on episodes in the histories of unions or political parties or on the careers of prominent working-class leaders. Biographies like my study of Victor Griffuelhes were particularly common undertakings. Indeed, the model for our scholarly endeavors was Goldberg's oppressively monumental *Life of Jean Jaurès* (Madison, 1962). This book thus was conceived in the shadow of Goldberg's *Jaurès*, and it continues to bear the imprint of the goals set for it in that far-off time: to rescue one of France's great early labor leaders from undeserved obscurity and, in the process, to shed new light on the development of French radical trade unionism in the pre-1914 era.

The present volume reflects the preoccupation of the political historians of labor in the 1960s with the strategy and tactics of trade-union leadership. In this it echoes to a great extent the concerns of the founders of French labor history, certainly the precursors, Edouard Dolléans and Maxime Leroy, but also their more or less immediate successors in the Second World War and early Cold War era, Georges Lefranc and Maurice Dommanget. Like Dolléans, an admirer of Proudhon, and Dommanget, a student of Blanqui and Vaillant, I believe that the interaction of labor leaders and militants with the economic, political, and social forces that shaped their times offers vital insights into working-class history. Like Leroy and Lefranc, I believe that the study of labor history also requires close attention to the evolution of the institutions created by workers for their defense in bad times and their advancement in good: trade unions and political movements. But this book also links forward, to take its place alongside Nicholas Papayanis' book on Alphonse Merrheim, which was an early product of Harvey Goldberg's seminar at Wisconsin and a penetrating study of the evolution of France's most prominent labor militant during the First World War era; it also aspires to kinship with one of the more eminent products of recent French scholarship in labor history: Jacques Julliard's study of Fernand Pelloutier and the origins of revolutionary syndicalism in France.[1]

Julliard's book sets out in great detail the project that informed Pelloutier's career as the progenitor of the *Bourse du Travail* movement, the nucleus of late-nineteenth-century French trade unionism. The French Bourses du Travail, or labor exchanges, were originally set up with municipal funding to

1. Nicholas Papayanis, *Alphonse Merrheim: The Emergence of Reformism in Syndicalism, 1871–1925* (Dordrecht, 1985); Jacques Julliard, *Fernand Pelloutier et les origines du syndicalisme d'action directe* (Paris, 1971).

combat the massive unemployment resulting from the Great Depression of 1873–1896; however, they soon became the headquarters of a trade-union movement dedicated to overthrowing the capitalist system. Pelloutier was concerned that the French proletariat serve an intensive apprenticeship in the great tasks that would be entrusted to it in future, when it would be obliged to take over from the bourgeoisie not only the organization and management of the economy and society, but the stewardship of French civilization itself. He thus prescribed a major educative role for the Bourses du Travail, not just in the technology of manufacturing but also in terms of a broad general culture—*la culture pour soi-meme,* as he put it. Pelloutier thought it was demeaning to limit workers' education to technical training; he saw the Bourses du Travail as a sort of modern-day equivalent of the medieval cathedral schools, but this time for the lowly among God's creatures.

Griffuelhes was also concerned with preparing workers for the day when they would inherit the earth, but unlike Pelloutier, he did not envision a long period of cultural apprenticeship. Already skilled producers, the working class would acquire the other talents required of it in the process of organizing and carrying out the crescendo of strike movements by which it was destined to wrest hegemony from the bourgeoisie. He wrote that the strike "is worth more than the contents of whole libraries; it educates, it hardens, it trains, and it creates."[2] This sentence is both a classic statement of revolutionary syndicalist tactics and a repudiation of what Griffuelhes saw as Pelloutier's "bourgeois" project of liberation through workers' education. Typically, Griffuelhes' project was a more activist undertaking: to forge a *parti du travail* (labor party) under the auspices of the CGT, a grand alliance of "workers of the mind and workers of the hand" outside the old party system, with the dual mission of destroying capitalism and overseeing the producers' commonwealth that would replace it.

Victor Griffuelhes also reflects the fascination of historians of French labor, in the 1960s and later, with the intellectual and other origins of revolutionary syndicalism. Interest in the subject was greatly stimulated by the May-June Revolution in France, whose ideology, amorphous though it was, appeared to have syndicalist antecedents. My own view has been that Annie Kriegel and Bernard Moss are correct in tracing the origins of revolutionary syndicalism to the theory and practice of the French sections of the First International in the 1860s. I thus reject the notion, less widespread today than it was in the

---

2. Victor Griffuelhes, "Romantisme révolutionnaire," *L'Action Directe,* 2nd ser., no. 15 (April 23, 1908).

early years of this century, that revolutionary syndicalism was primarily an offshoot of fin de siècle anarchism. This argument has been sustained in recent years by Christian de Goustine, Barbara Mitchell, and in more nuanced fashion, in some of the works of the late Jean Maitron.[3]

Finally, while I find his work extremely stimulating, I do not fully accept Jeremy R. Jennings' revisionist interpretation of the relationship between Georges Sorel and his coterie and the leadership of the revolutionary syndicalist CGT. I will concede that Griffuelhes and other CGT leaders had much closer ties to Sorel and his circle than has generally been recognized but remain convinced that revolutionary syndicalism shaped the thinking of Sorel and his disciple Edouard Berth, for example, much more than their ideas shaped the strategy and tactics pursued by the CGT. I maintain here that Blanquism played a more important role than either Sorelianism or anarchism in the emergence of revolutionary syndicalism as the dominant strand in pre-1914 French labor. In doing so, I am not breaking new ground. This position was asserted some time ago by Maurice Dommanget in his *Edouard Vaillant,* and has been defended in greater detail more recently in Jolyon Howorth's study of Vaillant.[4]

Although this current work has its roots in the working-class political and intellectual history of the 1960s, I completed the dissertation on which it is based in the 1980s, after a long hiatus, under the direction of Professor Lenard Berlanstein at the University of Virginia. Thus, the book also reflects to some extent the great changes that occurred in the study of labor history in the intervening decades. For example, it enters substantially into the debate launched in the 1970s over the role played by the "proletarianization" of artisans in the formation of the working class and the rise of labor movements. The opening gun in this debate was probably E. P. Thompson's magisterial *Making of the English Working Class,* which announced that the working class

3. See Annie Kriegel, "Vie et Mort de la I[re] Internationale," in *Le Pain et les Roses: Jalons pour une histoire du socialisme,* ed. Annie Kriegel (Paris, 1968); Bernard Moss, *The Origins of the French Labor Movement, 1830–1914: The Socialism of Skilled Workers* (Berkeley, 1976); Christian de Goustine, *Pouget: Les Matins noirs du syndicalisme* (Paris, 1972); and Barbara Mitchell, *The Practical Revolutionaries: A New Interpretation of the French Anarchosyndicalists* (Westport, Conn., 1987).

4. See Jeremy R. Jennings, *Georges Sorel: The Character and Development of His Thought* (New York, 1985), and *Syndicalism in France: A Study of Ideas* (New York, 1990); Maurice Dommanget, *Edouard Vaillant, un grand socialiste, 1840–1915* (Paris, 1956); and Jolyon Howorth, *Edouard Vaillant: La Création de l'unité socialiste en France: La Politique de l'action totale* (Paris, 1982).

was present at its own creation; Thompson located its beginnings in the destruction, by the process of industrialization, of England's handloom weavers in the late eighteenth and early nineteenth centuries.[5]

As far as French labor history was concerned, the high ground in the debate over the role of proletarianization was seized by Joan Scott's pathbreaking *Glassworkers of Carmaux.* Although highly untypical of its provenance and written in the teeth of considerable opposition from her mentor, Scott's book was the first product from Harvey Goldberg's 1960s workshop to reach a wider audience. She argued that the highly skilled glassblowers of Carmaux remained largely immune to unionization pressures or socialist politics so long as their hard-won skills commanded respect and a decent income; radicalization occurred only when industrial glassmaking began to make inroads on their profession.[6] Scott's insights were given broader application by Bernard Moss in his *Origins of the French Labor Movement,* which he subtitled *The Socialism of Skilled Workers.*

My own analysis of Victor Griffuelhes' experience, which was typical for many skilled workers of the period, argues for caution in applying the proletarianization thesis to the artisans of the Belle Epoque. Rather, the two main elements in the process that affected skilled workers like Griffuelhes and his artisan shoemaker comrades were falling incomes and frustrated upward mobility. The latter seems to have been especially galling to Griffuelhes, suggesting that perhaps thwarted social mobility deserves more attention as an impetus to radicalism than it has received so far.

My view of the impact of proletarianization to some extent parallels that of Jacques Rancière.[7] Griffuelhes, like Rancière's artisan "dreamers" of the 1840s, longed to escape from the world of labor, if not to write poetry or indulge in philosophical speculation, at least to make his way in the wider world of politics and labor activism. Unlike Rancière's artisans, however, Griffuelhes made no effort to idealize the artisan milieu he was leaving behind. His utopia was a world in which all producers would be machine tenders who made useful consumer items rather than luxury goods, items turned out as

5. For a wide-ranging, up-to-date survey of these changes, see Lenard Berlanstein, ed., *Rethinking Labor History* (Urbana, Ill., 1993). E. P. Thompson, *The Making of the English Working Class* (London, 1963).

6. Joan W. Scott, *The Glassworkers of Carmaux: French Craftsmen and Political Action in a Nineteenth Century City* (Cambridge, Mass., 1974).

7. See Jacques Rancière, *La Nuit des prolétaires* (Paris, 1981), and "The Myth of the Artisan: Critical Reflections on a Category of Social History," in *Work in France,* eds. Steven L. Kaplan and Cynthia J. Koepp (Ithaca, N.Y., 1986).

quickly and effortlessly as possible so as to offer the producer maximum free time to enjoy the fruits of his labors.

This study, aside from joining the discussion of Rancière's attempt to deconstruct the "myth" of the artisan, does not engage significantly in the current debate over the "linguistic turn" taken to a greater or lesser extent by today's cutting-edge practitioners of French labor history: Joan Scott, William Sewell, Donald Reid, and William Reddy, among others. Thus, my narrative has not followed Scott or Sewell in arguing for the primacy of discourse over class in the formulation of workers' politics and has not emulated Reid in decoupling working-class activism from material causation. Readers will, however, discern a partial accommodation with William Reddy's stimulating probe into the discourse of nineteenth-century liberalism, which helped me to understand better the roots of the 1903 "revolt" of textile workers in the Nord.[8] Victor Griffuelhes, who was much involved in this violent strike action, would have applauded Reddy's scorn for the relentless materialism that infused contemporary explanations of the event on both ends of the political spectrum. Ever aware of the "moral" dimension of his own authority and of the legitimacy of working-class struggle, he would have agreed with Reddy that workers of his day inhabited a world that had not yet been reduced to the parameters of the capitalist marketplace.

8. See William M. Reddy, *The Rise of Market Culture: The Textile Trade and French Society, 1750–1900* (Cambridge, Engl., 1984).

ACKNOWLEDGMENTS

In the twenty-six years that have elapsed since I first began writing about Victor Griffuelhes, I have accumulated many more debts, personal and otherwise, than I could ever acknowledge here. The assistance and encouragement of a number of persons have been invaluable to me, however, and they must be mentioned.

I have many reasons to be grateful to my friend and colleague, Dr. Blair Turner, chair of the Department of History and Politics at the Virginia Military Institute. I would like to thank Dr. Henry Bausum, the editor of *The Journal of Military History,* for his constant support and encouragement. Elizabeth Hostetter and "Sis" Davis of VMI's Preston Library have been unfailingly helpful in locating books for me through interlibrary loan.

I wish to express my deepest thanks to members of the Corcoran Department of History at the University of Virginia (UVa) who welcomed me in from the cold in 1986, especially Professor Lenard Berlanstein, my major professor, who kindly allowed me to continue with the dissertation on which this book is based, begun many years ago in a much different time and place. Professor Berlanstein patiently oversaw my labors and attempted to introduce me to the vast outpouring of research in European social history in the last two decades, most of which was unknown to me and too little of which has found its way into these pages. My thanks as well to Professor Emeritus Hans Schmitt, whose encouragement and counsel I have greatly valued, and to Professors Joe Miller and Duane Osheim, directors of graduate studies, who did so much to smooth my path through the Ph.D. program at UVa. My return to academic life was also made easier by the unstinting support and great good will of Dr. John T. O'Connor of the Department of History at the University of New Orleans.

There are many Europeans to whom I owe much, not least the scholars and archivists in Paris and Amsterdam who assisted me in researching "mon Griffuelhes." My greatest debts are to Professor Jean Maitron, the late director of the Centre d'histoire du syndicalisme; Mlle. Colette Chambelland, former *sous-directrice* of the Musée Social; Professor Jacques Julliard; Professor Claudie Weill of the Centre russe of the Ecole des Hautes Etudes; Mme. Denise Fauvel-Rouiff, *directrice* of the Institut Français d'Histoire social; and Dr. Tristan Haan, former director of the French Section of the incomparable International Institute for Social History in Amsterdam.

I am thankful to the Fulbright Scholar Program for helping to fund an unforgettable year in Paris, the French provinces, and Amsterdam in 1968–1969, where despite the many diversions of that exciting time, I did the bulk of the research on which this book is based.

I also wish to record my special thanks to two European trade unionists whose efforts on my behalf at a critical juncture in my life have given special meaning to the word *solidarity:* the late Ezio Canonica, general secretary of the Union Syndical Suisse, socialist, parliamentarian, and man of great courage; and the great labor publicist Dardis Clarke, of the Irish Transport and General Workers' Union, who used his formidable powers of persuasion to find a job for me when I desperately needed it.

I also acknowledge with sadness my great debt to two scholars and friends, the late Dr. Harvey Goldberg of the Department of History of the University of Wisconsin, and the late Dr. Georges Haupt of the Ecole des Hautes Etudes in Paris, whose premature departures have rendered our profession and our world much the poorer. It was Harvey Goldberg who, in one of the masterly missives he liked to dispatch to his graduate students from his sabbatical retreat in Paris, announced to me in December, 1967, that I would "do the Griffuelhes" (as he presumably had "done the Jaurès"). I have been doing it ever since. Georges Haupt, who replaced Harvey during his every-other-year absences in France, rendered me so many kindnesses that it pains me greatly to recall them now.

Deepest thanks go to Sarah Whalen, my copy editor, whose intelligent editing and gentle prodding have made this a much better book. I also wish to express my gratitude to the editorial team at LSU Press, whose professionalism shines through in this and every book they produce.

Finally, my thanks go to three women without whom this book literally would never have seen the light of day. My deepest thanks to Mary Egelberg Vandervort for the long hours of copying obscure documents in cold, dimly lit archives. To Ann Jablonski, my gratitude for precious insights into the First

International and Communard legacies to revolutionary syndicalism, too few of which have been included here. To my wife, Wendy Russell Vandervort, thanks are not enough. At her urging I returned to graduate school, and through her sacrifices I was able to continue. I hope she knows how grateful I am. I also hope that our children, Lucy and Nicky, know how much I regret the many times I could not be with them because of the demands of "Daddy's book."

Needless to say, none of these persons is in any way responsible for the inevitable shortcomings of this book. It has been "*mon* Griffuelhes" since the now long-ago day when Harvey Goldberg bequeathed it to me. It is done now, and I take full responsibility for it.

I

The World of
Victor Griffuelhes (1874–1899)

Being an exploited worker, I looked for ways to escape from my situation. But I came to realize that this search could only bear fruit in a continual struggle alongside others caught in the same trap as I was. So, I joined a union. . . . It was the union that gave me all my will to struggle and it was there that my ideas began to come together.
—Victor Griffuelhes, *L'Action syndicaliste*

The town of Nérac (Lot-et-Garonne) lies astride the Baise River in wooded hills some sixty miles southeast of Bordeaux. It was here, in this ancient capital of Jeanne d'Albret, queen of Navarre, and seventeenth-century stronghold of the Huguenots, that Victor Jean Griffuelhes was born on March 14, 1874.[1]

Victor was the youngest of three surviving children born to Guillaume Griffuelhes, an artisan shoemaker, and his wife Louise (née Noguès), a former household servant. The couple were married by a notary in Nérac on February 1, 1866. Their first child, a daughter named Marie-Amélie, was born June 4, 1869, and Victor's older brother, Dominique-Noguès, who would later change his name to Henri, was born on January 29, 1871. Victor grew up on the rue Puzoque at the edge of Nérac's medieval core, where most of the town's artisans and laborers lived and worked.[2]

The house in which the Griffuelhes family lived is indistinguishable from other workers' homes on the dank, cobble-stoned street: a narrow, two-story structure built of local stone and topped by the tile roof traditional to the region. Victor and his family occupied the two rooms on the top floor of the

---

1. Archives Municipales (AM), Nérac, Etat civil, 1874.
2. AM, Nérac, Etat civil, 1866, 1869, 1871.

house. At the foot of the rue Puzoque are the ruins of the riverbank tannery where Guillaume Griffuelhes and the other shoemakers of Nérac got their leather. At its other end, the rue Puzoque opens on to the town square, where Griffuelhes *père* peddled his shoes at the weekly market.

Guillaume Griffuelhes was more than just an independent craftsman, what French census takers call a *travailleur isolé*, he was also a "tramping artisan" or, as they say in the Nérac region, a *pélaroquet.* He roamed the surrounding countryside from one market day to another, pushing his wares before him in a crude wheelbarrow. In April, 1969, a childhood friend of Victor's pointed out the former Griffuelhes residence to the author and identified Guillaume as a pélaroquet, recalling that Victor once "borrowed" his father's wheelbarrow for a foray along the Baise River and got a thrashing for it.[3]

The Griffuelhes family was not native to the region; Victor's parents were mountain people of peasant stock who had come to Nérac during the years of the Second Empire. His mother, who was born in the village of Gazanc in the Hautes-Pyrénées Department some ninety miles south of Nérac, had followed the time-honored practice among her region's poor, single women of "descending to the plain" in search of work. She was thirty-five years old when she married Guillaume Griffuelhes; he was thirty-nine. Victor's father came of an even more famous wandering breed: the agricultural laborers of overpopulated Auvergne. He was born in Aurillac, the capital of the Cantal Department, where his father Joseph, described in public records as a "day laborer," appears to have settled temporarily in search of work. The ancestral home of the Griffuelhes family was the mountain village of Calvinet, some twenty miles south of Aurillac. The family name, which is quite common in the Haute-Auvergne region, means "the place where the holly grows" in the langue d'oc.[4]

Victor's mother was a fervent Catholic. She saw to it that the children were baptized at the parish church of Saint-Nicolas and, when the family could afford it, sent them to a nearby Catholic primary school.[5] This was not com-

---

3. These paragraphs could not have been written without the help of the late Jacques Héraut, who was in his nineties when I interviewed him in Nérac in April, 1969, and was probably the last surviving childhood playmate of Victor Griffuelhes. The term *pélaroquet* refers to the nearby town of Puylaroque (Tarn-et-Garonne), a center of leatherworking in the eighteenth century. Pierre Deffontaines, *Les Hommes et leurs travaux dans les pays de la moyenne Garonne* (Lille, 1932), xxxiii.

4. AM, Nérac, Etat civil, 1866; AM, Aurillac, Etat civil, 1827.

5. Victor Méric, "Victor Griffuelhes," *Les Hommes du jour*, no. 56, February 13, 1909, p. 2.

mon practice in late-nineteenth-century Nérac. The substantial bourgeois who dominated local politics through the Radical Party and the Masonic lodges, tended to be Protestant, while their peasant clients went largely un-churched. The Lot-et-Garonne was one of the regions most effectively "de-christianized" during the radical phase of the French Revolution, and the Church has not been very successful in reestablishing itself. "This is missionary country for us, just like Africa," a local priest lamented to the author in 1969. In the 1870s and 1880s, attendance at mass was often just another of the "signs" that distinguished "strangers" from the local population, not only immigrants from elsewhere in France like the Griffuelhes family, but most important, the Spanish migrant workers who inhabited the town's "little Madrid" quarter.[6]

In 1888, Victor Griffuelhes was taken from school to begin a three-year apprenticeship in the shoemaking trade under his father. Although he left no record of his reaction to this event, the shock of having to leave school and begin a life of labor at fourteen appears to have left a permanent scar on Griffuelhes' temperament. In later years, he would show a marked truculence in his relationships with certain middle-class intellectuals who dominated the French socialist movement and operated on the fringes of the CGT. Although he had plenty of ideological reasons for his differences with leading socialists, clearly Griffuelhes' envy of their educational attainments also played a part. Thus, while his doctrinal differences with Jules Guesde loomed larger than those with the more supple Jean Jaurès, the academician Jaurès most often was the target of Griffuelhes' formidable sarcasm. Griffuelhes once wrote, "Since I don't have the knowledge of a Jaurès, or the lifestyle of [wealthy socialist publicist] Gérault-Richard, or the needs of [steel and armaments magnate] Schneider, the fatherland doesn't mean the same thing to me as it does to them."[7]

Many of Griffuelhes' colleagues in the CGT expressed a similar anger and sense of loss at having been denied an education. Perhaps the most poignant example is Alphonse Merrheim, the metalworkers' leader, who tried to com-

---

Méric wrote under the pen name "Flax." My thanks to the Abbé Monjélet, curé of St. Nicolas Parish in Nérac, for allowing me to examine Victor Griffuelhes' baptismal papers, dated March 24, 1874.

6. Remark of the Abbé Louis Jouffroy, Nérac, April 8, 1969. Henri Dret, *La Chaussure* (Paris, 1927), 228; Dret was a custom shoemaker from Villeneuve-sur-Lot, the principal center of the leather industry in the Lot-et-Garonne, and a longtime associate of Griffuelhes on the executive committee of the National Leatherworkers' Federation in the pre-1914 era.

7. Victor Griffuelhes, *L'Action syndicaliste* (Paris, 1908), 38.

pensate by long hours of independent study for having to leave school at age ten.[8]

In 1891, his apprenticeship over, Victor Griffuelhes left Nérac to seek work in Bordeaux, the metropolis of the region. Although Victor Méric, in his account of Griffuelhes' early years, explains his departure as motivated by a "need for travels and adventure," he makes it clear that the young man had no regrets at leaving. "At age 17," Méric wrote, "he left his home town, never to return."[9] In fact, it appears that Victor consciously sought to suppress the memory of his youth spent in the Lot-et-Garonne. The word *Nérac* appears but once in the numerous pamphlets and articles he wrote in his lifetime.

But did Griffuelhes carry nothing with him of his early years? One legacy surely was a profound ambivalence toward his "southern" background and, by extension, toward provincial France in general. In later years, his writings contained unflattering remarks about the people of the South and their supposed frivolousness and lack of tenacity. He observed with characteristic bitterness that in the south of France "life seems sweet, easy; on the streets of its towns, one is immersed in a seemingly boundless gaiety, made to believe that a veritable paradise reigns there. . . . However, reality isn't always captured at a glance. Misery and suffering weigh heavily upon the working people of these regions, a misery and suffering made even more acute because they are . . . masked by the smile of the moment and the joy of the day."[10]

Not that Griffuelhes was less critical of the people of the North, whom he found to be dour and fatalistic. The point to be underscored here is that for young Griffuelhes and probably a great many of his fellow workers at the turn of the century, France was less a nation than a collection of regions, each with its own traditions, distinct, often antagonistic human types, and special types of industry and modes of agriculture. The unitary state theorized by Rousseau and idealized by the Jacobins and subsequent generations of bourgeois republicans was, to Griffuelhes' mind, an "artificial" construct, "shaped by the bloody hands of warriors," not the Rousseauean concept of a General Will of a sovereign people. If anything united the people inhabiting the diverse regions of this artificial creation, it was social class, not the institutions of the republic and certainly not universal manhood suffrage. The nation was not the framework that shaped workers' lives. "The life of the worker," Griffuelhes declared,

---

8. Papayanis, *Alphonse Merrheim*, 3.

9. Méric, "Victor Griffuelhes," 2.

10. Victor Griffuelhes, *Voyage révolutionnaire: Impressions d'un propagandiste* (Paris, n.d. [1910]), 5.

"is in the workshop and in his home, where he toils and where he eats."[11]

Griffuelhes' family also left Nérac during the 1890s. They settled in the Auvergnat ghetto in Aubervilliers, a Parisian suburb, where Marie-Amélie would marry in 1899.[12] Older brother Henri, meanwhile, took up residence in the apartment at 20, rue des Marais, in Paris' 10th arrondissement, that he and Victor would share for many years.

When Victor Griffuelhes arrived in Bordeaux in 1891, the city was still in the grip of the Great Depression of 1873–1896. Unemployment, which had been inflated by a 50 percent increase in the city's population between 1850 and 1870, was high everywhere, including the shoemaking trade. This would be young Griffuelhes' introduction to working life, and as Méric described it, it was a rude one: "In Bordeaux, he found work with a shoemaker. It was not an easy life. He earned little, just enough to live on. He stuck it out for a few months, then, tired of the long hours and meager pay, left Bordeaux and took to the road."[13]

Although Victor Griffuelhes' stay in Bordeaux was brief, it was nonetheless an important first step in his development as a skilled worker and a future trade-union and socialist militant. In a perceptive essay, Jean Maitron, the historian of French anarchism, argued that the main source of worker militancy in late-nineteenth-century France was not family influence or what was learned from books, but the worker's "first contact with the environment in which he would have to work. . . . After the satisfaction of his first pay check [had worn off], the young apprentice often came to feel that he was being exploited, condemned for life to miseries he had already known as a child." In Maitron's view, it was this experience that most often convinced young workers they were members of an exploited class and, in turn, brought them to the "not individual, but collective, struggle against a social order [they] perceived to be onerous and, above all, its most concrete expression, the enterprise for which [they] worked."[14]

---

11. Fédération nationale des Cuirs et Peaux (FNCP), *Compte rendu du 5ᵉ congrès national . . . Limoges . . . 1907* (Paris, 1907), 82, 86.

12. AM, Aubervilliers, Etat civil, Extrait du registre des actes de mariage, July 1, 1899.

13. Jürgen Kuczynski, *A Short History of Labour Conditions in France, 1700 to the Present Day* (London, 1946), 113; Méric, "Victor Griffuelhes," 2.

14. Jean Maitron, "La Personnalité du militant ouvrier français dans la seconde moitié du XIXᵉ siècle," *Le Mouvement social*, no. 33 (1961), 70.

Bordeaux had long been a modest center of leatherworking. In 1891, its 385 shoemaking concerns employed some 3,500 workers, 45 percent of whom worked at home. "Shoemakers ranked among the worst-off elements of the [Bordeaux] population." Part of the problem was the loss of lucrative military footwear contracts, as the government turned to cheaper sources, such as prison labor and army bootmakers.[15]

Victor Griffuelhes left Bordeaux in 1891 with few misgivings but with at least some hope the future would be kinder to him. While in Bordeaux he appears to have joined the ancient *compagnonnage,* or secret society of journeymen custom shoemakers (*cordonniers-bottiers,* or *bottiers* for short).[16] From Bordeaux, he set out on the two-year journeyman's *tour de France* required by his compagnonnage, first to Nantes, then to Blois, Tours, and finally Paris, presumably perfecting some aspect of his craft at each stop along the way.[17]

Griffuelhes must have arrived in Paris in 1893 with high expectations. He was, after all, a custom shoemaker or bottier, one of the "elite of his profession," or so a police report described striking bottiers in 1897.[18] Craft mythology supported the police assessment. The custom shoemaker usually worked at home, away from the discipline of the shop and the watchful eye of the boss. And he only made boots and shoes to order, usually for wealthy customers. But beyond that, his craft carried with it a certain social distinction that many workers in the trade still coveted. It was a genuine craft, attained only after painstaking preparation, a profession that assured status in the community. Thus, the bottier was expected to innovate, to experiment with different combinations of leather and new finishes, and to follow the styles and fashions of each successive commercial season.[19]

15. Claude Willard, *Le Mouvement socialiste en France (1893–1905): Les Guesdistes* (Paris, 1965), table, 660; Pierre Guillaume, *La Population de Bordeaux au XIXe siècle: Essai d'histoire sociale* (Paris, 1972), 43; Archives Départmentales (AD), Gironde, 1 M 474, n. 731, March 8, 1886.

16. Griffuelhes' membership in the "ardent" association of bottiers is attested by Emile Coornaert, *Les Compagnonnages de France* (Paris, 1966), 122.

17. Méric, "Victor Griffuelhes," 2.

18. Originally the term *bottier* applied strictly to craftsmen who made boots, which required more time and skill than shoemaking; later it came to refer to producers of high-quality, handsewn footwear in general. See Dret, *La Chaussure,* 27. The police report is in Archives de la Préfecture de Police (APP), B/a 1367, "Renseignements complémentaires sur la grève de la maison Costa & Cie.," August 4, 1897.

19. Henri Dret, "Enquete ouvrière sur la crise de l'apprentissage: Les Cuirs et Peaux," *Le Mouvement socialiste,* no. 197 (April 15, 1908), 247.

Paris was, in the 1890s as it had been for centuries, the capital of the quality shoe trade. If there was anywhere in France that an ambitious, highly skilled young craftsman from the provinces could expect to get ahead, aspire to become a master shoemaker, and perhaps eventually an employer, it was Paris.

These were the legends of the quality shoemaker's trade, and legends have their place in labor history. The reality of the craft as Victor Griffuelhes experienced it in the 1890s, however, bore little resemblance to these images from an earlier time. Griffuelhes did not thrive in shoemaking in Paris. "He found work with a small proprietor and settled down to it, but the conditions were the same [as before]: low pay and long hours." In 1899, only six years after arriving in the capital, Griffuelhes abandoned his profession. According to Dolléans, even though Griffuelhes stopped working on a regular basis that year, he continued to "ply the needle" when the family budget required it, "even during the year of the Congress of Amiens."[20]

There was no lack of work, however; unemployment in French shoemaking hovered around 4.5 percent from 1896 to 1901, below the national industrial average of some 7 percent for the same period. Seasonal joblessness *was* a persistent problem—shoemakers said the "good seasons" in the trade were March–June and October–December, or around 210 days a year in all. This situation would bulk larger in shoemakers' complaints as time went on.[21]

Albert Aftalion, in his contemporary survey of the clothing and allied trades (*vetement*), in which he included shoemaking, found that of the some twenty thousand shoemakers employed in the capital in 1896, around eight thousand, or just over one-third of the total, worked at home. This figure, while it may seem high, still represented something of a revolution in the profession. "Home working remained the dominant mode of production . . . during the third quarter of the nineteenth century. After 1875 and, especially, 1880, however, the workshop began to gain ground. In the last decade of the century particularly, the trend developed with remarkable speed. A profound transformation of the industry was accomplished in a relatively short time."[22]

Aftalion saw the decline of home working as evidence of a remorseless

20. Méric, "Victor Griffuelhes," 2; Edouard Dolléans, *Histoire du mouvement ouvrier* (Paris, 1939), II, 125.

21. République Française, Ministère du Commerce . . . , *Salaires et Durée du travail dans l'industrie française* (Paris, 1894–1915), I, 301; Kuczynski, *Short History of Labor Conditions in France*, 141; Fernand and Maurice Pelloutier, *La Vie ouvrière en France* (Paris, 1900), 288–89.

22. Albert Aftalion, *Le Développement de la fabrique et le travail à domicile dans les industries d'habillement* (Paris, 1906), 58 n. 1, 51.

trend toward factory production of shoes. Shoemakers themselves tended to agree with this forecast. Victor Griffuelhes, in the first speech of his CGT career, at the confederation's 1900 congress in Paris, used the example of the growth of factory production in shoemaking to underscore the urgency of union organization along industrial, as opposed to craft, lines. "The use of machines, by creating a division of labor," he reported, "has dictated that products once made by a single worker are today manufactured by several." In the old days, he said, "the shoemaker took the leather straight from the tanner and made a shoe to measure that you could walk away in. Today, because of the growing use of machinery, we have what they call a cutter, whose only job is to cut the leather, a stitcher who sews the uppers on a machine, and, finally, a specialized worker who makes the sole. Once, a single worker did all this."[23]

But, Griffuelhes added, the scale of machine production he had described was already being superseded. In some advanced shoe factories, as many as twenty-four different workers, using twenty-four different machines, were employed just to produce the sole. A year later, a Paris business publication reported that a plant operated there by the Dressoir and Prémartin Company, which had some twelve hundred workers on its payroll and was reputed to be the largest shoe manufacturer in France, employed ninety-two different specialized machine operators on each shoe it turned out.[24]

Aftalion concluded from all this that "factory production is growing at the expense of quality shoemaking, small shops, and the home worker." He was only partly right. Quality shoemaking did not decline, at least in the short term. In fact, the number of custom shoemakers employed in Paris increased between the 1890s and 1914, from some twelve hundred to around two thousand. The principal reason for this was that many manufacturers did not believe machines could produce high-quality shoes. A number of large shoe firms continued to employ artisans working at home to make handsewn, deluxe footwear. "Despite the much vaunted advances made in shoemaking machinery, manufacturers claimed that products requiring lightness and elegance were still best made by hand."[25]

23. Confédération générale du travail (CGT), *XIe Congrès national corporatif . . . Paris . . . 1900, Compte rendu* (Paris, 1900), 149, 161.

24. *Ibid.*; *L'Industrie progressive,* November 20, 1901, p. 102, quoted in Lenard Berlanstein, *The Working People of Paris, 1871–1914* (Baltimore, 1984), 85.

25. Aftalion, *Le Développement de la fabrique,* 54; Berlanstein, *Working People of Paris,* 78; Aftalion, *Le Développement de la fabrique,* 56; Berlanstein, *Working People of Paris,* 85.

The real source of the quality shoemaker's discontent was not the industrialization of the 1890s, which merely exacerbated an already unhappy situation, but the rise of a mass consumer market during the years of the Second Empire. A chicken-or-egg argument persisted over the origins of this mass market for shoes; "supply-siders" like Henri Dret believed that "the transformation of production preceded commercial organization," while opponents such as Aftalion tended to see mass production emerging in response to mass demand.[26] It seems clear that it was this development, which became full-blown by the mid 1860s, that ultimately deprived shoemakers like Griffuelhes of control over their work.

The relatively easy credit of those years favored the rise of large leather goods houses, which began to buy up small operators and bring their former employees and outworkers under contract. This meant that while skilled workers continued to work at home and to produce essentially the same range of quality footwear as before, they now did so to order, for retailers in the wealthier quarters of the city. Few, however, dealt directly with these outlets. Most worked under the arms-length but nevertheless real supervision of small masters who functioned as middlemen for the retailers. The master for whom Griffuelhes worked, for example, supplied handmade quality footwear to a large firm in the fashionable Faubourg-Saint-Honoré.[27]

When custom shoemakers became integrated into the mass consumer market, it was inevitable that they would sooner or later face competition from cheaper, machine-made imitations of their product. What this meant for such workers in the 1880s was underscored in testimony in 1884, before a Chamber of Deputies' committee investigating the causes and effects of the contemporary economic depression, by spokesmen for the elite handicraftsmen who made high-heeled or "Louis XV-style" pumps ("*chaussures en talons Louis XV*") in Paris.[28]

The witnesses, who represented the mutual aid society of their profession, told the deputies that they currently received eight francs per Louis XV shoe, which took fourteen hours to make by hand: four hours for the uppers and ten hours for the sole and heel. A pair of Louis XV shoes, they testified, sold

26. Dret, *La Chaussure*, 22; Aftalion, *Le Développement de la fabrique*, 51.

27. Georges Duveau, *La Vie ouvrière en France sous le Second Empire* (7th ed.; Paris, 1946), 415; Dret, *La Chaussure*, 29; O. Richard, "Victor Griffuelhes," *Revue de l'Agénais* (Fall/Winter 1951), 16–17.

28. Joseph Barberet, *Le Travail en France. Monographies professionnelles* (Paris, 1886–90), V, 137.

for Fr 45–50 in smart shops. In recent years, however, novelty shops had begun selling a lower-quality version of the shoe for Fr 30–32 a pair, and the department stores a cheap imitation for Fr 26.

There was pressure from employers, the spokesmen said, to force them and their fellow workers to accept lower piece rates, in order to compete with the cheaper goods. The only way that Louis XV shoemakers could continue to make a living in such circumstances, they declared, would be to increase daily output, and this could only be done by skimping on the quality of the product—a blow to their pride they found hard to accept.

The Louis XV shoemakers may have been a special case. Their product, a pump favored by clients with a powerful nostalgia for the Old Regime, was probably something of an anachronism by the 1880s. Bourgeois snobs might continue to buy a cheaper version of the shoe, but according to the artisans themselves, many traditional aristocratic clients were now buying their pumps in Brussels or London, where monarchies still ruled.[29]

That the problems faced by these "labor aristocrats" were being experienced by custom shoemakers as a whole, however, is borne out by the recollections of Henri Dret.

> To get an idea of the earnings of a bottier you have to understand the difference between what he could do and what he was expected to do. He was expected to produce veritable masterpieces. Light, solid shoes, with an impeccable finish. Of course, there are workers who are exceptionally quick, but they aren't the average. Now, and I'm speaking from experience here, let's say it takes 14 to 15 hours to make a pair of shoes. Most workers can only work efficiently for about eight hours a day. That means that the average handworker can turn out only about three pairs of shoes a week.[30]

Dret's remarks should make it clear that these shoemakers are not the type profiled in Jacques Rancière's stimulating but rather sweeping efforts to debunk the "myth" of the frustrated artisan as the quintessential nineteenth-century urban rebel. "Shoemaking was condemned as the last [least?] of the crafts," Rancière writes. "Or, rather, it was not really a craft at all: it was the occupation of concierges trying to supplement their incomes, or the appren-

---

29. *Ibid.*, 140–41.
30. Dret, *La Chaussure*, 34.

ticeship for orphans and the unfortunate; the craft most often taught in charitable institutions."[31]

Viewed in the context of the 1890s, Rancière's description may fit some marginal producers of cheap footwear; it does not fit the bottiers. Rancière is also wide of the mark when he argues it was actually the lack of a "real craft," rather than frustrated craftsmanship, that rendered shoemakers so prone to radicalism. He contends that shoemakers joined radical causes not *because of* professional ties or pride in their work, "but rather from the particular 'disponibilité' (freedom or detachment) of the workers . . . an intellectual detachment or freedom, as a result of the small intellectual and moral investment required to practice the craft. . . . And what is true for the common workers applies all the more to their leaders. These 'easy' trades were those where one was most likely to find men whose intellectual capacities and human aspirations were neither required nor satisfied in the workplace."[32]

But as Henri Dret recalled, it was not the "intellectual detachment" of their "easy" trade that drove handicraftsmen like Victor Griffuelhes to search "for ways to escape from [their] situation." Dret asked in 1908 why the number of custom shoe apprentices was declining; not, as Rancière states, because of the "small intellectual and moral investment required to practice the craft," but because, to the contrary, the handworker, low income notwithstanding, "today has to be a real artist and endowed with extraordinary patience to satisfy the boss and the clients. What is really scaring away the young is the limited reward available given the amount of time it takes to make a pair of handsewn shoes and the number of years you have to spend learning how to do it well."[33]

Rancière is on firmer ground in contending that the long "off-seasons"—what he calls the "enforced leisure"—of the shoe trade engendered discontent. By 1908, according to Dret, custom shoemakers were out of work about half the year, and during this "dead season" of three months in the summer and three in the winter, "there was constant suffering almost everywhere."[34] But seasonality had been a hallmark of the handworker's craft for a long time. What made the dead season so unbearable in the 1890s, when Victor Griffuelhes entered the trade, was the almost certain knowledge that earnings from

31. Rancière, "Myth of the Artisan," 319.
32. *Ibid.*, 319–21.
33. Dret, "Enquete ouvrière," 247.
34. Rancière, "Myth of the Artisan," 319–20; Dret, "Enquete ouvrière," 247.

the good season would fail to compensate for income lost during the months of idleness.

Although no specific data on the evolution of the handicraftsman's income in Paris in the 1890s is available, the general impression is one of stagnation, perhaps even decline. A good summary of the situation is given by Berlanstein in his *Working People of Paris:* "Assemblers and finishers in the shoe factories at the dawn of the twentieth century performed with machines only a segment of the work that domestic workers did by hand. Yet, the factory laborers earned 6.50 francs a day whereas the handicraftsmen earned at most this amount. Moreover, the factory operatives were able to advance their earnings, whereas the semi-artisans had to struggle against reductions. The use of personal skills at work put the traditional sorts of cobblers at a disadvantage with regard to earnings."[35]

Handworkers were also at a distinct disadvantage in seeking to advance professionally. Chances of becoming a master craftsman or a proprietor in the trade were becoming slim by the 1890s. Concentration of ownership in industry had progressed significantly under the Second Empire, especially in the 1860s. This compression exercised a predictably negative effect on social mobility. As Georges Duveau put it, during "the reign of Napoleon III, we are seeing the next-to-last generation of owners who rose from the people." Further, a growing number of the so-called proprietors in the leather trades of Victor Griffuelhes' time were in reality only middlemen, like the small master who supervised his work in the 10th arrondissement. Henri Dret summed up the situation: "If the worker acquires a certain professional skill, it doesn't follow that he can start dreaming about . . . becoming a proprietor in his own right. This happens less and less often with the development of modern industry, which demands a lot of capital."[36]

Albert Aftalion reported that, as a result of the "individual suffering" imposed upon the skilled handworkers, "the young are flocking to the factories." Handicraftsmen tried to fight back to protect their incomes and way of life. Even the Louis XV shoemakers, mutualists and labor aristocrats that they were, went on strike in 1882 in a bid to increase their piece rates.[37] In 1887

35. Berlanstein, *Working People of Paris,* 45–46.

36. Duveau, *La Vie ouvrière en France,* 208; Dret, "Enquete ouvrière," 250.

37. Aftalion, *Le Développement de la fabrique,* 291; a note in Archives Nationales (AN), F22 234, "Grèves en 1882," reports that the strikers won an increase in their piece rates from some employers, but another contemporary source suggests that the increase became a dead letter when employers supplying the department stores refused to apply it (République Française,

and again in 1896, Parisian custom shoemakers enrolled in a Blanquist-inspired union and attempted to organize shoemaking as a whole in order to redress their grievances. In 1897, the union struck one of the major employers in the trade, Costa and Company. Victor Griffuelhes was a member of the union at this point and possibly took part in the strike.[38]

However "trapped" Victor Griffuelhes might have felt in his situation as a custom shoemaker, he appears not to have begun his "search . . . for ways to escape" from it until some three years after his arrival in Paris. While "he already had very clear ideas on the situation facing workers in our capitalist society," Victor Méric wrote, "Griffuelhes wasn't much of an activist before he turned 21." Méric contends that young Griffuelhes made his debut as an activist during his year of compulsory military service in an infantry regiment at Lodève (Hérault) in 1895 where "the spectacle of the barracks helped . . . to reinforce his revolutionary convictions. . . . It was in uniform that he first tried his hand at propaganda, dangerous propaganda if ever there was such. He was lucky he wasn't caught."[39]

It is difficult to know how much credence to give Méric's account of Griffuelhes as a subversive in uniform. No doubt Griffuelhes held strong antimilitarist views later in life, views that went beyond the average trade unionist's dislike of the army for strikebreaking; these may indeed have originated in his reaction to the "spectacle of the barracks."

In assessing the influences that turned young Griffuelhes toward radicalism, it would be wise not to overlook the impact of the Parisian social environment he entered upon his arrival in 1893. Strolling around the neighborhood in which he lived from 1893 to 1906, one immediately notes the many institutional symbols associated with the early history of French organized labor that are clustered nearby; so many, in fact, that one is tempted to view that opening chapter as a simple neighborhood affair.

Thus, one finds in the 10th arrondissement: the Paris Bourse du Travail in the rue Chateau d'Eau; the rue Grange-aux-Belles, home of the CGT from 1906 to 1921; no. 96, quai de Jemmapes, where *La Vie Ouvrière,* the famous theoretical journal of revolutionary syndicalism, was published from 1910 to

Ministère du Commerce, Office du Travail, *Les Associations professionnelles ouvrières* [Paris, 1894–1904], II, 31).

38. APP, B/a 1367, "Renseignements complémentaires . . . Costa & Cie," August 4, 1897.

39. Méric, "Victor Griffuelhes," 2.

1914. These landmarks were a short walk from 20, rue des Marais, where Victor Griffuelhes and his brother, Henri—and after 1897, Victor's wife—would live until after Henri's death in 1906.

But other vital elements in the life of the young journeyman's neighborhood are not so evident to today's casual visitor. There is nothing, for example, to recall that the 10th arrondissement was a Communard stronghold in 1871. No monument attests to the electoral support it gave in the 1890s to the French socialist sects most consciously faithful to the Communard tradition, first the Allemanists (POSR), followers of Jean Allemane, one of the most famous of the surviving heroes of 1871, and then the Blanquists, whose leader Edouard Vaillant had been minister of education in the Communard government.

By the time Victor Griffuelhes arrived in Paris, the Allemanists were establishing an electoral base in the 10th, having won one of its four seats in the Chamber elections of 1893. Another leading POSR figure, the former Communard Eugène Faillet, was then serving as the municipal councillor from Griffuelhes' quartier, l'Hopital Saint-Louis. He and the newly elected Allemanist deputy, Arthur Groussier, remained as fixtures in the political life of the arrondissement even after they bolted the POSR in 1896 to help form a new party, the Revolutionary Communist Alliance (Alliance Communiste Révolutionnaire—ACR), which almost immediately tied itself to the coattails of the Blanquists.[40]

The political loyalty accorded these two figures by the 10th arrondissement clearly stemmed in part from their genuine plebeian credentials: Groussier was an industrial draftsman who defined himself as a workingman, and Faillet was a schoolteacher turned accountant. It could hardly have been otherwise in an area where artisans, petty bourgeois, and workers lived in the sort of

40. Jacques Rougérie, lists six different sections of the International Workingmen's Association (IWA), or First International, in the 10th arrondissement in 1870–71, making it one of the leading centers of IWA activity in the city ("L'A.I.T. et le Mouvement ouvrier à Paris pendant les événements de 1870–1871," *International Review of Social History*, XVII [1972] Pts. 1–2, pp. 22–23). On the Allemanists in the 10th, see Maurice Poujade, "Les Allemanistes à Paris (1890–1905)" (Diplome d'études supérieures [D.E.S.], Université de Paris, 1958), 23–24, 68. The emergence of the Blanquists/ACR as the major socialist sect in the 10th is covered in Arlette Marchal, "Le Mouvement blanquiste (1871–1905)" (D.E.S., Université de Paris, 1949), 128, but is treated most authoritatively in Howorth, *Edouard Vaillant*, 225–30.

rough intimacy that had been the stuff of Communard politics twenty years earlier.[41]

Faillet and Groussier also enjoyed the support of the powerful National Railwaymen's Union (SNTCF), which, with the Gare du Nord and the Gare de l'Est nearby, found it convenient to make its headquarters in the 10th. Eugène Guérard, the SNTCF's general secretary and future nemesis of Victor Griffuelhes and the CGT's revolutionary syndicalist wing, was at that time a key figure in the POSR and Griffuelhes' neighbor in the quartier l'Hôpital Saint-Louis.[42]

Victor Griffuelhes' early years in the 10th arrondissement coincided, then, with a remarkable conjuncture of events in that early "capital" of French organized labor: the establishment of a socialist beachhead in the 10th by the Allemanists; the birth there of the Alliance Communiste Révolutionnaire; and most important for our purposes, the government's use of armed force to shut down the Paris Bourse du Travail.

That blow had fallen in July, 1893, at the conclusion of a long and heated wrangle between the Paris municipal government, which paid an annual subsidy to the Bourse du Travail, and the unions who operated offices there. The city fathers, egged on by the minister of interior, who was upset by talk of a general strike that was emanating from the rue Chateau d'Eau, had insisted that the resident unions deliver the names and addresses of their officers to the police. This demand, if a bit unrealistic, was nonetheless legal; the law of 1884, which had finally given legal standing to trade unionism in France, had made such compliance part of the price of union recognition. Thus, the unions having proved recalcitrant, troops descended on the Bourse du Travail and, following a skirmish at the doors of the building, put its occupants into the street.[43]

The Bourse du Travail had served as headquarters for a number of Paris trade unions, and its closing was a severe blow. But for Victor Griffuelhes the event would come to have a special meaning. Two further armed invasions of Paris union headquarters in 1904 and 1905 convinced him that the French

41. Jean Maitron, ed., *Dictionnaire biographique du mouvement ouvrier français* (*DBMO*) (Paris, 1964—), XII, 157–60 (Faillet); 338–40 (Groussier).

42. Maurice Dommanget, *La Chevalerie du travail française, 1893–1911* (Paris, 1967), 118.

43. A useful sketch of the history of the Bourse du Travail movement can be found in Henri Dubief, ed., *Le Syndicalisme révolutionnaire* (Paris, 1969), 23–26. The authoritative account remains Fernand Pelloutier, *Histoire des Bourses du Travail* (Paris, 1902). The terms of the 1884 law are summarized in Dolléans, *Histoire du mouvement ouvrier*, II, 25.

union movement could no longer afford the luxury of allowing either government or private landlords to dictate to it. Thus, he arranged for the purchase of the building in the rue Grange-aux-Belles that served as CGT headquarters until after World War I. In 1909, his controversial handling of this transaction provided the pretext for his overthrow as CGT general secretary.

It was not the powerful Communard tradition, the electoral prowess of the Allemanists, or the military occupation of the Paris Bourse du Travail, however, that ultimately brought Victor Griffuelhes to the union movement or socialism. He never joined the POSR, despite its early strength in his arrondissement, although he did join the ACR—the rebels who bolted the Allemanists in 1896 and made the 10th an ACR stronghold. In later years, he was highly critical of the Allemanists. In his pamphlet *L'Action syndicaliste,* Griffuelhes praised the POSR for its leading role in creating a national federation of bourses du travail in 1892 and in founding the CGT in 1895. He criticized the Allemanists, however, for trying to control these organizations: "They were for the independence of [individual] unions, but they were not for the independence of the union movement." The final falling-out between Griffuelhes and the Allemanists came over their opposition to the merger of the federation of bourses du travail and the CGT in 1902. Griffuelhes charged that "because they lacked general ideas, the Allemanists failed entirely to foresee the powerful labor movement inherent in these two national organisms."

Nor was Griffuelhes overawed by the deeds of the martyred Communards, whose memory remained the touchstone of politics in the 10th. Although no stranger to the mystique of the Commune in the 1890s, Griffuelhes later came to believe that the Communard heritage hindered the French labor movement in dealing with new conditions posed by the industrialization of the French economy. He was referring to the negative impact of the Communard legacy when he wrote in a celebrated article in 1908: "The French working class continues to *see* in the past, to *reason* in the past, to *struggle* as it did in the past."[44]

If we take Griffuelhes' own testimony seriously, a more important source of his revolutionary politics lay in the rich radical traditions of the French shoemaking trade. Particularly significant for Griffuelhes was the long struggle of shoemakers and other leatherworkers to build an industrial union in the

---

44. Griffuelhes, *L'Action syndicaliste,* 5–6; Griffuelhes, "Romantisme révolutionnaire," *L'Action Directe,* 2nd ser., April 23, 1908 (reprinted in the May–June, 1908, number of *Le Mouvement socialiste,* 293–95). Griffuelhes' emphasis.

leather and hidedressing trades, a battle Griffuelhes himself was instrumental in bringing to a successful conclusion in the early years of the new century.

Griffuelhes could easily have reacted to his declining prospects as a custom shoemaker by joining the chorus of protest against machines and factory labor, lamenting the erosion of traditional skills, and calling upon France's nascent trade-union movement to take more vigorous measures to protect the crafts. Some workers, such as the elite Louis XV shoemakers, believed that a rein-vigorated craft unionism could roll back the tide of machine production. Griffuelhes, however, appears to have concluded relatively early in his working life that this strategy was retrograde and doomed to defeat. He attributed his more "forward-looking" attitude to membership of the shoemaking trade that, the Louis XV shoemaker mutualists notwithstanding, was in his view, "always open to the most advanced ideas and actions." Because "shoemaking was one of the first trades to undergo the implantation of machinery" and because trade-union "organizations did not exist when machines came along," shoe-makers had been forced to conclude that it was too late for unions now "to smooth out the [ill] effects" of mechanization. Besides, at least some shoe-makers were beginning to realize that "technical progress" held out consid-erable long-term promise for the worker.

Shoemakers, among the first French workers to experience mechanization, were also among the first to foresee its ultimate benefits, Griffuelhes believed. "While these [leatherworking] trades have suffered considerably from the in-troduction of machinery and have seen the numbers of workers drastically reduced, it is nonetheless true that they have never shown any desire to reject machinery." From its foundation in 1893, the National Leatherworkers' Fed-eration had stoutly resisted Luddism, Griffuelhes contended: "Their con-gresses, while noting the negative effects of machines, have concluded that these will disappear with the emergence of a more conscious working class, which is master of its own destiny."[45]

Griffuelhes came to see the machine, once it was "seized" by the workers, of course, as the instrument of worker emancipation from the wage system, a view he tended to attribute, not altogether accurately, to the whole of his profession.

But exaggeration aside, there was more than a little truth to Griffuelhes' assertion that shoemakers had a marked penchant for "advanced" ideas and

45. Griffuelhes, "La Fédération des Cuirs et Peaux," *Le Mouvement socialiste*, No. 200 (July 15, 1908), 28.

were among the most "enthusiastic and generous" of France's worker revolutionaries. From the revolutionary *journées* of 1792–1793 through the June Days of 1848 to Bloody Week in 1871, cobblers were in the forefront of every popular upheaval. Among the 214 identifiable artisans of the sansculotte sections and assemblies in 1793–1794, "no fewer than 41 were shoemakers." Of the 11,693 Parisians charged with "criminal acts" in the aftermath of the June Days of 1848, 416 were shoemakers, the third largest category of workers tried (after masons and joiners). And more than fifteen hundred shoemakers were sentenced by Versailles courts-martial in the wake of Bloody Week in 1871, moving historian Frank Jellinek to remark that the Commune was "curiously a cobbler's revolution."[46]

In 1896, Victor Griffuelhes joined the French Shoemakers' Labor Union (Chambre syndicale ouvrière de la Cordonnerie de la France—CSO), which appears to have been the union of choice for custom shoemakers. Founded in 1887, with branches in Paris and Lyon, it had merged with other shoemaker unions in 1891, and then resurrected itself in 1896, at the time of the reopening of the Paris Bourse du Travail.[47] According to his own testimony, this union imparted to Griffuelhes "all my will to struggle" and was where the ideas imbibed from other sources "began to come together." Thus, Griffuelhes' strong belief in industrial unionism may have come from his experience as a member of the CSO.

Griffuelhes' membership in the CSO indicates that at some point between 1893 and 1896 he had abandoned the custom shoemakers' compagnonnage. Dual affiliation would have been impossible, since the two organizations differed profoundly in ideology—the compagnonnages were bastions of mutualism and the gospel of self-help—and competed with each other for members. In addition, the sunset of these venerable secret societies, with their archaic rituals and traditions (*e.g.,* celibacy), was fast approaching. Even the editor of the movement's bulletin, *L'Union compagnonnique,* had to admit

46. *Ibid.*; Gwynn Williams, *Artisans & Sans-Culottes: Popular Movements in France and England During the French Revolution* (New York, 1967), 21; George Rudé, *The Crowd in History, 1730–1848* (New York, 1964), 175; Frank Jellinek, *The Paris Commune of 1871* (2nd ed.; New York, 1961), 381.

47. Office du Travail, *Associations professionnelles,* II, 38, 225–28.

that by the 1890s, "the *compagnonnage* is seen as an absurdity, even by its own members. Workers in the big cities consider it outmoded and laugh at it."[48]

Membership in the CSO also helps to explain Griffuelhes' early, vigorous opposition to the Government of Republican Defense, formed in 1899 by Premier René Waldeck-Rousseau to liquidate the Dreyfus Affair. Griffuelhes' ultimately successful battle to deny trade-union support to the Waldeck-Rousseau government's ambitious welfare-state program, perhaps more than anything else, propelled him into the leadership of the CGT. The CSO was one of a small number of unions that never accepted the law of 1884 legalizing trade unions, whose authorship had been Waldeck-Rousseau's first claim to fame. The CSO's rebirth on March 1, 1896, was motivated largely by anger at the law's acceptance by the unions with which the CSO had merged in 1891. Authorities had ruled that unions rejecting the Waldeck-Rousseau law would be barred from the Paris Bourse du Travail when it reopened in 1896.[49] At issue was the law's requirement that unions turn over to the police copies of their statutes and the names of their officers, but the CSO's opposition went beyond resentment at police surveillance, as Griffuelhes would later explain.

The law of 1884, he wrote, "sought to regulate the right to organize unions, to give them a narrow character and a limited role, and thus to paralyze them.... The law allows unions to do exactly what the government wants them to do and nothing else.... [By] establishing a legal framework like this, the bourgeoisie has created ... a dike to protect it against the workers' struggles."[50] For Griffuelhes and his CSO colleagues, the Government of Republican Defense was a continuation of Waldeck-Rousseau's attempt fifteen years before to confine the working-class movement within a legal framework conducive to "social peace."

The union probably also served as his entrée into the Blanquist wing of the French socialist movement. For workers like shoemakers, in transit from artisan to proletarian status, Blanquism possessed an especially potent appeal. Although it had become a full-fledged electoral party by the 1890s, with deputies in the Chamber and representatives on municipal councils, the Blanquist party, more than any other leftist political formation of the period, retained an aura of the revolutionary past. Its official title until 1898, the Revolutionary Central Committee (Comité révolutionnaire central—CRC), evoked mem-

---

48. Coornaert, *Les Compagnonnages en France*, 126–27, 123–24.
49. Office du Travail, *Associations professionnelles*, II, 38.
50. Griffuelhes, *L'Action syndicaliste*, 46.

ories of the conspiratorial societies and clubs of 1848 and 1871, where artisan shoemaker revolutionaries had rubbed elbows with the radical bourgeoisie and déclassé intellectuals. And its leader was one of the most prestigious of the surviving Communards, Edouard Vaillant.

But the CRC, renamed the Revolutionary Socialist Party (Parti socialiste révolutionnaire—PSR) in 1898, also proved attractive to younger militants such as Victor Griffuelhes, whose main concern was not the artisan past (though that exercised a pull on them as well) but the proletarian future. For them, the Blanquist party was congenial because it was the only socialist faction of the 1890s that was supportive of industrial unionism and, even more important, of efforts to establish an autonomous national trade-union movement that sought to overthrow the wage system.

The CSO had been launched by Blanquist militants and would remain a sort of trade-union auxiliary of Blanquism throughout its history. Under the leadership of the custom shoemaker François Capjuzan and Bernard Besset, a shoemaker from Lyon, the union had from its inception taken upon itself the formidable mission of uniting all shoemakers—and eventually all other leatherworkers as well—into one national federation. In 1892, Besset and Capjuzan were instrumental in forming a National Shoemakers' Federation; although the organization itself would not survive the 1890s, it was the direct inspiration of a broader-gauge body that would—the National Leatherworkers' Federation (Fédération nationale des Cuirs et Peaux—FNCP), founded in Paris in 1893.[51] The FNCP, in turn, would find its leader in another militant of Blanquist origins, Victor Griffuelhes.

Blanquism thus played a key role in the movement for unity and industrial unionism among the shoemakers' unions and those in the leather trades in general. This was in keeping with the contribution made by the CRC in creating national trade-union organizations in France. The Blanquists played an important part in the activities of the National Trade-Union Federation (Fédération nationale des syndicats—FNS), France's first central trade-union body, founded in 1885 under the auspices of the Guesdists (Parti ouvrier français—POF), as well as in those of the National Federation of Bourses du Travail, established in 1892 in opposition to the FNS.[52]

Blanquism's major contribution to the French syndicalist movement, however, was its role in founding the CGT in 1895, and especially in converting

51. On the careers of these two militants, see especially the dossiers personnels devoted to them in APP, B/a 991; Office du Travail, *Associations professionnelles*, II, 38, 30–31, 225–28.
52. Julliard, *Fernand Pelloutier*, 120–21.

the CGT to a revolutionary posture in the first years of the twentieth century. The latter evolution would be in some measure the work of Victor Griffuelhes, fresh from an unsuccessful run for the Paris municipal council under the Blanquist banner in May, 1900.

As Jacques Julliard, France's leading expert on revolutionary syndicalism, has written: "M[aurice] Dommanget is not mistaken in calling the leader of the CRC, Edouard Vaillant, the 'grandfather' of the CGT. . . . Throughout his life, he [Vaillant] remained true to this idea [of the total independence of the trade-union movement]; and he never demanded favors in return for the services he rendered the CGT as a municipal councillor or deputy."[53]

Julliard observed that the Blanquist doctrine of the two-track path to socialism, with unions operating independently of, but hopefully not in opposition to, the socialist parties, enabled it to play a crucial role in the shoemakers' union movement and in the formation and growth of the CGT. Vaillant's party was the only one of the socialist factions of the period that took this line, as he himself remarked: "We have always held the view . . . that in the struggle of the working class against the capitalist class, trade unions and political parties have different roles, and they are distinct bodies with different functions, which become more and more sharply defined as the proletariat grows in consciousness and power. For a long time, we spoke out in vain on this subject [to colleagues on the Left]."[54]

Although Victor Méric states that Griffuelhes joined "the Blanquist party, under the influence of [Alphonse] Delacour, a former Communard," this does not seem to have been the case. Griffuelhes was close to Delacour during this period, as police reports demonstrate, but careful checking did not show the old Communard to be a Blanquist; in fact, he appears to have been a Broussist, a member of the most moderate of the socialist factions of the 1880s and 1890s.[55]

Nevertheless, Griffuelhes' relationship with Alphonse Delacour was important to his future development as a socialist and labor militant. To begin with, Delacour was the stuff of which revolutionary heroes were made in the 1890s, and it is easy to imagine the respect, even awe, he must have inspired in young Griffuelhes. Although of artisan background, Delacour had served as an officer in the National Guard that defended the Commune in 1871. Twice cited for bravery, he was lying wounded when captured by Versailles

53. *Ibid.*, 130.
54. Dommanget, *Edouard Vaillant*, 459.
55. Méric, "Victor Griffuelhes," 2; APP, B/a 1028, Delacour dossier personnel.

soldiers during Bloody Week. His service to the Commune and his reputation as a "Red" during the 1860s subsequently earned Delacour a life sentence at hard labor on the Pacific island of New Caledonia. He was amnestied in 1879.[56]

Born in the Seine-et-Marne Department east of Paris in 1829, Delacour was nearly seventy years old when Griffuelhes met him. A contemporary police report describes the old militant: "Height 1m 60 [5'3"], white hair and beard, thinnish face; wears a black three-piece suit topped by a black derby." Although Delacour was working as a millinery salesman when Griffuelhes knew him, he had spent most of his life as a bookbinder, a craft renowned, not surprisingly, for its autodidacts. A self-taught student of socialism and contributor to the *Revue socialiste* edited in the 1880s by his friend, Benoit Malon, Delacour in 1893 had helped set up a small "socialist library" in the 6th arrondissement, his home from the 1860s until his death in 1904.[57]

Did Victor Griffuelhes make his way to Delacour's library at some point in his search for ways out of his situation? While plausible, a possible bookish bent on his part contradicts one of the more durable myths about Griffuelhes. In the shoemaking trade, which is almost as well known for its self-taught members as bookbinding, Griffuelhes stands out as a man of action who had no time for reading or readers.

This myth is largely of Griffuelhes' own making. When asked by Maxime Leroy, the amateur labor historian and theorist, what impact Georges Sorel had had on revolutionary syndicalism, Griffuelhes drily replied, "I read [Alexandre] Dumas myself." Griffuelhes' quip was probably a statement of fact, as well as a put-down of the too-cerebral Leroy. Dumas was prime reading fare among workers—and not just in his native France. Dick Geary remarks in a recent essay that borrowers from workers' lending libraries in Germany didn't go for "the Marxist classics . . . but preferred vocational textbooks which improved their skills, works of evolutionary biology and above all historical fiction, with the writings of Alexandre Dumas being especially popular."[58] Griffuelhes was defensive about his own lack of formal education, especially

56. *DBMO*, II, 337 (Delacour).

57. APP, B/a 1028, Delacour dossier personnel; *DBMO*, II, 337.

58. Dolléans, *Histoire du mouvement ouvrier*, II, 127. Leroy was doing research for his book *La Coutume ouvrière* when he put the question to Griffuelhes; see his "Griffuelhes et Merrheim," *L'Homme Réel*, no. 40 (April, 1937), 10. Geary's essay, "Socialism and the German Labour Movement Before 1914," is in *Labour and Socialist Movements in Europe Before 1914*, ed. Dick Geary (Oxford, 1989), 120.

as compared with the bourgeois intellectuals and professional men of French socialism. He also defended revolutionary syndicalism as a workingman's creed against claims that it was the brainchild of this or that bourgeois theorist— Sorel or Hubert Lagardelle, Edouard Berth or even Henri Bergson—and consistently went out of his way to downplay the intellectual influences on his own development and that of the movement he led.[59] Instead, he would stress the importance of day-to-day struggle and the accumulated experience of the working class in the evolution of revolutionary syndicalism.

Although Griffuelhes probably would not have been flattered by the comparison, his articulation of the development of trade unionism closely paralleled that of his American counterpart, Samuel Gompers. In 1898, Gompers remarked that trade unions "are not the creation of any man's brain" but rather "organizations of necessity of the working class, for the working class, by the working class."[60]

Most historians of French labor have taken Griffuelhes' defensive posture at face value, as did many of his fellow trade unionists, principally Pierre Monatte.[61] A closer look at Griffuelhes' career, however, offers considerable evidence of an interest in books and reading—when he had time for them. He also was more willing to turn to outsiders, even bourgeois intellectuals, for advice and guidance than he ever revealed, including Maxime Leroy, whom he had twitted about Sorel.[62] But the first outside influence on his thought and action was the self-taught artisan, Alphonse Delacour.

As a mentor, Delacour would have lent him books and pamphlets, advised him on what newspapers to read, and offered personal insights into the history of the French labor and socialist movements. Perhaps the most valuable of these insights for Griffuelhes' later development were those that stemmed from Delacour's own experience of the trade-union movement and the Paris section of the First International in the 1860s. In 1864, along with his close friend Eugène Varlin, later one of the best-remembered martyrs of the Paris

---

59. "As for the philosophy of Syndicalism, it was rooted in the anarchism of Nietzsche, had branched out into the *élan vital* of the Bergsonians, and finally come to flower in the *Reflexions sur la Violence* of M. Sorel" (George Dangerfield, *The Strange Death of Liberal England, 1910–1914*, [4th ed.; New York, 1961], 231).

60. Quoted in U.S. labor historian John R. Commons' autobiography, *Myself* (Madison, Wisc., 1963), 87; see Leon Fink, " 'Intellectuals' vs. 'Workers': Academic Requirements and the Creation of Labor History," *American Historical Review*, XCVI (April, 1991), 410.

61. Dolléans, *Histoire du mouvement ouvrier*, II, 127. Monatte, who was a proofreader by profession, told Dolléans that Griffuelhes was not a "reader" (*liseur*).

62. Leroy, "Griffuelhes et Merrheim," 10.

Commune, Delacour had helped found a bookbinders' craft union in Paris. The union affiliated en bloc with the Paris federation of the First International in 1868. When the International was outlawed by the imperial government on the eve of the Franco-Prussian War in 1870, Delacour and several of its leaders were imprisoned.[63]

Perhaps the first writer to try to establish a link between the Paris federation of the First International, in which Delacour was so deeply involved, and the CGT's revolutionary syndicalism in Victor Griffuelhes' day, was the Swiss anarchist James Guillaume. Guillaume, one of the leading figures in the Bakuninist wing of the First International and later perhaps its most authoritative historian, wrote that at its congress of La Chaux-de-Fonds in Switzerland in April, 1870, the International, to Karl Marx's dismay, had adopted a resolution declaring that the creation of federations of unions was "the sole means of ensuring the success of the social revolution." This, argued Guillaume, "is clearly the concept that was enshrined, more than a quarter century later, at the [CGT's] Congress of Amiens [in 1906, at which the "Charter of Amiens" presented by Griffuelhes was adopted], in that celebrated phrase: 'Syndicalism is sufficient unto itself.'"[64]

The link between the First International and the revolutionary syndicalist CGT claimed by Guillaume has been accepted, with some qualifications, by more recent historians. In his *Origins of the French Labor Movement*, Bernard Moss notes that under the leadership of "revolutionary collectivists" such as Delacour's friend, Eugène Varlin, in 1869, the French branch of the International, composed largely of trade unions, set about reorganizing itself into "a great socialist party." Another recent historian, Annie Kriegel, sees in the "Franco-Belgian model of the First International" the precursor of turn-of-the-century revolutionary syndicalism. "Like English trade unionism," she writes, "the French labor movement [of the 1860s] developed along authentic trade-union lines." But unlike their English counterparts, syndicalists such as Varlin were revolutionary because they "took it for granted that the economic structure of the society had to be overthrown and that the workers, because they alone were producers, would have to take production in hand."[65]

It was, then, in the era of the First International that the notion of the union movement as a labor party (parti du travail) with the mission of estab-

---

63. *DBMO*, II, 337.
64. *L'Action Directe*, 2nd ser., January 15, 1908.
65. Moss, *Origins of the French Labor Movement*, 56; Kriegel, "Vie et Mort de la Iʳᵉ Internationale," 127–28.

lishing—and managing—a cooperative commonwealth was born. Alphonse Delacour was a key figure in that movement and, we believe, helped to transmit its legacy to Victor Griffuelhes. If one thread can be said to connect the disparate phases of Griffuelhes' career, from the late 1890s to the early 1920s, it is his search for a genuine *labor* party, not one of middle-class intellectuals and professionals claiming to act on behalf of the workers, but a party of workers acting for themselves. This was not simply because Griffuelhes was antibourgeois, although clearly this was a strongly held sentiment on his part, especially early in his career. Listen to Griffuelhes as he denounces Alphonse Delacour's rival in the October, 1898, municipal council elections, as reported by the police: "Grifeuilhe [*sic*] [told the audience] that while there were two socialist candidates present—Delacour and Bernier [a Radical-Socialist, actually]—the latter is in fact a bourgeois and he therefore urged all present to vote for Delacour."[66]

What was vital, Griffuelhes felt, was to guard the autonomy of the working class against attempts at cooptation by business, the Church, and especially the ever more intrusive French government. The working class could trust only itself to carry out this task, he believed. Later, speaking on behalf of the revolutionary syndicalist majority in the CGT, he declared: "We contend that the organizing effort which is being forced upon [the workers] by their miserable condition, ought to involve only wage earners, ought to be led by workers for workers' ends. . . . Thus, militants must never subordinate the action of the workers to that of social forces [outside] their ranks."[67]

The socialist movement, at least as presently constituted, could not be counted upon to serve the interests of the working class, Griffuelhes argued. This notion was driven home to him in the course of the Dreyfus and Millerand affairs at the turn of the century, when the majority of socialists allowed themselves to be rushed into an alliance with the moderate bourgeoisie to save Captain Dreyfus and the Third Republic—at the expense of, in Griffuelhes' view, a burgeoning strike movement that held out far more promise for workers. It was a lesson Griffuelhes never forgot.

66. APP, B/a 1028, Delacour dossier personnel, report of October 12, 1898. This seems to be the first police report on Griffuelhes, and the misspelling of his name indicates he was not well known at the Quai des Orfèvres at this point.

67. Victor Griffuelhes, "Le Syndicalisme révolutionnaire," in "Les Deux Conceptions du syndicalisme: Controverse," *Le Mouvement socialiste*, no. 146 (January 1, 1905), 3.

II

Millerandism (1899–1901)

What did they [Millerand and Waldeck-Rousseau] want? To domesticate us! The result . . . was that the CGT took on a new life. A coalition of anarchists, Guesdists, Blanquists, Allemanists, and others formed to preserve the unions from State control. That coalition has endured; it is the life of the confederation.
— Victor Griffuelhes, speaking at the CGT Congress of Amiens in 1906

Victor Griffuelhes' rise to the top of the CGT hierarchy at the age of twenty-seven, after a scant seven years' trade-union experience, was an extraordinary feat and one that requires some explanation. Certain factors favored this meteoric rise. Clearly, one was his membership in the Blanquist movement, the only socialist faction in tune with growing demands among workers for an independent, worker-led trade-union organization. His professional background as a skilled worker in the shoemaking trade, with its long history of participation in revolutionary causes, also helped. These factors alone, however, would not have sufficed to propel Griffuelhes to the summit of the CGT. Rather, it was the combination of these factors, and his own personal dynamism, with a remarkable conjuncture of events in French political and social life at the turn of the century that explains Griffuelhes' extraordinary upward mobility. What really "made" Griffuelhes was his response to two great challenges that faced French labor as a consequence of the tumultuous Dreyfus Affair of 1894–1901. The first was the formation of the Government of Republican Defense in June, 1899, under the leadership of Premier René Waldeck-Rousseau, author of the controversial law of 1884 that legalized trade unions; this action brought a socialist minister into government for the first time since 1848—deputy and party leader Alexandre Millerand. The second was the takeover of the Paris city council, which was the administrator of the Paris Bourse du Travail that also served as CGT headquarters, by Anti-Dreyfusard nationalists in the May, 1900, municipal elections.

At the outset, Griffuelhes faced the challenges posed by the formation of the Waldeck-Rousseau government on two separate fronts. For most socialists, the main question raised by the creation of the Government of Republican Defense was: Did the republic face sufficient danger to warrant inclusion of one of their own in the government? Jaurès and the POSR were convinced that the Anti-Dreyfusard threat was serious and warmly supported Millerand's entry into the new government. The Guesdists and Blanquists strongly disagreed. They believed the Right was too weak to endanger the republic and that Millerand was an opportunist who deserved to be condemned along with the "ministerialism" he and his supporters espoused. As a loyal Blanquist, Griffuelhes dutifully inveighed against ministerialism at socialist congresses and on the hustings. More important for Griffuelhes, however, was the struggle he waged in meetings at the Paris Bourse du Travail and at CGT congresses against "Millerandism," the ambitious program of labor reforms formulated largely by Premier Waldeck-Rousseau and destined for implementation by his commerce minister, Millerand. Griffuelhes exhorted his fellow trade unionists to reject the reforms, charging that, like Waldeck-Rousseau's law of 1884, their goal was to foster "social peace" by bringing the unions within the grasp of the government and associating them "more closely with the State and ultimately with employers." In this way, it was hoped that "revolutionary syndicalism might be eliminated."[1] It was Griffuelhes' dogged uphill battle against Millerandism in union ranks that more than anything else secured him the post of general secretary of the CGT. When the tide turned against Waldeck-Rousseau and Millerand in 1901, it also turned against their supporters in the Bourses du Travail and the CGT. A new generation of militants swept into power, with Victor Griffuelhes at their head. Like him, they were often "new men"—young, of provincial origin, and fiercely antibourgeois.

The fight against Waldeck-Rousseau and Millerand was quite literally the fight of Victor Griffuelhes' life. He saw it as the most heroic stand of his career and never ceased to remind others that when the Waldeck-Rousseau government first tried to foist its program of social peace on the workers, he had been almost alone in the trade unions to oppose it. Griffuelhes believed that the "moral authority" he claimed to enjoy as leader of the CGT during

---

1. Judith F. Stone, *The Search for Social Peace: Reform Legislation in France, 1890–1914* (Albany, N.Y., 1985), 144.

its "heroic age" sprang from his principled opposition to Millerandism. But this struggle did not cease when the Waldeck-Rousseau government dissolved in 1902. It is no exaggeration to say that Griffuelhes never really stopped fighting Millerandism, since he continued to see welfare state policies of the type articulated by Waldeck-Rousseau and Millerand as the greatest threat to the autonomy of the working-class movement and to its fight to overthrow the capitalist system. Thus, when post–World War I French governments ushered in a social reform program that included the eight-hour working day, the unmet goal of the 1906 general strike he had led, Griffuelhes nonetheless rejected the program. It was a "nouveau Millerandisme," he wrote, another attempt by the State to coopt workers and divert them from their revolutionary task.[2]

A close examination of his activities makes clear that Griffuelhes played only a marginal—and reluctant—role in the Dreyfus Affair or, more precisely, in those aspects of the affair that have preoccupied its historians: the question of the guilt or innocence of Captain Dreyfus and the ensuing "civil war" between the Dreyfusards and their nationalist opponents.

Griffuelhes had no sympathy for the nationalist cause. Anti-Dreyfusard politics, he wrote, were rooted in "exploitation and the bestial egoism of the mob." He had nothing but contempt for the patriotic demagogy of the Anti-Dreyfusards. The words "fatherland" and "patriotism" in his view no longer reflected "generous sentiments" or served as "a stimulus to human development," as they may have done in the era of the Revolution of 1789. Today, he contended, "the word 'fatherland,' having become a synonym for 'property,' is meaningless to [the worker], since he owns nothing and everywhere enriches with the sweat of his brow property which belongs to others."[3]

No friend to the Anti-Dreyfusards, Griffuelhes was not much more sympathetic to the Dreyfusard cause, however. For him, the Dreyfus Affair was at best a diversion from and at worst an obstacle to the urgent task of organizing the labor movement on a more independent, combative basis and of coordinating for greater impact the unprecedented wave of strikes that coin-

2. Griffuelhes, "Le Nouveau Millerandisme," *La Revue communiste*, no. 1 (March, 1920), 30–33.

3. Griffuelhes, "Les Subventions du conseil municipal," *La Voix du Peuple* (*VdP*), no. 34, July 21–28, 1901, and "Le Valeur du mot," *VdP*, no. 60 (special issue, "Aux soldats") January, 1902.

cided with the penultimate phase of the affair. The strike wave began with a massive walkout of building workers in Paris in September–November, 1898, and continued through the important miners' strikes of 1901–1902. Griffuelhes' sentiments largely accorded with those expressed in the argot of the laboring man by Emile Pouget, a longtime anarchist militant and from 1901 to 1909 his closest collaborator at the helm of the CGT. Pouget wrote, "It's all right for the bourgeoisie to tie itself in knots over Dreyfus . . . I can understand that: The guy is one of theirs. . . . But us poor buggers? We've got other fish to fry!"[4]

For Dreyfusards and their opponents, 1898 was the year of the antisemitic riots and Emile Zola's "J'Accuse." For militant workers such as Griffuelhes, however, there were "other fish to fry." A police spy in Paris found that working-class attention in 1898 was focused on the strikes planned in the capital's building trades and on the nation's railways. "In these subversive circles," he reported, "the Dreyfus Affair is today of secondary interest; their main concern . . . is the solid organization of all the revolutionary elements against the bosses and capitalism."[5]

Some recent historians claim to have found a darker meaning in the indifference to Dreyfusism of trade-union militants like Griffuelhes. Israeli historian Zeev Sternhell, for example, attributes it to fear and dislike of "liberal democracy," which he sees as the guiding ethos of the Third Republic and progenitor of the Dreyfusard alliance. There is some truth to this, as for instance in Sternhell's contention that "syndicalist leaders like Emile Pouget and Victor Griffuelhes regarded the [Dreyfus] affair as an enormous hoax. . . . Once again, they said, as in 1789, 1830, and 1848, the bourgeoisie had utilized the revolutionary capacities of the proletariat to protect its own interests. . . . Once again in the name of liberty and the Republic, democracy and secularism, it had been cheated by its political leaders, who had persuaded it to save its own exploiters."[6] Pouget later changed course and rallied to the Dreyfusard cause; he was one of the labor signatories of an appeal in the leftist Dreyfusard newspaper, *Journal du Peuple,* calling upon workers to join a demonstration at the Longchamp race course to defend the republic against the nationalists.

---

4. Pouget, *Le Père Peinard,* no. 57, November 21–28, 1897, quoted in Goustine, *Pouget: Les Matins noirs,* 119.

5. AN, F7 12.496, report of October 4, 1898.

6. See Zeev Sternhell, *La Droite révolutionnaire, 1885–1914* (Paris, 1978), and *Ni droite, ni gauche* (Paris, 1984); quote is from the latter, in English translation as *Neither Right nor Left: Fascist Ideology in France,* trans. David Maisel (Berkeley, 1986), 18–19.

Griffuelhes, under protest, was ordered by his union to join the march on June 6, 1899, and was beaten up in the police riot that ensued.[7]

Where Sternhell goes awry is in trying to project a rationally conceived, historically conditioned mistrust of liberal democracy forward into a supposed antidemocratic "synthesis" between the authoritarian Right and elements of the labor and socialist Left that would in time produce fascism.[8]

What made the strike movement of 1898 so riveting, not only for workers but for a frightened public as well, was the spread over the previous decade of the notion of the "general strike" as labor's epic weapon for the overthrow of the class system. Although the theory of the general strike had its roots in ideas bandied about during the 1789 Revolution, its modern formulation came largely from anarchists in the trade-union movement. The most visible proponent of the general strike in the early 1890s was the anarchist carpenter, Joseph Tortelier, who traveled about France like an itinerant evangelist, preaching the gospel of "The Great Day." According to a police report, "By general strike Tortelier means the immediate and simultaneous stoppage of the whole system of production and exchange: factories, mines, canals, railroads, telegraph, the postal service; in a word, everything."[9]

By 1898, however, the earlier libertarian conception of the general strike as a spontaneous and universal folding of workers' arms had been refined somewhat. Vaillant, the Blanquist leader, and Fernand Pelloutier, the anarchist general secretary of the Bourse du Travail movement, had concluded that the proper strategy to pursue was that of the "generalized strike," *i.e.*, a work stoppage kicked off by a union in a leading sector of the economy, in which the rest of the trade unions would join. Vaillant had originally argued that the role of catalyst should go to the foodworkers' unions, apparently believing that the quickest way to the bourgeoisie's heart was through its stomach. Later, however, he came around to the view that the mission was best assigned to the miners or railway workers.[10] The strategy adopted by the CGT in 1898, as it turned out, was a variant of the generalized strike, but one dictated more by opportunity than by actual planning. Its lessons were not lost on young

---

7. Julliard, *Fernand Pelloutier*, 112; Méric, "Victor Griffuelhes," 3.

8. Sternhell, *Neither Right nor Left*, 52.

9. APP, B/a 76, note of November 15, 1889, quoted in Robert Brécy, *Grève générale en France* (Paris, 1969), 25.

10. Vaillant's evolving strategy for the general strike is recorded in two of his articles quoted in Howorth, *Edouard Vaillant*, 208–209; Pelloutier's strategy is given in Maxime Leroy, *La Coutume ouvrière* (Paris, 1913), II, 522.

Victor Griffuelhes, who would formulate a generalized strike strategy of his own in preparation for a second, more successful general strike eight years later.

Despite a promising beginning—some sixty thousand construction workers were idle in Paris the first week of October—the general strike of 1898 proved a dismal failure. Few other trades put down their tools, and the much-ballyhooed national strike of railwaymen lasted only three days, involving just 135 strikers.[11] Worse, it appeared that the ministry of interior, which had moved quickly to cut telegraph traffic between rail union headquarters in Paris and the provinces, had been tipped off to the strike plans by someone high up in the union. Suspicion fell on the union secretary, André Lagailse, who also served as general secretary of the CGT. The subsequent uproar, which resulted in the dismissal of Lagailse from both posts, devastated morale in the trade-union movement. The charges against Lagailse were never proved, but feeling ran so high against him, including in his own union, that he was obliged to retire from trade-union life.[12]

The 1898 general strike has the appearance of a dress rehearsal for the larger, more serious May Day general strike of 1906. In 1898 as in 1906, the government's response to the strike action was massive. Sixty thousand soldiers were drafted into Paris in October, 1898, to occupy struck building sites, a ratio of one soldier per striker. In 1906, the mining districts of the North were patrolled by thousands of troops, and Paris became an occupied city. And in both cases, the government sought to discredit the strike leaders by accusing them of plotting with the Right to overthrow the republic. In 1898, the government alleged a "plot" that brought together the Orleanists and the leaders of the building workers' and railwaymen's unions, Lucien Riom and Eugène Guérard respectively, while in 1906, the "conspiracy" involved the CGT leadership, including Griffuelhes, and the Bonapartists. Admittedly, the State's motives differed in the two cases. In 1906, the interior ministry's main concern seems to have been to secure a Radical victory at the polls. In 1898, though

11. The most detailed account of the 1898 building trades' strike is in Daniel Blume, "Recherches sur le syndicalisme ouvrier dans le Batiment à Paris (1892–1906)" (D.E.S., Université de Paris, 1957), 111–21. Blume's conclusions are conveniently summarized and commented upon in William E. McMechan, "The Building Trades of France, 1907–1914: An Exploration of Revolutionary Syndicalism," (Ph.D. dissertation, University of Wisconsin—Madison, 1975), 221–35. For the railway strike fiasco, see Syndicat national des Travailleurs des Chemins de Fer, *Compte rendu du Xe Congrès national, convoqué extraordinairement à Paris . . . 20 et 21 janvier 1899* (Paris, 1899), 7–22.

12. *DBMO*, XIII, 174–75 (Lagailse).

historians have generally ignored it, the government's action was dictated to a great extent by international considerations, namely the threat of war with Britain over Fashoda. At the very time the railwaymen were preparing to walk out, French troops were being entrained for the Mediterranean ports, en route to Africa.[13]

The 1898 strikes were also linked to the Dreyfus Affair. Dreyfusards were divided over whether to support the building trades' strike. Some like Georges Clemenceau, the future represser of the 1906 general strike, lent monetary and moral support to the strikers.[14] Others such as the reformist socialists around the newspaper *La Petite République,* perhaps the most important socialist journal of its day, saw the building trades' and rail strikes as provocations that could lead to a military coup d'état.[15] In a move that poisoned relations between the reformist wing of the socialist movement and the CGT for some time, the newspaper supported the charges of collusion between union leaders and the Orleanists. Six years later in 1904, Griffuelhes revived the issue during a feud with the reformist socialist leader, Jean Jaurès, accusing him of having inspired the *Petite République* campaign against Riom and Guérard.[16]

In June, 1899, Alexandre Millerand, labor lawyer, deputy, and leader of the moderate Independent Socialist faction, accepted the ministry of commerce, industry, posts and telegraph, which had primary responsibility for labor affairs, in the Waldeck-Rousseau Government of Republican Defense, thus provoking a row "between socialists . . . as bitter as those aroused in the French middle class by Dreyfus."[17]

The Blanquists, their proletarian "annex," the ACR, to which Griffuelhes belonged, and the Guesdists denounced Millerand's decision as betrayal of

---

13. Joseph Reinach, *Histoire de l'Affaire Dreyfus* (Paris, 1901), IV, 288; *DBMO*, XII, 342–43 (Guérard), XVI, 59–60 (Riom); Roger G. Brown, *Fashoda Reconsidered: The Impact of Domestic Politics on French Policy in Africa, 1893–1898* (Baltimore, 1970), 104.

14. APP, B/a 1397, note of October 6, 1898, quoted in Brown, *Fashoda Reconsidered,* 105.

15. The reformist socialists' fears were similar to those expressed by Captain Dreyfus' brother, Mathieu, in his unpublished "Souvenirs sur l'Affaire Dreyfus": "We were extremely uneasy because we knew that the General Staff desired disturbances in the streets. Grave trouble would justify the proclamation of a state of siege. And once the state of siege was decreed, all power would pass into the hands of the military" (*ibid.*).

16. For Griffuelhes' attempt to implicate Jaurès in the smear, see his article "Pas de réponse," *VdP,* no. 170, January 17–24, 1904.

17. James Joll, *The Second International, 1889–1914* (New York, 1966), 98.

the class struggle. "The socialist party, being a class party, has no business sharing power with the bourgeoisie, in whose hands the State can only be an instrument of conservatism and social oppression," they trumpeted in a joint manifesto of July 14, 1899.[18]

Millerand got firm support, however, from his own Independent Socialist group, which controlled the influential socialist daily newspaper, *La Petite République,* and the Broussists and POSR. Jean Jaurès put their case in his usual expansive fashion: "It is a great day in history when the bourgeois republic, at a time when its very existence is in danger, should itself admit that it has need of the energy of the socialists." The POSR position deserves extended comment here. Of all the socialist factions, the Allemanists were the most "profoundly republican," Michel Winock has written. "During . . . the Dreyfus Affair, the Allemanists were the first into the breach, going as far . . . in 1899 as supporting (with some rhetorical flourishes) the entry of Millerand into a bourgeois ministry! At this juncture there came alive within Allemanism a whole 1870-type freemason, freethinking, republican side: [the party] turned into a Committee of Public Safety, a fighting army of the *République en danger.*" [19]

Although weakened by the split of 1896, which produced the ACR, and by public coolness to its strident Dreyfusard stance in the 1898 Chamber elections, the POSR remained a formidable ally for the ministerialists. Allemanist endorsement of the Government of Republican Defense brought with it a solid measure of trade-union support. The POSR's tactical alliance with Fernand Pelloutier and the anarchist leadership of the National Federation of Bourses du Travail gave the Allemanists a pivotal position within the federation as long as Pelloutier lived. And within the CGT, their hold on the general secretary's post remained unbroken almost to the dissolution of the Government of Republican Defense, until November, 1901, when, battered by the ministerialist and Millerandist crises, they relinquished the office almost uncontested to the Blanquist Victor Griffuelhes.

There was a substantial political dimension to the trade-union struggle over the Millerand Affair. For Millerand supporters such as the POSR or for foes like the Blanquists, the Dreyfus and Millerand affairs were not unrelated events. These political sects and their trade-union allies regarded the latter

18. Georges Lefranc, *Le Mouvement socialiste sous la Troisième République (1875–1940)* (Paris, 1963), 106.

19. *Ibid.*; Michel Winock, "Robert Michels et la démocratie allemaniste," in *Mélanges d'histoire sociale offerts à Jean Maitron* (Paris, 1976), 282.

episode as simply a prolongation of the former; Blanquists would have said it was a logical culmination.

Whatever its political or union leaders might have thought, the French working class greeted Millerand's accession to the ministry of commerce with an enormous groundswell of support. Miners and railway workers, whose employers were for the most part concessionnaires of the State and who comprised a sizeable chunk of the labor force, welcomed the new minister as a longtime advocate of nationalizing the companies for which they worked.

Postal employees, whose boss he would become, looked to Millerand—with reason, as it turned out—to grant them improved wages and working conditions. But the socialist lawyer's support was not limited to State or quasi-State employees. In private industry as well, workers looked upon him as "their" minister and the defender of their interests within government circles. They viewed his arrival in office as a signal that, just as the Waldeck-Rousseau government would take action to bring the educational system, the Church, and the military into line with republican principles, so it would now also take steps to "republicanize" the workplace. The reception given the new government is reminiscent of that later accorded the Popular Front coalition of Léon Blum. In 1899–1900, as in 1936, French workers demonstrated their support for the incoming government by launching the biggest wave of strikes seen to date in France.

The last years of the nineteenth century saw a sharp rise in labor unrest. In 1897, there were 356 strikes involving 68,875 workers, while in 1898, 368 disputes idled 82,065 workers. The next two years brought a veritable explosion of strike activity in France. In 1899, the number of strikes jumped to 739 and the number of strikers more than doubled, to 176,772. The first year of the new century registered another major surge in strike activity, as 222,714 workers downed tools in 902 disputes.[20] More significant, however, are the comparative figures on workdays lost because of strikes during these years. In 1898, despite the long building trades' strike in Paris, approximately 1.2 million strike days were recorded. The following year, the number rose dramatically to around 3,550,000, and in 1900, it increased again to some 3,760,000.[21]

---

20. Figures from "Rapport fait . . . au nom de la Commission du Travail" of the Chamber of Deputies by socialist deputy Pierre Colliard, a member of the committee, on June 16, 1910, quoted in Allan Mitchell, *The Divided Path* (Chapel Hill, 1991), 187, table 6.

21. Edward Shorter and Charles Tilly, *Strikes in France, 1830–1968* (Cambridge, Engl., 1974), 361. The authors' table "Absolute numbers of strikes and strikers, 1830–1968," from which these

"France had never known a [strike] movement of such magnitude."[22]

To be sure, economic factors motivated many of the strikes during this period. The Great Depression of 1873–1896 was over and the economic conjuncture was propitious; company profits were high—in some sectors such as mining, exceptional—and workers were not slow to push for their share of the larger pie. In 1899–1900, about 62.5 percent of all strikes in France ended with at least some gains for the workers involved; over the 1894–1896 period, the average had been only 50 to 54 percent. But as observers at the time and since have noted, many of these strikes, including some of the most important, had no discernible economic motive. As Pierre Sorlin has written: "All of these facts indicate a general state of mind: The workers have confidence in the ministry; they expect moral and, if need be, even material support from it; they have the impression that for once the authorities are on their side. Justified or not, this feeling is important. Even if there were deeper reasons behind it, this strike wave was encouraged by the fact that workers no longer feared repression by the government."[23]

With this kind of hope abounding among the working classes, it is not surprising that Waldeck-Rousseau and Millerand also received the almost-unanimous endorsement of the top leaders of organized labor in the "honeymoon" period of their three-year term of office. The trade-union elite—Eugène Guérard of the railway workers, A. Baumé of the Trade-Union Federation of the Seine (TFS), Lucien Riom of the building trades, Edmond Briat the precision instruments workers, Pierre Coupat of the machinists, Auguste Keufer of the printers—moved quickly to assure the new minister of their personal support and that of the workers they represented. These union leaders also rallied to Waldeck-Rousseau and Millerand for political reasons, however. With the exception of Keufer, who espoused Comtean positivism, they were either Broussists (Baumé, Briat, and Coupat) or members of the POSR (Riom and Guérard) and thus committed by their parties to a program of republican defense. They were also reformists, either by conviction or as the result of chastening experience.[24]

---

figures have been taken, differs from French government data in that Algerian strikes and strikers are not included and totals for strikers have been rounded off.

22. Pierre Sorlin, *Waldeck-Rousseau* (Paris, 1966), 463.

23. Jean Bouvier, "Mouvement ouvrier et conjonctures économiques," *Le Mouvement social*, no. 48 (July–September 1964), 19; Sorlin, *Waldeck-Rousseau*, 472.

24. A. Baumé was general secretary of the Paris brushmakers' union in the 1890s and the

As can readily be seen, it took a certain brand of conviction to oppose Millerandism within the labor movement. Like Griffuelhes, most opponents came from the Blanquist camp or from the anarchist movement. Griffuelhes took part in the struggle from the beginning, first as his shoemaker union's delegate to the TFS, then as a TFS official.

In 1899, the Trade-Union Federation of the Seine grouped the 110 craft unions that Baumé had originally brought together when the Paris Bourse du Travail closed in 1893, to found an independent Bourse entirely funded and administered by the unions. Griffuelhes' union of French shoemakers had been an early member. In 1897, the TFS had returned to the Paris Bourse du Travail but had retained its structural integrity. Because it comprised the largest single bloc of unions affiliated with the Paris Bourse du Travail and was "composed of its most active elements," complained the police, the federation virtually handpicked the worker members of the administrative committee of the Bourse du Travail and saw to it that they stuck to their mandates.[25]

In the years 1899–1900, the TFS and thus the Paris Bourse du Travail were run by a coalition of Broussists and Allemanists. Fiercely protective of the administrative—if not necessarily the financial—independence of the Bourse du Travail, these officials, indeed the majority of the affiliated unions, looked to the new minister of commerce to curtail municipal control of the facility. They would be rewarded by his decree of July 17, 1900, which turned over administration of the Paris Bourse du Travail to a committee composed entirely of elected union representatives. The adverse consequences of this decree will be discussed in some detail below.

As a new delegate to the TFS, Griffuelhes quickly learned how solidly the Bourse du Travail crowd supported Waldeck-Rousseau and Millerand. He took up the fight against Millerandism in June, 1899, immediately after the Waldeck-Rousseau government took office. On this occasion, he waged a one-man, rearguard action against efforts by reformist and Allemanist labor leaders to offer official trade-union support to Millerand. At the CGT Con-

---

early years of the twentieth century (APP, B/a 1609, note of August 7, 1894). Coupat was a prominent reformist in the CGT and was "closely linked to . . . Millerand" in the period 1899–1902 (*DBMO*, XI, 272). Briat was appointed to the Supreme Labor Council in 1900 by Millerand as an ex-officio member, and although he was disavowed by his union and the CGT, he refused to give up his seat; in 1909, he became president of the Council after being purged from the executive board of his union (*DBMO*, XI, 57). In 1881, Keufer helped found the National Federation of Printing Workers (Fédération française des Travailleurs du Livre—known as Livre) and was a founder of CGT in 1895 and the leader of its reformist wing (*DBMO*, XIII, 143–45).

25. APP, B/a 1610, "Notice sur la Commission administrative de la Bourse du Travail et les

gress of Amiens seven years later, he recalled how he, then a simple delegate of his union, had stood alone against the old hands of the Bourse du Travail. "No sooner had Millerand taken office than a resolution appeared signed by Keufer, Baumé, [and] Moreau on behalf of their unions, approving his act [of joining the government]. . . . Then, at the Trade-Union Federation of the Seine, they decided to offer a banquet to Millerand. . . . I was the only one who opposed it."[26]

Victor Méric says that it was Auguste Keufer's idea to give a banquet for Millerand. He briefly describes the encounter between young Griffuelhes and the "big shot of the printers," who by 1899 was already a veteran of fifteen years as general secretary of the powerful union. "He [Griffuelhes] stood up and, in a few decisive words, rebutted Keufer's proposal. The latter didn't pursue the idea."[27]

A year later came the "Affair of the invitations." James Joll, in his book *The Second International,* offers the debate on this issue as evidence of the fanaticism aroused on the French Left by the Millerand Affair. "M. and Mme. Millerand were mocked for sending engraved cards to working men to invite them to a democratic reception by the Minister." What Joll does not tell us is that, aside from whatever reaction might have been provoked by "sending engraved cards to working men," there were serious objections to the timing of the invitations, which arrived after the strike at Chalon-sur-Saone in June, 1900, in which police killed three strikers. As Griffuelhes would later explain, "It was just after Chalon that members of the executive committee of the Bourse du Travail received . . . invitations to a reception given by the minister of commerce. Two days later, another invitation came—from Gallifet [minister of war] this time!—to a military review."[28]

Opposition to attending Millerand's "democratic reception" was not so widespread as Joll suggests. "Two of us protested and propagandized [against accepting the invitations]," Griffuelhes recalled. "We exposed their maneuvers and, little by little, we were able to make our comrades see the truth of the matter." On July 9, 1900, by which time Griffuelhes had become one of the

syndicats composant l'Union des Syndicats de la Seine," January 15, 1901; this report states that "the great majority" of the TFS leaders "are affiliated to groups of the POSR, the school [of socialism] called 'Allemanism.' "

26. Armand Moreau was an official of the Paris tramcar employees' union in the 1890s (*DBMO,* XIV, 137); CGT, *XVe Congrès national corporatif . . . Amiens . . . 1906 . . . Compte rendu des travaux* (Amiens, 1906), 167.

27. Méric, "Victor Griffuelhes," 3.

28. Joll, *Second International,* 98; the invitation's text, taken from the Geneva daily *La Suisse*

TFS assistant secretaries, a resolution was adopted stating that "elected officials of the organization can neither accept nor offer invitations from or to members of the government, municipal council, or parliament without authorization from its executive committee."[29]

However proud Griffuelhes may have been of his role in frustrating the government's alleged attempts to corrupt the Bourse du Travail, this would be a mere skirmish compared with the fight he waged against the social reforms proposed by Waldeck-Rousseau and introduced by Millerand, which had considerable backing within the labor movement, at least at the outset. In this contest also, Griffuelhes at first found himself in a distinct minority. Only gradually, by constant agitation and propagandizing, was he was able to gather around him a group of like-minded activists, most of them either anarchists or Blanquists like himself.

In 1899, however, Millerand went almost unchallenged in labor ranks. Opposition first emerged within the socialist movement. The issue was not one of republican defense; all the socialist parties, from the Marxist POF to the municipal socialists of Paul Brousse, agreed that the republic was worth fighting for and that its enemies must be brought to heel. Nor was the issue really that of ministerialism—the propriety of socialist participation in a bourgeois cabinet—even though the Guesdists, Blanquists, and ACR said as much in their July 14, 1899, manifesto, describing Millerand's entry into the Waldeck-Rousseau government as a betrayal of the class struggle. But this was only part of the story.

Griffuelhes' election as assistant secretary of the Trade-Union Federation of the Seine in November, 1899, plus reports of his principled stand against the Millerandists at the Paris Bourse du Travail the previous June, appears to have brought him to the attention of Edouard Vaillant. Consequently, the PSR chief asked Griffuelhes to represent a Blanquist constituency at the socialist unity congress to be held in Paris December 3–8, 1899. Thus, Griffuelhes made his first appearance at a socialist congress (he would attend three altogether) as the delegate of the *groupe socialiste* of Nérondes, a small community of timber workers (*bucherons*) and agricultural laborers between Bourges and Nevers in the Cher Department. This was the beginning of a

(no date given), is quoted in Michel Branciard, *Société française et luttes de classe*, 2 vols., Vol. I, *1789–1914* (Lyon, 1967), 161; CGT, *XVᵉ Congres national corporatif . . . Amiens*, 167.

29. CGT, *XVᵉ Congrès national corporatif . . . Amiens*, 167; "Invitation déclinée," *VdP*, no. 15, March 10–17, 1901.

long friendship between Griffuelhes and the Cher lumberjacks, the "silent men" he seems to have admired more than any other kind of workers.[30]

At the congress, Griffuelhes sat with the large Blanquist delegation, which included Vaillant and such PSR luminaries as the former student radicals Jules-Louis Breton and Marcel Sembat. As a student engineer in Paris in the early 1890s, Breton was a charter member of a Left Bank students' group who called themselves Etudiants Socialistes Révolutionnaires Internationalistes (ESRI); Jean Maitron believed they laid some of the theoretical foundations for revolutionary syndicalism. By 1898, Breton had graduated to electoral politics under the patronage of Vaillant, who found a safe seat for his protégé in his old constituency of Vierzon in the Cher. Once in the Chamber, however, Breton began to move steadily to the Right. Sembat, who held a doctorate in law but abandoned the bar for journalism, joined the Blanquists in 1895. A gifted writer and speaker, he became one of the leading lights of the Chamber socialist group in the prewar years. Griffuelhes, while leading the CGT, was always careful to keep channels of communication to Sembat open.[31]

Not surprisingly, the young shoemaker toed the party line on the issue that dominated debate at the congress—ministerialism. At the December 6 session, Griffuelhes voted with the majority—818 votes to 634—in support of a Guesde motion ruling out socialist participation in "bourgeois" ministries. (This was one of the very few occasions when Griffuelhes supported anything proposed by Jules Guesde.) The same day, he joined his party comrades in backing a compromise motion, superseding the Guesde text, stating that although there might be times when socialists would have to consider participating in a nonsocialist government, this was not one of them. "In the current state of capitalist society and socialism," the resolution stated, "all efforts of the party should be directed toward the conquest, in the commune, the department, and at national level, of elective offices alone." This motion, which won support from all but the hard core of the POF, enabled the congress to paper over its differences with respect to ministerialism and to form an all-party committee to pursue the quest for unity.[32]

---

30. *Congrès général des organisations socialistes françaises tenu à Paris du 3 au 8 décembre 1899. Compte rendu sténographique* (Paris, 1900), 428; Griffuelhes, *Voyage révolutionnaire*, 33.

31. Jean Maitron, "Le Groupe des étudiants E.S.R.I. (1892–1902): Contribution à la connaissance des origines du syndicalisme révolutionnaire," *Le Mouvement social*, no. 46 (January–March 1964), 3–26; *DBMO*, XI, 51–52 (Breton), XV, 152–55 (Sembat).

32. *Congrès général des organisations socialistes françaises*, "Annexe: Votes au Congrès."

More interesting for this study, however, was a report presented to the congress by Maxence Roldes, a journalist and one of the leaders of Griffuelhes' party, the ACR. Roldes' report concerned his role, along with Blanquist militant and fellow journalist Henri Turot, in the celebrated strikes at Le Creusot (Saone-et-Loire) and nearby Montceau-les-Mines in the autumn of 1899. According to the ACR leader, the two newspapermen had originally gone to Le Creusot to cover the strike and had ended up leading it. Roldes told the congress how he had convinced the striking metalworkers that any act of violence, even against scabs brought in by the employers, would cost them the support of public opinion and doom their cause to defeat; he and Turot had also successfully prevailed upon the workers to call off their strike and accept arbitration by the Waldeck-Rousseau government.[33]

Roldes' account of his and Turot's "takeover" of the strike at Le Creusot is highly suspect. As Pierre Sorlin has demonstrated, the Government of Republican Defense pursued a systematic policy of dispatching socialist deputies and militants to take over strikes from union leaders and to convince strikers to submit their grievances to binding arbitration; he cites Roldes and Turot's intervention in the Le Creusot strike as an example of this policy. It is interesting to note that the newspaper that sent Turot and Roldes to Le Creusot was *La Petite République,* the voice of Millerandism. A measure of the Blanquist movement's loose organization and lax discipline is that Roldes, the ACR's number two figure after its secretary, Arthur Groussier, and the other member, along with the PSR's Louis Dubreuilh, of the ACR-PSR liaison committee, was allowed to work for this rival organ in the first place. More curious still was Henri Turot's status. No mere pressroom hack, Turot had held stock in *La Petite République* since 1893 and was sitting on the newspaper's editorial board in 1899; he remained there throughout the ministerialist crisis and eventually was editor in chief, until the paper folded in 1914.[34] In conclusion, it seems likely that Roldes and Turot were sent to the strike zone by the government and its friends at *La Petite Republique* expressly to coopt the strike and stop it from spreading to other industrial centers, as more radical trade unionists hoped it would.

---

33. *DBMO,* XV, 81–82 (Roldes); Roldes' account of his role in the Le Creusot strike is corroborated by Jules Ratreau, "La Grève du Creusot," *L'Echo de Paris,* September 29, 1899.

34. Sorlin, *Waldeck-Rousseau,* 473–74; *DBMO,* XV, 258 (Turot); Jean Longuet, "Alliance communiste révolutionnaire," *L'Encyclopédie du mouvement syndicaliste,* no. 1 (January, 1912), 111; Claude Bellanger, ed., *Histoire générale de la presse française: De 1871 à 1940* (3 vols.; Paris, 1972), III, 373–74.

The minutes of the December, 1899, socialist congress provide no evidence of an objection by Griffuelhes or anyone else to Roldes' report, but it could not have pleased him. In May, 1901, he signed a resolution of the TFS executive committee criticizing workers who, during strikes, "call to their aid deputies, politicians, journalists, or others who may meet with their personal sympathies or preferences, as if these citizens know better than workers the suffering and needs of the proletariat, as if they had more experience of organizing workers than trade-union militants do."[35]

For Griffuelhes and his fellow revolutionary syndicalists, the conclusion of the Le Creusot strike of 1899 would serve as a notorious example of the duplicity of republican governments and their socialist supporters. Although the arbitration award in October, 1899, by Premier Waldeck-Rousseau obliged the Schneider family, which owned the Le Creusot complex, to accept formation of a works council in their factories, management quickly rendered the judgment null and void by breaking the local union and installing a company union in its place. Some three thousand "Reds" were fired from their jobs. Subsequently, as if in approval, Minister of Commerce Millerand presented a "promotion of industry" award to Emile Schneider, the "Prince of Steel" of Le Creusot, at the Paris Universal Exposition of 1900.[36] That these developments had somehow been made possible by the intervention at Le Creusot of his fellow Blanquists, Roldes and Turot, must have been deeply disturbing to Griffuelhes.

As Griffuelhes may have come to realize, the basic problem with the PSR and, to a lesser extent, the ACR was that the only cement holding them together was the prestige of their leaders, Edouard Vaillant and Arthur Groussier. The turn-of-the-century PSR was largely a creation of Vaillant's patronage system. Its leadership cadre was made up of young students and professionals—journalists being common among the latter—for whom Vaillant endeavored to find safe Chamber constituencies. In this sense, the Blanquist movement à la Vaillant, dominated by déclassé bourgeois radicals, differed little from that led by Blanqui fifty years earlier. Vaillant presided over his faction in benevolent, grandfatherly fashion and tolerated indiscipline in the ranks that would have been unthinkable in Guesde's POF, itself no model of

35. "Aux travailleurs syndiqués," *VdP*, no. 26, May 26–June 2, 1901.
36. For a sensitive account of the harsh fate of the Creusot strikers and its reverberations in the French working-class milieu, see Daniel Halévy, *Essais sur le mouvement ouvrier en France* (Paris, 1901), 37–47.

conformity despite its leader's well-known intolerance toward ideological deviation.[37]

Thus, neither the ACR nor the PSR proved to be as solidly opposed to Millerandism as their manifestos seemed to indicate. Leading figures in both parties, for example, worked more or less openly in support of the Waldeck-Rousseau government's objective of social peace. The activities of Maxence Roldes and Henri Turot have already been noted in this regard. In 1902, Jules-Louis Breton, Vaillant's young protégé, was expelled from the PSR for refusing to curtail his open support of Millerand's program of labor reforms, by then under serious attack from the trade-union movement. This, of course, contradicted not only Blanquism's official opposition to ministerialism but also its hands-off policy with respect to trade-union affairs.[38]

Griffuelhes' break with electoral socialism did not occur, however, before he had run the gamut of traditional political experience, attending two more socialist congresses as a member of the delegation of the PSR Seine federation's delegation, and actually running for public office. Griffuelhes attended the abortive socialist unity congresses of Paris (1900) and Lyon (1901) but apparently did not join the debates. The effort to unify the several socialist factions foundered over ministerialism. In 1901, the PSR, the ACR, and the Guesdists formed a Socialist Party of France (Parti Socialiste de France), in opposition to the French Socialist Party (Parti Socialiste Français) composed of Jaurès' Independent Socialists, the Allemanists, and the Broussists. The level of polemical violence attained by these rival parties after 1901 did much to discourage worker interest in socialist politics and, conversely, to encourage worker involvement in the revolutionary trade-union movement.[39]

In 1900, Victor Griffuelhes stood for political office, for the first and only time in his career. He ran as the ACR/PSR candidate in the May municipal

37. Vaillant's generous embrace of all comers assured the PSR a veritable rogues' gallery of ex-members, including Pierre Biétry, leader of the company unions (Dommanget, *Edouard Vaillant*, 269), and Pierre Laval, the future premier of Vichy France; see Bruce Vandervort, "The Early Political Career of Pierre Laval (1883–1927)" (M.A. thesis, University of Cincinnati, 1966), 36–43.

38. *DBMO*, XI, 51–52 (Breton); writing in 1909, Griffuelhes accused Breton of being responsible for the "moribund state of social movements [in Vierzon] for the last seven or eight years" (*Voyage révolutionnaire*, 33–34).

39. Georges Weill, *Histoire du mouvement social en France, 1852–1910*, (2nd ed.; Paris, 1911), 335.

elections, in the Quartier Saint-Vincent-de-Paul, adjacent to his home base, the Quartier L'Hopital Saint-Louis, in the 10th arrondissement. It was a disaster.

Griffuelhes was a reluctant candidate to begin with, having been drafted by his party at the last minute when Maxence Roldes decided to drop out of the race. Roldes had been unsuccessful in two previous electoral contests in the 10th and now was off to try his luck in the 11th arrondissement.[40]

The Anti-Dreyfusards scored a stunning upset in the 1900 Paris municipal elections. While the rest of the nation was returning largely republican city councils, nationalist candidates took forty-five of the eighty seats on the Paris council, ousting the Radical-Socialist coalition that had governed the capital for most of the two previous decades. One of their surprise victories came in the 10th's Quartier Saint-Vincent-de-Paul, where Camille Rousset, a candidate who presented himself as a *républicain progressiste nationaliste* and who was backed by one of the Anti-Dreyfusard leagues, La Patrie Française, squeaked by the Radical incumbent, Georges Villain, on the second round of balloting.[41]

Griffuelhes had left the race after the first ballot, obeying his party's instructions to stand down in favor of the better-placed Radical aspirant. On the first round, he polled just 582 votes out of a total of 5,674 valid ballots cast, coming in a distant third behind Villain (2,302 votes) and Rousset (2,280) and just 120 votes ahead of the Bonapartist anti-Semite (*plébiscitaire antisémite*) candidate, Kléber de Margerie.

The results must have been depressing for Griffuelhes. His total, barely 10 percent of the vote, was disappointing given the sizeable working-class population in the quartier; and there also was the knowledge that at least some of the votes he had received had helped elect Rousset, the nationalist candidate, on the second round. Rousset continued to represent the district into World War I but was nearly bankrupted by the war, since his export-import catalogue firm specialized in German and Austrian products.[42]

40. Roldes' withdrawal from the 10th arr. contest is noted in APP, B/a 693, report on "Elections municipales du 6 mai—candidats" (n.d.).

41. The nationalist victory in the 1900 municipal elections in Paris is analyzed in David R. Watson, "The Nationalist Movement in Paris, 1900–1906," in *The Right in France, 1890–1919*, ed. David Shapiro (London, 1962), 49–84; the names and affiliations of the candidates in the Quartier Saint-Vincent-de-Paul race are given in APP, B/a 693, "Elections municipales du 6 mai."

42. The first and second round totals for the various contestants were reported in *La Petite République*, May 8 and 15, 1900; APP, B/a 1535, note of January 18, 1915.

The nationalists would control the Paris city government for only two years. In 1902, voters in the capital returned a Radical majority to the city council. In the interim, however, the nationalists used their newly won power to make life extremely difficult for the Reds at the Paris Bourse du Travail.

Griffuelhes' participation in the struggle over ministerialism and his disastrous foray into electoral politics were peripheral to the battle against what he saw as the counterrevolutionary aims of Millerand's social reform program, undertaken during the latter's term of office, June 26, 1899–June 3, 1902. Griffuelhes never doubted that the main inspiration for the social reform program the world would label Millerandism was not the commerce minister, but the premier, Waldeck-Rousseau. To the end of his life, Griffuelhes believed that Millerand had been "placed at the head of a ministry by Waldeck-Rousseau" and "had been given the mission" of luring the labor movement into the embrace of the State.[43] This belief that Millerand was not just a renegade and traitor to socialism, but a mercenary hired for the specific purpose of destroying the independent trade-union movement, may help explain the virulence of Griffuelhes' reaction to him and his program.

But in the light of history, was Griffuelhes correct? Was Waldeck-Rousseau the real mastermind of Millerandism? To a large extent, yes. Marjorie Farrar, the most recent biographer of Millerand in English, exaggerates in describing the premier as a hesitant and reactive welfare stater. After all, as a disciple of Léon Gambetta, Waldeck-Rousseau held strong views on the "social question" and on the need to resolve it, if bloody upheavals like the Paris Commune were to be avoided in future. The whole thrust of his 1884 law on unions was to make unions strong enough to carve out a stake for the working class in society. He had wanted the law to allow unions to invest in enterprise and engage in commerce, but the Chamber had refused to go along. The grand purpose of such a reform was to promote the rise of the "worker-manager" or "worker-capitalist" of the future. "Having escaped from his proletarian condition, [the worker] will become an element of stability." The granting of a *personnalité civil,* or "civil personality" (a legal designation granting organizations the same rights and responsibilities as a private citizen), to the unions became something of an obsession for Waldeck-Rousseau in subsequent years. It was the subject of the only Millerandist reform bill that he actually drafted and sponsored before parliament. But this bill does not exhaust the premier's reform agenda over the years 1899–1902. It was Waldeck-

---

43. Griffuelhes, "Le Nouveau Millerandisme," 31.

Rousseau, not his minister of commerce, who actually proposed the system for compulsory arbitration of labor disputes that would earn Millerand so much ill will in trade-union and business circles. "The text [of the bill on compulsory arbitration] was drafted by Millerand, but under the superivison of Waldeck-Rousseau, who entirely rewrote it." [44]

With one exception, all of the minister of commerce's reforms were implemented through using his decree powers. Among these were decrees concerning:

—Wages and working conditions of State employees, which included the eight-hour day for postal workers (August 10, 1899)
—Reorganization of the Supreme Labor Council (Conseil Supérieur du Travail—CST), established in 1891 to oversee the application of labor legislation (September 1, 1899)
—Creation of bipartite regional councils to complement the CST and enable worker and employer representatives to "dialogue" on labor questions (September 17, 1900; January 2, 1901). [45]

The only piece of social legislation Millerand managed to push through the parliament was a revision of the 1892 law on child and female labor. The law had created problems in enterprises where women and/or children worked alongside adult males, since it limited the former to a ten-hour day while the men averaged twelve hours. Millerand got a ten-hour day for all accepted by the Chamber but ran into trouble in the Senate, which wanted a uniform eleven-hour day. In 1901, a compromise was struck with a ten-and-a-half-hour day, which would be implemented by April, 1904. The bill proved to be a mixed success, with Millerand being remembered in some quarters as the minister who had added a half-hour to the workday of women and children. [46]

Among the several ultimately unsuccessful bills championed by Millerand, two would be singled out for extensive adverse comment by Griffuelhes: the Millerand-Colliard bill establishing factory-level mechanisms for regulating strikes through compulsory arbitration (1900); and legislation amending the

44. Marjorie Farrar, *Principled Pragmatist: The Political Career of Alexandre Mitterand* (Oxford, Engl., 1990), 81–82 n. 49, and 84; Sorlin, *Waldeck-Rousseau,* 264, 267-68, 478 n. 178.

45. Farrar, *Principled Pragmatist,* 57–74; an older analysis of the origins and development of Millerand's reform program is Charles W. Pipkin, *Social Politics and Modern Democracies* (New York, 1931), II, 36–73.

46. Farrar, *Principled Pragmatist,* 62–63; Pipkin, *Social Politics,* 235–36.

1884 law recognizing unions, to allow them to own property and to engage in commerce (1900).

The government's program of labor reforms, Griffuelhes argued, was dictated by its desire for social peace. To achieve this end, the government was prepared to use force, as its suppression of strikes demonstrated, but its preferred weapon was what Griffuelhes called "corrupting liberalism": "[Waldeck-Rousseau] was too clever to stand steadfast in the path of social progress. Wasn't it a better idea . . . under the guise of liberalism, to regulate this progress, so as to diminish its flow and curb its force?" [47]

Griffuelhes' references to the government's desire to control the "flow and force" of social progress recall the backdrop against which the Millerand Affair was being played out—the strike wave of 1899–1902. These strikes were perhaps most worrying to employers and the government because they tended to be larger in scope and to affect the leading sectors of the economy more frequently than in the past.

Griffuelhes later reflected back on the hopes and expectations engendered in the labor movement by the strike wave that coincided with Millerand's term of office. In time, the strike wave began to take on a life of its own, one with revolutionary implications that went beyond demands for higher wages and improved working conditions or even republicanization of the workplace. "The number of strikes increased," he wrote, "their character became more focused, their importance grew. The life which developed around them was intensified through incessant practice and activity, drawing into the struggle militants long resigned to defeat, who brought along with them new trades and new activists." [48]

The mounting strike wave, with its growing complement of strikers in the major industries, revived expectations in some working-class circles of the revolutionary general strike, labor's own "practical and moral alternative to political socialism." [49]

That many of the strikes of the era were motivated by deeply felt anger and desperation, Griffuelhes knew from personal experience. One of the most violent strikes took place in his own trade, among the Breton shoe-factory workers of Fougères (Ille-et-Vilaine), France's leading center of industrialized footwear production. Paul Delesalle, Griffuelhes' future colleague on the CGT

---

47. Griffuelhes, *L'Action syndicaliste*, 8.
48. *Ibid.*, 7.
49. Alan B. Spitzer, "Anarchy and Culture: Fernand Pelloutier and the Dilemma of Revolutionary Syndicalism," *International Review of Social History*, VIII (1963), 379.

administrative bureau, has left an account of the sacking of the Doussin shoe factory in Fougères by some three thousand workers on July 23, 1900: "Everything was wrecked. Benches, chairs, tubs, doors, a barrel filled with white powder, jerrycans filled with gasoline and kerosene, brooms, a handcart, ladders, electric lamps, window shades, billing sheets, registers, scraps of leather, even whole machines, were thrown into the street and smashed."[50]

An article in *La Petite République* described what happened next. "The police came on in three successive waves, but the workers defended themselves with whatever fell to hand, and forced them to fall back. Finally, the cavalry arrived and charged full tilt into the crowd, trampling men, women, and children under the feet of their horses."[51]

To preserve social peace, Griffuelhes wrote, the State was prepared to use brute force, but it preferred to win over "the workers' organizations by trying to gain the cooperation of their militants and to convince them to confine their activity within a legal framework."[52] This task, in Griffuelhes' view, devolved upon the minister of commerce, with his network of contacts and allies inside the labor movement.

The first challenge in this area came with Millerand's decree reforming the Supreme Labor Council, the bipartite (workers and employers) body originally set up in 1891. Most unions had refused to participate in it, however, and it had become moribund. In September, 1899, the council was revived on new foundations with a more ambitious mandate. It was to be part of an overall structure to head off strikes through prior consultations on labor disputes. The reformed council would be tripartite, with equal numbers of worker and employer members and government appointees; the employer and worker delegates were to be elected by the members of their professional associations. Unions would have one vote for each twenty-five members.[53]

Further, the Supreme Labor Council was intended as the capstone of a system of regional councils—these limited to worker and employer participation—to advise the government on labor questions and to arbitrate enterprise-level disputes. Millerand spelled out the goals of this system of consul-

50. Allan Binstock, "The Shoemakers of Fougères: A Study of the Development of the Shoe Industry in the City of Fougères (Brittany, Department of the Ille-et-Vilaine)" (Ph.D. dissertation, University of Wisconsin-Madison, 1972); Jean Maitron, *Le Syndicalisme révolutionnaire: Paul Delesalle* (Paris, 1952), 119–20.

51. *La Petite République*, July 26, 1900.

52. Griffuelhes, "La Revue 'L'Action Directe' (1903–1904)," *L'Encyclopédie du mouvement syndicaliste*, no. 1 (January, 1912), 19.

53. Lefranc, *Mouvement socialiste sous la Troisième République*, 114.

tative bodies in an address in November, 1901: "The only way to reach the peaceful and legal solutions to these social problems that we all desire . . . is to . . . bring workers and employers together to closely examine social problems in order to resolve them in a reasonable and cooperative manner."[54]

The reformist leaders of the CGT and the Bourse du Travail responded enthusiastically to the plan to revive the Supreme Labor Council. Despite somewhat paranoid warnings from opponents that the elections to the council were simply a police plot to find out how many members the various unions had, in the spring of 1900 the CGT's two most powerful unions, both Allemanist-led, decided to elect representatives to the council workers' delegation. In April, Eugène Guérard was picked to represent the railway workers' union; in May, the building trades' union chose general secretary Lucien Riom as its delegate.[55]

Guérard, probably the most influential figure in the French trade-union movement at this point, now emerged as its leading spokesman for Millerandism. Taking part in the work of the Supreme Labor Council, he said, would give unions "a greater authority and soon make them indispensable to the normal workings of society." Even the partisans of the revolutionary overthrow of the capitalist system could profit from participation in the council, Guérard said, more than a little facetiously. "The unions who claim they are prepared to take over the government and administration of society ought to welcome contact which, by familiarizing them with the administration of things, can help train them for their future role."[56]

Victor Griffuelhes took a typically cynical view of the Supreme Labor Council and the role it was intended to play. He believed that the government hoped, by playing on the vanity and ambition of certain union leaders who liked hobnobbing with industrialists and government officials, "to turn organized labor into a new [government] instrument, a new social force, directed against the producing class." He realized, however, that there was little chance of boycotting the council. Motions to that effect failed at the CGT congresses

54. *Ibid.*, 115.

55. APP, B/a 1610, note of October 17, 1899. For Guérard's election, see Syndicat national des Travailleurs des Chemins de Fer, *Compte rendu du 11ᵉ Congrès national tenu . . . à Paris les 1ᵉʳ, 2 et 3 [avril] 1900* (Paris, 1900), 18–19; Riom's election is noted in Office du Travail, *Associations professionelles*, IV, 58.

56. Syndicat national des Travailleurs des Chemins de Fer, *Compte rendu du 11ᵉ Congrès national*, 18–19; Eugène Guérard, "Les Conseils du travail," *VdP*, no. 4, December 23–30, 1900.

of 1900 and 1901 (though by only a one-vote margin in 1901).[57] The strategy Griffuelhes fell back upon was one he would use repeatedly during his years leading the CGT—boring from within or *noyautage*. Thus, he and his cohorts would try to assure that future delegates to the council were trusted revolutionary syndicalists, who could be counted on to slow proceedings and render the institution as meaningless as it had been in the early 1890s.[58]

From the standpoint of revolutionary syndicalists like Griffuelhes, the supreme challenge, which they believed posed a threat to the very existence of the trade-union movement, came with the introduction in January, 1900, of the Millerand-Colliard bill on compulsory arbitration. This bill in effect completed the Supreme Labor Council–regional council edifice by providing for bipartite consultation at enterprise level; it called for elected councils in all plants with more than fifty employees to formulate and present labor demands to management. If no agreement on the demands could be reached at the level of the plant, the two sides would be obliged to submit the dispute to the relevant regional council for arbitration. Only in cases where employers refused arbitration could strikes be called and then only if half plus one of the workers involved voted in favor.[59]

Compulsory arbitration has never been very popular with unions, and the Millerand-Colliard bill was no exception. Even reformist trade unionists thought it was going too far, as Eugène Guérard admitted. "If we're not careful," he wrote, "the trade-union movement will be drawn off its course by these reforms." The revolutionary syndicalists, of course, were even more suspicious. In a two-part series in *La Voix du Peuple,* its editor, Emile Pouget, called compulsory arbitration "the most dangerous threat yet to the labor movement." Implementation of the reform would virtually rule out solidarity strikes and, most important, the general strike. The word *unions* appeared nowhere in the bill, and the proposed plant councils looked suspiciously like company unions, wrote Pouget. Whatever they turned out to be in actual fact, they would function as counterweights to CGT unions at enterprise level.

57. Griffuelhes, *L'Action syndicaliste,* 7; CGT, *La Confédération générale du travail et le Mouvement syndical* (Paris, 1925), 78–81.

58. See, for example, the campaign to replace Briat by Georges Yvetot, recounted in detail by Griffuelhes in "Méthode de corruption," *L'Action Directe,* 1st ser. (August, 1903); Griffuelhes' most extensive critique of the Supreme Labor Council is his "Le Conseil supérieur du travail," *Le Mouvement socialiste,* no. 129 (October 1, 1903), 225–44.

59. Lefranc, *Mouvement socialiste sous la Troisième République,* 115.

And they would make industry-wide organizing even more difficult than it already was, he concluded.[60]

Victor Griffuelhes saw the Millerand-Colliard bill as part of a new stage in the evolution of capitalist labor strategy. In an interesting piece on the advent of tripartite consultative machinery in the U.S.A. in the wake of the Homestead steel strike, he portrayed compulsory arbitration as one of the key elements in a new global strategy to "master" labor through legal methods.[61] Thus, "Waldeck, having understood that it is impossible to tame us by force, now wants to throw legal barriers in our path."

The premier had miscalculated, however. Unlike the U.S. "labor aristocrats" (as Griffuelhes termed the members of the American Federation of Labor), French workers were less interested in higher wages and better working conditions than in abolishing the wage system altogether. "The day when our American comrades understand that there is a social question and that its solution is not simply a problematic increase in wages or reduction in working hours," Griffuelhes wrote grandly, "the days of capitalism will be numbered in that country."

Parenthetically, Griffuelhes first spelled out in this context a theme that would become a constant in his pronouncements on labor grand strategy: that the trade-union movement had nothing to lose and much to gain from the concentration of capital. The growth of American-type trusts in France, he wrote, "shouldn't frighten us: They are an inevitable stage in the evolution of private property." The concentration of capital, he argued, would force the concentration of labor and thus hasten the coming of the "Final Battle."[62]

Griffuelhes also strongly opposed the government's plan to amend the law of 1884 to permit unions "to sign binding contracts, acquire and invest capital, and participate fully in judicial cases." Securing this "civil personality" for the unions had been a pet project of Waldeck-Rousseau's since the 1880s, and he

60. Guérard, "Les Conseils du travail," *VdP*, no. 16, January 6–13, March 17–24, 1901; Emile Pouget, "L'Etranglement de grèves," *ibid.*

61. Griffuelhes was referring here to the signing in May, 1900, of the Murray Hill Agreement between leading U.S. iron and steel manufacturers and the U.S. metalworkers' unions; the pact set industry-wide limits on working hours and set up national arbitration machinery for the sector. See David Montgomery, *The Fall of the House of Labor . . . 1865–1925* (Cambridge, Engl., 1987), 261–63.

62. Griffuelhes, "Phénomène capitaliste," *VdP*, no. 57, December 29, 1901–January 5, 1902; the ideas in Griffuelhes' piece appear to have been borrowed to a large extent from C.-A. Maybon's article, "Le Prolétariat devant les trusts," in *Le Mouvement socialiste*, no. 71 (December 1, 1901), 659–65.

was disappointed that the parliament had not extended these rights to workers' organizations in the 1884 law. In true Gambettist fashion, "as late as 1899, Waldeck confidently predicted that once the unions were allowed to receive and invest capital, they would become the agents of the future solution [to the social question of how to fit the working class into French society]: the accession of the salaried class to individual property and commerce." In March, 1900, Griffuelhes gave an interview to Clemenceau's newspaper *L'Aurore,* in which he charged that the aim of the amendment to the law of 1884 was to "divert the unions from their real task, [the] emancipation of all," by promoting "egoism" and greed for profits. "[Owning] capitalist property means social conservatism," Griffuelhes admonished. And like many other trade unionists, including some who supported the reform, he feared that if unions acquired property, it would encourage lawsuits by employers for alleged damages incurred through strikes. Finally, Griffuelhes saw the proposed amendment as one more proof that the Waldeck-Rousseau government sought to convert the unions into "an organ of the State charged with maintaining order in social conflicts."[63]

Griffuelhes' rise to prominence in the French trade-union movement, fueled primarily by his tough stand against Millerandism, also profited greatly from his position on the crisis that gripped the national Bourse du Travail federation in 1900–1901. Although Griffuelhes was active in the Bourse du Travail movement, he had strong reservations about its susceptibility to State and municipal control. Thus, he joined a campaign in 1900, with like-minded Blanquist militants, to wean control of the federation from its general secretary, Fernand Pelloutier, in the hope of moving the organization toward closer ties with the CGT. In 1901, his emphasis in the campaign switched to the controversy then raging over the crackdown on the Paris Bourse du Travail by the capital's newly elected nationalist city council. Nevertheless, the campaign's ultimate aim was the absorption of the Bourse du Travail federation into the CGT, an objective accomplished at the CGT Congress of Montpellier in September, 1902.

Fernand Pelloutier believed that the Blanquists wanted to take control of the National Federation of Bourses du Travail and use it for their political ends. In 1895, at the federation's congress in Nimes, he had succeeded in

63. Stone, *Search for Social Peace,* 145, 141–42; also see Sorlin, *Waldeck-Rousseau,* 461; Georges Laporte, "Le Projet de loi sur les syndicats," *L'Aurore,* March 7, 1900.

eliminating the Blanquists—general secretary Rieul Cordier and treasurer Bernard Besset—from leadership posts in the organization; Pelloutier himself succeeded Cordier.[64] Five years later, however, this coup would return to haunt him.

Besset had stuck with the Bourse du Travail movement, and by 1900, he and his Blanquist comrades were in de facto control of the Lyon affiliate.[65] At some point before the September, 1900, congress of the federation in Paris, the Lyon Blanquists learned that Pelloutier had accepted a research post in the Labor Office (Office du Travail) attached to Millerand's ministry of commerce. What followed was one of the more unsavory episodes in French labor history, and Griffuelhes was reportedly in the thick of it.

During the September 6 session of the congress, Jean Thozet, the Guesdist who served as general secretary of the Lyon Bourse du Travail and who was a front for Besset and his group, rose to ask Pelloutier how he could justify serving the Bourse du Travail movement and working for Millerand at the same time. Pelloutier, who had left his sickbed to attend the congress, related how, having suffered a tubercular hemorrhage and having no money for medical care, he had asked his friend Georges Sorel to go to Jaurès for help. Jaurès had found him the job at the Labor Office. Pelloutier said that the job only involved collecting data, and recalling his long years of disinterested service to the movement, he asked for—and got—a vote of confidence. Still, given the emotions aroused by Millerandism and despite the viciousness of the Blanquist attack, Pelloutier and the Bourse du Travail federation emerged diminished from the encounter.[66]

"Victor Griffuelhes took part in the unjust criticisms that the Lyon Blanquists levelled at Pelloutier," Edouard Dolléans has written, because "he saw a danger in any subsidy tying the Bourses to the municipalities or the State." Although he offers no proof of Griffuelhes' involvement, there is no reason to doubt it. It is also possible that there was more to his involvement than principled concern over the subsidies issue. As suggested earlier, removing Pelloutier would have been a big step on the road to CGT–Bourse du Travail fusion since, as Jacques Julliard has pointed out, by 1901 Pelloutier was the

64. Julliard, *Fernand Pelloutier*, 126–27.

65. Yves Lequin, *Les Ouvriers de la région lyonnaise, 1848–1914* (Lyon, 1977), II, 310–11.

66. *Ibid.*; *DBMO*, XV, 231 (Thozet). For the full debate on Pelloutier's sinecure, see Fédération Nationale des Bourses du Travail de France et des Colonies, *Compte rendu du 8ᵉ Congrès national, Paris, 5–8 septembre 1900* (Paris, 1900), 86–92.

major remaining obstacle to a merger.[67] That roadblock was removed by Pelloutier's death eight months later, but in the meantime, Griffuelhes had shifted to another tack.

On December 29, 1900, the nationalist-dominated Paris municipal council cancelled the city's annual subsidy to the Bourse du Travail, a sum totaling 110,000 francs and representing most of the organization's budget for the coming year. The council announced, however, that it would dole out funds on a case-by-case basis to unions that came forward to request them. No preference would be shown to unions affiliated to the Bourse du Travail and, of course, company unions would not necessarily be turned away.[68]

On January 4, 1901, a meeting of representatives of the unions affiliated with the Bourse du Travail, called by the TFS executive committee and chaired by Griffuelhes, voted to ignore the council. This position was reaffirmed at a second meeting of Parisian unions on January 16.[69] Griffuelhes explained the reasoning behind this strategy, which was very much his own, in a long article in the pro-Blanquist daily, *Le Petit Sou*, on January 9, 1901. To begin with, he wrote, the city council's decision to stop the subsidy was a political act that only indirectly concerned the working class. Its main target was the socialist minister of commerce, who had angered the nationalist city fathers the previous July by using his decree powers to turn over administration of the Bourse du Travail to a committee composed entirely of union men. "The municipal council," he said, "has remained faithful to its reactionary politics in this matter. It wanted to express its opposition to the [republican] government. This is just another round in the battle between the nationalists and the ministry. The unions have no business putting themselves between the log and the buzzsaw. Their task, and here is where I take my stand, is to stop asking for handouts and learn to live on their own resources."

The job of the trade unionist, Griffuelhes continued, was to build strong industrial unions, which depended on their members, not outside sources, for their funds. This was the only way to build a union movement that can "stand

67. Dolléans, *Histoire du mouvement ouvrier*, II, 118; Jacques Julliard, "Fernand Pelloutier," *Le Mouvement social*, no. 75 (April–June 1971), 17.

68. J.-B. Séverac, *Le Mouvement syndical* (Paris, 1913), 48–49, Vol. IV of Adéodat C. A. Compère-Morel, ed., *Encyclopédie socialiste, syndicaliste et coopérative de l'Internationale Ouvrière*, 12 vols.

69. APP, B/a 1610, note of January 5, 1901; Griffuelhes, "Bulletin syndical: Opinion," *Le Petit Sou*, February 3, 1901.

up to the power of the bourgeoisie and function like a state within a state, with a life of its own, above the battle of the political parties."

The municipal council's punitive action could turn out to be a blessing in disguise, Griffuelhes contended. If unions began to look to their own resources instead of to the State, they might soon have "a Bourse of their own, where the workers will truly be their own masters, like our comrades in Berlin."[70] An interesting comment from a man who would later gain—and to a large extent merit—a reputation as one of the CGT's leading Germanophobes.

The cutoff of subsidies to the Bourse du Travail did not have the immediate results Griffuelhes had hoped for. With the return of the Radicals to control of the municipal council in 1902, the subsidies were restored. Nevertheless, the interlude was something of a moral victory for Griffuelhes and the partisans of trade-union independence and unity. Militants were treated to the spectacle of union leaders lining up for handouts from the city council reactionaries.[71] What it all seemed to bear out, once again, was the inherent weakness in the Bourse du Travail movement—its reliance on sources outside its control for the facilities it used and the funding it needed to stay alive. The subsidies issue weakened a federation already on the defensive and further undermined its resistance to CGT calls for a merger.

On November 26, 1901, Victor Griffuelhes, just twenty-seven years old with only seven years of trade-union experience behind him, was elected general secretary of the CGT by the Comité confédéral, the organization's executive body.[72] The vote was 81–3, with three abstentions. Griffuelhes had been nominated for the post by his union, the National Leatherworkers' Federation, and he was the sole declared candidate. The postal and telegraph workers' union voted for Eloi Hardy, the moderate secretary of the blacksmiths' union who had not announced his candidacy, and the equally moderate retail clerks' union abstained.[73] To be absolutely precise, the title Griffuelhes inherited from his predecessor, Eugène Guérard of the railway workers' union, was somewhat less grand than general secretary. In statutory terms, he was simply the "secretary of the administrative bureau," and many in the confederation intended that the powers delegated to the post should remain

70. Griffuelhes, "Une Opinion," *Le Petit Sou,* January 9, 1901.

71. Or so the police reported, with undisguised satisfaction (AN, F7 12.890, note of March 7, 1906).

72. "Executive" in the sense of "executing" the resolutions passed by delegates at the confederation's biennial congresses, which were sovereign according to CGT statutes.

73. *VdP,* no. 53, December 1–7, 1901.

as limited as the title suggests. But Griffuelhes, who was not content to be a simple administrator, would change all that. His chances for increased power improved dramatically the next year, when revised statutes were adopted following the merger of the CGT and the National Federation of Bourses du Travail.

III

THE ORGANIZER (1902–1904)

The 1901–08 period . . . was one of continuous growth for the CGT. A new movement was built from the ground up. This was not a movement of ideas or theories; we already had plenty of those. It was a movement of action, created by the best militants and stimulated by groups full of the vigor and vitality of youth.

—Victor Griffuelhes, *Encyclopédie du mouvement syndicaliste*

The years 1902–1904 were perhaps the most constructive of Griffuelhes' eight years at the helm of the CGT. "The CGT was very active throughout the period," wrote Maxime Leroy, "one could even say that it was from 1902 to 1904 that it took definitive shape."[1] The first ten months of Griffuelhes' tenure were a veritable tour de force. At the CGT's Congress of Montpellier in September, 1902, his first as general secretary, he presided over the unification of the French trade-union movement, an objective that had eluded his predecessors for the better part of a decade.[2] The achievement of unity through the merger of the CGT and the National Federation of Bourses du Travail made Montpellier "the decisive congress of the confederation," in the view of Robert Brécy. Griffuelhes' report to the congress was "full of optimism and hope," recalled Pierre Monatte. Since his election as general secretary in November, 1901, Griffuelhes proudly reported, seventeen union federations

---

1. Leroy, *Coutume ouvrière*, II, 476.
2. This refers, of course, only to the "free" trade-union movement, *i.e.*, that part not sponsored or financed by the Church, companies, or the State.

had been coaxed back into the CGT and thirteen new ones had been added to the roster.[3]

The following year brought another triumph for Griffuelhes. In December, 1903, he orchestrated a demonstration of the practical value of direct action by organizing simultaneous rallies in one hundred cities to protest the Senate's footdragging on a bill to abolish private job placement bureaus. In 1904, the Senate finally passed the bill, thus satisfying a demand that had been on the French working-class agenda since the days of the Second Empire.[4]

By 1904, Griffuelhes had emerged as the dominant figure in the French trade-union movement. He would have argued that this achievement was the result of the "moral authority" he had acquired in leading the fight against Millerandism. Others might have noted his skills as an orator, debater, or propagandist, and some would have underscored his talents as an organizer. Another factor, however, which is less often cited, was his own highly visible activism.

From 1902 to 1904, he always seemed to be where the action was: in the middle of the ideological crossfire over the future of the powerful coal miners' union in the Pas-de-Calais (1902–1903); in the streets during the violent textile workers' strike at Armentières (1903); at the head of the nationwide campaign to abolish the private job placement bureaus (1903); at the center of a large agricultural laborers' strike in the Midi (1904). Activism of this kind had not been a hallmark of the CGT leadership in earlier years. Previous general secretaries, Parisians to a man, had only ventured beyond the capital to attend congresses. Nor had they gone into strike zones to offer support to the strikers, as Griffuelhes so often did.

Griffuelhes' activism during these years also underlines his strong commitment to building a genuinely national labor confederation, one organized around national industrial federations representing not only the traditional crafts that had dominated the old CGT but also the "big battalions" of modern industrial labor, *e.g.*, the miners and metalworkers. It also demonstrates his personal interest in organizing workers not yet in unions: the masses of textile workers, many of whom were still engaged in cottage industry, and the

3. Robert Brécy, *Le Mouvement syndical en France: Essai bibliographique* (Paris, 1963), 59; Pierre Monatte, *Trois Scissions syndicales* (Paris, 1958), 99.

4. Griffuelhes, "100 Meetings"; "Lettre au Sénat," *VdP*, no. 163, November 29–December 6, 1903; a brief historical sketch of the struggle to suppress the bureaus can be found in "Les Officines du placement," *VdP*, no. 1, December 9, 1900.

vast reservoir of agricultural labor, which until Griffuelhes became head of the CGT was almost virgin territory to union organizers.

Griffuelhes' determination to forge a national trade-union movement is clearly demonstrated in his effort to unite its two principal components, the CGT and the National Federation of Bourses du Travail. Faithful to the Blanquist view until around 1900 that the Bourses du Travail represented "the most powerful form of organization of worker militancy," Griffuelhes had entered trade unionism through the Bourse du Travail movement, not the CGT, but had quickly become disillusioned. As noted in Chapter II, he was shocked by the Bourse du Travail leaders' support for the Waldeck-Rousseau government and its subsequent program to bring the trade-union movement under government control. Moreover, the disarray caused by the nationalist city council's withdrawal in December, 1900, of the municipal subsidy to the Paris Bourse du Travail convinced him of the "danger [presented] by any subsidy tying the Bourses to the municipalities or to the public authorities." From this point on, Griffuelhes was convinced that the future of the French labor movement lay with the CGT, a conclusion reached at about the same time by the Blanquist chief, Edouard Vaillant, and that the number one item on the French working-class agenda for the immediate future was to merge the National Federation of Bourses du Travail and the CGT.[5] And convinced of the inherent weaknesses of the Bourse du Travail movement, Griffuelhes was determined that the senior partner in that merger would be the CGT.

The campaign to unite the two organizations was launched at the CGT Congress of Lyon in September, 1901. The motion for unification, presented by the Oise metalworkers' federation represented by the Blanquist Jean Majot, had failed to pass, principally because of strong opposition from the CGT general secretary, Eugène Guérard.[6] That obstacle, however, was removed two months later when Guérard was replaced by Griffuelhes. Now the cause of unity would have the general secretary of the CGT as one of its most dedicated partisans.

On the Bourse du Travail side, opposition to unification received a severe blow with the death of Fernand Pelloutier in March, 1901. Pelloutier, in ad-

---

5. Howorth, *Edouard Vaillant*, 103; Dolléans, *Histoire du mouvement ouvrier*, II, 118; Vaillant, "La Confédération du Travail," *Le Petit Sou*, September 20, 1901, quoted in Howorth, *Edouard Vaillant*, 200–201.

6. APP, B/a 1606, note of August 3, 1901; *DBMO*, XII, 333 (Majot); *L'Aurore*, September 25, 1901.

dition to believing that the two organizations had separate, incompatible missions—an educative function for the Bourses du Travail and an organizational one for the CGT—had also opposed unity because he saw it as yet another bid by the Blanquists to take over the union movement. Pelloutier's death, however, created a vacuum in the opposition ranks that no one else seemed able to fill. His successor, Georges Yvetot, while as opposed to unification as Pelloutier had been, did not enjoy enough prestige in the organization to combat it effectively.[7]

The major impetus toward unity within the Bourse du Travail ranks came from outside Paris, in the person of Louis Niel, secretary of the Montpellier Bourse. At the September, 1902, Congress of the National Federation of Bourses du Travail in Algiers, the pro-unity forces prevailed and a declaration was adopted stating, in part, that "the CGT is, from the material point of view, the unifying and activist force of the working class, both in terms of its immediate demands and its future aspirations." Niel was chosen to head the Bourse du Travail committee that would negotiate the terms of unification at the next CGT congress, to be held in his hometown, Montpellier, a few days later.[8]

Despite their recognition of the primacy of the CGT, the leaders of the Bourse du Travail federation did not intend to be swallowed up by the confederation. Niel had told the Congress of Algiers that the federation would "disappear as a central organization, but not in terms of its functions and services." What Niel and his confederates sought was a bipartite arrangement in which the two organizations would join forces without sacrificing the autonomy of either. The new CGT would be composed of two separate branches, a Section of Federations (the old CGT) and a Section of Bourses du Travail. Each would have its own bureau, headed by a general secretary; the two general secretaries would enjoy equal authority and would rotate as general secretaries of the CGT as a whole.[9]

Meanwhile, the Blanquists who now dominated the CGT leadership had maintained constant pressure on the Bourse du Travail federation. Just before the federation's congress at Algiers, the CGT newspaper, *La Voix du Peuple*, had published a draft of a "Proposal for Workers' Unity" from the Blanquist-led metalworkers' federation; while accepting that a "branch" of the unified organization would be reserved for the Bourses du Travail, the proposal made

7. *DBMO*, XVI, 346 (Yvetot).
8. CGT, *La CGT et le Mouvement syndical*, 44–45.
9. *Ibid.*; Leroy, *Coutume ouvrière*, II, 497.

clear that the CGT would hold the whip hand. Probably written by metal-workers' leader Albert Bourchet, it lambasted the Bourses for their "subordination" to the public authorities, their dependence on municipal funding, and their inability to keep out "yellow" or company unions.[10] Then, at the Congress of Algiers itself, the Lyon Bourse du Travail, dominated by Blanquists led by Bernard Besset, had proposed "the complete suppression of the Federation of Bourses."

Griffuelhes played little role in the debate on unity at Montpellier. He had no need to. Bourchet, who headed the CGT negotiating team, carried the ball very effectively, adroitly mixing conciliation and firmness. Thus in addressing the congress he declared, "We say to our friends of the Bourses du Travail: We recognize the immense services you have rendered to the proletariat and we know that, in the history of workers' organizations, you have a place that no one will contest; . . . we want to leave you as large a place as possible in the future." [11]

But Bourchet made clear that "as large a place as possible" did not mean sharing the top leadership of the CGT. The Bourses du Travail's dependence on municipal subsidies—some 350,000 francs a year, he estimated—rendered them unfit to lead a united working-class movement whose mission was to overthrow the capitalist system. "They live on these credits and it would be too easy [for the authorities] to create trouble and disorganization in our leadership if it was in the hands of the Bourses du Travail." This proved to be an unassailable argument; even reformist leaders of the CGT such as Pierre Coupat, who had been warm supporters of the pro-Millerandist leadership of the Paris Bourse du Travail, were unwilling to see Bourse officials at the head of the CGT.[12]

After "three meetings and fifteen hours of often passionate discussion," reported Bourchet, the committee on unity worked out a compromise. The new statutes of the CGT subsequently adopted by the congress conceded a substantial amount of autonomy to the Bourses du Travail within the new organization. Article 2 of the statutes declared that:

The [General] Confederation of Labor is composed of:

1. The national (or where necessary, regional) industrial or craft federations, and national unions;

---

10. *VdP*, no. 95, September 7–14, 1902.
11. *VdP*, no. 93, August 24–31, 1902, and no. 99, October 5–12, 1902.
12. Leroy, *Coutume ouvrière*, II, 473, 497.

2. The Bourses du Travail, considered as [representing] local or departmental or regional unions of different trades, it being understood that there will be no overlapping among them . . .

Article 5 of the statutes made the two sections autonomous and set out the mechanisms for their cooperation.

The first branch will be called "the Section of Industrial or Craft Federations. . . ." The second will be called "the Section of Bourses du Travail." . . . Each section will have its own bureau. Their work is delimited; they will meet separately once a month, when convened by their general secretaries. The executive committee, composed of the two sections, will meet every three months. It can be called into emergency session, in urgent cases. The administrative bureau is composed of the bureaus of the two Sections plus the secretary of each [standing] committee [*i.e.,* committees on *La Voix du Peuple;* on strikes and the general strike; and on finance].

The next sentence in the statutes, however, was the key one in terms of the new relationship between the CGT and the Bourses du Travail federation: "The secretary of the Section of Industrial or Craft Federations will have the title of general secretary of the confederation." [13] The Bourses du Travail would have the autonomy within the confederation that Niel had insisted upon. The new Section of Bourses du Travail would continue to hold congresses of its own and to add new affiliates at an uninterrupted pace; it would continue to perform the educative and ameliorative tasks that Pelloutier had ascribed to it, but it would not share power within the trade-union movement with the leaders of the old CGT.[14] That power had once been exclusively its own, while the CGT floundered. Now, power had definitely passed to the CGT. As Edouard Dolléans put it, "Working-class unity had been achieved. The confederation — and its executive body, the Comité confédéral — were reinforced. One man was prepared to use that force. That was the secretary of the Section of Federations, Victor Griffuelhes, whom this function made general secretary of the CGT." [15]

One of the principal tasks Griffuelhes set himself after his election as gen-

13. CGT, *La CGT et le Mouvement syndical,* 88–90.

14. "In 1902, [the CGT] included 83 Bourses du Travail and 30 trade unions; in 1904, the figures would show 110 and 52, respectively, or a total of 1,791 unions" (Leroy, *Coutume ouvrière,* II, 476).

15. Dolléans, *Histoire du mouvement ouvrier,* II, 56.

eral secretary in November, 1901, was to break the reformist socialists' grip on the national miners' union and, once this had been accomplished, to bring the miners into the CGT. Over the previous ten months, he had watched with increasing frustration as successive attempts to launch a nationwide miners' strike were undermined by those he called "the high priests of socialist opportunism," principally supporters of the Government of Republican Defense such as Emile Basly, deputy from Lens (Pas-de-Calais) and president of the large miners' union from that region, and Jean Jaurès, whose Tarn constituency included the miners of Carmaux. What frustrated Griffuelhes was that, in his view, a national miners' strike could have been "the signal for the general struggle so feared in government circles and elsewhere." For a long time now, he wrote, "we workers . . . have been waiting for the day when, behind a strong minority of our fellows who have finally seen what their true interests are, we could move to suppress the economic privileges [of the capitalists] and establish the real Republic." [16]

The coal miners had long been recognized as indispensable to building a strong, representative trade-union movement in France, yet in 1901, they were the only manual trade of any consequence that still had no membership in the CGT. At the turn of the century, the National Miners' Federation was the largest union in France; according to Rolande Trempé, the miners were the only true French industrial unionists in 1900. A report to the CGT Congress of Lyon in 1901 claimed that 60 percent of French coal miners, or somewhere between 80,000 and 100,000 men, belonged to unions; while the percentage figure is exaggerated, it is nonetheless true that miners had the highest level of union membership of any French trade during the period.[17]

Coal miners also enjoyed great respect among labor militants of Griffuelhes' generation. Their hard life, what Griffuelhes called "the life full of danger and weariness at the bottom of the pit," was one reason. But miners also had a reputation for toughness and militancy, a reputation no doubt enhanced by the novels of Emile Zola and Charles Malato. Georges Dumoulin, one of Griffuelhes' associates in the miners' movement during the prewar period, later recalled that "reading Zola and the POF brochures" convinced him to join the miners' union in the Pas-de-Calais in 1896. Zola's novel of the miners' struggle, *Germinal*, drew heavily on what he knew of the miners'

---

16. Griffuelhes, "La Grève des mineurs," *Le Petit Sou*, April 11, 1901.

17. Rolande Trempé, "Le Réformisme des mineurs français à la fin du XIXe siècle," *Le Mouvement social*, no. 65 (October–December 1968), 94; Dolléans, *Histoire du mouvement ouvrier*, II, 53 n. 2.

strike at Anzin (Nord) in 1884. Anarchist Charles Malato's novel *La Grande Greve*, which depicted the battle of miners at Montceau-les-Mines (Saone-et-Loire) to form a union in the 1880s and 1890s, was also among Dumoulin's favorite reading.[18]

The miner, wrote Jacques Julliard, was "the Worker par excellence . . . Until the turn of the century, he remained the avant garde of the proletariat, just as the building laborer would be a few years later or the metalworker in 1936. . . . The dangerous, back-breaking nature of his work; the scope and violence of certain miners' strikes (Anzin in 1884; Decazeville [Aveyron] in 1886); earned the miner a privileged place in the sentimental geography of the working class."[19]

To Griffuelhes' mind, the miners' union, massive, militant, and located at the heart of one of France's most critical industries, was the leading candidate to trigger the revolutionary general strike. To have that power under the umbrella of the CGT, where it could be channeled and coordinated, would considerably advance the revolutionary timetable. In an important article, written as a postmortem on the failed national miners' strike of October–November, 1902, Griffuelhes declared that "the miners' strike has demonstrated that the General Strike is possible, for it has refuted all the theoretical arguments that have been raised against it." The National Miners' Federation, despite an empty treasury and the loss of around one-third of its members when the more revolutionary elements departed the previous March, had still been able to bring out some 160,000 strikers, "in a movement admirable in itself and unique in our time." Why, then, had the strike failed? First of all, Griffuelhes argued, because the miners had "counted too much on themselves," when experience should have taught them that the more a movement "expands, the more manpower it has behind it, the more support it finds outside its own ranks, the greater will be its effect on production." The general strike, he wrote, is "the rapid and successive stoppage of industries through a natural and logical chain reaction, produced under moral pressure from the militant minority." Griffuelhes went on to state that "the miners' federation, the militant minority," had brought the mines to a standstill "and, if it had wanted to, could have brought out the metalworkers as well, and thus brought together the elements for an extension of the struggle."

18. Griffuelhes, "La Grève des mineurs"; *DBMO*, XII, 108 (Dumoulin); Georges Dumoulin, "La Fédération des mineurs," Pt. 1, *Le Mouvement socialiste*, no. 203 (October 15, 1908), 243.

19. Jacques Julliard, "Jeune et Vieux Syndicat chez les mineurs du Pas-de-Calais (à travers les papiers de Pierre Monatte)," *Le Mouvement social*, no. 47 (April–June 1964), 8.

In other words, the miners could have been the catalyst for a general strike, according to Griffuelhes. It could have happened, but it had not: Not only had the strike not spread to other trades, but "despite the grandeur of the effort, the results were meager" for the miners themselves. Why? To recap Griffuelhes' earlier point, the miners had not known how to "generalize" their strike nor understood the relationships among "the principal factors of production"; they had not realized the "natural and logical" linkages between their industry and metalworking, for example, a connection that Griffuelhes would make the cornerstone of his strategy for the general strike.[20] But even if all of this had been understood, Griffuelhes suggested, cooperation between the miners and other trades would still have been frustrated, and not so much because of the particularism of the miners, their "corporative egoism" and strong local and regional ties.[21] Although these factors certainly were present in the strike, the difficulties in cooperation occurred because key unions in the federation were controlled by reformist socialists whose real loyalties, in Griffuelhes' view, were to their parliamentary careers and to the republican regime.

Thus, Emile Basly had pulled the key Pas-de-Calais union out of the 1902 strike in its first days and opened negotiations with the local mining companies.[22] This move, apparently made under pressure from the government and reformist members of the socialist Chamber delegation, violated a pledge to conduct talks with management only at the national level, with the coal concessionnaires' association, the Comité des Houillères de France, and not to break off the strike until the demands of all participating unions had been met. In the end, Basly was obliged to submit his union's main demand, which was to restore bonuses to 1901 levels, to binding arbitration. The arbitration award, rendered on November 5, 1902, found "no justification for raising bonuses above the current [reduced] level." On November 13, after an attempt by outraged miners to disavow Basly and continue the strike was repressed by soldiers and police, work resumed in the coalfields of the Pas-de-Calais and

20. Griffuelhes, "Théorie en pratique," *VdP*, no. 112, December 28–January 4, 1902–1903.

21. Julliard, "Jeune et Vieux Syndicat," 8–9; Rolande Trempé, "Le Réformisme des mineurs français," 93–94, 102–106.

22. The most comprehensive account of Basly's actions during the months preceding the strike and in its opening days is given in Alain Besançon, "Le Mouvement syndical des mineurs du Nord et du Pas-de-Calais (1884–1914)" (D.E.S., Université de Paris, 1954), 107–16. See also Raoul Briquet, "La Grève générale des mineurs," Pt. 2, *Le Mouvement socialiste*, no. 114 (March 1, 1903), 171–73; and Dumoulin, "La Fédération des mineurs," Pt. 1, *ibid.*, no. 203 (October 15, 1908), 249–50.

the Nord.[23] Thus was the first national strike by miners—indeed the first industry-wide strike in French labor history—broken.

Griffuelhes reacted to Basly's action with cold fury: "The companies found in the violation of the pledge taken by the miners' national committee the conditions for their victory, the miners the conditions for their defeat."[24] Nevertheless, he believed that in the wreckage of the miners' strike were elements of a strategy that could wrest control of the miners' federation from the reformists and bring it into the CGT. His strategy was based on two pillars. First, he saw in the more radical unions, mostly from the Montceau-les-Mines and Saint-Etienne regions, which had left the National Federation of Miners in March, 1902, the nucleus of a force to drive out Basly and the federation's moderate general secretary, Gilbert Cotte, and take over the organization—*if* they could be convinced to return to the "old house" and battle from within. Griffuelhes was temperamentally and ideologically opposed to "splitting" as a solution to political or trade-union rivalries; noyautage or working from within was his preferred method. Here Griffuelhes believed he could rely upon the leader of the Montceau union, Etienne Merzet, syndicalist-inclined and closely associated with the Blanquists. Merzet was a disciple of the local deputy, the ex-miner Jean Bouvéri, who, although an independent socialist, was close to the Blanquist leaders Edouard Vaillant and Emmanuel Chauvière. The Blanquist PSR provided much of the strike fund for the January to July, 1901, walkout in Montceau-les-Mines, which inspired the movement for a nationwide miners' strike that year. Merzet led the strike in Montceau.[25]

Merzet, in turn, had strong support from fellow *montcelliens* François Chalmandrier and Jean-Baptiste Meulien, and from what one author has called the "Pleiades" of radical miners from Saint-Etienne: Marin Beauregard, Jules Escalier, Joanny Joubert, and Revol.[26] Together, the Montceau and Saint-Etienne unions gave Griffuelhes the nub of what might be called the "southern pillar" of his strategy to radicalize the miners' movement.

There was a "northern pillar" as well, which Griffuelhes believed could be

23. Briquet, "Grève générale des mineurs," Pt. 1, no. 113 (February 15, 1903), 69–70, and Pt. 2, pp. 171–72, 184; Besançon, "Le Mouvement syndicale des mineurs," 105–106; Dumoulin, "La Fédération des mineurs," Pt. 1, pp. 249–50.

24. Griffuelhes, "Manque de solidarité," *VdP*, no. 107, November 23–30, 1902.

25. *DBMO*, XIV, 73–74 (Merzet); XII, 31.

26. *DBMO*, XI, 158–59 (Chalmandrier); XIV, 77 (Meulien); X, 238 (Beauregard); XII, 141–42 (Escalier); XIII, 120 (Joubert) ; XV, 36 (Revol).

built from among angry union members in the Pas-de-Calais who had attempted to circumvent Basly and continue the strike on November 13. In
December, 1902, Griffuelhes toured the Pas-de-Calais, accompanied by the
treasurer of the CGT's Bourse du Travail section, Albert Lévy, and two militants from the metalworkers' federation, Jean Latapie and Alfred Klemczynski.
The presence of the two metalworkers underscores the importance Griffuelhes
attached to his idea of a natural link between miners and the metal trades.
Griffuelhes was struck by the big crowds he drew in what had been until then
"forbidden territory" to the CGT. The whirlwind tour (December 14–17) of
major mining towns to speak "on the general strike" and "make direct contact
with the miners of [the] department" did "useful work," Griffuelhes reported.
"We attracted new followers . . . in a milieu clearly hostile to the Confederation." [27]

That many of these "new followers" were members of the POF does not
seem to have bothered Griffuelhes at the time. He had worked with Guesdists
within the trade-union movement before; two of his closest associates on the
CGT Executive Committee, Alexandre Luquet of the barbers and Amédée
Bousquet of the foodworkers, were regular candidates for public office on the
POF ticket. No doubt he saw in Ovide Goudemetz, the Guesdist leader of
the dissident miners in the Pas-de-Calais, a man he could work with and
possibly bring around in time to a more syndicalist point of view.[28] Or perhaps
he believed the CGT had pulled off a coup against the POF by taking Goudemetz and his group under its wing. Whatever the case, this proved to be a
mistake. Guesdism as practiced in the Nord and the Pas-de-Calais did not
allow its trade-union adherents the latitude enjoyed by Luquet and Bousquet
in more cosmopolitan Paris, where the POF had, in any case, never been
much of a force. The POF seriously damaged its image in Paris trade-union
circles by being the only socialist faction that refused to condemn the government's closing of the Paris Bourse du Travail in 1893. Georges Lefranc
claims that Guesde, in an interview in *Le Matin,* said he was pleased with the
closure because it would disabuse workers of the notion that "emancipation

27. For Lévy's career in the CGT, see *DBMO*, XIII, 287–88, and for his participation in
the December, 1902, tour of the Pas-de-Calais see Griffuelhes, "Le Propagande dans le Pas-de-
Calais," *VdP*, no. 111, December 20–26, 1902, and "Les Réunions," *ibid.*, no. 116, February 1–
8, 1903. Latapie notes his and Klemczynski's role in the tour in his article, "Le Haut Baron de
Lens [*i.e.*, Basly]," *VdP*, no. 113, January 4–11, 1903.

28. *DBMO*, XIII, 322 (Luquet); XI, 26 (Bousquet), and *Le Petit Sou*, April 28, 1902; *DBMO*,
XII, 307 (Goudemetz).

is conceivable in any other way than through the conquest of the State." [29]

Griffuelhes had come away from the Pas-de-Calais with the impression that Goudemetz and his dissidents were determined to constitute themselves as a militant minority, rejoin Basly's union, and fight to take it over—and agitate "for the affiliation of the Pas de Calais Miners' Federation [Basly's union] to the CGT." No sooner had he returned to Paris, however, than the dissidents met on December 20 and voted to form a rival union, the Pas-de-Calais Miners' Trade-Union Federation, better known as the *jeune syndicat* ("young union").[30] This was a serious strategic error, in Griffuelhes' estimation. What he had learned during his swing through the Pas-de-Calais convinced him that Basly's position had been seriously undermined by the disastrous conclusion of the October–November national strike and that a good push would finish him off.[31] Goudemetz and his comrades' rival union would not accomplish this. Worse, they had divided the already weakened miners' movement in the face of its enemies, the powerful concessionnaires, into "Baslyites" and "anti-Baslyites," into "young" and "old" unions.

Griffuelhes soon learned, however, that Goudemetz had not taken this drastic step on his own initiative. "The party [POF] bosses in Lille," Guesde's bastion in the Nord, had intervened and imposed "the creation of a new union" upon the dissidents.[32] The jeune syndicat was a Guesdist front, more of an electoral machine to deprive Basly of his Chamber seat than a trade union. Thus, Griffuelhes was obliged to return to the Pas-de-Calais, this time to do battle with the Guesdists as well as Basly.

When the jeune syndicat held its first congress on January 25, 1903, Griffuelhes was there, flanked once again by Lévy and Latapie. In the preceding days, he had worked out a new strategy to deal with the schism in the Pas-de-Calais. The formation of the jeune syndicat, even though he believed it was a mistake, would have to be accepted. The question now was who would have the deciding influence in its councils, the POF or the CGT? Thus, Griffuelhes pledged the confederation's full support to the rebels in their battle

29. Claude Willard, *Les Guesdistes*, 354; Lefranc, *Mouvement socialiste sous la Troisième République*, 57 n. 2.

30. P.D., "Dans le Pas-de-Calais: Un Congrès," *VdP*, no. 116, February 1–8, 1903; this article is by an otherwise unidentified militant of the jeune syndicat.

31. Griffuelhes, "Retablissons," *VdP*, no. 113, January 4–11, 1903; Griffuelhes' assessment was shared by Rodière, the special agent of the Sûreté générale in Lens, who had frequent contact with Basly. See AD, Pas-de-Calais M 1795, dispatch to Sûreté générale, December 14, 1902.

32. Dumoulin, "La Fédération des mineurs," Pt. 1, p. 251; Dumoulin was active in the jeune syndicat at this point, as well as in the local section of the POF *(DBMO*, XII, 108).

against the Baslyites. Since the new union could not then afford a newspaper of its own to defend itself against attacks in Basly's journal, *Le Reveil du Nord*, he offered to print an extra run of the CGT newspaper, *La Voix du Peuple*, with a supplement featuring jeune syndicat news, for distribution in the Pas-de-Calais. This was, of course, more than a simple gesture of solidarity on Griffuelhes' part. Distribution of *La Voix du Peuple* in the Pas-de-Calais would open up a new and crucial region to CGT propaganda. And the offer of a regular supplement in the CGT newspaper would lessen the jeune syndicat's reliance on the POF's regional newspaper, *Le Travailleur du Nord*, to wage its propaganda battles.[33]

There was another, stickier problem to contend with, however. The jeune syndicat had adopted a motion on December 20, which was reaffirmed at its congress, seeking affiliation with the CGT. Griffuelhes' revised strategy for dealing with the jeune syndicat problem was mainly directed to this point. While publicly supporting the request, he appears to have privately convinced the leaders of the dissident union first to seek an alliance with the southern miners' unions that had split from the National Miners' Federation in 1902. Thus, the jeune syndicat was among the eight constituent unions—and the only one from north of the Loire—in the Federated Union of Miners founded at Grand'Croix (Loire) on May 7, 1903.[34]

Griffuelhes' relations with the jeune syndicat were made easier by the appearance of a new leadership cadre in its ranks. Goudemetz, already under fire from the POF for his cooperative attitude toward the CGT, faced total alienation when, in an abrupt about-face, Basly and the Guesdists made peace in a "socialist unity" conference in Lens in 1903. The marriage between the Guesdists and Basly's reformists was a shotgun affair, which came from a mutual desire to close ranks against "interference" by CGT Parisians, and was not destined to last. The alliance served its purpose during the Armentières textile workers' strike in late 1903, when the POF and Baslyites joined forces to send CGT "outside agitators" packing.[35]

The group that now came to the fore in the jeune syndicat was non-

---

33. Joachim Dercheville, "Dans le Pas-de-Calais," *VdP*, no. 116, January 25–February 1, 1903; Dercheville, the jeune syndicat's president, announced in this article setting out the agenda for the union's first congress that Basly had been invited to debate Griffuelhes—unfortunately, this debate never occurred. According to Dumoulin, when the jeune syndicat was founded, "The POF's Fédération du Nord printed [its] union cards and opened the columns of *Le Travailleur [du Nord]* to it" ("La Fédération des mineurs," Pt. 1, p. 251).

34. P.D., "Dans le Pas-de-Calais"; AN, F7 12.770 M/1009, report of "Louis," May 13, 1903.

35. Dumoulin, "La Fédération des mineurs," Pt. 1, p. 251.

Guesdist and led by Benoit Broutchoux. Broutchoux's rise to leadership of the union was also a considerable support for the southern pillar of Griffuelhes' strategy. Broutchoux was a southerner by origin, having come to the Pas-de-Calais only in 1901, after being fired for his participation in a strike in Montceau-les-Mines. He still maintained contact with his old comrades at Montceau, and in early 1903, he brought two of them, François Chalmandrier and Jean-Baptiste Meulien, to the Pas-de-Calais to propagandize for the jeune syndicat. Eventually, Broutchoux would be more of a burden than a blessing to the CGT. One of the more colorful "characters" in the history of French syndicalism, Broutchoux described himself as an anarchist, but Pierre Monatte, who knew him well, recalled: "His anarchism was not doctrinaire, . . . it was made up of syndicalism, anti-parliamentarianism, free thought, free love, neo-Malthusianism, and a lot of cheek." In early 1903, however, Broutchoux rendered a great service to Griffuelhes and the CGT by bringing the jeune syndicat into line behind the southern pillar of the strategy for radicalizing the miners' movement. Griffuelhes never forgot this. In 1908, when the CGT Executive Committee moved to disavow Broutchoux because of his stubborn opposition to miners' unity, which meant burying the hatchet with the reformists, Griffuelhes was almost alone in refusing to abandon him.[36]

Griffuelhes' strategy now called for, first, a united front among the dissidents from the National Miners' Federation, then a negotiated reunification of the two groups on terms favorable to the rebels and the CGT. The first condition was met with the establishment in May, 1903, of the Federated Union of Miners. The new organization, while still numerically weaker than the old group, contained some of the more dynamic figures in the miners' movement. Their leader was Etienne Merzet, but militants from the mines around Saint-Etienne were also prominent. All of these men shared a syndicalist perspective, but what most united them was the desire to avenge the alleged "treason" of the national federation's reformist leadership, principally Basly and his cohorts from the North but also their fellow southerner, the federation's general secretary, Gilbert Cotte from Saint-Etienne.

Griffuelhes feared this desire for vengeance might lead to a permanent schism within the miners' movement, rather than the unity under revolutionary auspices he was aiming for. Thus he dispatched Paul Delesalle, the veteran anarchist militant who was beginning to take his place in the inner

---

36. *DBMO*, XI, 73–74 (Broutchoux); XI, 159; XIV, 77; Monatte quoted in Julliard, "Jeune et Vieux Syndicat," 15; "Les Mineurs et la CGT," *L'Action syndicale* (Lens), July 28, 1908; *L'Action syndicale* was the journal of the jeune syndicat.

circle of the CGT, to the founding congress of the Federated Union of Miners in Grand'Croix to offer the rebels some advice on relations with the old house. Delesalle's pitch, which neatly sums up Griffuelhes' strategy for radicalizing the miners' movement, merits quoting in full.

> There must be only one miners' federation. The CGT doesn't want to admit you if you are divided. Return to the National Federation and take up the fight there on behalf of your ideals. There are enough of you so that you can secure the departure of some of the politicians who lead [the Federation]—and who are only too glad to be rid of you. Believe me, division is useless: There is only one enemy, the companies; it ought to have only one army facing it. Make concessions; the CGT pledges to you, through me, that it will see to it that the national federation makes some as well.[37]

The session in Grand'Croix preceded by one week the opening of the National Miners' Federation congress at Carmaux (May 20–24, 1903). Here the dissidents made their bid, with CGT support, to reunify the miners' movement on terms that would assure its radicalization. At Grand'Croix the dissidents had adopted proposals for changes in the statutes of the National Federation of Miners; their reentry depended on how many of these changes, which were revolutionary syndicalist in inspiration, were accepted by the congress. The key change proposed was the following: "No one can be a delegate to a congress if he is not a union member. . . . Persons holding political office cannot be members of the [administration of the federation] or delegates to congresses."[38] This proposed statutory change was, of course, aimed squarely at Basly. Its acceptance would depend on the extent to which the Federated Union's anger against Basly's "betrayal" of the 1902 national strike was shared within the larger federation.

Merzet and Revol of the Saint-Etienne unions were designated as emissaries to the Carmaux congress. That they acted under instructions from Griffuelhes is borne out by telegrams intercepted by the Sureté générale.[39] Reports by

37. AN, F7 12.770 M/1009, report of "Louis," May 13, 1903.

38. *Ibid.*, dossier "Congrès de Carmaux, 1903," reports of special agent (Albi) to Sureté générale, May 24, June 5, 1903.

39. A telegram from Merzet (Montceau-les-Mines) to Griffuelhes (Paris Bourse du Travail), May 19, 1903, read: "Chosen by Congress Grand'Croix to present new statutes to Congress Carmaux. Delegates accept discussion. Await your response before leaving" (AN, F7 12.770, dossier "Congrès de Carmaux, 1903").

agents of the Sureté, which paid close attention to the Carmaux congress, also indicate the seriousness of the challenge facing the Federated Union spokesmen and their CGT supporters at the congress. The federation's reformist leadership clearly did not intend to be taken by storm. The proceedings would take place in the presence of no less than seventeen friendly socialist deputies; all seventeen were affiliated with the more moderate Parti socialiste français and were members of the parliamentary Bloc des Gauches.[40] And, of course, the venue of the congress, a stronghold of Jean Jaurès, who led the socialist delegation, was a considerable advantage to the reformists.

To help even the odds somewhat, Griffuelhes dispatched his friend and colleague from the CGT Executive Committee, Auguste Garnery, to address the congress. "Garno," as he was known to his comrades in Paris, may not have been a wise choice, however; he was a well-known anarchist and antimilitarist, a militant who "knew how to get a strike off to a good start by putting a stick of dynamite in the right place." This might have impressed some of the Saint-Etienne miners, who appreciated this sort of talent, but it was not likely to have helped the CGT's cause with the sober reformists who dominated the federation. (In November, 1902, at the conclusion of the national miners' strike, angry miners in Saint-Etienne, convinced that the federation's general secretary, Gilbert Cotte, had not pushed the strike vigorously enough, sacked the local Bourse du Travail and attacked a café where he had taken refuge. Shortly afterward, Cotte transferred the federation's headquarters to Paris.) Garnery was a highly skilled artisan, a jewelry worker and a Parisian to boot, not the kind of horny-handed proletarian who would receive a sympathetic hearing from this gathering of miners from the provinces.[41]

The congress took a high-handed attitude toward both the Federated Union emissaries and Garnery. Merzet and Revol were not allowed to defend their statutory proposals, which were debated and rejected in their absence. On the last day of the congress, after the vote had been taken, Merzet, Revol, and Garnery were finally permitted to speak. Their pleas for miners' unity and "proletarianization" of the federation were greeted with scorn. Garnery was particularly roughly handled, principally by the head of the Carmaux miners' union and local mayor, Jean-Baptiste Calvignac, a protégé of Jaurès, and Charles Goniaux, leader of the Nord miners and a close ally of Basly.[42]

40. AN, F7 12.770, dossier "Congrès de Carmaux, 1903," May 5, 1903.

41. Maitron, "La Personnalité du militant ouvrier français," 68; *DBMO*, XI, 268 (Cotte); XII, 249 (Garnery).

42. AN, F7 12.770, reports of May 24, June 5, 1903.

Round one to the old house. The split in the miners' movement created in 1902 and confirmed at Carmaux would continue for another five years.

The reformists, however, turned out to be the big losers at Carmaux—at least in the short term. The old house continued to lose members, while the Federated Union gained strength under Merzet's leadership, affiliating, for example, the iron miners' union of Longwy (Lorraine) in 1905. By 1906, the reformists were ready to admit defeat. A Sureté agent wrote: "[The Federated Union] has around 21,000 members. This number seems destined to grow with each passing day, and the time is not far off when the National [Miners'] Federation will be little more than a skeleton, with no influence in the ranks of the mine workers."[43]

The rank and file of both organizations were weary of the struggle, and at St.-Etienne in June, 1906, reunification was achieved along the lines of the proposals made by Merzet and Revol at Carmaux. Most important, it was decided that political officeholders could not represent unions at miners' congresses. In October, 1906, the newly reconstituted National Miners' Federation duly applied for membership in the CGT, believing that by restoring unity it had met the CGT Executive Committee's criteria for admission.[44] It was in for a rude shock.

Like their political counterparts, trade-union leaders must be circumspect in their personal loyalties and enmities. It is not good to be seen as either too indulgent or too thin-skinned. In December, 1906, Griffuelhes erred in both directions. A row erupted in the Pas-de-Calais between Broutchoux's jeune syndicat and the rival union of Emile Basly, that effectively disrupted movement toward reunification of the two unions. Basly had started the row by accusing Broutchoux and his cohorts of pocketing funds collected to help the widows and orphans of miners who died in the Courrières disaster of April, 1906; such a charge usually was reserved for the buccaneers of capitalism. A commission of inquiry was formed—composed of two members each from the CGT (one was Griffuelhes), the National Miners' Federation, and the *vieux syndicat* ("old union")—to examine Basly's charges. The socialist deputy also called into question the honor and good faith of the CGT leadership in the uproar that followed.[45]

43. A.N., F7 13.788, dossier "Fédération Nationale des Mineurs–Congrès de St.-Etienne," report of June 28, 1906.

44. *Ibid.*, dossier "Mineurs: Congrès Paris—octobre 1906," report of October 9, 1906.

45. Emile Basly, "Au pilori," *Le Reveil du Nord*, December 8, 1906; "Chez les mineurs," *L'Echo du Nord*, December 25, 1906.

Griffuelhes' reaction was to strike a "him or me" pose with respect to Basly, while at the same time pledging his unequivocal support for Broutchoux. The miners' federation, he declared, would be admitted into the CGT only when the vieux syndicat publicly disavowed the "traitor" Basly. It is no exaggeration to say that Griffuelhes almost singlehandedly kept the miners out of the CGT for the next two years. His loyalty to the jeune syndicat leadership was equally unrestrained. In November, 1907, he told a rally in Lens: "All my sympathies, all my friendship, go to the Fédération syndicale [jeune syndicat] and, whatever happens, I will always be at its side." [46] In the end, he got his way—the Pas-de-Calais miners of the vieux syndicat disavowed Basly—but it was a pyrrhic victory.

However miners regarded Basly and his journalistic diatribes, he was one of their own and they were reluctant to see him humiliated by an outsider. Many believed that Griffuelhes should have reciprocated for the disavowal of Basly by abandoning Broutchoux, whose increasingly erratic leadership and refusal to accept fusion with the Baslyites had alienated even former comrade Georges Dumoulin. But Griffuelhes did not relent. When the miners were finally admitted into the CGT, he was in prison, accused of leading a rebellion against the State, and it was Alphonse Merrheim, the metalworkers' leader, who more than anyone else saw to the formalities of their affiliation. Jacques Julliard has written that "perhaps the personal influence of Griffuelhes over the executive committee would have convinced its members to postpone the decision yet again. . . . Broutchoux later claimed that the miners would not have been admitted had Griffuelhes been present." [47]

Griffuelhes could not have been happy with the outcome of his efforts to bring a radicalized miners' movement into the CGT. To be sure, the miners had come in, some 65,000 strong, to swell the ranks of the confederation but not to reinforce its revolutionary wing. Internecine warfare of the type that had raged among French miners for nearly seven years is a great "eater of men," and most of the radical leadership Griffuelhes had relied upon had been swallowed up: Etienne Merzet, worn out and eventually pushed aside by younger militants; Benoit Broutchoux, undone by his freewheeling life,

---

46. Griffuelhes, "Basly et ses domestiques sont des menteurs sans scrupules," *L'Humanité*, January 8, 1907; Augustin Dehay, "La Voix confédérale sympathique au jeune syndicat malgré tout," *L'Action syndicale*, November 24, 1907.

47. Dumoulin, "La Fédération des mineurs," Pt. 2, pp. 333–38; for an overall picture of the deterioration of the "broutchoutistes," see Julliard, "Jeune et Vieux Syndicat," 26–30. Jacques Julliard, *Clemenceau, briseur de grèves* (Paris, 1965), 108–109.

careless bookkeeping, and inability to compromise; Ovide Goudemetz, broken by his party's distrust and company blacklisting, and forced to emigrate to the United States, where he met an early death in the coal mines of Pennsylvania. The new leadership of the miners was reformist. Casimir Bartuel and Jean Bouchard from the Loire emerged as leading spokesmen for reformist causes on the CGT Executive Committee and at CGT congresses. When Griffuelhes was driven from office in February, 1909, Bouchard saluted his departure as a "triumph of trade unionism over anarchy."[48]

In October, 1903, Griffuelhes was back in France's industrial northeast once again, this time as a participant in the massive textile workers' strike that began in the Armentières (Nord) region. This proved to be a much more dangerous assignment than his December, 1902, and January, 1903, visits to the neighboring Pas-de-Calais. Several thousand soldiers were on duty in the region when he arrived there, and a rally he addressed turned into a riot in which a number of people were injured by charging cavalry. Warring Guesdists and reformist socialists put aside their quarrels long enough to mount a joint campaign to drive him and other CGT representatives back to Paris. He found himself branded in the local socialist press as an "anarchist," "foreigner," and "outside agitator." Years later, Griffuelhes still believed that a speech by Jaurès in the Chamber of Deputies toward the end of the strike, in which the socialist leader labeled him a "dangerous agitator," had nearly sent him to prison under the antianarchist laws, the so-called *lois scélérates* of 1893–1894. In 1907, during a tour of French-speaking Switzerland, Griffuelhes revived this charge in Bienne (Jura), apparently to counter an earlier visit by Jaurès. Jaurès' subsequent denial led to a confrontation in the deputy's office, after which Griffuelhes stated that he "gave me the impression of a man who was surprised he had said such things."[49]

By the time he arrived in the Nord, the strike had already spread far beyond its point of origin. Most of the textile industry of the Nord, France's largest and most concentrated producer of cottons, woolens, and linens, was on strike. "Like a whirlwind, more than 15,000 strikers had fanned out over the textile region and, like an irresistible torrent, had dragged along in their wake

48. *DBMO*, XIV, 74; XI, 73–74; Willard, *Les Guesdistes*, 626; *DBMO*, X, 215 (Bartuel), 344 (Bouchard).

49. Marc Vuilleumier, "Quelques documents sur les conférences de Jaurès en Suisse (1907)," *Bulletin de la Société d'Etudes Jaurésiennes*, no. 18, pt. 2 (July–September, 1965), 103.

the workers of La Gorgue-Estaires, Frelinghein, Bailleul, Hazebrouck, La Madeleine, Lomme, Halluin, Lille, and Roubaix. . . . Over 40,000 workers of both sexes, spinners, carders, dyers, weavers, workers in linen, wool, or cotton, found themselves on strike, without clearly formulated demands, without income, and without strike funds."[50]

The official explanation of the "explosion" in the Armentières region has it stemming from the crisis in which the French textile industry found itself at the start of the twentieth century. Competition had intensified among French textile manufacturers, in part because of a loss of markets to foreign producers, and had led them to cut costs by reducing workers' wages. In the Armentières region, the thirty-nine industrialists who dominated the local linen trade responded to the crisis by introducing differentials in the wages paid to spinners and weavers. Up to 1903, the manufacturers had generally observed a uniform wage structure negotiated with the local textile workers' union in 1889 (the "Schedule of 1889"). Thus, according to one observer, "the principal cause of the strike was the diversity of wage scales and the desire of the workers to make them more uniform." And behind the question of wage differentials lurked another problem of concern to workers and employers alike. The Millerand law of 1900, which had established a ten-and-a-half-hour workday in factories where women and children worked alongside men, had stipulated that the workday would be reduced to ten hours in April, 1904. Workers were determined that shorter hours would not mean lower wages, as some mill owners, citing "unfair" competition from cottage industry, had threatened. Another issue said to have figured in the dispute was the attempt by some manufacturers to introduce new products at piece rates lower than those traditionally paid.[51]

Dissatisfaction had been smoldering among mill workers in Armentières and surrounding towns, such as Houplines, for some time, however, and a number of small strikes had already taken place in the area. What appears to have ignited the more violent and widespread strike of October–November, 1903, was an event seemingly unrelated to the economic issues at stake: the

---

50. Fédération nationale de l'Industrie Textile, *Compte rendu du VIe Congrès national ouvrier de l'Industrie Textile, tenu à Reims les 14, 15 et 16 aout 1904* (Lille, 1904), 7; from the activities report of the federation's general secretary, Victor Renard, most of which is devoted to the Armentières strikes of October–November 1903, and April, 1904.

51. Paul Louis, *Histoire du mouvement syndical en France: De 1789 à 1918* (Paris, 1947), 139. Léon de Seilhac, "Les Grèves dans l'Industrie Textile—dans le Nord (en 1903)," *La Quinzaine* (September 16, 1904), 264–65; Peter N. Stearns, *Revolutionary Syndicalism and French Labor* (New Brunswick, N.J., 1971), 91.

"expulsion by a landlord of a couple with ten children," which had "disgusted the whole community."[52]

Griffuelhes, in articles he wrote both at the time and later, saw reasons for the strike that transcended the contemporary dispute over wages. Looking back on the strike years later, he remarked on "the pitiful wages" of the textile workers and also on their "miserable existence." To understand the workers of the Nord, he wrote, "You have to be present when they come and go at the factories, to see the long lines of men and women workers, to read the suffering on their faces. . . . These are no longer men and women, but so many flocks of sheep, whose energy is entirely absorbed by their work, who have only enough strength left to worship a god who can do nothing for them and politicians who mock them."

But there was a limit to the patience and resignation of even these "sheep," as the Armentières strike demonstrated. "Thus, when, under the pressure of anger so long built up and repressed, these proletarians rise up, spontaneously, just as quickly do the killers of energy fall upon them, frightened to see their troops revolt without their consent."[53]

Griffuelhes saw the workers of the Nord through a southerner's eyes, hence the often unflattering regionalist overtones that color his observations. He frequently made unflattering remarks about his fellow southerners as well. Thus, if the Nord workers were too passive, their southern counterparts lacked seriousness. His ideal worker would have combined the southerner's "zest" with the northerner's "capacity to endure." Despite this, his comments reveal an understanding of what motivated the Armentières strike of 1903 that eluded most local politicians and trade unionists. Thus, while the latter—and government officials both on the scene and in Paris—chose to believe that the strike was over wages and that its aggressive, sometimes violent aspects were due to the influence of agitators, homegrown or imported, Griffuelhes saw it as a spontaneous, popular *revolt* that was against political, religious, and economic repression and for an independent working-class movement with its own leaders, agenda, and means to resolve the problems besetting it.

Griffuelhes' analysis of the Armentières strike hews closely to that offered by William Reddy in his insightful study of the nineteenth-century French textile industry, *The Rise of Market Culture*. Outside observers, including socialists, Reddy writes, "failed to understand the insurrectionary tone of textile strikes" because their "analysis of wage labor remained a classical one: It was

52. Seilhac, "Les Grèves dans l'Industrie Textile," 264–65.
53. Griffuelhes, *Voyage révolutionnaire*, 8–9.

because of competition that the laborer suffered, suffering was caused by low remuneration, therefore textile strikes were short-term (and usually irrational) outbursts of discontent." Reddy, who says nothing about unions in his account of the strike, claims that along with "all socialist factions, . . . after 1896 [1895, the year CGT was founded?] the syndicalist Confédération générale du travail . . . constantly emphasized wages and hours." This probably was the view of many CGT leaders and militants, especially among the reformists; others, however, either because of experience or informed imagination, knew better than to confuse an insurrection with a wage dispute, as Griffuelhes' analysis bears out.[54]

Actually, market forces had very little to do with textile workers' demands, says Reddy, for the simple reason that "there was very little about life in French industry that fit the market mold." Fin de siècle France "was an illiberal society stuffed into a liberal box." State officials, some owners, and most politicians of whatever stripe were "blinded by the [classical] liberal vision." Laborers, however, "did not act in markets. . . . To indicate a desire to bargain, to utter a word deemed disrespectful meant almost certain dismissal, blacklisting, unemployment, loss of income, probable ostracism from one's town and trade. Yet when changes in industrial organization threatened laborers' vital informal arrangements in the shops, they were told they were free to go elsewhere. For all that they demanded from the laborers, the owners claimed to owe only wages in return." What the textile workers of Armentières were fighting for in 1903, "was the way of life of the working community."[55] This was reflected, of course, in the angry outburst over a poor family's ejection from their home, which appears to have touched off the conflict.

Whatever its source, the strike caught the textile employers completely by surprise. By the time Griffuelhes arrived in Armentières, most of them had taken refuge in Lille, where they were resisting pressure from the prefect of the Nord to go back and negotiate. Jules Guesde's POF, which dominated local government in most of the textile centers, had lost control of the situation. Guesdist mayors such as Emile Sohier in Houplines or Désiré Daudrumez in Armentières, swept along by the torrent, proved unable or unwilling to obey increasingly frantic directives from the POF citadel in Lille to restore order and to obtain "reasonable" demands from the strikers.[56]

54. Reddy, *The Rise of Market Culture*, 296, 297.
55. *Ibid.*, 323–24.
56. Marius Gabion, "Les Grèves du Nord," *Le Temps*, October 14, 1903; *DBMO*, XV, 170–71 (Sohier); XI, 312 (D. Daudrumez).

Spontaneous strikes were anathema to Guesde. They served the interests of the bourgeoisie, he wrote, by furnishing "moribund capitalism with the popular bloodletting it needs to survive," and thus postponed the hour of deliverance. That deliverance could only come through conquest of the State; in that perspective, only disciplined strikes that advanced the party's political agenda were permissible. This philosophy guided the Guesdist response to the Armentières strike, and as Griffuelhes learned to his considerable dismay, it also guided the action of the CGT-affiliated National Textile Workers' Federation, whose newly elected general secretary, Victor Renard, was a leading member of the POF.[57]

The federation, usually referred to simply as "Textile," had been founded by the Guesdists in 1891. Subsequently, the POF seems to have lost interest in union organizing in the textile industry—or any other industry, for that matter—unless a rival political party attempted to set up a union on its turf. In November, 1900, for example, the Guesdists broke a tulle workers' strike in Calais by establishing a rival union; the original tulle workers' union, founded in 1893, allegedly was sympathetic to Jaurès.[58] This kind of behavior—placing political rivalries above workers' economic interests—made the Guesdists the most disliked of the socialist currents as far as revolutionary syndicalists were concerned. Griffuelhes somewhat unfairly blamed Guesdist indifference to unions for the deplorable conditions of workers in the Nord, France's most heavily industrialized region.

Revival of the textile workers' federation in August, 1901, was not the work of the POF but of the CGT Executive Committee. The driving force behind its resuscitation was the secretary of the Paris ribbon makers' union, Desjardins, who ranks, along with Albert Bourchet of the metalworkers, as one of the unsung pioneers of the revolutionary syndicalist CGT. Desjardins moved quickly to bring the textile workers' unions in the Lyon and Saint-Etienne regions into the federation. His approach to rebuilding the organization was industrial unionist, an interesting stance given the large number of craft subdivisions within the trade and its persistence as a cottage industry in many regions. "We need to devote all our energy to organizing all the textile workers," Desjardins said in Lyon. "When that is done, we can then go on

---

57. Lefranc, *Mouvement socialiste sous la Troisième République*, 53, 56; *DBMO*, XV, 27 (Renard).

58. Maxime Leroy, *Coutume ouvrière*, I, 31; Léon de Seilhac, *Syndicats ouvriers, Fédérations, Bourses du Travail* (Paris, 1902), 104, 145. Tulle is a sheer, often stiffened net used for veils and ballet costumes.

to talk about how best to go about satisfying our demands." He accompanied Griffuelhes to the Nord in 1903 and was one of the leaders of the fight to forestall a Guesdist takeover of Textile following Renard's election as general secretary and the transfer of its bureau to Lille.[59]

What brought Victor Griffuelhes into the Nord on October 12 was the impression, entirely accurate as it turned out, that Renard was cooperating with Guesdist efforts to take over and choke off the Armentières strike. In his report to the Textile congress in Reims in August, 1904, Renard explained how he and the Textile bureau in Lille had tried to cope with the unforeseen strike in Armentières. On October 5, two days after the strike began, he sat down, not with representatives of the strikers or the CGT, but with Sohier, the Guesdist mayor of Houplines and head of its textile workers' union, and Gustave Delory, the Guesdist mayor of Lille, "to find the best way to deal with this difficult situation." The meeting in Lille, Renard added, "took place in the presence of citizen Guesde." He did not talk to representatives of the strikers, who had formed a steering committee by this time, because, according to Renard, they were under the spell of the reformist socialists of the French Socialist Party, specifically Basly's crowd in the Pas-de-Calais.[60]

With upwards of fifteen thousand mill workers in the streets and the strike beginning to spread across the Nord, the best that Renard, Sohier, Delory, and Guesde could do was echo proposals being put forward by the Nord prefect. They produced a plan for negotiations with the employers that comprised restoring the wage structure of 1889 wherever it had been violated by the employers and forming a joint commission of workers and employers, which would adjust wages to compensate for cost of living increases and the workday reduction [to 10 hours] that would take effect in April, 1904.

In the meantime, the Armentières-Houplines steering committee had circulated its own plan. Totally ignoring Textile and its POF advisers, the committee announced that it was declaring "a general strike of all the trades and categories of the textile industry"; that it had drawn up a new, uniform wage schedule embracing all textile workers in the Nord (making clear this was necessary to circumvent the employers' contention that they could not pay mill workers more because of competition from low-wage cottage industry in

59. CGT, *Rapport du comité confédéral pour l'exercice 1900–1901 et rapport de* La Voix du Peuple, *23–27 septembre 1901* (Paris, 1901), 6–7; Fédération national de l'Industrie Textile, *Compte rendu du Congrès de l'Industrie Textile, tenu à Paris les 20, 21 et 22 septembre et à Lyon les 27, 28 et 29 septembre 1901* (Paris, 1901), 63; *DBMO*, XII, 34 (Desjardins).

60. Fédération nationale de l'Industrie Textile, *Compte rendu du VIe Congrès*, 6.

the surrounding countryside); and that it was calling upon textile workers throughout the Nord to "stop all work until the conflict has ended." The committee's circular did not propose forming worker-employer committees to work out new wage rates; the strikers clearly intended to impose their own. "They [the steering committee] did nothing less than substitute themselves for the federation," protested Renard. "During the whole strike, they treated us as if we were guests in a conquered country."[61]

On October 13, Victor Griffuelhes arrived in Armentières, apparently invited by the steering committee as a representative of the CGT General Strike Committee.[62] His mission, as he saw it, was to try to save the generalized strike movement of the Nord textile workers from government interference and POF meddling. His intent was to ensure the strike retained its trade-union character, a task that should have been carried out by the Textile bureau in Lille but was not, because of Renard's collaboration with Guesde and Delory. Griffuelhes' mission was complicated by the fact that two days before his arrival, on October 11, the riots began which would give the Armentières strike its reputation as the most violent labor dispute of the pre–World War I era in France. His and Desjardins' presence during the most agitated period of the strike quickly made him and the CGT the scapegoats for the violence and the difficulties the government and the POF encountered in trying to get the textile workers to call off the strike.

The riots in Armentières and Houplines began the afternoon of October 11 and continued into the evening. Maurice Daudrumez, the son of the Guesdist mayor of Armentières, later recalled some of the events of that time. "The Verley-Decroix bank was sacked. [The rioters] tried several times to burn down the Notre Dame cathedral. They set fire to the home of a rent collector nicknamed Jesus Christ, who barely escaped being burned alive."[63]

These incidents and similar ones in Houplines added up to "the most generalized violence in the whole [prewar] period," according to Peter Stearns, who cannot be accused of exaggeration. The riots, he found, were largely the work of "thousands of poor linen weavers" whose violent behavior was "usually spontaneous, influenced indirectly at most by doctrines or excited speeches." Stearns offers no evidence as to what did motivate the Armentières rioters, but he does provide a clue in an account of another riot that occurred

---

61. *Ibid.*, 7, 10.
62. Gabion, "Les Grèves du Nord," *Le Temps*, October 14, 1903.
63. *DBMO*, XI, 312 (M. Daudrumez).

about the same time in nearby Lille, which he does not connect to the Armentières strike. Some six thousand textile workers in Lille, "rioted when they learned that manufacturers had not answered their demands. They roamed all over town, looking for their own employers, seized and burned cloth in the factories, and in the evening blocked off the streets and doused street lights to impede the police, and then set many fires."[64]

Taken together, these two incidents indicate that the striking textile workers who, according to Stearns, did most of the rioting were angry first at their employers, who refused to respond to their demands, but also at others they held responsible for their miserable circumstances, such as banks and the Church. Their behavior fits rather well Griffuelhes' analysis of the riots as a spontaneous release of pent-up anger at those he called the "killers of energy."

Griffuelhes, then, went to the Nord just as authorities, including the Guesdist deputies and local officials, were beginning to increase pressure to conclude the strike. There were twenty thousand troops in the region, about one soldier for every two strikers. The prefect, under orders from Paris, had proposed a referendum on a return to work, along with a pledge to mediate negotiations personally between workers and employers once work had resumed. This proposal had the support of the POF and its reformist socialist opponents, who shortly began to appear on rostrums in the Nord alongside the Guesdist deputies to urge a speedy end to the strike.[65] These appeals were accompanied by increasingly virulent attacks in the socialist press on the CGT emissaries and members of the Armentières-Houplines strike committee who sought to keep the strike alive.

On October 14, Desjardins and Griffuelhes spoke in Armentières and in Houplines, where they shared a rostrum before a crowd of six thousand with the Guesdist mayor, Sohier. The workers attending these rallies were not ready to accept the prefect's offer. Desjardins, who had arrived a day earlier, Griffuelhes, and Mayor Sohier counseled them to participate in the referendum but to vote to continue the strike. What else Griffuelhes said is open to some doubt. The local stringer for Basly's journal, *Le Reveil du Nord*, reported that Griffuelhes called upon the crowd "to vote the revolutionary general strike . . . and it was carried by acclamation," but curiously, the reporter of the Paris daily *Le Temps* does not mention this.[66] Since it seems unlikely that any re-

64. Stearns, *Revolutionary Syndicalism*, 68–69.

65. "Les Grèves—dans le Nord," *Le Reveil du Nord*, October 26, 1903.

66. *Ibid.*, October 13, 14, 1903; Gabion, "Les Grèves du Nord," *Le Temps*, October 14, 1903.

porter worth his salt would have missed a turn of events of this magnitude, one must charitably conclude that Basly's man in Armentières confused a call for continuing the strike with an appeal for the general strike.

For the moment, the strikers in Houplines and Armentières were holding firm; elsewhere, however, resistance was crumbling. In Lille, "the strikers are showing a great desire for conciliation; they are making concessions one after the other"; in Roubaix, "the strikers [on October 15] refused to allow . . . M. Griffuelhes . . . to speak at their meeting." On October 16, *Le Reveil du Nord* opened up on Griffuelhes. In an unsigned article headlined "Griffuelhes et Cie.," the newspaper repeated its dubious account of how the CGT general secretary had "obtained, by his beautiful phrases, the vote of a revolutionary general strike" in Armentières and accused him of having incited "a violent clash" between strikers and cavalrymen after the rally. "These anarchosyndicalists . . . these Parisians," the author wrote, "are lice who prey on the trade unions of the provinces and the strike movements of the proletariat of the departments." Textile workers of the Nord should shun these "cardboard revolutionaries from the capital"; in the Pas-de-Calais, they had sponsored "in opposition to the admirable miners' organization [of Basly] a caricature of a union [the jeune syndicat]," run by "jailbirds and thieves."[67]

A week later, the Guesdist press moved to the attack, although in somewhat more restrained language. Griffuelhes' efforts had been "fruitless" and "the [POF], as well as the socialists sometimes called reformists, are unanimous in criticizing the efforts of these Parisian delegates. Both are happy to learn that citizen Jaurès has responded to the appeal of the Armentières [strike] committee to give some strictly economic speeches under the chairmanship of the mayors of Armentières and Houplines."[68]

By the last week of October, the Guesdists, with the temporary support of their erstwhile reformist foes, had succeeded in bringing the Armentières and Houplines strikes under their control. On November 4, the strikes ended. The results were "poor, it's true," acknowledged Renard. "In addition to the proposals made at the beginning by [Renard] and Delory, which were finally accepted, the strikers were promised an eight percent wage increase in April"; this would compensate for income lost due to the reduced working hours that were to come into effect then. This was only partly true. What the employers actually promised was that the wage increases would be implemented only "if

67. Gabion, "Les Grèves du Nord," *Le Temps*, October 16, 1903; *Le Reveil du Nord*, October 16, 1903.

68. *Le Travailleur du Nord*, October 23, 1903.

competing manufacturers of the region agreed to equivalent sacrifices"; presumably this included those employing cottage labor, among others. When April 1 came, the employers of Armentières and Houplines, in fact, refused to implement the wage increase, and a second strike, this time involving some eighty thousand workers, was required before a final settlement could be reached.[69]

Victor Griffuelhes' forays into the Pas-de-Calais and Nord Departments in 1902–1903 had for the first time given the CGT something approaching a national presence. Strikers in the provinces could now reasonably expect that an urgent telegram to Paris would produce a flying visit from Griffuelhes or one of his lieutenants, to help stiffen resolve and boost morale. But the general secretary's journeys into the hinterland had not been only to show the CGT flag. In the Pas-de-Calais miners' dispute and to a lesser extent the Nord textile strike, he had used the authority of his office and the resources of the confederation to support local trade-union radicals against their reformist leaders. Both initiatives proved controversial and brought down upon Griffuelhes' head the condemnations of local union bosses and politicians who resented outside encroachments on their bailiwicks. At the national level as well, reformist labor leaders, who understood perfectly well where Griffuelhes' policy of noyautage was leading, mobilized to fight back. The stage was thus set for the first major confrontation between the CGT's revolutionary leadership and the aroused reformist opposition—at the CGT Congress of Bourges in October, 1904.

---

69. Fédération Nationale de l'Industrie Textile, *Compte rendu du VIe Congrès*, 8; Seilhac, "Les Grèves de l'Industrie Textile," 275; Fédération Nationale de Textile, *Compte rendu du VIe Congrès*, 9–10. See also Griffuelhes, "Les 10 heures," *VdP*, no. 182, April 10–14, 1904; and "Résultats," *ibid.*, no. 186, May 8–15, 1904.

IV

BOURGES (1904)

Tricked, misled, betrayed for centuries, the worker today counts *only on himself* in the struggle for his emancipation. . . . Free from all governmental influence, from all political influence, anarchists and socialists struggle together, committed to pursuing their goal on the terrain of revolutionary syndicalism, which is their common ground.
—Victor Griffuelhes, "Le Congrès syndical de Bourges"

For Paul Delesalle, the assistant general secretary of the CGT's Bourses du Travail section, the CGT Congress of Bourges from September 12–20, 1904, was destined to become "a significant date in the history of the proletariat." Delesalle's counterpart in the CGT Federations section, Emile Pouget, called it "the most important trade-union congress ever held in France." For both of these anarchists turned revolutionary syndicalist, the Bourges congress took on such monumental significance because it appeared to have answered definitively the most important question then facing the French working-class movement: "Which current [of trade-unionism] responds best to the aspirations of the workers, the 'reformist' or the 'revolutionary'?"[1] Bourges provided the arena for the long-awaited showdown between reformist and revolutionary syndicalists; there the reformists had posed a fundamental challenge to the dominance of the revolutionary majority, and they lost by a decisive margin.

What made this outcome even more significant, Delesalle wrote afterward,

1. Paul Delesalle, "Le Congrès [de Bourges] et l'Opinion ouvrière," *Le Mouvement socialiste*, no. 142 (November 1, 1904), 72; Emile Pouget, "Les Débats du Congrès [de Bourges]," *ibid.,* 34.

was that more delegates and more unions had participated in this congress than in any other in the CGT's history. According to his calculations, over four hundred delegates, representing 1,204 unions, had attended the congress.[2] And, added Griffuelhes, no doubt remembering his rough reception in the Pas-de-Calais and the Nord the year before, "of the more than 400 delegates, provincial delegates numbered around 350 . . . , [which] discredits the tactic being used to sow terror in the provinces: raising the spectre of the Parisian 'outside agitator'—a revolutionary agitator, of course."[3]

Not only was there a record turnout of delegates and the participation more broadly representative of French organized labor than in the past, but, Griffuelhes noted with pride, because member unions had received the documentation for the congress three months in advance, the "points on the agenda were the subject of extensive discussions in the trade-union press and in *La Voix du Peuple.* The votes cast therefore could only have been the considered positions of the organized workers, reached after much reflection."[4]

But even before the congress documents became public, concerned union members and the public at large were aware that a confrontation between the reformist and revolutionary camps of French syndicalism was in the offing. The reformists, on the defensive since the Congress of Lyon (1901) and Griffuelhes' takeover of the CGT leadership two months later, had been unable to come to grips with their adversaries in public debate in the years following. The Congress of Montpellier in 1902 had been devoted almost entirely to the question of unity between the CGT and the National Federation of Bourses du Travail, which had the support of most reformists as well as revolutionaries. In the meantime, reformists had the impression of being under unremitting attack from the revolutionaries. The entire administrative apparatus of the CGT was in the hands of their enemies and was being used in an effective— and in their view entirely partisan—way to advance the revolutionary cause. Griffuelhes, who was denied the right to intervene directly in the internal affairs of member federations by CGT statutes, was using the General Strike Committee as a cover for his forays into the provinces, most of which seemed to be aimed at subverting reformist union leadership. He had already seriously

2. Delesalle, "Le Congrès [de Bourges]," 72.

3. Griffuelhes, "Le Congrès syndical de Bourges," *Le Mouvement socialiste,* no. 142 (November 1, 1904), 76.

4. *Ibid.,* 78.

weakened the reformists' hold on the miners' movement in this way; less successfully, he had similarly challenged the reformist (in practice, if not in theory) leadership of the textile workers' federation.

In addition to his boring-from-within campaign directed against existing moderate unions, the general secretary had been instrumental in forming new federations with revolutionary credentials, *e.g.,* those of the timber workers in the Centre and the agricultural laborers in the Midi. The reformists also felt shut out of the official newspaper of the confederation, *La Voix du Peuple,* which in Pouget's hands seemed to devote more space to revolutionary propaganda and attacks on reformist socialists and trade unionists than to labor news. And as if this were not enough, in July, 1903, the revolutionaries had launched *L'Action Directe,* a periodical devoted to antireformist polemics and criticism of the positivist philosophy espoused by the reformist boss, Auguste Keufer of Livre.[5] Finally, the reformists were disturbed by growing evidence of close ties between the CGT's revolutionary syndicalist leadership and the so-called socialist-syndicalist wing of French socialism. This link provided the CGT revolutionaries with yet another key propaganda outlet—*Le Mouvement socialiste,* the prestigious monthly review edited by Hubert Lagardelle, a leading light of the socialist-syndicalist circle.

This relationship mainly involved Griffuelhes, Pouget, Yvetot, and Merrheim on the CGT side and Lagardelle, André Morizet, and Ernest Lafont from the socialist-syndicalist group. (Robert Louzon, who will be discussed in Chapter V, was a lesser participant in the relationship.) Lagardelle, Morizet, and Lafont had begun to build bridges to the CGT revolutionaries following Millerand's entry into the Government of Republican Defense in 1899, which they strongly opposed. The original bond between them was Lagardelle's *Le Mouvement socialiste,* whose contributors included a number of leaders and militants from the CGT, among them Victor Griffuelhes. The trio became more closely associated with the CGT leadership in 1905, when Morizet founded *L'Avant-garde,* a weekly review whose politics were spelled out in its subtitle: *Socialiste-Syndicaliste-Révolutionnaire.* This review's collaborators also included a number of leading figures from the revolutionary syndicalist wing of the CGT. Lafont, Lagardelle, and Morizet remained active in the socialist

---

5. Griffuelhes, Albert Bourchet, Paul Delesalle, Jean Latapie, Pouget, and Alexandre Luquet were the main trade-union collaborators on this monthly, which ceased publication in February, 1905. There is no direct link between it and the weekly of the same name that appeared in 1908, to which Griffuelhes also contributed. Brécy, *Mouvement syndical,* 140, 142; Griffuelhes, "La Revue 'L'Action Directe' (1903–1904)," 18–19.

movement as well, occupying a position on its extreme Left from which they defended the CGT from attacks by the Guesdists and agitated for formation of a labor party along the lines of the parti du travail advocated by Griffuelhes.[6]

Thus, it was known well in advance of the congress that the key reformist leaders—Keufer, Eugène Guérard of the railwaymen, and Pierre Coupat of the machinists, for example—were preparing an assault on the very nexus of revolutionary control of the confederation, in the form of a motion to base votes at CGT congresses on proportional representation, *i.e.,* on union membership, rather than the one-union, one-vote system in effect since the CGT was founded in 1895. The reformists believed the power of Griffuelhes and the revolutionaries rested on support from numerous small unions—the so-called militant minority (*minorités agissantes*)—who they thought had little to lose by adopting a radical posture. The bigger unions, they contended, were reformist but were forced to support dangerous and fruitless revolutionary initiatives because the voting system at congresses was rigged against them. The reformists had begun their campaign for proportional representation almost as soon as the tide began to turn against Millerandism within the labor movement, raising the issue at the Lyon congress in 1901, where it garnered only twenty-six votes, and again at Montpellier the next year, where it won seventy-four.

During the summer of 1904, the reformists set about organizing a bloc of delegates in favor of their proportional representation motion. At the Bourges congress and after, the revolutionary syndicalists accused them, particularly Livre, of trying to pad Bourse du Travail delegations, buying votes, and keeping unions within their ranks that did not support the reformist line from attending. While these charges were probably exaggerated, Griffuelhes was clearly right in stating that "the congress was the object of careful preparation" by the reformists. Livre came to Bourges 128 unions strong; only thirty had shown up at Montpellier. Keufer, who had not attended a CGT congress since 1900, served as the main reformist spokesman at Bourges. The other leading reformist federation, the railwaymen's union, sent representatives of forty-six member unions, compared to "a mere handful" at earlier congresses.[7]

---

6. *DBMO*, XII, 172–73 (Lafont) ; XII, 175–77 (Lagardelle); and XIII, 145–46 (Morizet); the ideological dimension of the rapprochement between these intellectuals and the CGT leadership is elucidated in great detail in Chapter 1 of Jeremy Jennings' *Syndicalism in France*.

7. Griffuelhes, "Le Congrès syndical de Bourges," 76–78; Pouget, "Les Débats du Congrès [de Bourges]," 49–51; Delesalle claimed Keufer had not attended a trade-union congress for "nearly 10 years" ("Le Congrès [de Bourges] et l'Opinion ouvrière," 73).

The revolutionaries, however, had not been idle before the congress, either. Griffuelhes and Pouget made the rounds of federation congresses, ostensibly to show the CGT flag but no doubt to drum up support at Bourges as well. In May, 1904, Griffuelhes published an article in *La Voix du Peuple* that indicated the majority did not intend to be on the defensive at the congress. There had been enough talk about winning the eight-hour day, he wrote, and now it was time to do something about it. Although he gave no specifics, Griffuelhes strongly suggested that a proposal for a concerted campaign to win the eight-hour day, involving strike action, would be made at Bourges.[8] Such a proposal was certain to arouse opposition from the moderates, who could be expected to denounce it as hasty and provocative, but their opposition would also appear to be against one of labor's most cherished reforms.

Any remaining doubts as to the seriousness of the issues at stake at Bourges were dispelled by a much-publicized—and afterward much-noted—debate on July 29, 1904, between the veteran leader of Livre, Auguste Keufer, and Griffuelhes. The debate was a no-holds-barred affair in which the main differences between reformists and revolutionaries were clearly set out and the points of confrontation at Bourges neatly prefigured. Griffuelhes led off with a speech of the type that was to make him such a formidable propagandist in working-class circles. His strength was his ability to portray revolutionary syndicalism as the working class's only logical response to conditions imposed upon it against its will and to demonstrate this in simple, reasonable terms, buttressed by apt contemporary examples.[9]

The differences between reformist and revolutionary syndicalists were fundamental, Griffuelhes declared, and stemmed from their basic disagreement over the nature and ultimate fate of the capitalist system. Reformists, he suggested, believed that workers could achieve the freedom and well-being they desired within the framework of capitalism, through negotiations with employers and reforms enacted by parliament. It logically followed, therefore, that reformists "organized [unions] for the purpose of seeking an entente with the employers, so as to demonstrate to them the need to make a few conces-

---

8. CGT, *XVe Congrès national corporatif . . . Amiens*, 27; Griffuelhes, "Besoin d'agir," *VdP*, no. 134, May 1, 1904, p. 185.

9. The text of this debate was probably more widely read abroad than any other French syndicalist document; I have seen reference to translations into Dutch and have reason to believe it was also translated into German and Spanish. In 1905, Keufer's union published an edition entitled *Les Deux Méthodes syndicalistes: Réformisme et l'Action directe*, which served as the basis for translations.

sions, but without undermining in the least the privilege" of the capitalists. Thus, reformists placed their trust in and actively collaborated in State institutions that supposedly brought workers, employers, and civil servants together to work out reforms of the workers' condition, but that were, in fact, only intended to "deflect [the] action of the working class" and place it "under the tutelage . . . of the bourgeois State." These institutions included the Millerandist creations, the Supreme Labor Council and regional labor councils, and the arbitration panels and joint committees foisted upon the miners and textile workers by the Combes government. The result was perpetuation of the capitalist system and continued subordination of the producer to the nonproducer.

Revolutionary syndicalists, on the other hand, believed that the capitalist system was forced upon the working class "by violence and that only violence can suppress it . . . , not because violence pleases us, but because it is made necessary by the conditions that characterize the workers' struggle." Since employers are unlikely to satisfy workers' demands "out of the kindness of their hearts, the worker is forced to struggle." And since "the nonproducer, *i.e.,* the employer, the capitalist, can only prolong the existence of his prerogatives by keeping the producer, *i.e.,* the worker, subordinate," the struggle must continue until its ultimate cause—the exploitation of the workers—disappears.

This struggle can only be the "work of the workers themselves" if it is to achieve its goal of emancipating the working class. "For us revolutionary syndicalists," declared Griffuelhes, "the struggle is based on interests and needs, not sentiments." And it was in the very nature of the capitalist system and the class relationships characterizing it that no one else could be expected to look after the workers' "interests and needs" but the workers themselves. "We say that the organization [of the workers], which is being forced upon them by their miserable conditions, ought to involve only wage earners, ought to be led by workers for workers' ends. . . . To that end, militants must never subordinate the action of the workers to that of social forces [outside] their ranks."

The revolutionary syndicalist strategy, Griffuelhes declared, was direct action culminating in the general strike. Direct action was a workers' strategy, derived from concrete experience accumulated over decades of workers' struggle. "Through direct action, the worker himself creates his struggle; it is he who conducts it, relying not upon others but only upon himself to liberate himself."

Despite current theorizing about the meaning of direct action, concluded

Griffuelhes, there was nothing abstract or mysterious about it. Using a favorite example that suited perfectly his polemical purposes, he declared that everyone in his audience was familiar with perhaps the most dramatic example of direct action of the times: "the agitation carried on in France to liberate Captain Dreyfus. If it had been left to the legal system, his liberation might never have been achieved. It was thanks to agitation, through press campaigns, rallies, meetings, protests, and street demonstrations, some involving bloodshed, that public opinion was aroused. . . . It was crowd action, which put pressure on the authorities and set the slow-moving judicial machinery in motion, which freed the captain." [10]

Keufer's rejoinder provided a foretaste of the line of attack that the reformists would use at Bourges. With the advent of the revolutionary syndicalist majority, he contended, the CGT had fallen into the hands of "anarchists" who "have become trade unionists only for the purposes of . . . making a tabula rasa of the present society so as to put in its place the most complete communism." Griffuelhes and his anarchist allies, he added, "see the trade union as . . . an instrument of social demolition, destined to disappear when its work . . . of demolition is complete."

Their advocacy of the use of force, he continued, was irresponsible and dangerous for the working class. "If we have not allowed ourselves to indulge in these excesses, it is because we have always believed that violence inevitably begets violence, and that it is the workers who pay the heaviest price." Besides, the preaching of direct action "drives away from the unions many workers who prefer a humdrum, peaceful existence to the prospect of uncertain improvements by way of revolutionary means. . . . The masses are generally inert and indifferent, rather than hungry for action, with its only momentary thrills, its worries and letdowns."

In contrast, Keufer reiterated his positivist faith as an example of constructive reformism. "I am a partisan of organic, peaceful trade unionism, which works through constant effort toward a more perfect society, . . . a system that scientific experiments and data reveal to be mankind's normal state . . . while respecting the rights of individuals." Behind their revolutionary rhetoric, "the pontiffs of direct action" behaved little differently in the daily struggle from the reformists they were so critical of. They curry favor with politicians, negotiate collective agreements, and petition for social legislation. Revolution "or what others call Renovation," he concluded, will not be accomplished by

10. Griffuelhes, "Le Syndicalisme révolutionnaire," in "Les Deux Conceptions du Syndicalisme," 2–15.

these "false prophets" but by the "incessant labors of the proletariat, scholars, and philosophers"; it will be "the gradual work of generations." [11]

Accounts of CGT congresses have not paid enough attention to the impact of congress venues on the deliberations. In the case of the Congress of Bourges, for example, the setting worked to the advantage of Griffuelhes and the revolutionary syndicalist faction. Put succinctly, they were on friendly ground. The city of Bourges was the capital of Edouard Vaillant's longtime electoral fief, the Department of the Cher, and the region's politics and trade unionism bore a strong Blanquist imprint. Griffuelhes was well acquainted with the area and its working people, having represented the Blanquist timber workers and farm laborers of Nérondes, a commune between Bourges and Nevers, at the Salle de Japy socialist congress in 1899. He had taken a keen interest in the long, painful struggle of the timber workers of the Cher and the neighboring Nièvre Department to build a union, and had attended their congresses in 1902 and 1904. The secretary of the Bourges Bourse du Travail, Pierre Hervier, was one of his heroes. He "is an incomparable militant," Griffuelhes wrote. "Every Bourse ought to have [a secretary] like him." [12] Hervier would host the Bourges congress.

The mood of the delegates as they arrived for the congress was also important to its outcome. A substantial strike was underway in Marseille as the congress began, and many delegates probably also had in mind the recent events at Cluses, just across the border from Geneva, where on July 18, 1904, the sons of a local clock manufacturer had fired on a peaceful demonstration of workers and their families, killing three persons and wounding 43. [13]

The reformists began their attack against Griffuelhes and the revolutionaries as soon as the congress started on September 14. In the debate following Griffuelhes' report from the CGT Executive Committee, the reformists called for rejection of the report on the grounds that, contrary to CGT statutes, the leadership's activities were in large part politically motivated. For those who had heard or read about the Keufer-Griffuelhes debate in Paris in July, the reformists' arguments offered few surprises. Keufer repeated his earlier charge

11. Auguste Keufer, "Le Syndicalisme réformiste," in "Les Deux Conceptions du Syndicalisme," 21–40.

12. Griffuelhes, "Le Congrès des bucherons," *VdP*, no. 83, June 15–22, 1902; Griffuelhes, *Voyage révolutionnaire*, 36; see CGT, *La CGT et le Mouvement syndical*, 481, on Hervier's remarkable career.

13. Griffuelhes and Georges Yvetot, "La Grève de Marseille," *VdP*, no. 203, September 4–11, 1904; Justinien Raymond, "Un Tragique Épisode du mouvement ouvrier à Cluses (Haute-Savoie) en 1904," in *Mélanges d'histoire sociale offerts à Jean Maitron*, esp. 202–203.

that anarchists had infiltrated the CGT leadership and were using the confederation as an instrument to smash the State and establish a communist society. Their advocacy of "violent direct action is dangerous for the workers," he said. "It will inevitably lead to reprisals [and] break up the workers' organizations." Instead of working to unify the CGT membership, Keufer continued, the leaders were using their positions to undermine reformist unions such as the miners' and his own printers' federation.[14]

The railwaymen's Eugène Guérard, the other leading spokesman for the moderates, went straight for Griffuelhes, though perhaps out of courtesy he did not refer to him by name. His concern was not the anarchists among the CGT leadership but the political influence exerted over it by "*une personnalité*" (Griffuelhes) whose first loyalty was to his political party (the Blanquists) and its agenda, which he described as "pure antiministerialism." This influence, Guérard contended, was detrimental to the working class because it introduced politics into the CGT and thus set worker against worker and encouraged rejection of government reforms, for purely partisan political reasons, that benefited workers, such as laws on job-related accidents and pensions.[15]

Guérard's attack on Griffuelhes was more than a little hypocritical. His own articles in *La Voix du Peuple* during his tenure as general secretary clearly reveal his effort, as an Allemanist supporter of Millerand, to rally labor backing for the ministerialist cause. Although Griffuelhes tried to remain above the fray at congresses as much as possible and let others make his points for him, he felt obliged to respond to Guérard's personal attack. There was no love lost between the two men, as everyone, including the police, was aware. Still, Griffuelhes did not reply in kind, finding instead the weak link in Guérard's argument—something he seemed to have an unerring nose for—and using it to demolish his opponent. The railwaymen's chief had offered as proof of Griffuelhes' unrepentant antiministerialism the latter's public charge that the Combes government had been responsible for the police invasion of the Paris Bourse du Travail on October 29, 1903. This, suggested Guérard, was a transparent attempt to discredit the Bloc des Gauches, the reformist Socialist–Radical Party coalition that supported Combes in the Chamber of Deputies.[16]

14. CGT, *XIVᵉ Congrès national corporatif . . . à Bourges du 12 au 20 septembre 1904. Compte rendu des travaux* (Bourges, 1904), 92–93, 95–96, 132.

15. *Ibid.*, 110–12.

16. See Eugène Guérard, "Les Conseils du travail"; "Chacun chez soi," *VdP*, no. 4, Decem-

Guérard might have chosen a better example. Parisian militants were still angry over the police raid, which had left one person dead and 140 injured. Nor had it increased their respect for the Bloc des Gauches; on October 30, thirteen reformist socialist deputies had joined the governmental majority in absolving the Combes ministry of responsibility for the raid. Griffuelhes did not dwell on this, however. Instead, he deftly turned the tables and asked delegates to recall a similar incident at the Paris Bourse du Travail in 1901 and the subsequent letter of protest addressed to then Premier Waldeck-Rousseau and signed by Pouget and Guérard, the CGT general secretary at the time. Griffuelhes seemed to be saying that Guérard supported Waldeck-Rousseau, yet when police invaded the Bourse du Travail, as CGT general secretary he protested in his official capacity to the premier. Now, Griffuelhes had done the same and was accused by Guérard of acting from purely antiministerialist motives. Consequently, the reports presented by Griffuelhes and other CGT officials were approved by the congress by a vote of 825–369.[17]

The debate over the reports, however, was a mere skirmish compared to the confrontation over proportional representation (PR) that took place September 16. In terms of the range of issues raised and the fundamental points of trade-union structure and activity addressed, the debate on PR at Bourges was one of the most important in the history of the prewar CGT. The only debate of greater significance during the period was in 1906, on relations between the CGT and the French Socialist Party, which produced the Charter of Amiens. In a number of ways, however, the 1906 debate was only a continuation and amplification of the reformist-revolutionary controversy formally engaged at Bourges two years before, which was, in turn, largely an outgrowth of the division within the trade-union movement caused by Millerandism. Also noteworthy about the PR debate is the extent to which the arguments, especially on the reformist side, were directed to an international audience, which had not been done at previous CGT congresses. That this occurred at Bourges indicates the reformist minority's need for moral support within the CGT, not only from the French reformist socialists to whom they customarily turned, but from the moderate trade unions of Britain and Ger-

---

ber 23–30, 1900; "Every militant knows about Guérard's enmity toward Griffuelhes, which goes back to the [CGT] Congress of Lyon (September 1901)" (APP, B/a 1686, "Le Mouvement social en mars 1906," 46); CGT, *XIVᵉ Congrès national corporatif... Bourges*, 112.

17. Aaron Noland, *The Founding of the French Socialist Party (1893–1905)* (Cambridge, Mass., 1956), 157–58; CGT, *XIVᵉ Congrès national corporatif... Bourges*, 137–38, 143.

many as well. That this sort of appeal came forth at Bourges rather than earlier was no doubt because the CGT had joined the International Secretariat of National Trade-Union Centers (ISNTUC) at its Dublin conference in 1903.[18]

As most participants and observers were aware, the PR debate was not really over voting rules. What was at stake was the leadership of the confederation. Whether adopting PR would have had much immediate impact upon CGT voting patterns is not at all clear; the evidence does not altogether support the reformists' portrayal of themselves as the actual majority in terms of membership, but one denied leadership because of a voting system that favored smaller, more radical unions. As Griffuelhes and other revolutionary syndicalists argued, there was no correlation between union size and ideology. CGT figures on dues-paying membership as of May 31, 1904, for example, show that the largest union in the confederation at the time of the Bourges congress was a solid member of the revolutionary camp—the State and naval arsenal workers' federation, with twelve thousand paid-up members. The second largest, Guérard's railway workers' union (11,450), was of course reformist. In a three-way tie for third, the tobacco workers, Livre, and the metalworkers' federation all claimed ten thousand dues-paying members; the first two were reformist, while the metalworkers' federation, one of the CGT's fastest-growing unions, definitely was not. Nor were all small unions radical. The auto chauffeurs' and mechanics' union (one thousand members) was expelled from the CGT in 1901 for membership in a yellow Bourse du Travail. At the Amiens congress of 1906, Griffuelhes announced the expulsion of the cooks' union (also one thousand members) for accepting master chefs and restaurateurs as members.[19]

But while adoption of PR at Bourges might not produce a new reformist majority within the CGT in the near term, as reformists argued it would and some revolutionaries seemed to accept, it threatened to do so in the longer term so long as unions with large membership bases remained under reformist leadership. Thus for Griffuelhes and the revolutionary syndicalist majority, beating back the PR motion at Bourges was a holding action, a means of gaining time to expand the noyautage process begun in the miners' federation.

---

18. In June, 1902, the ISNTUC had held a preliminary conference at Stuttgart, Germany, in conjunction with the annual congress of the German social-democratic unions; Griffuelhes attended both this meeting and the Dublin session as a CGT delegate.

19. CGT, *XVᵉ Congrès national corporatif . . . Amiens*, "Rapport financier de la Section des Fédérations," 32–33, 24, 29–30.

A major target in this regard would be Guérard's railwaymen's union, which probably had the greatest potential for membership expansion of any organization in the CGT, greater even than the miners, metalworkers, or building workers. By contrast, reformists pointed out that many unions in the revolutionary camp did have very small professional bases. Philippe Henriot, who represented the matchworkers' federation, the revolutionary syndicalist union that would produce Léon Jouhaux, pointed out that his union of only fifteen hundred members, for example, had already organized 95 percent of the workers in the State match monopoly.[20]

This was not, of course, how opponents argued against PR at Bourges. Their main thrust was that it would enable the bigger unions to "crush" the smaller fry, many of whom had organized most of the workers in their trade and thus earned the right to an equal voice in the confederation's deliberations. Reformist speakers countered that granting an equal voice to small unions — and here they usually focused on the more revolutionary unions such as the barbers — perpetuated craft unionism and alienated the "real" proletariat from the trade-union movement. "What we're asking the little unions," said Lucas of the reformist clerks' union, "is to give up their selfish craft pride." Pierre Coupat of the machinists and Keufer, meanwhile, charged that unless the larger trades could be assured their views would have the weight they deserved in CGT councils, they would not rally to the confederation. Keufer's cohort from Livre, Jacques Maroux, went somewhat further, and in so doing, weakened the reformist case. He argued that some professions, thinking no doubt of his own printing trade, have "greater utility" than others and therefore should have a greater voice in CGT decision making.[21]

This sally, of course, produced an uproar among the revolutionaries and provoked an equally unwise retort from Louis Niel of the Montpellier Bourse du Travail. How does one decide which trade is the most useful? he asked, and then condemned the whole exercise of assigning mathematical values to unions as an "Anglo-Saxon," un-French invention. "These mathematical notions are all right for the English, Americans, or Germans," Niel declared, "but they don't suit liberty-loving, sentimental Frenchmen." Somewhat more

20. Between May 31, 1904, and May 31, 1906, the railwaymen increased their membership in the CGT from 11,450 to 24,275 (CGT, *XIVe Congrès national corporatif . . . Bourges*, "Rapport financier," 32, 154).

21. *DBMO*, XIII, 319 (Lucas); CGT, *XIVe Congrès national corporatif . . . Bourges*, 153 (Coupat); 156–57 (Keufer); 144–45.

to the point, he argued that adoption of PR would create a "labor aristocracy" in France, presumably like that in Britain where trade unions employed PR.[22]

Indeed, both sides in the debate used examples drawn from foreign trade-union experiences to buttress their cases. In order to save time, each side in the PR debate was limited to five speakers, and all five reformists contended that adoption of PR had provided British and German unions with mass bases, while failure to employ PR was responsible for the CGT's comparative numerical weakness. Only Niel among the revolutionaries responded to this argument directly. As numerous French revolutionary syndicalists, including a not quite convinced Griffuelhes, would do later, he argued that the British and Germans might well have "quantity" and were welcome to it; but the CGT had "quality," *i.e.,* the most combative workers, in its ranks and foreign unions should emulate that instead of the other way round.[23]

The Guesdist Alexandre Luquet, secretary of the much-belabored barbers' union, raised the issue that would make the PR debate a landmark in the history of revolutionary syndicalism. Just as Maroux had argued that some trades were more useful than others and thus merited a stronger voice in the councils of labor, so Luquet now rose to say that some unions were more revolutionary than others, indeed serving as militant minorities, a vanguard, example, and guide to the proletariat, and therefore deserved special consideration. To give them anything less than an equal voice in the CGT's decision-making process would stifle the struggle to emancipate the working class.

Thus was raised for the first time in public debate the argument that seemed to justify the worst fears of reformists in the CGT, the French Socialist Party, and in trade unions and socialist parties abroad. Critics concluded from the revolutionaries' line of argument that the CGT leadership was opposed to mass unionism and, hence, dedicated to dictatorial control of the trade-union movement by a radical elite. Thus, despite the solid socialist credentials of Luquet, his intervention could now be used to vindicate the charges that anarchists had taken over the CGT. The reformists now began to organize for propaganda purposes, to counter the influence of *La Voix du Peuple* and *L'Action Directe* by reaching out to French workers in a publication of their own. This was the monthly *Revue syndicaliste,* founded by Albert Thomas, the trade-union expert of the reformist wing of French socialism and labor

22. CGT, *XIVᵉ Congrès national corporatif... Bourges,* 164–65. On PR in British unions, see Pouget, "Les Débats du Congrès [de Bourges]," 62.

23. CGT, *XIVᵉ Congrès national corporatif... Bourges,* 151 (Maroux); 153 (Coupat); 160 (Keufer); 162, 169 (Lucas); 182 (Lauche-Machinists); 164–65 (Niel).

editor of *L'Humanité*, "after conversations with militants at the Congress of Bourges."[24] In this publication the ongoing polemic over the supposed elitism and craft-unionist ethos of revolutionary syndicalism was first developed in a systematic way. At the outset, it was a strictly national debate. By late 1905, however, with publication in its pages of a slashing attack on revolutionary syndicalism by Paul Umbreit, the editor of *Correspondenzblatt,* the official organ of the German Freie Gewerkschaften, the dispute took on the international dimensions it has never lost.[25]

What gave urgency to the reformist campaign was the third consecutive defeat of PR by a large margin at Bourges. Although the pro-PR forces were probably destined to lose, Griffuelhes adroitly sealed their fate by announcing to the weary delegates, no doubt eager to leave after the day-long debate on PR, that before the vote, "it should be understood that we are voting on the *principle* of PR and, that if we adopt the principle, we will still have to figure out how to apply it." Hungry, thirsty, and with Niel's argument about the French aversion to mathematical formulas ringing in their ears, the delegates promptly voted down PR by 822 to 388, with one abstention.[26]

As its pre-congress propaganda suggested, the CGT majority came to Bourges with a proposal for a national direct-action campaign for an eight-hour workday and the six-day week, although the latter was a secondary demand. The motion was made by Raymond Dubéros, one of Luquet's barber militants and the Blanquist secretary of the Lyon Bourse du Travail. The campaign that Dubéros outlined, however, was really the brainchild of Emile Pouget, who had been interested in the eight-hour day since American building trades' workers agitated for and won it in 1886. Like many revolutionary syndicalists, Pouget had been scornful of the eight-hour day campaign of the socialist Second International; led in France by the Guesdists, it had consisted mainly of peaceful marches, speeches, and petitions to local mayors on May 1. What Pouget wanted and what Dubéros proposed was direct action. "We're not saying to the working class: 'We'll give you the eight-hour day,'" Pouget wrote. "We're saying: 'Have the strength to impose your will on the bosses; . . . you'll have [the eight-hour day] when you refuse to work more than eight

24. CGT, *XIV* Congrès national corporatif . . . Bourges,* 176–77, 188–90; Félicien Challaye, *Syndicalisme révolutionnaire et Syndicalisme réformiste* (Paris, 1909), 151; Challaye says that the reformists used German, Austrian, and U.S. labor publications as their models for *Revue syndicaliste.*

25. Paul Umbreit, "Des faits!," *La Revue syndicaliste,* no. 7, November 15, 1905.

26. CGT, *XIV* Congrès national corporatif . . . Bourges,* 190, 192. Griffuelhes' emphasis.

hours.' " [27] According to Edouard Dolléans, Griffuelhes questioned the wisdom of the campaign, with its rigid timetable and all-or-nothing overtones; "What if we fail?" he asked. Griffuelhes, who knew better than Pouget what the shopfloor worker thought, also had some less strategic reasons for hesitating. In his postmortem on the campaign at the CGT Congress of Amiens in 1906, he remarked that "the working class was, for the most part, hostile to a shorter working day. Shorter days meant a reduction in wages. . . ." [28] Griffuelhes had encountered this reasoning among the Nord textile workers in 1903, where imposing the ten-hour day had been joined with a demand for maintenance of income; this amounted to a demand for higher wages and exposed workers to the charge by employers of asking for "more pay for less work." Griffuelhes' early coolness, then, derived in part from his realization that the struggle for eight hours would require a major effort to educate workers and the public about the value of the reform.

Such a campaign would also demand a much greater organizational effort than any yet undertaken by the CGT. Was there sufficient manpower for the organizational and propaganda effort and enough money for the thousands of leaflets, posters, etc., and for bail and lawyers' fees when the inevitable confrontation with government came? Here Griffuelhes' fears were justified. Although Dubéros proposed a levy of fifty centimes per one hundred members per year from affiliated unions to finance the campaign, the congress, faithful to the penuriousness of French labor that so frustrated Griffuelhes, would only agree to voluntary contributions. Nevertheless, despite his reservations, Griffuelhes rallied to the idea of the eight-hour-day fight, apparently with some nudging from Pouget, and would devote most of his time as general secretary to the campaign over the next two years.

Dubéros proposed that on May 1, 1906, all workers in industries where the CGT had members would cease work after eight hours and stay out until their employers conceded the eight-hour day and the six-day week. Dubéros' resolution placed the eight-hour day squarely in the category of what modern-day labor strategist André Gorz has called "non-reformist reforms." "Agitation for the eight-hour day," Dubéros said, "is a step toward the ultimate task of complete emancipation [of the working class]." The campaign would be organized by a special committee of fifteen members, including Griffuelhes, his

---

27. Maurice Dommanget's *Histoire du premier mai* (Paris, 1972) remains the best source on the eight-hour-day movement in France; CGT, *XIVᵉ Congrès national corporatif . . . Bourges*, 210.

28. Dolléans, *Histoire du mouvement ouvrier*, II, 121–22; CGT, *XVᵉ Congrès national corporatif . . . Amiens*, 2–3.

assistant Pouget, Georges Yvetot, general secretary of the Bourses du Travail section, his assistant Paul Delesalle, and the irrepressible Luquet.[29]

Reformists expressed hesitations about the proposal but did not refuse outright to support it. Keufer said it would have been wiser to proceed by stages, with a nine-hour-day target in 1906. Guérard, too, thought 1906 was too soon for eight hours. Regardless, the Dubéros resolution was adopted by acclamation and the stage was set for France's first general strike and the CGT's major prewar confrontation with the French State.[30] Despite an illness that would sideline him for nearly nine months in 1905, Victor Griffuelhes threw himself into the eight-hour-day campaign with characteristic energy. Although his long illness precluded day-to-day organizing of the campaign, he became its symbol—a notoriety he would pay for. On May 1, 1906, when thousands of French workers left their ateliers and factories after eight hours' work, Griffuelhes was in prison, accused of plotting with the Bonapartists to overthrow the Third Republic.

29. André Gorz, *Strategy for Labor* (New York, 1969), esp. 12 and 32; APP, B/a 1686, "Le Mouvement social en mars 1906," 37.

30. CGT, *XIVᵉ Congrès national corporatif. . . Bourges*, 207–209 (Keufer); 216–17 (Guérard); 220.

V

May Day (1906)

The failure of [general strikes] is in no way an argument or justification for opposing them. . . . We will even go so far as to say that in order to achieve final triumph, there must be failures along the way. But these failures will be fruitful only if we gain from them more confidence in ourselves, in our strength, and in the value of the struggles which produced them.

—Victor Griffuelhes, *Les Objectifs de nos luttes de classe*

At the Congress of Bourges in September, 1904, the revolutionary syndicalist leadership of the CGT received a mandate to pursue the most ambitious campaign undertaken by French organized labor before World War I. The campaign would take nineteen months, and the committee chosen by the congress to organize and direct it held its first meeting at CGT headquarters in Paris on November 29, 1904. In addition to Griffuelhes, Pouget, Yvetot, and Delesalle, it included Raymond Dubéros; Albert Lévy, treasurer of the CGT; Jean Latapie, a secretary of the metalworkers' federation; Léon Robert, Guesdist secretary of the painters' union; and Jules Roullier, secretary of the Paris electricians' union and member of the TFS executive committee. Apparently, Dubéros replaced the head of the barbers' union, Alexandre Luquet, on the committee.[1]

While the membership of the committee would not change during its tenure, its leadership, at first confided to Pouget who originated the idea of the campaign, gradually devolved upon Paul Delesalle, the assistant general secretary of the Bourses du Travail section. The reason for this was Griffuelhes'

1. APP, B/a 1686, "Le Mouvement social en mars 1906," 37.

sudden, serious tubercular attack in January, 1905, which incapacitated him for much of the year; from January until early August, Emile Pouget served as acting general secretary of the CGT.

Griffuelhes' illness seems to have been hastened by fatigue from his involvement in a large agricultural workers' strike in the Midi in December, 1904. Between its Montpellier and Bourges congresses, the CGT had succeeded in setting up a Southern Agricultural Workers' Federation (Fédération des Travailleurs Agricoles du Midi—SAWF) largely through the efforts of Louis Niel of the Montpellier Bourse du Travail, and a remarkable young man named Paul Ader. Ader was a farm laborer who lived most of his short life in the village of Cuxac-d'Aude, deep in the wine-growing country of the Aude Department; he would become one of the great peasant leaders of the Belle Epoque. Most important from Griffuelhes' point of view, Ader favored merging the farmworkers into a broader federation of rural laborers, including timber workers and market gardeners.[2]

Ader became secretary of the Southern Agricultural Workers' Federation in November, 1904, just in time to direct the Midi's first major farmworkers' strike. The issues in the strike, which principally affected the Aude and Hérault departments, were increased wages, rehiring vineyard workers made jobless by the current surplus of wine, and union recognition. Throughout December, the strike leaders—Ader and CGT representatives Griffuelhes and Niel—traveled from village to village as a sort of peripatetic strike committee, boosting morale, baptizing new unions, and helping in negotiations with the winegrowers.

The strike must have been exhilarating for Griffuelhes, who understood perhaps better than anyone else in the CGT leadership the importance of rural workers in the French economy and the necessity for bringing them into the CGT. The show of solidarity between the urban workers of Narbonne and the farm laborers that brought the strike to a successful conclusion would have been particularly heartening to him, but the long hours he spent in the Midi appear to have exhausted Griffuelhes, by his own admission. Sometime in January, he fell ill and was forced to leave Paris for a long rest in the country. On February 6, 1905, Pouget told a meeting of the CGT Federations section that Griffuelhes' health was improving but "a complete cure will take a long time."[3]

2. *DBMO*, X, 116–17 (Ader).

3. Griffuelhes, *Voyage révolutionnaire*, 31; AN, F7 12.890, note of July 11, 1905; *VdP*, no. 241, May 26–June 4, 1905.

It was not a good time to be out of harness. The work of the Eight-Hour-Day Committee was going on without him. Perhaps more important in the long term, the warring French socialists, prodded by their comrades of the socialist Second International, finally achieved unity at this time. Even though Griffuelhes had himself participated in the socialist unity movement in 1899–1901 and had long complained about the negative effects of socialist factionalism upon the working-class movement, he would have been hard-pressed now, in 1905, to see anything positive for the CGT in the socialists' newfound unity. Unity had been imposed on the French socialists at the Amsterdam congress of the Second International in August, 1904, by the powerful German Social Democratic Party (SPD), and this seemed to mean that Jules Guesde's POF, the SPD's French protégé, would have the upper hand in the new unified party, known as the French Section of the Workers' International (Section Française de l'Internationale ouvrière—SFIO). This was not good news for the CGT revolutionary syndicalists. Although Griffuelhes had little love for Jaurès and the reformist wing of the party, he knew that Guesdism was the real enemy of trade-union independence. By reducing the unions under their control in the Nord and Pas-de-Calais region to largely mutualist functions, the Guesdists discouraged union membership; through their monopoly of the left-wing press in these areas and their harassment of local revolutionary syndicalist militants, they made CGT recruitment extremely difficult. Now, certain POF militants within the CGT were trying to impose Guesde's design upon the confederation. A socialist party dominated by the POF was unwelcome news indeed.

Besides, in a very significant way, socialist disunity had made possible the growth of the CGT and the rise to power of Griffuelhes' revolutionary faction within it. Workers' weariness with socialist feuding had turned their attention to the CGT to such an extent that—especially after unification with the Bourse du Travail federation at Montpellier in 1902—the CGT could begin to see itself as France's labor party (parti du travail). Now that a unified socialist party had emerged with its own daily newspaper, Jean Jaurès' *L'Humanité*, parliamentary socialism would be a much more serious force to contend with. The rise of the SFIO would certainly require rethinking CGT strategy, but in what direction? Should the CGT bring its considerable moral force to the aid of the anti-Guesdist wing of the party, in which Vaillant would now find himself, or was the risk of "electoralist" contagion too great in even such a limited gesture? The CGT's great strength and its attraction for working people was precisely its refusal to be a pawn in electoral politics; thus its proper strategy in the face of this new force was perhaps to reaffirm and strengthen this position above and outside of the electoral battle. Answers to these questions would await Griffuelhes' return to Paris, but in the meantime, he probably had already firmly concluded that socialist unity made imperative a good showing on May 1, 1906, if the CGT's moral authority was to be preserved.

Other pressing problems bedeviled the general secretary's convalescence. The issue that would have weighed most heavily on Griffuelhes' mind in the first six months of 1905 was the threat of war. Syndicalist militants believed war was the worst calamity that could befall the labor movement, and not only because the working class and peasantry traditionally did most of the fighting and dying. It was almost an article of faith among revolutionary syndicalists that wars are the ultimate diversionary tactic for regimes under pressure to make fundamental changes. The Russo-Japanese War in the Far East had gone badly for France's Russian ally since its beginning in February, 1904. When it began, the CGT had issued a manifesto signed by Griffuelhes and Yvetot denouncing both belligerents and branding the war as an imperialist struggle over China. In the Executive Committee report to the Bourges congress in September, 1904, Griffuelhes had added, significantly, that the tsarist regime had entered the war "to silence her proletariat in a wave of nationalism."[4] Early in the war, however, suspicion mounted on the French Left that the French government was contemplating joining the conflict on the side of its Russian ally to "save" the massive loans made to her over the years and to avoid weakening France's (at the time) sole alliance partner.

A new dimension was added to the French Left's concern over the Russo-Japanese War in January, 1905, just as Griffuelhes became ill. In Russia, popular anger at mismanagement of the war combined with war-induced hardship led to mass protests against the government. On Sunday, January 22, troops fired on demonstrators outside the tsar's Winter Palace in St. Petersburg, killing ninety-six people. "Bloody Sunday" was the spark that set off the Russian Revolution of 1905, which would have considerable impact upon socialist and trade-union movements in other parts of Europe. In France, the Left rushed to declare its solidarity with the Russian protesters, partly from fear that the French government might intervene to forestall the collapse of its only European ally. Edouard Vaillant, who was one of the most tireless critics of the tsarist regime, proclaimed that the 1905 revolution in Russia would have the same effect "on the proletarian revolution of the 20th century as the French bourgeois revolution of the 18th century had upon the rise of the middle

4. CGT, *XIVᵉ Congrès national corporatif . . . Bourges,* 5–6.

class." The CGT, meanwhile, "organized a big rally" on May 10, 1905, to celebrate, somewhat prematurely, "the victory of the Russian revolutionaries over the government of the Tsar," probably in response to news of the formation of the first soviet in St. Petersburg.[5] These organs of popular power in Russia, which resembled the French syndicat (in its postrevolutionary function as coordinator of the production and distribution of goods, thus becoming the government), captured the imagination of CGT militants in France.[6] Syndicalist fascination with the soviet would contribute enormously to French workers' positive reception of the Bolshevik Revolution in 1917–1920, as will be shown in Chapter XI.

Worries over this threat to peace were abruptly superseded at the end of March, 1905, by a major diplomatic crisis involving France and Germany, which concerned the quasi-independent Sultanate of Morocco. The Germans rightly viewed France's steady encroachments on the sultanate, technically a dependency of the crumbling Ottoman Empire, as a bid to add Morocco to its North African empire, which already included Algeria and Tunisia. Germany, which had hopes of expanded trade with Morocco and colonial ambitions of its own in Africa, made it clear that it would resist French aggrandizement at the expense of the sultanate.[7]

For Griffuelhes and the CGT leadership, the Moroccan crisis had been brought on by competition between French and German capital in North Africa. The French colonial lobby, they argued, had powerful friends in the government, principally Foreign Minister Théophile Delcassé. The CGT's analysis was spelled out in the text of the poster it issued in January, 1906, entitled "War on War" (*Guerre à la Guerre*): "For five years a French colonial lobby of which Delcassé was the linchpin, has been preparing for the conquest of Morocco. Capitalists and army officers pushed for the conquest of this country, the first in search of booty and profits, the second in search of medals and promotions."[8] What bothered them most, however, was the apparent

---

5. *L'Action Directe*, 1st ser., December 3, 1905; APP, B/a 1686, "Le Mouvement social en mars 1906," 40.

6. See Paul Avrich, *The Russian Anarchists* (Princeton, 1967), 72–90.

7. The standard account of this crisis is Eugene N. Anderson, *The First Moroccan Crisis, 1904–1906* (Chicago, 1930), and new information is given in Christopher Andrew's insightful *Théophile Delcassé and the Making of the Entente Cordiale: A Reappraisal of French Foreign Policy, 1898–1905* (New York, 1968). Reactions to the crisis on the Left in France are extensively catalogued in Vol. I of Georges Oved, *La Gauche française et le Nationalisme marocain, 1905–1955* (Paris, 1984).

8. CGT, *XVᵉ Congrès national corporatif . . . Amiens*, 8.

willingness of Premier Maurice Rouvier's government to court war over this issue. Was Morocco the Rouvier government's real concern in keeping the crisis alive? In brief, CGT leaders suspected that the government's brinkmanship had internal as well as external motives. In France, momentum was building (or so the CGT leaders hoped) toward the May 1, 1906, national strike for the eight-hour day. What better way for the French government to defuse this growing social unrest, they reasoned, than to escalate a colonial dispute into an international confrontation, in which national honor and security were engaged? Griffuelhes, for one, apparently believed that the French government was dangerously close to declaring war at the end of 1905, and he devoted much of his activity in December, 1905, and January, 1906, to efforts to save the peace.

In his first article in *La Voix du Peuple* since falling ill in January—a September 17 morale booster for the eight-hours' campaign—Griffuelhes indicated his immediate priorities.[9] Much had been done in his absence to get the campaign underway. The Paris police, who kept a close watch on the preparations, were especially interested in the committee's purchase in March, 1905, of "an immense sheet of calico bearing the slogan 'After May 1, 1906, we will work only eight hours,' which was draped across the façade of the [Paris] Bourse du Travail." [10]

In early October, 1905, police reported that the Eight-Hour-Day Committee's program was "thrown into disarray" by the CGT's expulsion from the Paris Bourse du Travail, an action apparently prompted by the disturbing news that the CGT intended to make union rights for State employees an issue in the campaign.[11] This was no idle threat. That same month, the CGT formed a Joint Committee to Secure the Right to Organize (Comité d'entente pour le conquete du droit syndical) for government employees, and in January, 1906, the CGT organized rallies in sixty cities around the country to convince State and local government employees to join the confederation and support the May 1 strike.[12] Ever since the passage of the 1884 law granting official recognition to unions, successive governments had strenuously resisted unionization of civil servants on the grounds that such action could lead to paralyzing the State through strikes.

The expulsion of the CGT from its headquarters in the Paris Bourse du

9. Griffuelhes, "Les Huit Heures," *VdP*, no. 257, September 17–24, 1905.
10. APP, B/a 1686, "Le Mouvement social en mars 1906," 38–39.
11. *Ibid.*, 40.
12. Griffuelhes, "Pour la liberté syndicale," *VdP*, no. 272, January 1–7, 1906.

Travail meant that Griffuelhes had to interrupt more serious work to go house-hunting. After what appears to have been a hurried search, office space was rented at 10, Cité de Riverin, in the 10th arrondissement not far from the Bourse du Travail. The confederation's new lodgings were somewhat less than grand. Police agent "Roy," who quickly nipped around to inspect the new headquarters, found the mighty CGT housed in "four modest rooms, two of which," he added hopefully, "have a view of the city." Griffuelhes called it "a stinking slum." The entire CGT leadership—Griffuelhes, Pouget, Lévy, Yve-tot, Delesalle—was crammed together in one room, and the other three rooms housed the confederal archives, the Section of Federations, and the CGT's placement office. Worse, "when the landlord learned that he had rented to the CGT, he gave us notice and we had to leave," apparently assisted by the police, who "came to order us out." The experience was humiliating for the proud Griffuelhes, who commented years later, "What a miserable situation we were in then!" [13] In January, 1906, resolved that the CGT would never again be dictated to by private or public landlords, he set about forming a private company to buy, with borrowed funds, a proper home for the CGT. This controversial venture provided the ammunition used by Griffuelhes' enemies to drive him from office in 1909 and will be discussed in detail in Chapter VIII.

With the CGT's housing problem temporarily, if unsatisfactorily, resolved, Griffuelhes now turned his attention to another issue that had cropped up in his absence: a row between the CGT and the German Freie Gewerkschaften. Nationalist sentiments among workers, ideological differences, feuding over the proper functions of the new trade-union international, and German labor's downplaying of the gravity of the Moroccan crisis had all helped sour relations between the French and German unions. Jolyon Howorth concludes that internationalism "may well have inhabited the minds of many European workers prior to 1914, but . . . at least as far as . . . French workers . . . are concerned, nationalism occupied their hearts and guts." He blames this lack of internationalism largely on the "nationalist conditioning" of workers in the schools and believes the negative effects of schooling were supplemented by the "clash of political cultures" between a "relatively docile party-union [SPD-Freie Gewerkschaften] tandem" in Germany that accepted the "paternalist

13. APP, B/a 1686, note of October 23, 1905; B/a 1603, note of June 3, 1909; B/a 1686, "Le Mouvement social en mars 1906," 40; B/a 1603, note of June 3, 1909; Griffuelhes quoted in *Le Travailleur du Batiment*, February 1, 1910.

state" and a "libertarian movement [in France, *i.e.,* the CGT] which rejected all states."

The CGT had insisted, in vain, that the issues of the general strike, anti-militarism, and the eight-hour day be placed on the agenda of the conference in Amsterdam on June 23–25, 1905, of the trade-union international, which had the cumbersome title of International Secretariat of National Trade-Union Centers (ISNTUC). The Germans felt that if these issues were to be debated at all, it should be within the political framework of the Socialist International. Although differences over these issues were real enough, it would become increasingly clear that the real thrust of the dispute was who would preside over the destinies of the international labor movement: German social democrats or French syndicalists. The CGT operated at a considerable disadvantage in this contest. ISNTUC headquarters were in Berlin and its secretary was Carl Legien, president of the Freie Gewerkschaften. By 1913, Germany was also home to twenty-two of the existing twenty-six international trade secretariats, sectoral groupings such as the International Metalworkers' Federation.[14]

The domestic ramifications of the relationship may have been equally important. The CGT revolutionary syndicalist leadership probably began to suspect the German unions of offering unofficial support to their reformist foes in the confederation at least as early as the Congress of Bourges in September 1904, when several reformist spokesmen used the Freie Gewerkschaften as proof of the advantages of proportional representation.

The German unions also had reason to complain about CGT interference in their internal affairs. Even before the Congress of Bourges, *Le Mouvement socialiste* had opened its pages to Dr. Raphael Friedeberg, Germany's noisiest exponent of the general strike and spiritual leader of its small revolutionary syndicalist movement, the Localists or Lokalisten. But what no doubt irked Carl Legien and company most was the space the monthly review accorded, beginning in early 1905, to Robert Michels, later one of this century's most prominent sociological theorists but in 1905 the leading German spokesman for revolutionary syndicalism and a talented polemicist. In a series of articles, Michels took the German union leadership to task for ignoring growing sen-

14. Jolyon Howorth, "French Workers and German Workers: The Impossibility of Internationalism, 1900–1914," *European History Quarterly,* XV (January, 1985), 73, 77–78, 88; Susan Milner, *The Dilemmas of Internationalism: French Syndicalism and the International Labour Movement* (Oxford, 1990), 168.

timent in labor ranks for direct action as opposed to the parliamentary variety. His international airing of the controversies afflicting the German unions—and the SPD—was an unwelcome addition to the already considerable challenges being faced by the German labor establishment.[15]

Griffuelhes waded into the controversy with the Germans not long after his return to Paris. Jolyon Howorth dates his involvement from December, 1905, but it actually began in early November with a polemical piece in *La Voix du Peuple* in which Griffuelhes argued that direct action produced more tangible benefits for French workers than reformist action did for German workers. He was responding to an article in *Correspondenzblatt,* the official journal of the Freie Gewerkschaften, by its editor, Paul Umbreit, who stated in essence that revolutionary syndicalists were long on talk but short on results. When Umbreit's article was reproduced in the CGT reformists' monthly, *La Revue syndicaliste,* on November 15, 1905, Griffuelhes riposted with a three-part series in *La Voix du Peuple,* lambasting the German union leadership for "having been in dereliction of their international duties" in refusing to discuss the general strike and antimilitarism at international labor conferences and in declining "to support the Russian Revolution and peace initiatives from the SFIO and CGT" during the continuing Moroccan crisis.[16] What seems to have most upset Griffuelhes, however, was what he called the "utter pretentiousness" of Umbreit's claim that the German unions were a model for all Europe to follow.

January, 1906, was the most tragic month of Victor Griffuelhes' life. On New Year's Day his beloved brother Henri died. A police spy who attended Henri's burial on January 4 reported that "the [general] secretary of the CGT appears to have been devastated by the death of his brother, which can only worsen his already precarious state of health." Agent "Roy" of the Paris Préfecture de Police concurred. "The death of Henri Griffuelhes, treasurer of the [National] Leatherworkers' Federation, caused by tuberculosis, has profoundly affected his brother, Victor," he reported, adding in a remarkably prescient statement: "The days of the latter are henceforth numbered, and they [the CGT leadership] have already designated his successor, who will be none other

15. *Le Mouvement socialiste,* nos. 137–138 (June 15–July 5, 1904); Robert Michels, "La Grève générale des mineurs de la Ruhr," *ibid.,* no. 152 (April 1, 1905), and "Le Congrès syndical de Cologne," *ibid.,* no. 158 (July 1, 1905).

16. Griffuelhes, "Des chiffres," *VdP,* no. 263, October 29–November 4, 1905; Howorth, "French Workers and German Workers," 79–80; Umbreit, "Des faits!"; Griffuelhes, "Dans l'Internationale," *VdP,* 3 pts., nos. 271–73, December 24–31, 1905, January 1–7, 7–14, 1906.

than [Louis] Niel, secretary of the Bourse du Travail of Montpellier."[17] Niel did succeed Griffuelhes as CGT general secretary in March, 1909. The police agent's remark makes one wonder if the government's scheme to push Griffuelhes out of the CGT leadership and replace him with a moderate—with, in fact, Niel—was as much of a last-minute operation as has been alleged. Niel's long-term relationship with the police has been documented and will be discussed in Chapter VIII.

No sooner had Henri been buried than the Franco-German imbroglio over Morocco heated up once again. In early January, Griffuelhes and the CGT leaders received information from "very well informed" sources that relations between France and Germany over Morocco were far worse than the Rouvier government was willing to admit. The news was sufficiently alarming to warrant sending Victor Griffuelhes to Berlin on January 12 to seek joint French-German trade-union demonstrations against the threat of war.[18]

More was riding on the outcome of the general secretary's rendezvous with the Germans than peace in Europe, important as that was. Griffuelhes' mission was the only direct action undertaken by the European Left to avert war during the Moroccan crisis; if successful, it clearly would have buttressed the CGT's claim to be France's only genuine parti du travail. Throughout 1905, the newly united SFIO had tried through the machinery of the Second International and its relations with the SPD to organize a joint antiwar campaign; but the SPD had refused to take the war threat seriously, and in July 1905, the German government had barred Jaurès from going to Germany to speak for peace.[19] In this context, perhaps Griffuelhes' Berlin mission was, in part at least, an attempt to upstage the SFIO.

It also seems likely that the CGT leaders saw the mission as a way to enhance the confederation's power and influence and to increase the momentum of its eight-hour-day campaign, now entering the countdown. Along these same lines, one suspects that Griffuelhes thought a successful mission would outflank the increasingly troublesome labor and socialist Ultra-Left, the Hervé crowd and the International Antimilitarist Association, by showing

17. AN, F7 12.890, report of January 3, 1906; APP, B/a 1601, note of January 3, 1906.

18. APP, B/a 1601, note of January 9, 1906. Oved identifies the CGT's "very well-informed" source as Maurice Sarraut, Paris bureau chief of *La Depeche de Toulouse*, a mass-circulation daily close to the Radical Party and Jaurès' wing of the SFIO (*La Gauche française et le Nationalisme marocain*, I, 80).

19. Georges Haupt, ed., *Bureau socialiste international, comptes rendus des réunions, manifestes et circulaires, (1900–1907)* (Paris, 1969), I, 145–46, 150, 155–56, 175–76, 184.

that in spite of the latter's violent rhetoric, it was the CGT leadership that got things done regarding antiwar agitation.

The Berlin mission, Jolyon Howorth writes, "was a total failure; worse, it was a humiliating failure." The leaders of the Freie Gewerkschaften gave Griffuelhes a less than friendly reception and turned a deaf ear to his call for joint antiwar protests. In his report on the Berlin trip to the CGT's Executive Committee, he allegedly recalled that "the trade-union militants I talked to said that no one in Germany believed there was a danger of war, and that they didn't see any need for a demonstration." The chances of war were remote, they contended, and even if they weren't, German law forbade unions to participate in "political" demonstrations of the sort he was proposing. Thus, Griffuelhes later wrote, "I returned to Paris bearing a categorical refusal." [20]

Griffuelhes' overwhelmingly negative impression from his failed mission stemmed from more than resentment at his German hosts' lack of comprehension and cooperation. According to a police spy, who apparently sat in on the general secretary's report to the Executive Committee, the overriding lesson Griffuelhes brought back from Berlin was that rather than demonstrating their solidarity with their French comrades in the event of war, "the German people will leave us in the lurch when war comes." Years later, attempting to explain his support of the war in 1914, Griffuelhes wrote that his experience in 1906 convinced him that "in time of war, all Germany would march against us. It could not have been otherwise." There is some evidence that Griffuelhes' subsequent bitter dislike of the Germans rested on more than resentment at what he saw as their lack of solidarity. The day after he left Berlin, he made a brief, unscheduled stop at the first station on the French side of the border, just long enough for a meal at the local railway café. The event was significant for future relations between the French and German labor movements. As he would later tell his cronies on the Executive Committee, he had become so bitter toward the Germans while in Berlin that he felt compelled to take the first opportunity possible to console himself with traditional French beefsteak and fried potatoes (*un steack-frites national*). [21]

20. Howorth, "French Workers and German Workers," 80; APP, B/a 1686, note of "Ric," January 26, 1906; Griffuelhes, "L'Internationale syndicale," *L'Action Directe*, 2nd ser., May 13, 1908.

21. APP, B/a 1686, note of "Ric," January 26, 1906. I wish to thank Jacques Julliard for sharing this anecdote with me; he heard it from Alfred Rosmer shortly before the latter's death in 1964. Both Julliard and I find this significant because it demonstrates that Griffuelhes' rejec-

Back in Paris, Griffuelhes threw himself into the eight-hours' campaign. On March 10, 1906, it took an unexpected, dramatic turn with a coal mine explosion at Courrières (Pas-de-Calais) that left over eleven hundred miners dead, the biggest catastrophe in the history of French mining. The disaster, blamed by some workers and local union officials on company negligence, led to a strike in the Pas-de-Calais coalfields that rapidly spread to the Nord mines and then to metal- and glassworks in the region.

Griffuelhes and the CGT leadership in Paris quickly realized that the Courrières disaster was a bonus for their campaign and also their long-term effort to wrest control of the workers' movement in the Pas-de-Calais and the Nord from the reformist socialist deputies Emile Basly and Arthur Lamendin and the Guesdists, respectively. In the aftermath of Courrières, as angry workers took to the streets, the syndicalist minority in the North tried to position itself to lead the agitation, as it had done in the wake of the failed miners' general strike of 1902.[22] It now also appeared possible for the CGT to graft the miners' agitation onto the eight-hours' campaign, thus giving the countdown to May 1 the emotional dimension and momentum it badly needed.

Griffuelhes grasped all this and moved swiftly to take advantage of the situation. What he appears not to have understood clearly is that the State, whose police apparatus was now under the direction of the stern Jacobin, Georges Clemenceau, would not stand idly by while disorder gripped the nation's principal industrial region and threatened to enhance further the CGT's strength and prestige; its challenge to established authority in industry and government was already worrying enough. Nor did the sitting Radical government want the country in turmoil on the eve of the May 6 national elections. A major, prolonged strike in the North could only accentuate popular fears that the government was unable to keep order and was too soft on labor. The stage was set for the first major confrontation between the revolutionary syndicalist CGT and the French State.

Repression mounted as the miners' strike in the Pas-de-Calais gathered strength and fury—with the inevitable reprisals of strikers against scabs and their families—and the agitation spread to the neighboring Nord Department, where it affected not only the coal basin but, in a classic demonstration of Griffuelhes' 1902 theory of linkages among industries, the metallurgy and

---

tion of the Germans was as much cultural as ideological, and therefore more visceral (Julliard to author, August 5, 1987, author's files).

22. The most detailed account of the Courrières disaster and its aftermath is Heinz-Otto Sieburg, *Die Grubenkatastrophe von Courrières 1906* (Wiesbaden, 1967).

glassmaking trades as well. The government's response was to order in large numbers of troops—just under eight thousand in the Lens area alone—and to begin arresting local revolutionary syndicalist leaders. Benoit Broutchoux, head of the jeune syndicat, was sentenced to three months in prison for incitement to violence; before the Pas-de-Calais strike ended in early May, some forty leaders and militants of the jeune syndicat were behind bars.

On April 17, a strike was declared in the Nord mining and metallurgical center of Denain. On the eighteenth, the local union sent a telegram to CGT headquarters in Paris: "Four thousand strikers acclaim CGT. Miners' and metalworkers' steering committee calls for support. Send delegate as soon as possible." To which Griffuelhes immediately wired back: "Merrheim arrives tomorrow morning 11 o'clock." The telegram must have been music to Griffuelhes' ears. Since 1902, he had argued that natural linkages between the mining and metalworking sectors could be used to advantage in general strikes. In February, 1906, he had urged that Etienne Merzet's tour of the northern mining areas on behalf of the Eight-Hour-Day Committee should be coordinated with a visit by metalworkers' delegates to the metallurgical centers of the Nord.[23] The events now unfolding in Denain, where mines and mills were being struck simultaneously, seemed to offer dramatic proof of his theory.

Alphonse Merrheim, secretary of the CGT metalworkers' union, arrived in the Nord on April 19 and went straight to a large rally in Denain. Merrheim's message to the strikers, as reported by the Baslyite newspaper, *Le Reveil du Nord,* was the same as that being pushed by Griffuelhes and his emissaries in the Pas-de-Calais: Political and occupational divisions among the workers must now be transcended; the CGT is not an agent of division; it represents *all* workers, regardless of politics, craft, or creed.[24]

But on April 21, Clemenceau arrived in the Pas-de-Calais, accompanied by Emile Hennion, chief of the Sureté générale. The ostensible reason for the visit was to investigate increasing violence between strikers and strikebreakers, but there appears to have been another, more important goal to his mission. With the possibility fading for a peaceful settlement of the agitation and the twin deadlines of May 1 and May 6 approaching rapidly, it must have been clear to Clemenceau and his entourage that drastic measures were now re-

23. AD Nord M 626/62, notes of April 17–18, 1906; the telegrams were intercepted by the Sureté and copies sent to the Nord prefect in Lille; APP, B/a 1601, note of February 3, 1906.
24. *Le Reveil du Nord,* April 20, 1906; AD Pas-de-Calais, M 1796, note of April 20, 1906.

quired. But what measures and how to implement them without painting the government as an oppressor of labor and handmaiden of capital?

The Paris newspaper *La Presse,* looking back on developments from hindsight on May 10, provided an interesting if speculative account of how Clemenceau arrived at a solution. The newspaper claimed that during his April 21 inquiry into the violence in the Pas-de-Calais, Clemenceau was told by local miners: "The rioters aren't our people; they're strangers to this region." Whereupon, "M. Clemenceau looked at M. Hennion, who smiled back. Together they had hit upon the idea of a 'plot.' "[25]

The *Presse* account, while colorful, offers an unnecessarily complicated explanation for the antigovernment plot now cooked up by Hennion and Clemenceau. As the interior ministry archives make clear, the two men had no need of xenophobic miners in the Pas-de-Calais to suggest the story line of their "plot." Clemenceau and his chief of security had two missions: to maintain order and to assure a government victory in the general elections beginning May 6. Order was being challenged by the strikes in the North and the impending CGT general strike; meanwhile, the Radical government believed its parliamentary majority was threatened by a resurgence of the authoritarian Right, galvanized into action by outrage at the just-commenced separation of Church and State. Pressed for time, Clemenceau and Hennion now set themselves to kill these two birds with one stone, with a plot that went something like this: The strikes in the North had been fomented and financed by the CGT with money provided by elements of the extreme Right, whose aim was to disrupt the May 6 elections. The next step was to accumulate sufficient evidence of rightist-CGT collusion to convince the Sarrien government to authorize the arrest and detention of the principals involved. This evidence, I believe, was provided from Sureté files.

On April 22, Clemenceau put his plot theory to a cabinet meeting where he sought and received endorsement of a police dragnet to disrupt the alleged conspiracy; by that time, those slated for detention had already been chosen. On the CGT side, Clemenceau proposed to arrest CGT leaders Griffuelhes and Lévy, plus union militants who could be charged with direct responsibility for the disorders in the North, *e.g.,* Pierre Monatte, Alphonse Merrheim, and Charles Delzant. As for the rightist conspirators, Clemenceau, using Sureté files, centered his attention on Count Louis Octave Durand de Beauregard,

25. *La Presse,* May 10, 1906.

a former army reserve officer and Bonapartist activist in Paris who had the added distinction of being a multimillionaire. Bracketed with Durand de Beauregard was Louis Bressolles, a onetime socialist agitator who had acted as intermediary in the count's efforts to buy worker support for the Bonapartist cause. With the exception of Merrheim and Delzant, all of the above were arrested between April 23 and 28.

The document that brought all of these threads together, and which I believe became the prize exhibit in the "evidence" Clemenceau submitted to the cabinet ministers on April 22, was a note dated August 23, 1905, by Sûreté agent "Bruxelles," to the effect that "Bressolles, who has been mentioned in previous reports and who is [Durand de] Beauregard's man in Toulouse, is on his way to Paris. His mission is to bring around [Amédée] Bousquet [head of the food workers' union], Pouget, and Griffuelhes to the idea of launching a workers' movement which would coincide with the elections in early 1906. Important sums for this purpose will be placed at his disposal by the Bonapartist party."[26]

Durand de Beauregard had long been known to the police, although the Paris Préfecture de Police had more extensive knowledge of him than the Sûreté and tended to dismiss him as something of a joke. In early 1906, a préfecture agent reported that "the Count ... poses as a man of action, but what he really is is a *naive conspirator who is the only one to take himself seriously*. Nobody in his party thinks he has any real value and no one would pay any attention to him if he wasn't a millionaire." His personal fortune was estimated by police at eleven million francs.[27]

The police operation Clemenceau demanded got under way the day after the cabinet session, with the arrest of Pierre Monatte in the Pas-de-Calais. That same day, seemingly unaware of the wave of arrests about to engulf them, CGT leaders called upon the interior minister to determine the government's intentions regarding the planned May 1 general strike. According to press accounts of the meeting, Clemenceau denied charges that police surveillance had been tightened on CGT leaders and militants in recent days and blandly asserted that the government had no plans to make preventive arrests of CGT officials in the time remaining before May 1. This was the carrot, but as was so often the case in State relations with the unions under the Third Republic,

26. AN, F7 12.867, dossier "Impérialistes—1905."
27. APP, B/a 1061, dossier personnel Louis Octave Durand de Beauregard, notes of November 8, 1875; January 28, 1902; October, 1904; January 11, 1906 (agent's emphasis); November 8, 1905.

there was also a stick. The interview appears to have come to an abrupt close when Clemenceau turned to Griffuelhes and said: "Your method is to create disorder, while my job is to preserve order. My duty is to oppose you. We are on opposite sides of the barricade and the best thing now is for each of us to take his place."[28]

The campaign of repression that now unfolded had comic opera aspects. Investigators soon discovered that Bressolles, the alleged intermediary between Durand de Beauregard and the workers, actually had been blackmailing the count for some time and had been bought off in January, 1906, four months before troubles began in the North. Further, they learned that the rightist money trail led to the yellow or company-union movement, not the CGT. As early as February, 1906, the Paris police knew that Bressolles had deserted the Bonapartists to join Pierre Biétry's yellow trade-union movement; the count himself was involved with them three years later, when the Paris police listed him as "one of the influential members of the Federation of Company Unions [Fédération des Jaunes]."[29]

Finally, one supposedly incriminating piece of evidence found in a search of Durand de Beauregard's villa, a list of ministers slated to take power following a Bonapartist coup, had to be discarded when it was discovered that one of the "ministers" had been dead for two years. Farcical as it was, Clemenceau's stratagem proved remarkably successful. As Georges Wormser, Clemenceau's longtime aide and hagiographer, has observed, the interior minister's top priority upon assuming his post in March, 1906, was to, in Wormser's phrase, " 'make' the elections of May 1906." In this regard, the veteran Jacobin more than fulfilled his mandate. The incoming Chamber boasted 115 Radical deputies instead of a previous 96, while the Radical-Socialist delegation increased from 119 to 132 and the right-wing opposition lost 58 seats. How much the electoral victory owed to Clemenceau's success in selling the Bonapartist-CGT plot to the public is unclear, but coupled with the vigorous action he took to repress the May 1 general strike, one can surmise that it had a considerable effect.[30]

28. *L'Action*, April 24, 1906; Georges Wormser, *La République de Clemenceau* (Paris, 1961), 210.

29. APP, B/a 1061, note of January 11, 1906; *Petit Parisien*, May 1, 1906; APP, B/a 1061, April 24, 1906; APP, B/a 1061, note of January 5, 1909.

30. *L'Eclair*, May 2, 1906; Wormser, *La République de Clemenceau,* 209–10. Even the generally admiring David R. Watson, Clemenceau's most recent English-language biographer, concedes that his manipulation of public opinion before the elections "certainly did much to give

Victor Griffuelhes was arrested on April 30, along with Pouget and Lévy, and incarcerated in Santé Prison. The arrest was made at the Griffuelhes family's newly rented flat at 20, Place de Gambetta (20th), following police searches of the flat and Griffuelhes' office at CGT headquarters over the previous days. The general secretary remained in prison until May 6, when he and Lévy were released without bail. By this time, of course, both the May 1 general strike and the first round of the general elections were over. Griffuelhes' early release may have been prompted by ill health; the day of his arrest, his wife Marie convinced the judge to have him transferred to the prison infirmary, and on May 3, Griffuelhes petitioned for temporary release on grounds of ill health. The prison stay did not improve it; a police spy reported that he "came out more worn out than ever. He is suffering from a fistula," very likely a lesion in the lungs from his tuberculosis.[31]

In the weeks preceding May Day, 1906, the right-wing Paris daily, *L'Echo de Paris,* ran a series of articles collectively entitled "The Coming Revolution [*La Revolution qui vient*]," casting the upcoming general strike in a lurid insurrectionalist light. These sensationalist articles, combined with government claims to have uncovered a labor-Bonapartist plot to overthrow the Republic, induced the greatest mass panic seen in Paris since the days of the Commune. "The propertied classes were in something of a panic on the eve of May 1, in many cases actually fearing a social revolution. Where possible, capital was converted into movable form. Provisions were stored away as if for a siege, and the peasants finally refused to bring their produce in to the Paris markets, lest they be plundered."[32]

In all, an estimated 150,000 Parisian and provincial workers took part in the May Day strike.[33] In Paris, "the streets were deserted," not surprisingly, since they were patrolled by forty thousand cavalry and infantry ordered in

---

Clemenceau his reputation for Machiavellianism" (Watson, *Georges Clemenceau, A Political Biography* [New York, 1976], 176).

31. APP, B/a 1601, notes of April 28, April 30, 1906; APP, B/a 1601, note of April 30, 1906; BB 18, 2335, dossier 382 A06, memorandum of Procureur-général de la République to the minister of justice, June 9, 1906; APP, B/a 1601, note of May 7, 1906.

32. The police believed that the *Echo de Paris* series was intended to scare the populace into voting for the Right in the upcoming elections (APP, B/a 1601, note of April 6, 1906); Wilfred H. Crook, *The General Strike: A Study of Labor's Tragic Weapon in Theory and Practice* (Chapel Hill, N.C., 1931), 40.

33. Dolléans, *Histoire du mouvement ouvrier,* II, 135; Dolléans' figures come from the CGT Executive Committee report to the Congress of Amiens in October, 1906. See CGT, *XVᵉ Congrès national corporatif . . . Amiens,* 15.

by Clemenceau, the most imposing show of military force in the capital since 1871. In the provinces, pitched battles occurred between strikers and police in the port city of Brest and the metallurgical center of Montluçon. An estimated ninety-three different unions actually participated in the strike, with the largest single contingent of fifty thousand coming from the metalworkers' union. Some unions, such as the jewelry workers and the Paris branch of the printers, remained on strike for several weeks after May 1; the Paris printers and the metalworkers of Hennebont in Brittany were still on strike when the CGT Congress of Amiens convened in early October.[34]

Many historians have viewed the May Day strike as a disaster for the CGT, in that almost none of the unions involved succeeded in gaining the eight-hour day. "May Day 1906 was a 24-hour strike for the 8-hour day, and a failure," concluded American historian Val Lorwin. Another American historian, W. H. Crook, pointed to the low level of involvement in the strike of France's biggest unions—the railwaymen and miners, for example—and the strike's high cost to those unions that did participate—an estimated five million francs (presumably calculated on the basis of strike contributions and lost income). Bernard Moss has drawn attention to the high price of the campaign in terms of the repression it engendered; the CGT had "given the government and bourgeoisie an unnecessary fright."[35]

Griffuelhes and the CGT leadership, of course, presented a more positive view of the outcome of the strike. The conclusions drawn in the report of the Executive Committee, signed and presented to the Congress of Amiens by Griffuelhes, highlighted the mobilizing and consciousness-raising aspects of the campaign. In the report's view, the turnout on May 1 had been greater than might have been expected, given the odds against it. "At the outset of the agitation, the [Eight-Hour-Day] Committee was struck by the attitude taken by certain organizations. These organizations did more than just try to criticize or discredit [the strike]. Their aim was to stifle—or at least paralyze—the movement before it could even be launched." But in spite of the obstacles posed by "these organizations," clearly a slap at certain reformist unions, the

34. Crook, *The General Strike*, 40; Lewis Levitski Lorwin, *The Labor Movement in France* (New York, 1912), 177; CGT, *XVᵉ Congrès national corporatif . . . Amiens*, 15. On the long and bitter Hennebont strike, see Nicholas Papayanis, "Alphonse Merrheim and the Strike of Hennebont: The Struggle for the Eight-Hour Day in France," *International Review of Social History*, XVI (1971), 159–83.

35. Val R. Lorwin, *The French Labor Movement* (Cambridge, Mass., 1954), 45; Crook, *The General Strike*, 40; Moss, *Origins of the French Labor Movement*, 148.

report continued, "Who today would dare to say that this task has not borne fruit? . . . What needs to be underscored is that never before had there been such agitation. The working class, under the leadership of the more active unions, rose up to demand shorter hours and more leisure. Let's admit it: the events of the day and of those which followed astonished and surprised many comrades, sympathetic and unsympathetic alike."

The report concluded that the strike had been important not for the material gains made but for the heightened level of consciousness it produced among the participating workers, many of whom were not even union members. "We hope that militants will have digested fully the social import of the events we have just been through. . . . It cannot be said too often: It is only in agitations of this kind and extent that the sense of struggle, still so lacking in many parts, will be developed." [36]

The CGT leadership line was, first, that it was the struggle itself—which as Griffuelhes later wrote "educates, hardens, emboldens, and creates"—that mattered, not the success or failure in achieving its goal, and second, that the strike was a "moral victory" because it was the first *national* strike movement in French history and it served notice on a frightened bourgeoisie of the growing strength and élan of the working class. In lines that reflect Griffuelhes' sarcasm and *ouvriérisme,* the report commented: "Just think back on the fright that seized the bourgeoisie! There was an amusing flight of capital, sent abroad in the name of the purest patriotism. There was the stockpiling of provisions in cellars, which later had to be gorged down, causing indigestion to the delicate stomachs of the cowardly hoarders. Who will recount those days, the fear of the bourgeoisie, their cretinism and cowardice? There is material aplenty here for someone with a facile pen." [37]

This, then, was the official view of the CGT leadership, the verdict it rendered for public consumption. But did the leaders' private judgments match their public statements? Did Griffuelhes, for example, really consider May 1, 1906, a victory, albeit a moral one, or did he privately concur in later historians' verdict of a defeat? The evidence is mixed. Police reports mention worries at CGT headquarters over declining membership in some unions due to disappointment with the outcome of the general strike. There also seems to have been a consensus among the leadership that the eight-hours' campaign would not be repeated in 1907. But police reports also note a greater sense of

36. CGT, *XVᵉ Congrès national corporatif . . . Amiens,* 10, 13, 15.

37. Griffuelhes, "Romantisme révolutionnaire"; CGT, *XVᵉ Congrès national corporatif . . . Amiens,* 14.

confidence among the leaders of the CGT revolutionary majority in the weeks before the Congress of Amiens than had been observed before the one in 1904 in Bourges, despite the fact that they anticipated a stiff fight with the reformists at the congress over the outcome of the eight-hours' campaign and with the Nord trade unionists over a motion for closer ties to the SFIO.[38]

Griffuelhes' own judgment on the May Day strike may shed some light on his colleagues' mixed reactions. Although he was not enthusiastic about the campaign when it was first proposed, he was brought around to supporting it by Pouget. He feared that more was being promised to the rank and file than could be delivered, thus risking disillusionment and demoralization when results failed to match expectations. The general secretary also seems to have suspected that the campaign would be viewed in some quarters as a prelude to revolution, thus raising even more dangerous false hopes and, in addition, increasing chances for a violent confrontation with the government that the CGT was not strong enough to win. This last fear proved unjustified because the campaign remained largely focused on strictly trade-union issues from beginning to end; government provocations mostly went unanswered. Even so, police reported that Griffuelhes was among those CGT leaders most adamant that this sort of eight-hours' campaign should not be repeated.

Nevertheless, Griffuelhes did see a positive side to the campaign. There is no reason to doubt, for example, the sincerity of his claim that the May Day strike was a moral victory. Indeed, Griffuelhes was probably one of those most "astonished and surprised" by the response to the strike call. Nothing on this scale had ever before been attempted by a French labor organization; that 150,000 workers, many of whom were not union members, responded was no mean accomplishment. Other positive aspects included the CGT's emergence from the struggle with its moral authority enhanced; for at least a month, it commanded public attention to an extent few would have thought possible when the campaign began, thanks to Clemenceau's extravagant conspiracy charges and troop movements and the hysteria of the right-wing press. Finally, it could be claimed—and Griffuelhes appears to have believed this—that the CGT, not Clemenceau, emerged the winner of the contest of wills, despite the latter's success in "making" the May general elections. His so-called plot had become a subject of amusement and ridicule, even in the Radical press. The Radical newspaper *L'Action,* for example, in a June 9, 1906, piece signed by party stalwart Arthur Ranc, savagely attacked the Sarrien

38. AN, F7 12.493, note of July 12, 1906; APP, B/a 1601, note of June 6, 1906; AN, F7 12.493, note of September 30, 1906.

government for perpetuating a hoax. The imprisoned CGT leaders, Griffuelhes included, had acquired the aura of martyrdom, and not only in the eyes of the trade-union rank and file.

Griffuelhes seems to have approached the Congress of Amiens in October, 1906—perhaps the most important congress in the history of the French trade-union movement and certainly the most important in his own career—with unusual and unexpected serenity. Some of this may have been due to a growing fatalism. In the summer of 1906, he again fell ill and was obliged to spend some weeks in the country recovering. Already unnerved by his brother's death and afflicted himself by the disease that had killed Henri, he began to talk of impending death.[39] But there was also the sense that his star was rising. Following his recovery, in the summer and fall of 1906, he appeared at union congresses to drum up support for the revolutionary agenda at Amiens; everywhere, he was greeted with standing ovations. Amiens would be Griffuelhes' greatest personal triumph—and his last.

39. During his imprisonment, Griffuelhes was reported to have said of charges that he had conspired with the Right: "For the few months I still have to live, I would have been the most miserable of mortals if I had committed such a cowardly act" (APP, B/a 1601, note of April 30, 1906).

VI

AMIENS (1906)

On the political plane, the working class was for a long time the prey of parties or sects which fought each other for the honor of leading it to its final emancipation. The working class took part in those cheap masquerades. [At Amiens,] we undertook to achieve the unity of the working class on the economic plane: no more Jaurèsists, Guesdists, Allemanists, or anarchists: just syndicalists marching in unison in the same class struggle.

—Interview with Griffuelhes in *L'Humanité,* September 23, 1920

The CGT Congress of Amiens, which was held October 8 to 16, 1906, has long been regarded by labor historians as the seminal event in the history of French revolutionary syndicalism, perhaps in the history of the French trade-union movement as a whole. The congress dealt a crushing defeat to the enemies of revolutionary syndicalism—the Guesdist wing of the French Socialist Party, who sought to profit from what they saw as the May 1 defeat to finally bring the CGT under SFIO control. In the process, the CGT congress approved by a near-unanimous majority the Charter of Amiens, the manifesto of trade-union autonomy and self-reliance in the struggle to overthrow the wage system.

Commentators on the life and career of Victor Griffuelhes see Amiens clearly as his greatest claim to renown. The Charter of Amiens, co-authored by Griffuelhes and Emile Pouget and placed on the agenda by Griffuelhes, would be known by many as simply the "Griffuelhes motion"; it would determine ideological and personal affinities within the trade-union movement into the 1920s and beyond by the degree of attachment to its principles.

Griffuelhes, despite all he did and wrote over the remaining sixteen years of his life, would be remembered largely as "the man of the Charter of Amiens."

Amiens represents the high tide of revolutionary syndicalism, the apogee of Edouard Dolléans' so-called Heroic Age in the history of the French trade-union movement. Many of those who attended the congress, observed or read about it, supported the CGT or loathed everything it stood for, believed that the CGT and its revolutionary syndicalist majority had become a potent force in French public life and were gathering strength for the revolution they had threatened for so long. Few realized that the CGT would never again be so united as it seemed then or that revolutionary syndicalism would never again dominate French trade unionism as it did in October, 1906, led by Victor Griffuelhes. Just two years later, the CGT would have its second head-on confrontation with Georges Clemenceau, this time with many dead and injured, and there would be no rebound as in the aftermath of May Day, 1906. The spirit of the Charter of Amiens, the apparent unity it brought, and the élan it engendered, were broken at Villeneuve-Saint-Georges in the summer of 1908.

"The debates at the Congress of Amiens," wrote Pierre Monatte, who attended the congress as a delegate, "were dominated by two major events: 1) The eight-hours' movement of May 1, 1906, preceded by the miners' strike in the Pas-de-Calais and the Nord . . . and 2) The accomplishment of socialist unity the year before, which had encouraged the Guesdists to think it would be possible to achieve in France the link between the socialist and trade-union movements which prevailed in countries where the workers' movement was under the influence of social democracy." [1]

Although the Congress of Amiens accomplished much significant work, for the public at large, the press, and the CGT leadership and delegates all else paled in comparison to the debates on the eight-hours' campaign and, especially, relations between the CGT and the newly unified socialist party. The latter debate, which led to adoption of the charter, monopolized attention most. It was clear well before the congress opened that the CGT would finally have to take a position on the question of relations with the SFIO. Since at least July, 1906, the CGT leaders had been aware that Guesdists in the Nord were campaigning for closer ties between the socialist party and the trade unions and were angling to have the question raised at Amiens by their loyal

1. Pierre Monatte, "Souvenirs [sur le Congrès d'Amiens]," *L'Actualité d'Histoire*, no. 16 (October, 1956), 8.

supporters in the textile workers' federation. At its August, 1906, congress in Tourcoing (Nord), the federation voted to instruct its secretary, Victor Renard, to present a motion at Amiens calling for establishment of "ad hoc relations" between the CGT and the SFIO. Renard's actual resolution at Amiens continued in this vein: "The executive committee is invited to consult, whenever circumstances demand, by means of ad hoc or permanent delegations, with the national committee of the socialist party for the purpose of more easily securing the principal social reforms [under consideration in parliament]." [2]

Historian Germaine Willard is correct in observing that the "Renard motion explicitly recognized the existence of two specific organizations, struggling on two different fronts," and therefore did not in itself constitute "a new attempt by the Guesdists to subordinate the trade unions to the socialist party." Griffuelhes, who would make one of the most important fights of his career against the "motion Textile," admitted as much, writing that it "said nothing specific in and of itself." [3] Why, then, was Renard's motion so bitterly contested at Amiens?

Part of the answer lies in a development that paralleled the textile workers' congress, which appears to have escaped Willard's attention but presumably not that of the prospective delegates to Amiens. It certainly did not pass unnoticed by Griffuelhes. "No one would have suspected anything," he wrote, "if the socialist Fédération du Nord hadn't asked that the same question [Renard's motion] be placed on the agenda of the socialist party congress in Limoges [set for November 1–4, 1906]. It was, in fact, the same people in the two organizations who had undertaken this double initiative." Griffuelhes can be excused if he saw in the "double initiative" a somewhat more sinister design than the content of the Textile resolution seemed to suggest. Willard's colleague, Maurice Moissonnier, has underscored the importance of the two-pronged Guesdist offensive to the subsequent debates at Amiens. "If the discussion focused as specifically as it did on the attitude to take toward the socialist party," he observes, "it was because [the SFIO] congress at Limoges also had on its agenda the [question of what] attitude to take toward the CGT." Certainly, the double initiative gave some credence to Griffuelhes'

---

2. Fédération nationale de l'Industrie Textile, *Compte rendu du 8ème Congrès national . . . Tourcoing . . . 12 au 15 aout 1906* (Lille, 1906), 20–21; CGT, *XVe Congrès national corporatif . . . Amiens*, 135–36.

3. Germaine Willard, "La Charte d'Amiens et les rapports entre syndicats et partis politiques," in *1906: Le Congrès de la Charte d'Amiens*, ed. Jean Maitron (Paris, 1983), 66; Griffuelhes, *L'Action syndicaliste*, 43.

charge that "while the Guesdists demanded the subordination of the unions to the party, we wanted the autonomy and independence of the unions!"[4]

But Griffuelhes had a second and equally important reason for his forceful opposition to the Textile motion, a reason captured in Monatte's insightful analysis: "To understand the exact significance of the Congress of Amiens, you have to go back a bit in history. It [the congress], in fact, represents the culmination of the struggle against Millerandism."[5]

While I regard the confrontation at Amiens as a stage in rather than the culmination of the battle over Millerandism, Monatte's point remains well taken. Griffuelhes appears to have carefully read the report to the textile workers' congress in Tourcoing on which Renard's mandate was based, and to have closely followed the debate it engendered. Since he did not attend the congress and would not have had access to its published minutes at this early date, he probably relied for his information on opponents of Textile's Guesdist leadership, such as his old comrade-in-arms, Desjardins, head of the Paris weavers' union, or Charles Dhooghe, secretary of the Reims textile workers' union. The Textile congress, Griffuelhes wrote, had made it clear that the collaboration it sought between the CGT and the SFIO was for the precise purpose of carrying forward the Millerand program of social reforms. That Griffuelhes was not exaggerating is borne out by the mandate approved by the Tourcoing congress, which stated: "The bourgeois parliamentarians themselves have declared that the current legislature (1906–1910) will be a legislature of social reform," then listed a series of such reforms for which party and trade unions should battle in tandem. These included: (1) an amendment of the 1884 law to allow unions to own property; (2) legislation fostering collective agreements; (3) a State-managed workers' pension plan, to which workers would be expected to contribute; and (4) Millerand's projected Labor Code. What probably grabbed Griffuelhes' attention, however, was reference to "a second, even more important, proposal from the same author [Millerand] tending toward the peaceful resolution of differences over working conditions, *i.e.*, regulation of the right to strike." The text goes on to say: "Two other bills on this same question will be proposed by the socialist party. These bills would establish a system capable of preventing conflicts which develop between man-

---

4. Griffuelhes, *L'Action syndicaliste*, 43; Maurice Moissonnier, "Le Syndicalisme français à l'heure du Congrès d'Amiens," in *1906; Le Congrès de la Charte d'Amiens*, 56; Griffuelhes, *L'Action syndicaliste*, 44.

5. Monatte, "Souvenirs," 6.

agement and labor and, in cases where they cannot be avoided, of finding a prompt solution."[6]

Little wonder, then, that Griffuelhes could assert: "Adversaries of the government at the political level, servants of the government at the trade-union level, such is the . . . syndicalist theory of the militants of the Nord." Or that he concluded the Guesdists, among the most fervent opponents of Millerand's entry into the Waldeck-Rousseau government in 1899, had now adopted "the social program of Waldeck-Rousseau." At the Congress of Amiens Griffuelhes framed his rebuttal to Renard's motion in terms of a stern warning against Millerandist "corruption," declaring, "the danger still exists. There are still attempts to draw the unions into the embrace of the government—and it is this which will break the moral unity of our movement."[7] Griffuelhes did battle at Amiens as much to combat resurgent Millerandism as to proclaim trade-union independence from party rule, a point I believe not sufficiently appreciated by historians who have interpreted the significance of the Congress of Amiens and its charter.

In the months preceding the Amiens congress, Griffuelhes met the double initiative of the Guesdists with one of his own. Within the CGT, he set about forming a tactical alliance with the reformists against the Textile resolution, reminding them that "since the beginnings of the [modern] French trade-union movement, all of its tendencies have had to battle against the authoritarianism of the Guesdists and their contempt for unions, which they considered inferior organizations." He also tried to foster opposition to the motion within the SFIO, to be presented at Limoges by the Fédération du Nord. Whenever possible, Griffuelhes tried to kill both birds with one stone. Thus in July, 1906, he showed up as the CGT's fraternal delegate to the congress of the pottery workers' federation in Limoges. The pottery workers, perhaps more than any other union outside the Nord, favored close ties between the CGT and the socialist party, a policy they had implemented in their Limoges stronghold where party and union leadership were virtually interchangeable. There was a difference, however. The pottery workers' union was close to the Jaurèsist, not the Guesdist, wing of the SFIO and thus tended to view the

6. *DBMO*, XII, 51–52 (Dhooghe); Griffuelhes, *L'Action syndicaliste*, 45; Fédération Nationale de l'Industrie Textile, *Compte rendu du 8ᵉᵐᵉ Congrès national*, 20–21.

7. Griffuelhes, *L'Action syndicaliste*, 45; CGT, *XVᵉ Congrès national corporatif . . . Amiens*, 167.

party-union relationship as one of cooperation, rather than subordination.[8] Although the minutes of the pottery workers' congress are mute on what Griffuelhes actually did in Limoges, one suspects that he spent much time trying to convince union leaders—and perhaps socialist deputies in attendance as well—of the divisive nature of the Guesdist double initiative. It is worth noting that at Amiens, pottery workers' delegates withdrew their own motion on CGT-SFIO cooperation and rallied to the Charter of Amiens, although the union subsequently voted against its local application.[9]

In September, 1906, just a month before the Amiens congress, Griffuelhes attended the glassworkers' federation congress in Albi (Tarn), in the heart of Jaurès' constituency. The minutes of this congress provide some idea of Griffuelhes' strategy on the eve of Amiens. On the next-to-last day of the congress, he spoke at a banquet in nearby Carmaux presided over by Jaurès himself. One would not have suspected the frequent enmity between the two men. "All eyes were on the rostrum as the president introduced comrade Griffuelhes, general secretary of the CGT." The ostensible purpose of Griffuelhes' speech was to convince the Carmaux glassworkers to resurrect their union, defunct since 1895, and join "your brothers in struggle and misery, in the national federation [of glassworkers] and the CGT." But he seems to have had another purpose as well—to extend an olive branch to the Carmaux trade unionists and the Jaurèsist wing of the SFIO, considered enemies of syndicalism just a few months earlier. Now, for Griffuelhes Carmaux was "this city which has contributed so much to the growth of the trade-union movement, a city cited everywhere as a model because of the struggles it has waged." The report of the proceedings concludes: "Griffuelhes' speech made a profound impression. There was sustained applause." Joan Scott says that Griffuelhes tried to "shame" the glassworkers, lulled by relatively high wages on one hand and bullied by management on the other, into reviving their old union, but interest proved slight. In fact, she states that most of his enthusiastic audience were local miners.[10]

8. Monatte, "Souvenirs," 16; Kathryn Amdur, *Syndicalist Legacy: Trade Unions and Politics in Two French Cities in the Era of World War I* (Urbana, Ill., 1986), 36.

9. Griffuelhes' presence at the congress is noted on p. 1 of Fédération nationale de la Céramique, *Compte rendu du VIe Congrès (14 juillet 1906) et Ier International (15 juillet 1906) tenus [à] Limoges* (Limoges, 1906); CGT, *XVe Congrès national corporatif . . . Amiens*, 140–41, 160–61; Amdur, *Syndicalist Legacy*, 38.

10. Fédération (nouvelle) nationale des Travailleurs du Verre, *Compte rendu du XIe Congrès national (Ve de la Fédération nouvelle), tenu à Albi les 6, 7, 8, 9, et 10 septembre 1906* (Lille, 1906),

Would Griffuelhes be applauded at Amiens? His forays into the provinces to seek reformist support against the Guesdist double initiative may have given him a foretaste of what to expect at Amiens, as well as an idea of what strategy to pursue there to build a consensus in favor of trade-union independence. The real test, however, would come at the congress itself, and even though police reports describe a serene Griffuelhes as the date approached, he must have faced it with considerable apprehension. Police agents reported that "serious workers" were fed up with the CGT leadership's radical and "non-trade-union" program and were ready to work more closely with the SFIO. Monatte also worried about the "reformist elements who, at Bourges two years before, had carried on a vigorous struggle against the administrative bureau over the issue of proportional representation. Would the Keufer-style reformists join with Renard's Guesdists?" Not even the traditional bloc of revolutionary syndicalists could be counted on, police reports asserted. "The rather pitiful result of CGT efforts on May 1 has had a great impact on a number of anarchist-syndicalists who, after believing that trade-union action was all-powerful, now see that they were misled about this by Pouget, Griffuelhes, and consorts." The poor showing on May Day had also disappointed the metalworkers, among the CGT leadership's staunchest supporters, a police spy wrote. Their union "will only send about 20 delegates to Amiens, compared to the 56 it sent to the Bourges Congress." [11]

If Griffuelhes and his allies felt apprehension before the congress, it seems to have dissipated once it got underway. Police forecasts of a much smaller turnout at Amiens than at Bourges proved unfounded; the Amiens congress seated 297 delegates, as against 300 at Bourges. [12] The number of unions represented was down from 1,214 at Bourges to 1,040 at Amiens, although the latter figure is somewhat misleading. The Amiens congress turned away forty-seven unions that had not met the "triple obligation" imposed at Bourges in 1904: membership in the federation of unions representing their industry; membership of their regional federation or Bourse du Travail; and subscription

---

100–101; Scott, *Glassworkers of Carmaux*, 177; Fédération (nouvelle) nationale des Travailleurs du Verre, *Compte rendu*, 101.

11. AN, F7 12.493, notes of September 30, July 12, 1906; Monatte, "Souvenirs," 8; APP, B/a 1686, note of September 14, 1906; AN, F7 12.493, note of September 30, 1906. In fact, forty-seven metalworker delegates attended the Amiens congress (CGT, *XVe Congrès national corporatif . . . Amiens*, xvi–xix, 471).

12. There is some controversy about the number of delegates who attended the Amiens congress. Brécy puts the number at 350 (*Mouvement syndical*, 64); however, both *L'Humanité* and *La Petite République* reported 297 delegates in attendance on October 9, 1906.

to the CGT organ, *La Voix du Peuple.* Other unions present at Bourges were not represented at Amiens because they had disappeared in the interim through mergers or absorption into industrial unions. Nor did the delegates prove to be ready for closer ties to the SFIO. "On arriving in Amiens," Monatte wrote, "you could see that the Textile resolution had not won over the provincial unions. On every side, you could feel a clear hostility to it."[13]

The first major hurdle for Griffuelhes and the revolutionary syndicalists was the debate on the report of the Section of Federations and the Executive Committee, drafted and signed by the general secretary. Its most controversial item was the CGT leadership's handling of the May Day, 1906, general strike. Griffuelhes had done his best in the report to present the strike as a moral victory, fully aware that even some of his closest associates considered it, in Maurice Moissonnier's apt phrase, "a semi-defeat (or a semi-victory)." After three days of relatively congenial sparring—too congenial for some firebrands such as Henri Dret of the leatherworkers—Griffuelhes' reports were passed by a vote of 781 to 115, with twenty-one abstentions and ten contested ballots. Most of the negative votes came from Textile and other unions from the Nord. Police spies quickly interpreted the unexpectedly wide margin of approval for the Griffuelhes reports as a personal victory for the general secretary. The reports of Pouget (*La Voix du Peuple*) and Yvetot (Bourses du Travail Section) fared much less well, noted the Sureté's "Louis"; Pouget's report was approved by 638–292 (thirty-four abstentions) and Yvetot's by 675–214 (forty-eight abstentions). Observed "Louis": "The difference in the confidence accorded Griffuelhes, Pouget, and Yvetot was clearly shown in the number of votes each received." He concluded that this "shows that if the majority of the confederation accepts the revolutionary method, it does not accept anarchist theories to the same extent." Or did it show that Griffuelhes' offer of an olive branch to Keufer and the reformists had paid dividends? Or that for the moment at least, Pouget and Yvetot were easier marks for the reformists than Griffuelhes? One police observer at Amiens leaned toward the latter interpretation, writing that the only reason the "big unions [*e.g.,* Livre, the railwaymen] remain in the CGT is because they hope to wrest control of it from the revolutionaries."[14]

After three days of debates on the leadership reports, the stage was now set

13. *XVᵉ Congrès national corporatif . . . Amiens*, v–xxiv, xxv; Monatte, "Souvenirs," 8.

14. Moissonnier, "Le Syndicalisme français à l'heure du Congrès d'Amiens," 52; CGT, *XVᵉ Congrès national corporatif . . . Amiens*, 177, 253–63, 264–87; AN, F7 12.493, notes of October 11, 19, 1906.

for the pièce de résistance of the congress, the eagerly awaited debate on the Textile motion, "Relations between the Unions and Political Parties." The morning of October 11, Textile's secretary, Victor Renard, took the floor, and his case, Monatte reported, "was very ably stated." The veteran Guesdist's main point was that some sort of partnership between the trade unions and the socialist party was inevitable, because "the union is no more than the law [of 1884] wants it to be: an organ for the defense of wages, workers' dignity, living conditions, etc. The union cannot depart from this sphere without having a sword of Damocles suspended over the heads of its administrators."[15]

Unions thus cannot engage in politics without running the risk of dissolution, Renard continued. But, "When you preach antimilitarism or antipatriotism, when you preach abstention from voting, you are making politics. . . . These things can only be done by political groups. We [in the Nord] are antimilitarist, but we leave our political groups to deal with that." Renard chose recent developments in the British trade-union movement to make his point. The unions in Britain had been using direct action for thirty years; they had won high wages, were highly organized, and had large strike funds. But all of this had been for nothing when the Taff-Vale judgment outlawing picketing was handed down. "It was then that the English workers were obliged to take a political stand and to elect union members to Parliament in order to get laws passed favorable to the workers."[16]

"We want [the CGT] to avail itself of all possible avenues of action, just as we do in the Nord," Renard declared. "We believe that it is necessary to combine trade-union, cooperative, and political action," a combination that had paid off in the Nord, where "we have 315 unions, with 76,000 members, 12 cooperative leagues with 30,000 members, 300 [political] groups with 8,500 paying members. We have numerous municipal councillors, eight deputies, and 105,000 socialist voters. If everybody knew how to work together like this, we could achieve great results."

The Textile motion, which Renard now read out, had been shorn of the explicit references to Millerandist legislation so prominently featured in the mandate given him by the Tourcoing congress. "All we want [is] occasional, or permanent, consultations" between the CGT Executive Committee and the SFIO National Committee for purposes of "achieving legislation which

---

15. Monatte, "Souvenirs," 14; CGT, *XVᵉ Congrès national corporatif . . . Amiens*, 134–35.

16. CGT, *XVᵉ Congrès national corporatif . . . Amiens, ibid.;* for details on the Taff-Vale judgment, see Henry Pelling, *A History of British Trade Unionism* (Harmondsworth, Engl., 1963), 123–26.

would improve the social condition of the proletariat, and perfecting its means of struggle against the capitalist class." The examples of legislation that might be pursued were carefully chosen: bills on the eight-hour day, the right of civil servants to belong to trade unions, abolition of night working, and a minimum wage.[17]

In closing, Renard could not resist a parting shot at Griffuelhes. What Textile was proposing, he said, was no more than formal recognition of relations that already existed between the CGT leadership and the socialists. "Isn't it true," he asked, "that Griffuelhes and others enter into relations with certain socialist deputies, when they [the deputies] need material for an interpellation?"[18] Griffuelhes would be obliged to respond to this charge, which insinuated that he enjoyed privileged relations with "certain" socialist deputies, principally friends in the Blanquist wing of the party.

The debate that followed, from the afternoon of October 11 through the morning of October 13, demonstrated that Monatte was correct in observing that "the Textile motion had not won over" the delegates. Aside from Renard and Philippe of the Lille retail clerks' union, no one rose to support the motion. This left the floor to its opponents. Almost all who spoke against it expressed suspicion of Guesdism or at least of Guesde, whose jibes at unions now came back to haunt Renard and his friends. Louis Niel, for example, recalled Guesde's remark at the London congress of the Second International ten years before: "Creating a union? Poof, that's not hard; all you need is a 25-centime rubber stamp."[19] There was also a general desire to keep politics out of the union movement, although what that meant varied from speaker to speaker; a common denominator on this point may have been a wish to finally close the books on the Millerand Affair. As the debate on the Textile motion unfolded, Griffuelhes and the CGT leadership, now that the defeat of Textile seemed apparent, undoubtedly scrutinized what was said, searching for elements of a consensus to serve as the basis for a more unified CGT—elements of a "charter" for syndicalism.

The coup de grace to the Textile resolution was delivered by Alphonse Merrheim, like Renard, a northerner. In one of the more celebrated speeches at the CGT prewar congresses, Merrheim recalled that, "Renard said, among other things: 'We have 315 unions, 76,000 members,' and concluded by saying, 'Voilà, this is what *we* have done.'" He charged that Renard's total included

17. CGT, *XVe Congrès national corporatif . . . Amiens,* 135–36.
18. *Ibid.,* 136.
19. *Ibid.,* 157, 143.

"at least 130 'yellow' unions," which he hoped the Textile leader was not intending to take credit for. Merrheim also drew on his personal knowledge of the Nord—he continued to serve as secretary of the metalworkers' union in his hometown of Roubaix—to show that Renard had inflated the figures on union membership as well. It did not help Textile's cause that Renard later had to admit that Merrheim's data were "correct."[20]

Merrheim spoke during the afternoon of October 12. Earlier that day, since no morning session was held, members of the CGT administrative bureau and certain of their associates gathered at the local railway café to draft the resolution that would become known as the Charter of Amiens. Apparently, the CGT leadership was convinced that the Textile motion was lost and that the time and mood were right to move adoption of a countermotion that would, in Griffuelhes' words, proclaim "the independence of the trade unions."[21]

The next day when the resultant "motion Griffuelhes" was brought to a vote, and for some time afterward, no one seems to have been particularly concerned about the identity of its author or authors, the general impression being that someone from the CGT administrative bureau wrote it.[22] Authorship of the charter became an issue only after World War I, when the document became the touchstone of syndicalist purity for the various factions then contending for control of the CGT (see Chapter XI). The controversy raged through the 1930s into the post–World War II era, as part of an effort by various groups within the French labor movement to use the charter as an ideological counterweight to communism. Now ninety years later, the dispute seems to center on two questions: (1) Who was present at the drafting of the charter? and (2) who was responsible for its wording? The answer to the first question would seem to provide the key to answering the second, but this logic has not satisfied all observers.

The first question was apparently answered definitively in 1938, when Paul Delesalle sent historian Edouard Dolléans a photo he took showing four men around a table on the terrace of the Amiens railway café where, Delesalle

20. See *ibid.*, 152–54, for Merrheim's speech; Renard claimed that the figures he gave were only indicative, *i.e.*, intended to demonstrate that the Nord had "the second largest number of unions in France," after the Seine region (*ibid.*, 165).

21. Griffuelhes, *L'Action syndicaliste*, 48.

22. The only speculation on the charter's authorship I have found for the prewar period is from Mermeix (Gabriel Terrail), a contemporary critic of socialism and the trade-unions, who thought he saw in Griffuelhes' motion "the expert pen of his [Griffuelhes'] comrade Pouget" (*Le Syndicalisme contre le Socialisme* [Paris, 1907], 209).

wrote in a letter dated May 27, 1938, "we put the finishing touches [*le coup de pouce*] to our motion." Dolléans concluded from this evidence that "the motion was written" by Delesalle and the four men in the photo: Griffuelhes, Pouget, Louis Niel, and André Morizet. Delesalle, however, does not actually say this in his cover letter or in a second one sent to Dolléans explaining what had transpired. In the second letter, dated June 1, 1938, Delesalle wrote that the charter represented "the point of view of and was the emanation of the administrative bureau alone." Taken literally, this would seem to rule out Morizet and Niel's participation in drafting the motion. Niel was not at this point a CGT administrator; Morizet was not even a trade unionist but one of the left-wing journalists covering the congress (for whom is unclear, but he was writing for both *L'Humanité* and *Le Mouvement socialiste*). In fact, in the May 27 letter, Delesalle recalled that "at the first reading [of the motion] Pouget held the pen" while he and Griffuelhes bickered over points in the text; he does not mention Morizet or Niel.[23]

Delesalle's correspondence with Dolléans in 1938 may have been motivated by the latter's desire to restore credit for the charter to the men of his so-called Heroic Age of French trade unionism that he admired. By the late 1930s, Griffuelhes and Pouget, those he most wished to honor, were dead and others were being thrust into the limelight. Eugène-Jules Marty-Rollan, who had been a young delegate from a Toulouse textile workers' union at Amiens and by the 1920s had become a leader of the CGT reformist wing, wrote articles in 1933 on the charter that put Alphonse Merrheim at the center of events. In Marty-Rollan's version, Merrheim, the postwar convert to reformism, held the pen, while Pouget, Griffuelhes, and others looked on. This account coincided with the contemporary elevation of Merrheim, who had died in 1925, to the role of saint and martyr of CGT reformism. Since no other proof exists of Merrheim's presence at the café on October 12, 1906, one can only assume that Marty-Rollan heard the story from Merrheim himself, who claimed at the CGT Congress of Orléans in 1920 that "because I was from the Nord they insisted that I become a part of the group of comrades who drew up the Charter of Amiens." In 1937, Georges Lefranc embroidered on Marty-Rollan's account, introducing Jean Latapie as well as Merrheim into the circle at Amiens.[24] It was probably Lefranc's version featuring Latapie, the "revolutionary

23. Dolléans, *Histoire du mouvement ouvrier*, II, 135, 136 n. 1; *DBMO*, XII, 146 (Morizet).

24. CGT, *XVe Congrès national corporatif . . . Amiens*, xiii; Eugène-Jules Marty-Rollan, "Exposé historique sur la Charte d'Amiens," *VdP*, n.s., no. 158, November, 1933; also see his brochure, *Comment fut élaboré la Charte d'Amiens* (Paris, 1933), esp. 24; CGT, *XXIe Congres national*

turncoat" accused of plotting with Aristide Briand to bring down Griffuelhes in 1909, that finally goaded Dolléans to set the record straight.

The Cold War brought yet another twist to the story of the Amiens charter: the supposed presence (in flesh or spirit) of a "sixth man" at the railway café. The anticommunist authors of these new accounts possibly wanted to add lustre to the charter by ascribing it to intellectuals of the pre-1914 era, rather than mere workers, demonstrating that syndicalism, too, had its Marxes and Lenins. Thus, Roger Hagnauer, writing in 1956, attributed the charter to Charles Guieysse, founder and editor of the influential *anarchisant* weekly, *Pages Libres;* Hagnauer also accepts Merrheim's claim to have played a role in drafting the charter. A year later, it was author Maxime Leroy's turn to be cast as the sixth man. Leroy was an acquaintance of Griffuelhes and Merrheim, but his reminiscences about them give little suggestion of a close relationship with Griffuelhes that would have included him in CGT decision making. And even though Leroy's ties to Merrheim were closer, I do not believe that Merrheim was involved in writing the charter. In 1957, Boris Souvarine, Comintern agent turned professional anticommunist, wrote: "Few survivors of [the pre-1914] epoch and the two wars know that Maxime Leroy, who discreetly attended the Amiens Congress, helped to draw up the charter about which so much ink has been spilled." Finally, in 1967, Georges Lefranc claimed that the inspiration for the charter had come from the ex-Blanquist Ernest Lafont, labor lawyer, prominent socialist-syndicalist intellectual, and Griffuelhes' friend and legal defender.[25]

What is striking about all of this latter-day speculation is that it ignores, as does Dolléans, a prime piece of evidence in the case—the testimony of the two persons along with Delesalle whose presence at the café in Amiens everyone seems agreed upon: Griffuelhes and Pouget. This testimony, well known and easily accessible, was part of an interview by Amédée Dunois with Griffuelhes, Pouget, Delesalle, and Georges Yvetot published in *L'Humanité* in September, 1920. It was, in fact, this interview that apparently prompted Merrheim to claim he had been involved in drafting the charter. When asked

---

corporatif . . . Orléans . . . 1920. Compte rendu (Villeneuve-St. Georges, n.d.) 135–36; Georges Lefranc, *Histoire du mouvement syndical français* (Paris, 1937), 256 n. 2.

25. Roger Hagnauer, *L'Actualité de la Charte d'Amiens* (Paris, 1956); Leroy, "Griffuelhes et Merrheim," 9–14; Boris Souvarine, contribution to "In Memoriam: Maxime Leroy," *Le Contrat social,* I (November, 1957), 279; Georges Lefranc, *Le Mouvement syndical sous la Troisième République* (Paris, 1967), 142. This version departs radically from Lefranc's pre–World War II account, in which the charter was the product of the CGT working-class leadership.

by Dunois who had authored the "motion Griffuelhes," the former general secretary replied brusquely: "Pouget and I." None of the other interviewees, two of whom had been present at the drafting, contradicted Griffuelhes. In light of this, I agree with Jean Maitron's conclusion that "Griffuelhes and Pouget . . . drafted . . . the charter of syndicalism," with assistance from Paul Delesalle.[26]

Finally, there is the matter of bourgeois journalist André Morizet's presence at the railway café when the charter was drawn up. Unlike Dolléans, I do not believe he participated in the actual drafting of the document. Even though Morizet was well known to the CGT leadership, especially Griffuelhes and Pouget, it is doubtful that his editorial services were required. The notion that a document as celebrated as the Charter of Amiens could not have been written by workers without help from sympathetic intellectuals is arrogant and ignores the fact that the charter was not conceived as a timeless manifesto, which many union leaders, militants, and intellectuals years later took it to be, but as a motion composed under a deadline to win support from a labor congress. Griffuelhes, Pouget, Delesalle, or even Niel needed no help in drafting such a motion because all had served lengthy apprenticeships in that line of work. Indeed, if the motion's basic intent was to secure backing from the majority of the delegates at Amiens—a purpose it admirably served—then perhaps no persons in France were better equipped to do so than the team assembled at the Amiens restaurant. If the motion needed to retain the support of anarchist-syndicalists in the ranks and on the fringes of the CGT, Pouget or Delesalle could accomplish this, and if language to accommodate the reformists without alienating the more revolutionary elements was required, who better to consult than Niel, who was moving from his youthful anarchism to reformism? And Griffuelhes, who had contacts with Vaillant and the ex-Blanquist faction, with the socialist-syndicalist group, and inside the SFIO, would have been invaluable in deterring the Guesdists without alienating socialists as a whole. I believe that the tactical sense of the men present, not the metaphysics of a Guieysse or the legal expertise of a Leroy or a Lafont, was crucial in drafting the "motion Griffuelhes," as the finished product clearly demonstrates.

Morizet's presence at the rendezvous was possibly not as an editor or even a reporter but as the liaison between the socialist-syndicalist group around Hubert Lagardelle and Lafont and the CGT leadership. Morizet was a charter

26. Amédée Dunois, "Une Conversation sur la motion d'Amiens avec l'ançien bureau confédéral," *L'Humanité*, September 23, 1920; Maitron, *Paul Delesalle*, 112–13.

member of this group, and he may have been covering the Amiens congress for Lagardelle's *Mouvement socialiste*. Relations between the socialist-syndicalists and the leaders of the CGT, principally Griffuelhes, Pouget, and, increasingly, Merrheim as well, had been close since at least 1904. Thus, it seems plausible that Morizet was called in once the motion was drafted to give a second opinion on how the different factions in the SFIO were likely to react to it when they met in Limoges in November. Perhaps Morizet was also given advance notice of the motion as a fraternal gesture to revolutionary syndicalism's closest friends in the socialist camp.

The "motion Griffuelhes" came to the floor of the Amiens congress the afternoon of October 13, after two long, grueling sessions devoted to debate on the Textile resolution. In the interim, the three-hundred-odd delegates had heard Merrheim demolish what he referred to as the socialist "cathedral" of the Nord, then Keufer and Coupat's careful presentation of the reformists' price for a truce with the CGT's revolutionary leadership. Keufer's motion, countersigned by Coupat of the machinists, declared that "it is proper to banish all political, philosophical, and religious discussions and preoccupations from the confederal organization." The CGT, it continued, "has no more business becoming an instrument of anarchist and anti-parliamentary agitation than it has establishing official or informal, permanent or temporary, connections to any political party or philosophical organization whatever." [27]

Keufer's resolution, although it laid to rest Monatte and the CGT leadership's residual fears of a tactical alliance between the reformists and the Guesdists, was no offer of compromise to the CGT revolutionaries. Essentially a restatement of the position maintained at the Congress of Bourges two years earlier, the "motion Livre" made it clear that the reformists' stand was a principled one from which they would not budge. From their point of view, antimilitarist and antipatriotic campaigns were as much "political" intrusions upon trade-union business as was socialist electioneering. The claims of CGT leaders such as Pouget that antimilitarism and antipatriotism were "economic" issues were, to reformists, simply a device for smuggling anarchist politics on to the trade-union agenda, for using the trade unions, in Keufer's phrase, "as an instrument for social demolition." [28]

The reformist hard-liners placed Griffuelhes in a difficult position, from

27. CGT, *XVe Congrès national corporatif . . . Amiens*, 154–57.
28. Keufer, "Le Syndicalisme réformiste," 22.

which he was only partially successful in extricating himself at Amiens. By making an explicit issue of antimilitarism and antipatriotism, topics that already were at the top of the agenda not only for anarchists and anarchosyndicalists but for the SFIO's increasingly influential Hervéist wing as well, Keufer and his allies had reduced Griffuelhes' room to maneuver. Any concession to the reformists on these points would drive a wedge between the CGT leadership and its erstwhile allies on the Left, some of whom had already begun to grumble about faint hearts in the administrative bureau. But to make no effort to conciliate the reformists would be equally unwise under the circumstances. Rumors abounded that Clemenceau was acceding to the premiership, from whence he could be expected to conduct an effective campaign to "contain" the CGT. The reformist-revolutionary split had seriously weakened the unions in their May Day confrontation with the "Tiger"; the need to restore at least a modest sense of common purpose to the confederation seemed even more imperative now, as Clemenceau moved to bring the whole apparatus of government within his grasp. The task facing Griffuelhes, then, was to placate the reformists enough to lower the level of hostility between them and the revolutionary majority without alienating key elements of that majority.

When Griffuelhes spoke for the first time in the debate on relations with the socialist party, the morning session of October 13 was coming to a close. He began by drawing upon his own experiences in the Nord in 1903–1904 to add to Merrheim's critique of the Guesdist stronghold there. As for Renard's citing current British trade-union practice as proof of the value of party-union cooperation, he stated, "There is a contradiction here that runs counter to your [Textile's] purpose." Renard himself had said that the high wages and short workdays won by the British unions were the result of using direct action. "As for the results of parliamentary action there, well, the most one can say is that this remains to be seen." Griffuelhes now cleared the decks for the main thrust of his speech by replying to charges of "backstairs relationships between the CGT and members of the parliament." This supposed link, which was being used to justify the Textile motion, actually amounted to two consultations with deputies who "asked me to provide them with documentation to use in debate." The deputies in question were Marcel Sembat and Albert Willm, both members—as reformist critics such as Eugène Guérard would have been quick to note—of the ex-Blanquist wing of the SFIO. Excuses were unnecessary: "I did it and every time a deputy . . . asks for information, I will provide it with pleasure."

Renard, however, was not the main target of Griffuelhes' speech. "Over

and above the motion proposed by Renard, which raises questions of fact,"
he said, "there is a more important one, Keufer's, which addresses the question
of moral unity, and reproaches the CGT for having destroyed it." Keufer's
notion of "moral unity" was an illusion, Griffuelhes declared, in a rare venture
into the realm of Hegelian dialectics. "In every group, there is conflict, but
this does not mean there is division. Acceptance of [Keufer's] motion would
constitute a negation of life, which is made up of the clash of ideas."

Moreover, Keufer "insists too much on the presence of anarchists in the
[Executive Committee]; they are less numerous than legend would have us
believe." In any case, the charge was not serious. "It is a tactic to arouse fear
of an anarchist peril, in order to create a coalition to eliminate that peril." If
division existed in the ranks of the trade-union movement, the anarchists were
not responsible, Griffuelhes continued. Here, he recalled for delegates "some
little-known facts" concerning the collaboration of the reformists, including
Keufer, in Waldeck-Rousseau and Millerand's attempt to "domesticate" the
CGT: "They maneuvered in those days to insinuate the government into the
affairs of the [Paris] Bourse du Travail—and it was in reaction to their maneuvering that the CGT began to take life and grow."

Griffuelhes was nearly finished now with Keufer and the reformists. It was
not the so-called anarchists who were creating disunion in the CGT, he declared, but those who wanted "the organization to march to the government's
tune." Put simply, "There are those who look to the government on the one
hand, and those who want complete autonomy from the bosses and the State
on the other. The CGT has acted in the latter way, and its considerable growth
as a result belies Textile's thesis. . . . There is no need to change an organization
that has proven itself; instead, we should be demanding that the CGT remain
what it has been these last years."

Neither of the two main motions before the congress merited passage,
Griffuelhes declared. The Textile motion would oblige the CGT to enter into
relations with the State through the back door, since it advocated ties to a
party "which deals with the State, because it undergoes the influence of the
State." Keufer's motion, meanwhile, would limit activity to the purely econ-
omist sphere and bring the CGT down to the level of British trade unionism.
"It would mean retracing our steps and foregoing our dream of social change."
The congress, Griffuelhes said confidently, "would not want that." [29]

The delegates then voted on the Textile resolution, defeating it 724–34

29. CGT, *XVe Congrès national corporatif . . . Amiens*, 166–68.

with thirty-seven abstentions.[30] Griffuelhes again took the floor and read the following motion.

> The Congress of Amiens reaffirms Article 2 of the CGT statutes, which says: "The CGT unites, regardless of political belief, all workers conscious of the struggle to be carried on for the disappearance of the wage system and the employing class."
>
> The Congress believes that this declaration is a recognition of the class struggle which, in the economic realm, places the workers in revolt against all forms of capitalist exploitation and oppression, material and moral.
>
> The Congress clarifies this theoretical affirmation by the following specific points:
>
> In its day-to-day demands, the union movement seeks the coordination of workers' efforts, the increase of workers' well-being by the achievement of immediate gains, such as the shortening of hours, the raising of wages, and so forth.
>
> This effort, however, is only one side of the work of the union movement. It prepares for the complete emancipation which can be achieved only by expropriating the capitalist class. It endorses the general strike as a means of action to that end. It holds that the trade union, which is today a fighting organization, will in the future be an organization for production and distribution, and the basis of social reorganization.
>
> The Congress declares that this double task, the day-to-day task and that of the future, arises from the position of wage earners, which weighs upon the working class and creates for all workers, regardless of their political or philosophical opinions or attachments, the duty to belong to their basic organization, the trade union.
>
> As far as the individual member is concerned, therefore, the Congress affirms his complete liberty to take part, outside of his union, in whatever forms of action correspond to his philosophical or political views. It merely asks him not to bring up in the union the opinions he holds outside it.
>
> As for affiliated organizations, the Congress declares that, since economic action must be directed at the employers if the union movement is to attain its full results, the unions should not concern themselves

---

30. *Ibid.,* 170.

with the parties and sects which, outside and parallel with the unions, may in their own free way strive for social transformation.[31]

The motion had been countersigned by forty-three militants, including many whose names had been associated with Griffuelhes over the years: Merrheim, Delesalle, Pouget, Garnery, Luquet, Dret, Merzet (Montceau-les-Mines miners), and Ader (Midi farmworkers), among others. And there were two whose names would provoke surprise in just a few months—Jean Latapie and Albert Lévy.[32]

Henri Jusserand, one of Keufer's lieutenants, read a statement on behalf of the printers. "We will vote for the Griffuelhes motion," he said, "while expressing our most serious reservations on the question of the General Strike, to which Livre is at the moment opposed. This is because we are opposed to the intrusion of all forms of politics into the unions and the CGT."[33]

The printers having fallen into line behind the "motion presented by the administrative bureau," as Louis Niel termed it, assured its passage by a sizeable margin. No one, however, was prepared for the near unanimity of the vote. By a margin of 830 to 8 with a single abstention, the "motion Griffuelhes" passed into history as the Charter of Amiens.[34]

For the police, at least, the lopsided vote was another personal victory for Griffuelhes. In a post-congress memoir to his superiors, agent "B.T." of the Sureté wrote that of all the orators who spoke at the congress, "it's undeniable that it was Griffuelhes who made the strongest impression. A cold, sober, incisive orator, he speaks with a frankness and conviction which overwhelm his adversaries. I know very well that it's all flimflam, that he only says what he wants to say and that he knows how to slide over points which embarrass him. Still, I have observed that there was no one else of his stature at Amiens. His word alone carried authority."[35]

Griffuelhes, too, saw the enormous majority for his motion as something

31. This translation of the charter is from Val Lorwin, *French Labor Movement*, Appendix B, 312–13; the article reaffirmed is actually Article 2.1 of the CGT statutes.

32. See CGT, *XVe Congrès national corporatif. . . Amiens*, 170–71, for the motion's text and the names of the co-signers.

33. *Ibid.*, 171.

34. *Ibid.* The "no" votes came from four textile workers' unions, two unions of Livre, and one union each of the paper workers and retail clerks; twenty-two textile workers' unions supported the motion. For a breakdown of the voting, see CGT, *XVe Congrès national corporatif. . . Amiens*, 295–304.

35. AN, F7 12.493, note of October 19, 1906.

of a personal victory. "The congress, by adopting the text I presented, came around to my point of view," he wrote. The general secretary did not, however, make extravagant claims about what had been accomplished by the Charter of Amiens. He believed it had "proclaimed" the independence of the unions, but this was not a new or revolutionary departure in Griffuelhes' eyes. "My task as spokesman for the confederation was limited to defending the status quo, that is, the absence of all ties [with parties or sects], whether local or national," he said modestly. Further, "My argument was inspired by the sole desire to block all changes in the way the confederation operates." There is a sense of *culmination* in Griffuelhes' view of the charter; by adopting it, the Congress of Amiens had finally legitimized what had been the thought and practice of the CGT since he acceded to its top post in 1901. Thus, he took great comfort that Article 2.1 of the statutes had been reaffirmed in the motion, for "this article is an affirmation of the class struggle [against] all the forces of oppression, material as well as moral"; no change occurred "on this key point," this "basic and theoretical part" of the CGT statutes.[36]

The second important section of the charter, to Griffuelhes' mind, spelled out the "double task imposed upon the worker by virtue of his status as a wage-earner," a task he could accomplish only by joining his trade's union. This double task, of course, was the day-to-day struggle for better wages and working conditions *plus* the longer-term struggle to abolish the wage system. Again, there is a sense of *culmination* here, of commitment in a congress document to tasks long regarded as part of revolutionary syndicalist practice.[37]

Third was the section on the union member's rights and obligations with respect to his political or philosophical creed. Outside the union, a worker was free to believe what he chose, but he was "asked in turn, as a consequence of his standing as a wage-earner, to bring into the union only concerns that reflect that standing." No more politics in the unions, in other words.

The final paragraph of the charter, however, drew Griffuelhes' greatest attention. "The last part is explicit," in stating categorically that affiliated unions "should not concern themselves with . . . parties and sects"; doing so kept the union movement from attaining "its full results," which could only be accomplished by "economic action . . . directed at the employers." Thus, the congress had declared that "local or national ties" with political parties

---

36. Griffuelhes, *L'Action syndicaliste*, 48–49; Terrail [Mermeix] interpreted the section reaffirming the class struggle as a sop to the Nord Marxists (*Le Syndicalisme contre le Socialisme*, 211).

37. Griffuelhes, *L'Action syndicaliste*, 49–50.

"were harmful" and likely to "erode the power of the union movement" in the class struggle.

For Griffuelhes, the Charter of Amiens' overriding significance was its consolidation in a few paragraphs of the essential principles and practices of revolutionary syndicalism that he believed had been part of the life of the CGT since the turn of the century. The charter was for Griffuelhes, then, a *conservative* document in the strictest sense of the term, a conserving of "the status quo."

As a tactician, what did Griffuelhes see as the Charter's immediate practical value, which would have been of primary concern to him? For one thing, he appears to have believed or at least hoped that adoption of his motion would dissuade the socialists once and for all from any plans to co-opt the CGT. Thus, he wrote that "the socialist congress of Limoges, coming after the trade-union congress of Amiens, could only wisely take note of [our] decisions." When the Guesdists once more brought up the question of relations with the unions, however, at the SFIO Congress of Nancy in 1907, Griffuelhes was furious. "This means war," he blustered.[38]

Within the CGT itself the question remained of what role the charter would play in relations of the CGT leadership, increasingly cast in a centrist role between the confederation's reformist Right and its anarchist-insurrectionist Left. On this topic, Griffuelhes remained silent, no doubt for good reason. Already an incident had occurred at Amiens that demonstrated how fragile unity of purpose was within the CGT and how difficult it was to impose the terms of the charter upon its warring clans.

The last major item on the congress agenda was a motion on antimilitarism and antipatriotism, the issues with the greatest potential for disrupting whatever harmony had been achieved by passage of the "motion Griffuelhes." Georges Yvetot, whose current primary allegiance was to the International Antimilitarist Association, had announced his intention to present a motion denouncing both militarism and patriotism. Later, the police would claim that Griffuelhes had tried to dissuade Yvetot from presenting his motion and had even threatened to deny him the floor. If so, his efforts were to no avail. Yvetot's speech was delayed for half an hour as delegates booed and hissed at one another.[39] His motion, which called upon the CGT to intensify its antimilitarist and antipatriotic propaganda, could not have been better designed to arouse resentment among the reformists in attendance.

38. *Ibid.*, 50, 52.
39. AN, F7 12.493, note of October 13, 1906.

A vote was finally taken, by show of hands. Yvetot's resolution was approved by only 488 votes to 310 with forty-nine blank ballots and twenty-three abstentions. Even delegates from the radical metalworkers' federation declared they did not consider the resolution binding because it had not won a majority of the 991 mandates represented at the congress.[40] Griffuelhes was not pleased. "I overheard Griffuelhes say after the vote that the whole moral effect of the congress was destroyed," reported agent "B.T." Merrheim supposedly added that the CGT was in for a rough two years.[41] He was right.

40. CGT, *XVᵉ Congrès national corporatif . . . Amiens*, 175–77; for a breakdown of the vote see 304–14.
41. AN, F7 12.493, note of October 13, 1906.

VII

VILLENEUVE-ST.-GEORGES (1907–1908)

The working class continues to see in the *past,* think in the *past,* struggle in the *past.*
Knocked to the ground, it has struggled back on to its feet, not, however, to get on
with life, which is constantly changing, but to fight once again the battles of the *past.*
— Griffuelhes, "Romantisme révolutionnaire"

Early French labor historians such as Edouard Dolléans tended to regard the
Congress of Amiens as the high-water mark of revolutionary syndicalism and
the Charter of Amiens as its holy writ. But it is doubtful if the CGT leadership
took such an exalted view of the results of the Amiens congress. Certainly
Griffuelhes did not believe his motion and the impressive display of unity it
engendered there had saved syndicalism from its enemies: the newly united
socialist party; the increasingly influential Ultra-Left represented by Gustave
Hervé; or the State, which had lately taken a more muscular approach to labor
relations under Clemenceau's direction. Nor could the "spirit of Amiens" be
interpreted as anything more than a brief hiatus in the continuing struggle
for power with the reformists within the CGT. The charter's intended purpose
was to preserve the moral authority of the CGT revolutionary majority against
its many opponents, and Griffuelhes could be reasonably assured that it had
been served, for the time being at least. Indeed, he and his majority looked
stronger and more secure as 1906 shaded into 1907 than at any time since his
accession to power in 1901. Yet just over two years later, in February, 1909,
the general secretary's revolutionary majority would be in disarray, and he—
his moral authority dissipated—would be forced to resign. The agents of his
demise would be precisely those elements within the CGT against whom the
Charter of Amiens had been directed: the reformists and the Ultra-Left.

It was during this period that the only personal sketch of Griffuelhes as trade-union boss was penned. In late 1907, two Paris journalists, M. Leclerq and E. Girod de Fléaux, interviewed Griffuelhes at CGT headquarters. He was an authoritarian figure, they wrote, supremely self-confident, "tall, thin, bony, a bit pale, slightly hunched over, [and] if not stylish, at least correctly attired. . . . He has the air of an intellectual, with his dark, carefully parted locks, stiff, pointed Van Dyke beard, and smooth cheeks."[1]

The test of strength between Clemenceau and the CGT, begun so dramatically in the spring of 1906, continued on into 1907 without letup. Although there were far fewer strikers or workdays lost from strikes than in the previous year, and no repetition in 1907 of the May, 1906, general strike, the actual number of strikes did not fall appreciably, declining from 1,309 in 1906 only to 1,275 in 1907.[2] The strike statistics, however, hardly tell the whole story of the continuing battle between the CGT and the premier. The 1907 strikes, even if shorter and more localized, were nonetheless bloodier than the more massive engagements of 1906 had been. Almost every strike during 1907 had its complement of troops, with the year's balance sheet showing nine strikers killed and 167 wounded by soldiers or gendarmes. The heaviest toll was registered among members of a shoemakers' union newly affiliated to Griffuelhes' leatherworkers' federation. The union, composed of shoe factory employees at Raon-l'Etape (Vosges), had struck in early July, 1907, for a minimum wage of 32 centimes an hour and a maximum workday of ten hours. By mid July, three battalions of infantry and two squadrons of cavalry were on the scene. On July 28, the soldiers fired on a crowd of strikers, killing two and wounding thirty-two.[3]

Publicly, the CGT engaged in a ceaseless propaganda war against what it described as a policy of violence and provocation directed against the working class. Following the killings at Raon-l'Etape, the CGT Executive Committee distributed a poster entitled "More Bloodshed!" (*Encore du Sang!*) in which it charged: "Whether it is in a milieu where revolutionary action has been implanted for some time, or in a half-peasant milieu where trade unionism is

1. M. Leclerq and E. Girod de Fléaux, *Ces Messieurs de la CGT (Profils révolutionnaires)* (Paris, 1908), 99.

2. Louis, *Histoire du mouvement syndical en France*, I, 270.

3. Dolléans, *Histoire du mouvement ouvrier*, II, 145; Georges Airelle, "Les Événements de Raon-L'Etape," *Le Mouvement socialiste*, no. 194 (January 15, 1908), 14–33.

only beginning—such as Raon-l'Etape—the method of the government is always the same: violence and shooting. No such system of government—no matter how bloody it is—will ever succeed in stopping the growth of the workers' movement." [4]

Privately, however, Griffuelhes believed there were certain advantages to having Clemenceau as an adversary. According to "Lyon," a police spy, "[Griffuelhes] said, and all of his comrades agreed with him, . . . 'I prefer Clemenceau a hundred times over, despite his bloody-mindedness, his changes of mood, and his mania for causing trouble for us, to a man like Millerand. There are certain things Clemenceau won't do to us. Millerand would have tried anything." [5] Although Griffuelhes' opinion of what Clemenceau was willing to do would change drastically over the coming year, his basic notion—that the premier's reliance on force was a losing strategy in the long term—never wavered. He believed that the crucial left wing of the governmental coalition was not prepared to stomach a continuous diet of repression and that given enough time and rope, Clemenceau would hang himself. All the CGT needed to do was to avoid being provoked into action that could be portrayed as "insurrectionalist" and to continue hammering away at the government's alleged violations of civil and human rights. [6]

But in the summer of 1907 the government and nation's attention shifted to the Midi, where a protest movement against deteriorating economic conditions, which had been festering since the turn of the century and had furnished part of the backdrop to the farmworkers' strikes of 1903–1904, suddenly took on the proportions of a revolt.

The government would profess to see the hand of the CGT in the Midi disorders, but this was not the case. "The CGT is very interested in what is going on in the Midi and corresponds continually with the Bourses du Travail at Narbonne, Béziers, and Montpellier," police reports noted, but the news the CGT leaders received could not have been comforting. For contrary to the government's suspicions, the CGT had been hostile to the agitation that swept the South from Narbonne to Perpignan because it was organized and led by employers—in its first phase by the Comité d'Argéliers, a small owners'

---

4. Quoted in Dolléans, *Histoire du mouvement ouvrier*, II, 144.

5. APP, B/a 1601, note of May 7, 1907; but the same police spy reported earlier that Griffuelhes had said, "It's a hundred times better to face a moderate government than one presided over by a man who amuses himself by dragging us through the shit" (*ibid.*, note of April 27, 1907).

6. *Ibid.*, note of March 12, 1908.

group led by Marcellin Albert, and later by the Confédération générale des Vignerons (CGV), a large winegrowers' organization. Indeed, to the CGT's dismay, these organizations, although employer-led, had quickly turned into mass movements that threatened to decimate its own Southern Agricultural Workers' Federation. The farmworkers' unions deserted the federation in droves to follow Albert and then the CGV. What gave the owner-led movement its mass appeal, federation leader Paul Ader admitted ruefully, was its ability to exploit the latent enmity of the southerner for the North and its capital, Paris, and to convince the southern masses that the problems of the Midi's wine industry were caused by northern neglect. Ader paraphrased their arguments thus: "The prices of all staples are rising, except for wine; [the government] is protecting butter against margarine, they've put up tariffs on imported wheat, they've granted enormous subsidies to the [beet] sugar industry. What have they done for wine? Nothing! . . . The Midi has a right, just like the North, to a place in the sun."[7]

The regionalism of the winegrowers' movement and its contention that all the Midi's problems, including those that ranged employer against farmworker, could be solved if wine sales were increased, won it an enormous following. Demonstrations of support swelled in size: on May 5, 50,000 people demonstrated in Narbonne; on May 12, 150,000 turned out to protest in Béziers; then on June 9 came the monster rally in Montpellier—700,000 people. Clemenceau's response was predictable. In late June, when the agitation was at its height, he sent large contingents of troops into the area. This time, however, the government's strategy backfired. The movement the soldiers faced was a popular revolt involving a broad swath of the local population, not a wage earners' strike. In addition, most of the troops were from the region, and they were loath to use force against their own people. On June 20, soldiers refused to fire on a crowd at Montpellier. At Narbonne on June 21, they did fire, killing one person and injuring several others, but the same day, in the great wine-trading center of Béziers, the 17th Regiment not only refused to fire on a crowd but threw down its rifles and fraternized with the demonstrators.[8]

It was the event the antimilitarists and antipatriots in the anarchist movement, the Hervéist wing of the SFIO, and at the CGT had been waiting for. On one day in June, 1907, deep in the Midi, all of their agitation, rallies, and

7. *Ibid.*, notes of June 2 and 22, 1907; Paul Ader, "La Crise viticole et la Classe ouvrière," *Le Mouvement socialiste*, no. 193 (December 15, 1907), 436–38.

8. Julliard, *Clemenceau briseur de grèves*, 24.

jail sentences appeared justified. And to some, the revolution seemed a step closer. In the coming weeks and months, many a speaker would be interrupted by cries of "*Vive le* 17ᵉ *!*" and those who felt the CGT leadership was not bold enough in its contest with Clemenceau began raising their voices as well. This would bring increased pressure from the Ultra-Left inside and outside the CGT to force abandonment of Griffuelhes' cautious strategy for dealing with the government's provocations. Although Griffuelhes did not bend to this pressure, eventually he was overwhelmed by it, and the result was the bloody defeat at Villeneuve-Saint-Georges in July, 1908.

Griffuelhes was not in the Midi during the winegrowers' revolt because he was in the Landes Department, successfully organizing yet another contingent in the great Federation of Landworkers (Fédération des Travailleurs de la Terre) that he and Ader dreamed of forming: the *résiniers,* the workers who gathered pitch from the pine forests that stretched south from Bordeaux to the Basque country. Griffuelhes then moved on to the Midi to help Ader pick up the pieces of his farm laborers' federation in the wake of the winegrowers' upheaval. By the time he arrived there in early November, the CGV was beginning to fall apart under the weight of internal contradictions. Some growers had refused to honor a pledge to maintain a floor under wine prices, with the result that the market had weakened and many vineyard owners had begun to lay off workers or cut their wages.[9] This provided an opening for Ader and the CGT to wean back some of the farmworkers who had deserted the federation for the employers' movement.

By the time Griffuelhes returned to Paris in November, the fallout from the Midi events was beginning to accumulate. The government embarked upon a policy of silencing those it blamed for incidents such as the mutiny of the 17th. In February, 1908, Clemenceau escalated repression, using the antianarchist laws enacted in the 1890s. The CGT had just put out another poster, the first of two bearing the provocative title "*Gouvernement des Assassins!,*" that blasted Clemenceau's government for the year's toll of dead and wounded workers; it was signed by seventy-seven union leaders and militants, including the general secretary. Now, the premier turned to his new minister of justice, Aristide Briand, and asked him to choose which signatories should be charged with breaking the law.[10] Thus, instead of arresting all seventy-seven

---

9. Griffuelhes, "Le Mouvement des ouvriers résiniers des Landes," *Le Mouvement socialiste,* no. 187 (June, 1907), 494–506; Ader, "La Crise viticole," 440–41.

10. Julliard (*Clemenceau briseur de grèves,* 25) says Clemenceau ordered the judge in charge of the case to choose whom to prosecute, but according to police spy "Lyon," Alphonse Mer-

signers of the poster, only twelve were jailed and these included, not surprisingly, most of the CGT leadership: Griffuelhes, Pouget, Delesalle, Merrheim, Monatte, and Luquet, along with six others whose presence on the list probably stemmed from their membership in the International Antimilitarist Association.[11]

It was Griffuelhes' second arrest by Clemenceau's police in less than two years. The first time, the prosecution elected to drop the charges, but this time charges were pressed and on February 20, 1908, "The Twelve," as the press called them, went on trial in Paris. According to a reporter for the mass-circulation daily, *Le Matin,* Griffuelhes "admitted his part of the responsibility—1/77th—for the poster," which he said had only expressed "common thoughts and aspirations. . . . We were all agreed on expressing, in a concise text, our indignation at the massacre at Narbonne." Stressing the Narbonne shootings was perhaps an attempt to play on public awareness of and possible sympathy with the Midi revolt; if so, it certainly did not harm the case of the Twelve, who were acquitted three days later. One of Griffuelhes' codefendants, Clément Beausoleil, a leader of the Paris clerks' union and a CGT founder, took advantage of the trial to observe that if he and his colleagues were guilty, it was only of having taken seriously Clemenceau and Briand's preachments on social issues, referring no doubt to the premier's turn-of-the-century plea for action on the social question (*La Mêlée sociale*) and to Briand's career in the 1890s as France's best-known proponent of the general strike.[12]

For Griffuelhes, the year 1908 was dominated by the tragedy of Villeneuve-Saint-Georges. The July 30 encounter in this Seine-et-Oise hinterland of Paris, which left four workers dead and nearly one hundred wounded, led to the arrest of the CGT leadership three days later, just six months after the trial of the Twelve.

The Villeneuve-Saint-Georges incident has been dealt with in exhaustive detail by Jacques Julliard in his *Clemenceau briseur de grèves;* therefore I will

---

rheim believed it was "someone who knows us well—that is, Briand —who told Clemenceau who to prosecute" (APP, B/a 1602, note of January 9, 1908).

11. Julliard, *Clemenceau briseur de grèves,* 25.

12. *DBMO,* X, 239 (Beausoleil); for an account of the trial, including Griffuelhes and Beausoleil's remarks, see "La CGT aux Assises: L'Affiche déchirée, 77 = 12," *Le Matin,* February 21, 1908.

not dwell on its complex origins and ramifications but seek rather to demonstrate how and why Griffuelhes and the CGT leadership lost control of confederation strategy. They sought to avoid a confrontation with Clemenceau, in the expectation that his hard line would wear thin in the Chamber, but were instead forced to stand by helplessly while the CGT's most militant union, the newly reunited Building Workers' Federation (Batiment), suffered a crushing and demoralizing defeat. The defeat at Villeneuve-Saint-Georges also played a key role in the "Affair of the Maison des Fédérations" that drove Griffuelhes from office in February, 1909, and helped produce the "crisis in the unions" (*crise syndicaliste*) that dominated CGT activity to 1914.

Batiment, the CGT's militant spearhead during the prewar era, was at the center of these events. The reunification of the organization, which in 1900 had split up into a series of craft unions following nearly a decade as one of the French labor movement's first industrial federations, had been high on Griffuelhes' list of priorities in the campaign to wean the CGT from its craft-union past. He was among those who had pushed through an ultimatum at the Congress of Amiens in 1906, calling upon the construction trades to reunite. He had attended the new federation's first congress, held in Paris from March 31 to April 3, 1907, and also its congress in April, 1908, during a much-publicized lockout of building workers in the capital by a newly constituted construction employers' association. Appearing as a fraternal delegate of the CGT, Griffuelhes addressed the opening session of the 1908 congress on a cautionary note. The federation had made great strides since reunification a year earlier, he declared, but perhaps its progress had been "too rapid" and could "constitute a danger" for the federation's future, in the sense that whereas Batiment had clearly grown in numbers, its cohesion had not kept pace.[13] This was a poorly disguised reference to the fact that the brunt of the battle against the employers' lockout was being borne by the masons, the best-organized branch of the federation, with little help from its other elements. The CGT administrative bureau had expressed this concern to Batiment leaders earlier. Griffuelhes' point was that the current lockout had been provoked by Batiment before it had achieved the structural cohesion and unity of purpose necessary to face down the employers. Now, he intimated, the federation

13. CGT, *XVᵉ Congrès national corporatif . . . Amiens*, 186–91; Fédération nationale des Travailleurs de l'Industrie du Batiment, *Compte rendu du 2ᵉ Congrès national tenu à . . . St. Etienne, les 19, 20, 21, 22 et 23 avril 1908* (Courbevoie, 1908), 35; on this point, see also Griffuelhes, *Voyage révolutionnaire*, 17.

faced defeat, a defeat it—and the labor movement as a whole—could ill afford.[14]

Other concerns lay behind Griffuelhes' somber warning to the Batiment congress. On April 23, the day it concluded, *L'Action Directe* published a piece by Griffuelhes entitled "Romantisme révolutionnaire," which is perhaps the best known of the dozens he wrote over the years. In it, he took aim at the *braillards* (literally, "squalling brats") outside the trade-union movement who "preach revolution from the safety of their firesides," a clear reference to Gustave Hervé and the crowd associated with his popular newspaper, *La Guerre sociale,* and to assorted other revolutionaries who presumed to advise the CGT on how to conduct its business. Griffuelhes was no more sparing of the "romantic revolutionaries" within the CGT. He recalled that at the turn of the century general strike enthusiasts saw within "every strike, in no matter how small a workshop, the makings of The Revolution," but they could conceive of it only in terms of the Commune, a type of insurrection doomed by the machine gun and other modern instruments of oppression. Revolution in the modern industrial era would take new forms, adapted to the new age, not those of the past, and these would become evident only as a result of experience in struggle. There was no formula for them; they could not be learned from books. "The day is not far off," he wrote, "when all militants will recognize that the real revolutionary action is that which, practiced each day, increases the revolutionary potential of the proletariat. The strike, wielded by a working class made strong by its struggles, thanks to powerful and active unions, is worth more than the contents of whole libraries; it educates, it hardens, it trains, and it creates."[15]

Explicit in Griffuelhes' attack on the braillards and nostalgics was a plea for patience, for attention to organization and preparation, and for consideration of the consequences of actions undertaken. Patience, Griffuelhes would say on more than one occasion, was a commodity in short supply in the French working class, as was concern for organization—assembling structures and resources to enable unions to carry on protracted struggles like resistance to the lockout Batiment was now facing. The building contractors' association, formed in 1906 in the wake of the May 1 general strike, clearly intended its lockout to break the union. In advance, it sent emissaries to Berlin to study a successful lockout in the building industry that took place there in

14. APP, B/a 1602, note of March 24, 1908; Batiment, *Compte rendu du 2ᵉ Congrès national,* 35.

15. Griffuelhes, "Romantisme révolutionnaire."

late 1906. Bank credits were arranged to cover anticipated losses, and agreements were made with building materials suppliers to cut off employers who did not join the lockout. Griffuelhes followed these preparations with great interest and even some admiration for what he saw as an unusual display of dynamism by French employers.[16] But most important, Griffuelhes—echoed by many other union leaders at one time or another—was saying that unions must never allow anger, impetuousness, or self-confidence to cloud their judgment as to the timing of a strike and they must never launch a strike except when and where they chose, no matter how great the provocation.

Griffuelhes' article, "Romantisme révolutionnaire," is the most informative and eloquent witness to pressures from the Ultra-Left that were building in the spring and summer of 1908—pressures to strike back at Clemenceau, to tap the presumed wellspring of working-class anger and frustration at his provocations and turn it into an insurrectionary thrust. Braillards like Hervé and his lieutenants, Eugène Merle and Miguel Alméreyda, may have been talking most along these lines, but Griffuelhes knew that many strategically placed militants within the CGT were listening, none more assiduously than those of Batiment.

In mid May, the construction industry lockout in Paris ended in partial victory for the union. Although some workers had gone back on the old terms, others had gained raises and a cap on overtime, the federation's main strike demands. No doubt relieved that matters had turned out as well as they had, Griffuelhes proclaimed the strike results a "great victory" for Batiment.[17] Almost immediately, however, the federation was plunged into another conflict. Throughout the spring, an affiliated building materials workers' union had been on strike against employers in the Draveil-Vigneux region in the Seine-et-Oise Department not far from Paris. Now that the big dispute in the capital was over, Batiment could turn to helping these sand-and-gravel workers, whose central demand was recognition of their union. The employers, meanwhile, had begun bringing in strikebreakers, or *renards* ("foxes"). Building workers have a reputation in most countries for being especially intolerant of strikebreakers, and France was no exception. Soon a "*chasse aux renards*" was underway at Draveil-Vigneux, which

16. See Griffuelhes' remarks in Fédération nationale des Cuirs et Peaux, *Compte rendu du 5ᵉ Congrès . . . Limoges . . . septembre 1907*, 89–90; for the French contractors' visit to Berlin, see [Christian Cornelissen,] "L'Internationalisme des patrons," *Bulletin international du mouvement syndicaliste*, no. 13, December 1, 1907.

17. Griffuelhes, "L'Action ouvrière dans la Maçonnerie," *VdP*, no. 319, May 10–17, 1908.

brought the police on the scene to protect the "right to work" guaranteed under law. This was the opening act in the drama of Villeneuve-Saint-Georges.

On June 2, local police went hunting for a striker accused of harassing a renard. Thinking he had entered a building where a union strike meeting was in progress, the policemen entered the foyer and demanded admission to check identities. Refused entry on the grounds the meeting was a private affair that they lacked a warrant to interrupt, the officers went back outside and began firing through the windows at the workers within. When the shooting was over, one worker was dead, another dying, and ten were wounded. The police claimed they had been shot at first, but proof of this was never found, nor was it ever ascertained that the striker they sought had been in the room, known as the Salle Ranque. A subsequent judicial inquiry concluded that the policemen had "lost their heads," but no punishment was meted out.[18]

Predictably, rage swept the ranks of organized labor in Paris. On June 3, the day after the killings, the CGT plastered the walls of the capital with yet another poster entitled "Gouvernement des Assassins!" "After the massacre of Narbonne and the butchery of Raon-l'Etape, the government has killed again," it charged, and those responsible for the deaths were "the trio of Clemenceau-Briand-Viviani."[19] In the week following the Salle Ranque incident, crowds of workers and other activists from Paris descended on Vigneux to demonstrate. Police were stoned, local officials jostled and berated. Pressure mounted on the CGT and Batiment to "do something" to respond to the "provocation" of June 2. Griffuelhes called for a twenty-four-hour general strike in the capital, to appear to be taking action and to shift the focus away from the dangerously escalating situation in Draveil-Vigneux. But the general secretary insisted the strike must be prepared—he was not willing to rely on mass "spontaneity," as he had made clear in his April article—and demanded that strategically placed Parisian unions commit themselves to action. This seems a tactical maneuver on Griffuelhes' part, since he was clearly aware that most of these key unions—the gas workers, transport workers, railwaymen—were controlled by reformists and would not respond to a strike call. Apparently, he aimed to shift blame for inaction to the reformist unions and thus preserve his own moral authority and that of the CGT's revolutionary syn-

18. This account of the Draveil-Vigneux strike and the June 2 killings is based on Jacques Julliard's meticulous reconstruction of events in *Clemenceau briseur de grevès*, 36–53.

19. *Ibid.*, 9–10. Independent socialist René Viviani was France's first minister of labor; his functions had been carried out earlier by the ministry of commerce.

dicalist majority. In any case, at a meeting on June 6, the CGT Executive Committee could not agree on plans for a strike because the reformist-led unions refused to commit themselves. Batiment also declined to take action, its troops and treasury exhausted by the recent lockout and its leaders wary of the agitation at Draveil-Vigneux.[20]

There are certain ominous overtones to these developments. First and most obvious, the "consensus" between revolutionaries and reformists supposedly sealed by the almost unanimous adoption of the Charter of Amiens one and a half years earlier was no longer in effect—if it ever had been. The only reformist union to show even a glimmer of interest in the projected strike activity was Livre, and this only because its Paris branch was traditionally more radical than the union leadership. Second, the events immediately following June 2 suggest a diminution of the CGT leaders' authority, whether because of a growing dislike for Griffuelhes' "dictatorial" manner—as one police spy reported—or because the initiative had passed to his critics at *La Guerre sociale* or the "hard core" in Batiment, "a veritable bastion of anarchism in the working-class world."[21] Third, there is evidence of a widening split within the CGT leadership between the devotees of spontaneity, such as Bourse du Travail leader Georges Yvetot (who was now closer to Hervé's circle than to the CGT) and those Julliard has dubbed the *politiques*. This group, led by Griffuelhes and including Pouget, Merrheim, Monatte, Luquet, and others who had become "permanents" of the administrative group, preached patience and the necessity of organizing strong and solvent unions. Their manifesto might well have been Griffuelhes' "Romantisme révolutionnaire," in which he argued for the urgent need to detach "the working class from its revolutionary mysticism so as to confront it with reality and the day-to-day task" of building a real movement.

The CGT leaders' difficulty was to achieve balance between solidly anchored unions with regular dues structures on one hand and élan and combativeness on the other—a sort of cross between Keufer's Livre and the building laborers. In the best of all possible trade-union worlds, leaders and militants dream of a harmonious dialectic between organization and spontaneity; this, no doubt, is what Griffuelhes and the politiques had in mind the spring of 1908. But labor history demonstrates—and events soon to follow in France bear this out—that this combination is an extremely elusive one;

20. APP, B/a 1602, note of June 9, 1908.
21. *Ibid.*, notes of July 18, 1908, by two different police spies; Julliard, *Clemenceau briseur de grèves*, 64.

the two qualities are more frequently in opposition than conjunction. Beyond speculation, however, the stance of the politiques ran counter to a very real urge for retaliation against Clemenceau's provocations in important sectors of the working class, at least in Paris. Much blood had been spilled, and many workers believed the honor of the working class and its organizations was at stake. To counsel patience and organization at this point was to risk charges of bureaucratism, backsliding, even betrayal. Forces were waiting in the wings who were only too ready to make those charges: those whom Griffuelhes had alienated by his sharp tongue and authoritarian manner; reformists who had long waited for an opportunity to seize control of the confederation; and various elements of the Ultra-Left, who condemned Griffuelhes and his associates for standing in the way of the revolution.

These problems and conflicts remained largely latent during June, 1908. A month later, however, in the crucible of Villeneuve-Saint-Georges, they surfaced dramatically, provoking a near schism in the CGT and leading to Griffuelhes' resignation as general secretary.

In the meantime, the situation at Draveil-Vigneux was daily becoming more explosive. The employers had hired two professional strikebreakers from the Ardennes to speed up the importation of scab workers. This, of course, led to more worker reprisals and a growing risk of confrontation with the authorities as more police were brought in to protect the scabs. Equally dangerous, local union leadership was on the verge of losing control of the strike to outside elements. Gustave Hervé's insurrectionalist wing of the socialist party had moved quickly to capitalize on the anger aroused by the Vigneux killings. On June 7, the day after the victims' burial, Hervé lamented in his popular *journal d'action, La Guerre sociale:* "A crowd of several hundred strikers and not a revolver among them!" This oversight, Hervé wrote, was due to the unhealthy influence of the "preachers of calm," *i.e.,* the leaders of the CGT and Batiment. He offered the paper's assistance in "redressing the balance." [22]

Individualist anarchists, as well, had become permanent fixtures on the site, including one Marceau Raimbault, who would be arrested on July 30 for inciting the crowd at Villeneuve-Saint-Georges to violence and then unmasked in October as an agent provocateur in the pay of the Paris Préfecture de Police. Raimbault, a leading militant in the newly founded Anarchist Fed-

---

22. APP, B/a 1602, note of July 18, 1908; Julliard, *Clemenceau briseur de grèves,* 67–68.

eration in Paris, later wrote that his role at Draveil-Vigneux was to "oppose the tactics" of the "so-called 'leaders' of the CGT . . . most of whom are Free-masons," and to "inoculate" the unions "with a strong dose of the anarchist virus," including the tactic of sabotage.[23]

Of more immediate concern, the local union's leadership was being up-staged by a young firebrand named Ricordeau who opposed negotiations with the employers and seemed to relish scuffling with the police. Although disa-vowed by both the CGT and Batiment leadership, Ricordeau had become the strikers' de facto leader at Draveil-Vigneux by the end of July, 1908.[24] Thus, his arrest, along with five other militants, for interfering with police on July 28 presented the Batiment federation and the CGT with a serious di-lemma. Not responding to this new provocation would diminish the already reduced credibility of the CGT and Batiment leaders, whose failure to launch strike action following the deaths at the Salle Ranque had already stirred charges of irresolution and worse among Ultra-Left critics. Agent "Brossier," the best of the Préfecture de Police's spies on the labor beat, reported: "For the last four years, but especially since the Amiens Congress (1906), [the CGT] has taken a turn that displeases many militants. They say the confederation is weakening."[25] In other words, Griffuelhes' policy of avoiding confrontation was under fire.

But to respond with a twenty-four-hour general strike, an option under consideration by the CGT administrative bureau, also presented substantial risks. In the present heated atmosphere, the chances of another, even bloodier confrontation with the police were great. Some said Clemenceau was spoiling for a showdown and that he was eager to smash the CGT once and for all.[26] A further risk, as Griffuelhes had carefully pointed out, was that the strike call, if it came, would not be followed; he was convinced that, except for Batiment, no real sense of solidarity with the strikers at Draveil-Vigneux ex-isted in Paris. Julliard remarks that, in the event of arrests such as those of

23. Marceau Raimbault, "Le Mouvement anarchiste en France," *Bulletin de l'Internationale anarchiste*, no. 5, June, 1908; for the details of Raimbault's "unmasking," in which Griffuelhes played a part, see Julliard, *Clemenceau briseur de grèves*, 163–66.

24. In the aftermath of Villeneuve-Saint-Georges, there were charges that Ricordeau also had acted as an agent provocateur, but apparently this was not the case; rather, he seems to have been excessively zealous (Julliard, *Clemenceau briseur de grèves*, 167–74).

25. APP, B/a 1602, note of July 18, 1908.

26. *Ibid.*, July 28, July 29, 1908; agent "Lesieur" claimed that Ricordeau's "excesses aren't at all displeasing to M. Clemenceau, who is only waiting for a chance to 'lock up' the CGT."

July 27, "Batiment had earlier pledged to take action and could not now back away without losing face."[27] The general secretary also doubted the wisdom of appearing to be acting on behalf of Ricordeau, whose behavior had not been in the movement's best interests.

The evening of July 28, the Batiment secretariat summoned the leaders of its member unions (carpenters, painters, masons, building laborers, stonecutters, etc.), the executive board of the Trade-Union Federation of the Seine, and the CGT administrative bureau to a meeting at 60, rue Charlot in Paris, the offices of the stonecutters' union. It was not open to the public. Its purpose was to decide whether to call a twenty-four-hour strike in retaliation for the arrests of July 28 and, if so, whether it should be a general movement or one confined to Batiment. CGT representatives included Griffuelhes, Pouget, Lévy, Merrheim, Henri Dret, and Garnery.

One by one the Batiment chiefs spoke, the majority declaring themselves in favor of a strike. When their turn came, none of the spokesmen for the other unions could pledge participation. Griffuelhes then took the floor and indulged in some of the sarcasm for which he was by now famous. "No one should be too surprised at the negative or evasive responses we've just heard," he said. "The movement we're discussing is just too new for French trade unionists; you can't expect big things from amateurs." The general secretary then proposed a twenty-four-hour strike limited to the building trades and, anticipating the next stage of the debate, recommended it be confined to Paris. These proposals appear to have emanated from discussions held by the CGT administrative bureau that afternoon.[28]

With no pledges of support forthcoming from the TFS or CGT affiliates represented at the meeting—even Merrheim's usually ebullient metalworkers declined—it was unanimously agreed that Batiment would go it alone. The debate now moved to its final, crucial stage: the Batiment leaders' vote on whether to combine the strike with a demonstration at Vigneux. Griffuelhes' intervention on this point is important since he was later arrested and charged with inspiring and directing the Villeneuve-Saint-Georges action because of his presumed decisive role at the meeting.

The minutes taken by Batiment clearly show that Griffuelhes argued against the demonstration at Draveil-Vigneux: "Griffuelhes is not in favor of an expedition to Draveil because of the obstacles the government would not

27. Julliard, *Clemenceau briseur de grèves*, 76.

28. *Ibid.*, 77; Griffuelhes' remarks are quoted from the minutes of the meeting drawn up by the Batiment secretariat; APP, B/a 1602, note of July 28, 1908.

fail to place in the way of the departing Parisian workers." Journalists who covered the closed meeting from the street concurred. Later, the judge in charge of the Villeneuve-Saint-Georges investigation questioned reporters from newspapers as diverse as the republican-socialist *La Petite République* and the monarchist *L'Action Française* about Griffuelhes' role; they believed Griffuelhes had spoken out against the "exodus to Draveil."[29] A police informer on the spot reported Griffuelhes' disillusionment with the outcome of the meeting, providing at least indirect confirmation of the reporters' statements.[30]

The ball, however, was now in Batiment's court and Griffuelhes could only suggest what action to take; the decision would be Batiment's alone. By a vote of ten to seven, the building trades' leadership decided to hold a demonstration at Vigneux on July 30. Reported agent "Lyon," "The results surprised the bosses of the confederation, [who think] it is a bad tactic to act now, since it is inevitable that people will accuse them of going to bat for Ricordeau, who is useless." This view had not been well received in the meeting, however, according to the spy. The CGT leaders were "severely attacked" by the "violent ones" who said, in effect, "If we take that attitude, the Revolution will never come."[31]

The morning of July 30, some four thousand Parisian workers, most of them members of the building laborers' union, took trains from the Gare de Lyon to Villeneuve-Saint-Georges, from whence they marched to the nearby village of Vigneux. Accompanying them at a distance were Victor Griffuelhes and other CGT leaders: Emile Pouget, Jean Latapie, and Alphonse Merrheim. It was Batiment's show, not the CGT's. The only non-Batiment official to march with the crowd that day was Henri Dret, the ferocious antimilitarist who had succeeded Griffuelhes as head of the leatherworkers' federation. He would pay dearly for his beliefs.

We can imagine Griffuelhes' sense of foreboding as he trudged along on the fringes of the mass of workers. As they listened to speeches in an open field near the strike headquarters of the sand-and-gravel workers' union in Vigneux, they could see cavalry maneuvering near the rue de Paris, which led from the village back to Villeneuve-Saint-Georges. Griffuelhes had done all

---

29. Julliard, *Clemenceau briseur de grèves*, 77. See reporters' comments in *L'Humanité*, October 23, 1908; Henri Dadoune of the *Petite République*, who apparently slipped into the meeting unnoticed, said he actually heard Griffuelhes "suggest that rallies be held in various quartiers of Paris in preference to [staging] a demonstration in Vigneux."

30. APP, B/a 1602, note of July 29, 1908.

31. *Ibid.*

in his power to discourage this adventure. The previous day, following the rue Charlot meeting, he had written a piece about the purposes and tenor of the demonstration, hoping to lessen the chances of a bloody confrontation, and even as the building laborers descended on Vigneux, many Parisians would be reading it on the front page of the mass-circulation daily, *Le Matin*. In it he tried to put the day's events into an understandable perspective.

First, he sought to de-emphasize the demonstration by placing it in the broader context of the twenty-four-hour strike called by Batiment. "Today [Paris] will witness a sectoral general strike. So the trades of Batiment have decided," he wrote, taking pains to make clear the strike was declared by Batiment, not the CGT. The purposes of the strike were clear and legitimate—and limited. "Some of its own having been murdered, stirred by a fierce indignation, the working class has felt the need to express its anger and cry out its protest." He asked, "Will the government take advantage of the occasion to make arrests among the strikers? There are rumors to that effect." Griffuelhes added that by striking, the Batiment workers aimed for more than protest and intended to demonstrate "their power, to make clear their role as producers, to show that this world is what it is only because of their labor." By these means alone, which were their own, and not through universal suffrage or acts of parliament, could workers achieve "final liberation."[32]

In the Seine-et-Oise countryside, the demonstrators had now decided to march back to Villeneuve-Saint-Georges and hold a rally in the cemetery where the Salle Ranque victims were buried. On the way, the cavalry descended and tried to disrupt their line of march. The workers massed on a raised railroad bed, gathering around the red flag of the building laborers' union. When they began showering rocks on the cavalry, some of the soldiers dismounted and advanced on the crowd. There was some hand-to-hand fighting, but the Seine-et-Oise prefect, Autrand, separated the combatants and the marchers continued on their way.

More cavalry now appeared, cuirassiers under the command of a full general, Virvaire, and just outside the railway station at Villeneuve-Saint-Georges, the workers found themselves surrounded. The desperate men ransacked a nearby building site for steel bars and pieces of timber; others raided a café across the way for bottles and bits of furniture. Using whatever fell to hand, the workers began to throw up barricades. According to witnesses, Griffuelhes and Pouget now ran into the mass of workers, "repeatedly imploring them

---

32. Griffuelhes, "Dans l'attente de la manifestation d'aujourd'hui," *Le Matin,* July 30, 1908.

. . . to tear down the barricades . . . saying that it was madness, folly." Their efforts were in vain, and likewise, orders to disperse were greeted by showers of rocks and bottles. Troopers fired a salvo of blanks in the air, to no effect, then leveled their carbines at the demonstrators. After several challenges more, they fired, but additional volleys and hand-to-hand fighting were required to dislodge the demonstrators, who streamed into the railway station; from there they eventually returned to Paris with their wounded. It was a bloody day's work. Four union men were killed and nearly one hundred wounded; sixty-nine cavalrymen were treated for wounds. Among the wounded was Henri Dret, who had taken a bullet in the shoulder; his arm was later amputated.[33]

Griffuelhes and his colleagues returned to Paris, along with the mass of roughly handled building laborers, all undoubtedly convinced that a rough reception awaited them. Arrests of those held responsible for the clash were virtually certain; government attempts to dissolve the CGT altogether could not be ruled out. On July 31 and August 1, desperate efforts were made to organize a general strike in Paris to respond to the "massacre" of Villeneuve-Saint-Georges. An automobile was sent to the Vendée to bring back the secretary of the Paris electrical workers' union, Emile Pataud, from vacation. Pataud was wildly popular among Parisian workers, who called him the "Prince of Darkness" because of the spectacular way he had secured a new wage agreement for his union in 1906. When the city council refused to accept union proposals, Pataud forced the issue by turning off the lights during a performance at the Paris Opera in honor of the King of Portugal. The new contract was signed between acts. If nothing else, the CGT Executive Committee apparently reasoned, at least the lights could be doused.[34] Pataud agreed to cooperate and an electrical workers' strike did take place on August 6, but too late to forestall government action against the presumed leaders of the demonstration at Villeneuve-Saint-Georges.

On August 1, Pierre Tesche, a former trade unionist and now an editor at *L'Humanité,* brought the news that arrests of the CGT leadership had been ordered for early the next day. "Everywhere," reported a police spy, "they [CGT officials] are getting their files in order or burning papers they fear could be compromising." Those who believed they would be arrested took

---

33. Witnesses to Griffuelhes and Pouget's intervention included some journalists who later testified concerning Griffuelhes' role in the affair, according to police spy "Lyon" (APP, B/a 1602, note of September 16, 1908); details of the "battle" of Villeneuve-Saint-Georges are from Julliard, *Clemenceau briseur de grèves,* 85–94.

34. APP, B/a 1602, notes of July 31, August 1, 1908; *DBMO,* XIV, 214–15 (Pataud).

whatever precautions they thought necessary. Pierre Monatte fled to Switzerland, where he hid out under the name "Baud" with a friend, the anarchist doctor Fritz Brupbacher. Three of the Batiment chiefs, Rousselot, Clément, and Raymond Péricat, fled to Brussels. The CGT general staff, however, elected to remain. "Griffuelhes will spend the night in his office," noted the police spy "Brossier."[35] At dawn on August 2, police cordoned off CGT headquarters, and rumors circulated that those inside were prepared to defend themselves. As the arresting officers approached the building, somewhat gingerly no doubt, they were met at the door by the concierge Mazeau who, quickly ascertaining that the policemen had no arrest warrants, refused to admit them.

Finally, the Paris prefect of police, Louis Lépine, arrived, "flanked by his whole staff," to serve the warrants. The suspense now ended as Griffuelhes, Pouget, and François Marie, secretary of the typographers' union, "walked out to the cheers of militants gathered in the courtyard."[36] The CGT leaders were taken to the prison at Corbeil, in the Seine-et-Oise, where they were charged with plotting and leading an insurrection and where some would remain almost five months, until November 30, 1908.

35. APP, B/a 1602, note of August 1, 1908; Julliard, *Clemenceau briseur de grèves*, 103.

36. Julliard, *Clemenceau briseur de grèves*, 102–103; a warrant was also served on Henri Dret in the hospital, where he was recovering from the amputation of his arm.

VIII

RESIGNATION (1909)

I left because I felt that if I had wanted to stay—and I could have if I had wanted
to—it would have been hard for me to carry on my work as I had done in the past.
A confused situation had developed . . . and I chose to leave, to turn over the job to
others, in the hope that it might be possible for them to carry on the work I had
pursued for seven years and to which I was so fiercely attached.
                    —Victor Griffuelhes' statement at the CGT Congress of Toulouse in 1910

Victor Griffuelhes remained in Corbeil Prison from August 1 to October 31,
1908—the longest, and last, of his three detentions. After some pondering
among government officials and the examining magistrate charged with the
Villeneuve-Saint-Georges case, they decided to forego the charge of conspiracy
to overthrow the Republic, which had been used to detain the CGT leadership
in 1906. In the end, Griffuelhes, seven other CGT and union officials, and
eight less prominent defendants were charged with disorderly conduct. Thus,
writes Jacques Julliard, the CGT leaders were held in prison for three months
on the same charge as that brought against one Madame Auclaire, "accused
of striking a dragoon's horse with an umbrella" at Villeneuve-Saint-Georges.
An article in *La Voix du Peuple,* based on detailed information apparently
leaked by the detainees' lawyer, Ernest Lafont, revealed that the case against
them was weak, which forced the Clemenceau government finally to release
them pending further investigation. Eventually all charges were dropped, including those against Pierre Monatte and the Batiment leaders who had fled
the country. Remarks Julliard: "The tough approach favored by Clemenceau
had produced no tangible results save one: It had permitted the detention of
the CGT leaders for three months, and the surfacing of an internal crisis

[within the CGT] which would be extremely serious." "When all is said and done," declared Alphonse Merrheim when he heard the prisoners were being released, "the important thing is that Griffuelhes is coming back. It's high time."[1]

The internal crisis that came to a head during Griffuelhes' enforced absence was indeed serious. It would cost the general secretary his job just four months later. In October, 1910, at the CGT Congress of Toulouse, Griffuelhes gave his version of what had transpired during his stay in Corbeil Prison. "While I was in jail, they [his enemies] profited from the occasion to drag my name through the mud. But since my administration was above reproach, they went after me in roundabout ways. They didn't dare challenge me to my face, so they planted doubts and raised delicate questions, about money matters for example, thinking 'This way, we'll create such an atmosphere that Griffuelhes will have to clear out.' "[2]

While obviously self-serving, Griffuelhes' statement is a good introduction to the "Affair of the Maison des Fédérations" that brought him down, for it suggests that the Affair, which centered on Griffuelhes' alleged mishandling of CGT funds, was only the pretext for the campaign that led to his resignation. Historians of the French labor movement have long realized there was more to the Affair than missing money. Taking their cue largely from the general secretary and his supporters, they have concluded that Griffuelhes was pushed out as a result of pressure from a coalition of reformist and Ultra-Left enemies directed by the man who had been Clemenceau's minister of justice, Aristide Briand. Briand had begun his political career as an intimate of Fernand Pelloutier and one of France's most notorious proponents of the general strike. But, writes Julliard, "The minister [of justice] had retained almost nothing from his tumultuous youth, save a tenacious reputation as a renegade and, also, solid friendships in working-class circles." According to Edouard Dolléans, who devised the standard version of Griffuelhes' resignation, "Briand wanted to get rid of Griffuelhes because he saw in him the incarnation of revolutionary syndicalism. He hoped that getting rid of him would make it easier to break up the trade-union movement"—thus he plotted with certain of his trade-union contacts to oust Griffuelhes.[3]

---

1. Julliard, *Clemenceau briseur de grèves*, 120–21, 133; APP, B/a 1602, note of December 14, 1908; AN, F7 12.915, note of October 30, 1908, from a Sureté spy.

2. CGT, *XVIIᵉ Congrès national corporatif . . . Toulouse . . . 1910. Compte rendu* (Toulouse, 1911), 132.

3. Julliard, *Clemenceau briseur de grèves*, 182; Dolléans, *Histoire du mouvement ouvrier*, II,

Labor historians also generally agree on the identity of Briand's "solid friendships" in the workers' movement. They were revolutionaries, wrote Griffuelhes some eight months after his departure, in an article comparing the intrigues of Briand, who by then had succeeded Clemenceau, to the seductions practiced by Alexandre Millerand in 1899–1901: "M. Millerand directed his attentions toward moderate militants in the working-class movement. . . . The new premier intrigued with militants known for their revolutionary ideas."[4] The two individuals identified as Briand's co-conspirators were Albert Lévy, the CGT treasurer, and Jean Latapie, a secretary of the metalworkers' federation. Both had long-term reputations as revolutionaries, having come into positions of influence in the trade-union movement as part of the radical wave that brought Griffuelhes to power in 1901. And both had served alongside Griffuelhes and knew him well: Lévy was Griffuelhes' principal troubleshooter in the Pas-de-Calais in the battles with the Baslyites in 1902–1903 and in 1906, while Latapie had served as one of the CGT's chief emissaries to the Nord metalworkers during the same period. Presumably, however, the three men had had a falling-out in subsequent years, and Briand used this estrangement to recruit Lévy and Latapie for his scheme to unseat Griffuelhes.

For Dolléans, "Lévy was Briand's puppet," blinded to his "villainous task" by "the hatred he bore for Griffuelhes." Griffuelhes "was intolerant; his comrades' failure to grasp certain things exasperated him; his impatience was expressed, in their presence, by judgments that were wounding"; Lévy probably had been a frequent target of Griffuelhes' scorn. Latapie's case was somewhat different. While the evidence connecting Lévy to Briand is mostly circumstantial, Latapie clearly had been a close friend of the politician for several years. So well known were Latapie's ties to Briand, comments Julliard, that "many of the revolutionary militants who reproached him [Latapie] for them nevertheless did not hesitate to contact him whenever they got into a scrape with the law."[5] Furthermore, like Briand, Latapie had been moving steadily toward the Right, a process hastened by his observations at Villeneuve-Saint-Georges. Thus, if Lévy presumably served Briand out of hatred for Griffuelhes,

---

153. Lefranc generally accepts this thesis as well (*Le Mouvement syndical sous la Troisième République*, 148).

4. Griffuelhes, "La Leçon du Passé," *La Vie Ouvrière* (*V.O.*), 1st ser., no. 1, October 5, 1909.

5. Dolléans, *Histoire du mouvement ouvrier*, II, 153; Julliard, *Clemenceau briseur de grèves*, 184.

Latapie seems to have acted out of friendship for Briand and a growing reformism.[6]

This standard version of the events leading to Griffuelhes' dramatic resignation as CGT general secretary in February, 1909, needs revision on a number of points. In general terms, it is too simplistic; it relies on the conspiracy of a few individuals, but the Affair was considerably more complex than this. In addition, the standard explanation, while criticizing Griffuelhes for irascibility and sloppy bookkeeping, for example, generally portrays him as the largely blameless injured party. I believe his ouster was to a considerable extent a self-inflicted wound. Finally, Dolléans and others have tended to view the Affair almost exclusively in terms of Victor Griffuelhes' fate and largely within the context of events that transpired between October, 1908, and February, 1909. Much more was at stake, however, than the loss of Griffuelhes' leadership, important as it may have been to the revolutionary syndicalist cause. The Affair is best viewed, I am convinced, as a stage in the power struggle within the CGT that originated in the Millerand Affair of 1899 and would only reach a first dénouement in the CGT schism of 1921–1922.

The storm clouds began gathering around Griffuelhes even before the Villeneuve-Saint-Georges tragedy. In April, 1908, Albert Lévy was released from prison after a year's detention for inciting a riot. When Lévy first looked at the CGT books following his return, he discovered that 4,178.40 francs were unaccounted for. "When [Lévy] protested, Griffuelhes, *très grand seigneur,* counted out 18.40 francs on the spot and signed an I.O.U. for the rest."[7]

Predictably, Griffuelhes' lordly, proprietary behavior did not sit well with Lévy, a "scrupulous treasurer" whose accounting skills had won praise at CGT congresses. Nor is it difficult to understand that Griffuelhes' persistent refusal to explain where the money had gone aroused Lévy's suspicions that the general secretary had simply pocketed it. Julliard attempts to explain Griffuelhes' silence by contending that he "was both too honest and too proud to allow

---

6. Latapie gives his own account of his evolution in "Diplomates syndicalistes et révolutionnaires," *L'Humanité,* December 15, 1908. In his speech at the CGT Congress of Marseille, during Griffuelhes' imprisonment, he said, "I am one of the people who will no longer lead the workers to the slaughterhouse [referring to Villeneuve-Saint-Georges] . . . just because three or four men decide it ought to be done" (CGT, *XVIe Congrès national corporatif . . . Marseille . . . 1908. Compte rendu sténographique des travaux* [Marseille, 1909], 50).

7. Julliard, *Clemenceau briseur de grèves,* 137.

his rectitude to be called into question" by Lévy.[8] This may have been true, but it is only part of the story. The missing francs were, as Griffuelhes later observed at the CGT Congress of Toulouse, part of a "delicate" matter he did not want to have to explain, for the following reasons.

It will be recalled that in December, 1906, immediately following its expulsion from the Paris Bourse du Travail and temporary relocation at 10, Cité Riverin (10th)—Griffuelhes' "stinking slum"—the CGT had gone looking for more commodious quarters. The search was conducted by Griffuelhes, Pouget, and Albert Lévy. On January 28, 1906, Griffuelhes reported the team had found "a building close by that could serve our purposes nicely." It was an abandoned chemicals plant located at 33, rue Grange-aux-Belles (10th), and was available at an annual rent of 8,000 francs. Griffuelhes sought authorization from the CGT Executive Committee to set up a private company, with himself as director, to rent and manage the property; it would be called the "Maison des Fédérations."[9]

Griffuelhes' proposal was not so unorthodox as it may sound. Article VI of the 1884 law that gave unions legal status and allowed them to form confederations stipulated that only individual unions could rent property, and then only to provide themselves with facilities for meetings, job placement, libraries, and so on. No trade-union organizations were permitted to own property, and confederations such as the CGT could neither rent nor own property in their own name. The only way around the law was to set up a private company like the one Griffuelhes was proposing.[10] As noted earlier, there was a precedent for such a step and presumably Griffuelhes knew of it. When the municipally owned building occupied by the Paris Bourse du Travail was closed by the minister of interior in 1893, its secretary, A. Baumé, set up a company in his own name to rent space for a "Bourse du Travail autonome," which functioned until 1898.[11]

In any case, the Executive Committee approved Griffuelhes' plan and thus was born the "Société Victor Griffuelhes et Cie.," with Griffuelhes as director. Griffuelhes proposed to pay the rent and fund repairs to the property—the

8. *DBMO*, XIII, 387 (Lévy); Julliard, *Clemenceau briseur de grèves*, 137.

9. APP, B/a 1601, note of January 29, 1906.

10. In 1899, however, when Premier Waldeck-Rousseau proposed revising the 1884 law to permit unions and confederations of unions to own property, Griffuelhes and the CGT revolutionary syndicalists had rejected this reform (see Chapter II) because (1) they saw it as part of a government scheme to "domesticate" the unions, and (2) they feared that union property might be claimed by employers seeking compensation for losses of property during strikes.

11. APP, B/a 1609, note of August 7, 1894.

latter estimated at 100,000 francs—with profits from a printing plant to be set up on the premises and rent to be paid by a wine retailer, a clinic to treat workers, and CGT unions that would relocate to the Maison des Fédérations from the Paris Bourse du Travail.[12] It was a shoestring venture; none of the proposed sources of income was guaranteed, and in fact, all would fall short of expectations. So adamant was Griffuelhes that the CGT have an independent headquarters, after years of government meddling in the administration of the Paris Bourse du Travail and the disastrous interlude at 10, Cité Riverin, that he appears to have been given virtual carte blanche to handle the Maison des Fédérations project as he saw fit. From this point on, it became a one-man show.

Apparently, almost from the beginning Griffuelhes wanted to buy the property at 33, rue Grange-aux-Belles. He was afraid the owner, a widow Chatenet, might get skittish about having revolutionaries as tenants and break the lease, as the CGT's previous landlord had done; thus, on June 5, 1907, the property was purchased in the name of one Robert Louzon for 90,000 francs and turned over to the Société Victor Griffuelhes. At first, Griffuelhes refused to tell his CGT associates where the money had come from, in a useless attempt to protect the benefactor's identity.[13] But the police had the story in only a week.

Louzon, they discovered, was a "very intelligent, serious, proper young man" who had graduated from the prestigious Ecole des Mines and was currently employed at the Paris gas company as an engineer. Explaining why a young man of good family—Louzon's deceased father had been a lawyer at the Paris Court of Appeals—decided to assist the CGT in circumventing the law seems to have caused the police some concern. Even though police investigators learned that Louzon had been active in the Allemanist wing of French socialism since around 1900 and was involved in the Paris municipal employees' union, they concluded he had "thrown himself into the socialist and trade-union movements more out of snobbism than conviction." Snob or no, Louzon's gesture on behalf of the CGT was not appreciated, and sometime in the summer of 1907, he was fired from his job at the city gas works.[14]

12. APP, B/a 1602, notes of July 7, October 27, 1906; January 7, 1907.

13. *Ibid.,* note of December 24, 1908.

14. APP, B/a 1686, Robert Louzon dossier personnel, note of June 17, 1907; *DBMO,* XIII, 316 (Louzon); this entry mistakenly gives 1906 as the purchase date of the rue Granges-aux-Belles property and Louzon's subsequent victimization.

By mid 1907, the CGT finally had a home of its own; the Société Victor Griffuelhes, however, was deeply in debt. Besides having to pay interest on Louzon's loan, Griffuelhes required further outlays to renovate the old factory, build a meeting hall next door, and make payments on three printing presses and equipment for the workers' clinic. He later claimed he had tried to obtain money for purchasing and furnishing the property from the CGT federations but had been turned down. "Every time I asked the comrades for money, they complained they were broke and ended up saying 'Sorry, you'll have to look for it somewhere else.' " Presumably, they wanted an independent CGT headquarters but were not willing to pay for it. The penuriousness of French trade unions often exasperated Griffuelhes, but perhaps his project was too grand or risky in their eyes. Whatever the case, the comrades' lack of support clearly accounts for much of Griffuelhes' bitterness and sarcasm over the course of the Affair. In remarks made at a Batiment executive committee meeting in January, 1910, nearly a year after his resignation, he stated: "I had to knock on a lot of doors. I even had to take money from the CGT treasury; I don't deny it. For two years [*sic*], I carried on this juggling act. Finally, I went to see some bourgeois. I prefer certain bourgeois to certain workers."[15]

Embedded in this characteristically provocative account of how he kept the Société Victor Griffuelhes and the Maison des Fédérations afloat are two of the elements that caused the general secretary so much trouble during the Affair. First is his admission that he diverted CGT funds to pay the Société's bills—the first such avowal I have found in the record. This was what he refused to tell the incredulous Lévy in April, 1908, possibly out of pride or anger that his integrity was questioned, as Julliard contends. Griffuelhes was proud to a fault, there is no doubt, but it does not appear that the diverted money was misused, as Lévy and others later claimed. There were additional problems, however.

For one, Griffuelhes had become used to running the CGT as if it were his own business and had not bothered to ensure that accurate accounts of his transfers and expenses were kept. He was not directly involved in book-keeping in Lévy's absence but left it to an interim treasurer, a typographer named Tennevin who apparently had few qualifications for, and less interest in, the job.[16] He probably could not have provided a clear accounting of the money even if he had wanted to. And he had not wanted to because of the

---

15. Minutes of meeting of executive committee of the Building Trades Federation (Batiment), January 10, 1910, published in *Le Travailleur du Batiment,* no. 37, February 1, 1910.

16. Julliard, *Clemenceau briseur de grèves,* 135.

second element that would plague him—a crucial point overlooked by both Griffuelhes' contemporaries and subsequent historians: the necessity of maintaining the legal fiction of the distinction between the CGT and the Société Victor Griffuelhes. Griffuelhes was extremely sensitive to this point, but unfortunately in his arrogance and pride, he did not explain it clearly to the comrades.

Griffuelhes' statement in early 1910 raises a third and in some ways even more serious question about his handling of the Maison des Fédérations project. Needing money and turned down by the comrades, Griffuelhes says he "went to see some bourgeois." The problem was not that he had obtained bourgeois money for a workers' cause, although some colleagues, such as Raymond Péricat of Batiment, took exception to this.[17] The problem lay in the "certain bourgeois" he turned to.

In their dossier on Louzon, the police failed to establish—and it was a capital oversight—his connection to Griffuelhes. Pure chance had not brought Griffuelhes knocking on Louzon's door in search of a loan. Louzon was a member of the socialist-syndicalist crowd around *Le Mouvement socialiste* with whom Griffuelhes had been associated since at least 1904. Both men had been on the editorial board of the socialist-syndicalist review, *L'Avant-garde,* from April, 1905 to March, 1906. It can be assumed the two were fairly close because Griffuelhes was so incensed when he heard Louzon had been fired by the Paris gas company, he vowed he "would not rest" until the person he considered responsible for "denouncing" Louzon, Louis Lajarrige, the reformist secretary of the majority union at the gas works, had been "brought down."[18] As noted earlier, Griffuelhes' connections to the socialist-syndicalist circle were manifold and close, closer than he ever admitted, at least. One of the group's leading figures, and a future SFIO deputy, was Ernest Lafont, his lawyer. Another prominent member, André Morizet, journalist and a founder of *L'Avant-garde,* had been the only bourgeois present at the drafting of the Charter of Amiens, as if to give the circle's imprimatur to the document.

17. Péricat's response to Griffuelhes' remark was: "Since you like the bourgeoisie so much, you ought to go with them and stay there" (*Le Travailleur du Batiment,* no. 37, February 1, 1910). He opposed Griffuelhes during the Affair because of the latter's authoritarian style, declaring after Griffuelhes' lordly refusal to explain the whereabouts of the missing funds, "I want no gods in the CGT" (CGT, *Compte rendu de la conférence extraordinaire . . . 1–3 juin 1909* [Paris, 1909], 65).

18. *DBMO,* XIII, 316 (Lajarrige); other board members were Ernest Lafont, Hubert Lagardelle, and André Morizet of the socialist-syndicalist circle, and Georges Sorel's disciple, Edouard Berth (Brécy, *Mouvement syndical,* 140); APP, B/a 1602, report of December 26, 1908.

These ties, I believe, prolonged Griffuelhes' links to the Blanquist wing of French socialism and exposed him to attacks from CGT reformists at the congresses of Bourges and Amiens. They were also disquieting to radicals within the confederation, including erstwhile allies such as Georges Yvetot.[19] But the problem was not simply that Griffuelhes' political ties to the leftist socialist-syndicalist faction of the SFIO seemed to violate the spirit, if not the letter, of the Charter of Amiens. His increasingly obvious connections to the socialist-syndicalists seemed to reintroduce into the trade-union movement the kind of socialist factionalism that revolutionary syndicalism was supposed to banish.

That process had begun with certain CGT militants rallying to Gustave Hervé and the SFIO's insurrectionalist wing in 1905–1906, and Griffuelhes' ever closer ties to the socialist-syndicalists, who were rivals of the Hervéists for power on the SFIO Left, can be seen as a defensive reaction to that trend. Nevertheless, these contacts gave the appearance that Griffuelhes and key members of the Executive Committee such as Alphonse Merrheim were now running the CGT in tacit partnership with the socialist-syndicalists. Thus when the source of the 90,000-franc loan to the Société Victor Griffuelhes was revealed as Robert Louzon, more than one CGT militant might have concluded that the Maison des Fédérations was the instrument for a takeover of the CGT by "certain bourgeois." If police reports can be trusted, Griffuelhes did not help his cause by initially refusing to divulge where the money had come from, telling his colleagues instead: "If you want to know so badly, give me the money to pay them back and I'll tell you."[20]

The socialist-syndicalist connection is one of the murkier aspects of the Affair of the Maison des Fédérations and one largely disregarded by historians of the pre-1914 French labor movement. Nevertheless, it is a crucial element in the story because it explains better than any other factor—Briand's manipulation or Griffuelhes' nasty disposition, for example—the hostility to the general secretary from the CGT's radical Left during the Affair. His links to the socialist-syndicalists, viewed as a clique of Parisian bourgeois intellectuals and politicos, aroused strong resentment among younger militants, especially in the provinces. Marius Blanchard, the metalworkers' leader in the Meurthe-et-Moselle region, was representative of these militants who believed the CGT administrative bureau had become, in Albert Lévy's words, a camarilla more

19. See Yvetot's response to the "Enquete" on "La Crise syndicaliste [trade-union crisis]," *Le Mouvement socialiste*, no. 217 (January, 1910), 60–61.

20. APP, B/a 1602, note of December 24, 1908.

interested in playing politics and advancing its own interests than in leading the workers' struggle. Blanchard and his group also seem to have represented what one police spy called a "regionalist" or "localist" tendency within the CGT. They opposed the CGT leaders' push to create industrial unions, apparently fearing these national organizations would have more power in the trade-union movement than regional labor federations or local Bourses du Travail.[21]

In a very real sense, Griffuelhes was now being tarred with his own brush. Just as he and his young band of rebels from Lyon and the Cher had once pushed aside an older "Parisian" leadership whom they accused of senility and political opportunism, so now he himself had become the target of young radicals from the provinces. These militants did not need a Latapie or a Lévy—or a Gustave Hervé, although some at least were admirers of the "Sans-Patrie"—to lead them in opposing those they called the "pale faces" (*visages pales*), the CGT administrative bureau who had become indifferent to struggles in the provincial industrial centers. Blanchard and his faction blamed the CGT leadership for the failure earlier in 1908 of a bitter, four-month-long strike in the metallurgical industry at Monthermé in the Ardennes. Significantly, the CGT official who acted as liaison with the strikers was Théophile Sauvage of the molders' union, a close associate of Griffuelhes and a director of the Société Victor Griffuelhes.[22] Latapie's importance to the young militants, rather, lay in his ability to act as a bridge between them and the traditional reformist wing of the CGT, which had its own longstanding reasons for wanting Griffuelhes out. The hard core of leftist opposition to Griffuelhes came from the metalworkers' union; thus Latapie was well placed, as one of its secretaries, to bring this faction into a tactical alliance with the reformists, an alliance that would topple Griffuelhes and bring the CGT close to the brink of schism.

None of this explains the role played in the Affair by Albert Lévy. Although Lévy was an insider of the CGT administrative bureau and almost as much of a pale face as Griffuelhes himself, he attacked Griffuelhes' mismanagement of the CGT treasury, which provided a safe issue on which to challenge him. It was a virulent attack, as a police spy reported: "For several months, Lévy, who is crazy and who, moreover, has a very wicked tongue, has been spreading

21. André May, *Les Origines du syndicalisme révolutionnaire* (Paris, 1913), 120–28; Jennings, *Syndicalism in France*, Chapter 1; for Lévy's description, see APP, B/a 1603, note of January 6, 1909; APP, B/a 1602, note of "Brossier," September 10, 1908.
22. APP, B/a 1602, notes of December 14 and September 21, 1908.

about the worst kinds of accusations against Pouget and Griffuelhes, even while they were in Corbeil prison, accusing them of 'selling out' to the government. . . . He said, moreover, that Griffuelhes is a thief and that to purchase the building in the rue Grange-aux-Belles, he involved himself in dubious commercial operations from which he skimmed off scandalous profits."[23]

Such virulence seems to justify Dolléans' view that Lévy was motivated by hatred for Griffuelhes. A number of other explanations have been advanced for it as well. The police generally regarded Lévy as "crazy" and also suggested more than once that he was an alcoholic. Colleagues on the CGT administrative bureau commented on his excitability; Pierre Monatte, for example, called him "nervous as a cat."[24] Another aspect of the Lévy case, however, deserves some consideration.

Lévy was a Jew, an exceedingly rare commodity in the upper echelons of the CGT. He became active in the trade-union movement during the Dreyfus Affair, when he served as a liaison between the League of the Rights of Man and the Citizen and labor leaders sympathetic to the Dreyfusard cause. There is some evidence that by 1908, on the eve of his run-in with Griffuelhes over the CGT accounts, Lévy had begun to feel he was a victim of anti-Semitism. He described in a revealing piece in *Le Mouvement socialiste* how, during his 1907–1908 prison term, officials had responded grudgingly to his requests to see a rabbi; he also related how oppressive he had found the crucifixes that adorned the prison walls. The atmosphere around CGT headquarters must have been oppressive to him at times as well. First were Griffuelhes' little jokes about how, in his search for funds to launch the Maison des Fédérations, he had "even tried to tap the Rothschilds." Or Griffuelhes' threat, if Clemenceau got rough, to tell the world that the Tiger's newspaper, *L'Aurore,* was financed by "Jewish money" during the Dreyfus Affair.[25]

This was low-grade stuff, however, compared to views expressed by some of Lévy's other colleagues. Clément Beausoleil, a fellow militant of the retail clerks' union and one of the defendants in the celebrated trial of the Twelve in February, 1908, for example, was an anti-Semite of long standing. During

23. APP, B/a 1603, note of January 15, 1909.

24. See, for example, APP, B/a 1601, report of August 19, 1907; Monatte, *Trois Scissions syndicales,* 131.

25. APP, B/a 1601, report of August 19, 1907; Albert Lévy, "Syndicalisme et Anticléricalisme," *Le Mouvement socialiste,* nos. 189–90 (August 15–September 15, 1907), 166–69; APP, B/a 1601, notes of April 30, 1906, April 27, 1907.

the Boulanger Affair of the 1880s, Beausoleil, although a fervent republican, had "attacked the Jewish element, whose monopoly of capital, he said, was impeding reforms [and had] called for laws of exception against Jews." Paul Delesalle, a colleague of Lévy's on the administrative bureau and one of the CGT's leading figures, was fired by the anarchist newspaper *Les Temps Nouveaux* in May, 1906, for writing a scurrilous anti-Semitic article. Finally, there was the case of Robert Louzon, the benefactor of the Maison des Fédérations himself. In July, 1906, *Le Mouvement socialiste* published an article by Louzon whose thesis is evident from its title: "The Bankruptcy of Dreyfusism or the Triumph of the Jewish Lobby."[26] It seems logical to ask if knowledge that Louzon was funding the Société Victor Griffuelhes added to the fury of Lévy's attack on Griffuelhes.

That anti-Semitism was more than a peripheral factor in the duel between Lévy and Griffuelhes and his camarilla is convincingly borne out in an exchange that occurred during the January 20, 1909, session of the CGT Executive Committee; Lévy was then seeking reelection as CGT treasurer against Griffuelhes' candidate, Théophile Sauvage. "Brossier," the most reliable of the Préfecture de Police's labor spies, reported: "I want to draw attention to an intervention by Monatte, who reproached Lévy for being 'l'homme des juifs' ["the man of the Jews"]." As noted earlier, Monatte had commented on Lévy's nervousness; perhaps he was aware of the origins of this disorder.[27]

Organized opposition to Griffuelhes and his allies within and outside the CGT first appeared at the CGT Congress of Marseille in October, 1908. Reformist criticism was somewhat muted at the congress due to an unspoken

26. APP, B/a 956, Clément Henri Beausoleil dossier personnel, note of October 30, 1888; Maitron, *Paul Delesalle*, 125–27; Robert Louzon, "La Faillite du Dreyfusisme ou le Triomphe du parti juif," *Le Mouvement socialiste*, no. 176 (July, 1906), 193–99.

27. APP, B/a 1603, note of January 20, 1909. On the question of anti-Semitism among revolutionary syndicalists, see Edmund Silberner, "Anti-Jewish Trends in French Revolutionary Syndicalism," *Jewish Social Studies*, XV (July–October 1953), 195–202, and also Paul Mazgaj, *The Action Française and Revolutionary Syndicalism* (Chapel Hill, 1979), 128–49. To my knowledge, no one has yet probed attitudes toward Jews among the CGT leadership, as opposed to those of marginal figures such as Emile Pataud, Emile Janvion, and Francis Delaisi. A more positive account of the Jewish experience in pre-1914 French trade unionism is Nancy L. Green's "The Contradictions of Acculturation: Immigrant Oratories and Yiddish Union Sections in Paris Before World War I," in *The Jews in Modern France*, eds. Frances Malino and Bernard Wasserstein (London, 1985), 54–77.

agreement "to refrain from attacking the men who were still behind bars" and the tendency of Griffuelhes' partisans "to treat critics of the administrative bureau as accomplices of the government." This left the field to the radical dissidents from the provinces. Their targets were the socialist-syndicalists and those members of the CGT leadership who were not in prison, principally Merrheim. Although he was not a union member, Ernest Lafont had rather unwisely wangled a union mandate allowing him to sit with the delegates; he was "unmasked" by the radicals and obliged to retire to the press gallery.[28]

The dissidents' main target, however, was what they saw as the fading revolutionary esprit of the CGT leaders. Apparently inspired by the *Guerre sociale* faction, they pushed for a motion declaring that workers should make an insurrection in case of war. This thrust forced Merrheim and the administrative bureau to draft a resolution on antimilitarism that reflected the workers' widespread dislike for the army as strikebreaker but went further in the direction of insurrectionary politics than the leaders wanted, considering how divisive the issue was. Merrheim's resolution on antimilitarism, which would remain the CGT's official position until the outbreak of war in 1914, ended as follows: "The Congress recalls the formula of the [First] International: The workers have no fatherland! . . . The Congress declares that it is necessary, from the international point of view, to educate the workers so that, in case of war between the Powers, the workers will respond to a declaration of war with a declaration of the revolutionary general strike." The motion passed by a vote of 681 to 421, with forty-three abstentions. As F. F. Ridley has observed, however, the resolution committed the CGT "to no more than propaganda" and to a revolutionary general strike only if antiwar agitation became "international."[29]

Nevertheless, Merrheim was furious at the tenor of the Marseille congress; it gave the impression of a CGT out of control, one that could only hearten the reformists. A year later, he stated, "One had to live through, as I did, the days of this Congress, to appreciate how it encouraged our adversaries to think they could now take charge of the confederation." Frustrated at Marseille by the moratorium on direct criticism of the imprisoned CGT leaders and by yet another rejection of their cherished goal of proportional representation— by a vote of 741 to 383—the reformists could nevertheless look to the future with confidence, Merrheim declared. "Full of this assurance, aided by certain

---

28. Julliard, *Clemenceau briseur de grèves*, 125; APP, B/a 1602, note of October 10, 1908.

29. CGT, *XVIᵉ Congrès national corporatif . . . Marseille*, 213, 215; F. F. Ridley, *Revolutionary Syndicalism: The Direct Action of Its Time* (Cambridge, Engl., 1970), 138.

so-called revolutionary militants, who acted only out of *personal hatred* for Griffuelhes, it was through the 'Affair of the Maison des Fédérations' that they would try to take their revenge for Marseille." [30]

Opposition to Griffuelhes began to mount in December, following the first session of the CGT Executive Committee after the leaders' release from prison. At the meeting, Griffuelhes threw down the gauntlet, declaring: "While I was in prison, I was accused of being a thief. Now, our job is to find out if there is a thief and, if so, throw him out. If on the other hand, it turns out that we have a false accuser, I demand that we throw him out." With Griffuelhes' declaration of "Lévy or me," wrote Merrheim, "the whole physiognomy of the executive committee changed. Guérard and many others [in the reformist camp] who had not set foot in the committee *since the Congress of Bourges* [1904], now reappeared. They came back, not to discuss the interests of the proletariat, or workers' action, but because the 'Affair of the Maison des Fédérations' was in the air." [31]

In a report from early December, 1908, "Brossier" dilated on the dim prospects of Griffuelhes and the CGT leadership as they looked to the New Year. The reformists, with fresh wind in their sails because of Lévy's charges, now had support from within the revolutionary syndicalist camp as well. The latter's concern was the leadership's "collaboration with bourgeois elements, such as Lafont, the lawyer, or the engineer [Francis] Delaisi, etc. . . . The real pivot of this movement is Latapie, now in accord with the reformists." This report, the first by police spies in which Delaisi's name appears, indicates that the leftist dissidents, led by militant metalworkers from eastern France like Blanchard, were gunning for Delaisi's friend Merrheim as much as Griffuelhes. The two were collaborating at this time on studies of the structure and political economy of the French metalworking industry, resulting in their first joint articles. Blanchard and his cohorts apparently believed that such a collaboration was carried on at the expense of trade-union activities. [32]

The struggle came to a head in January, 1909, at a series of CGT Executive

---

30. Merrheim, response to the "Enquete" on the trade-union crisis in *Le Mouvement socialiste*, no. 216 (November–December, 1909), 295; CGT, *XVIᵉ Congrès national corporatif . . . Marseille*, 175; Merrheim, response to the "Enquete," 295. Merrheim's emphasis.

31. Griffuelhes quoted in Dolléans, *Histoire du mouvement ouvrier*, II, 154; Merrheim, response to the "Enquete," 295. Merrheim's emphasis.

32. APP, B/a 1602, note of December 11, 1908; for the Merrheim-Delaisi articles, see "L'Organisation patronale en France," "La Métallurgie," and "La Comité des Forges," in *Le Mouvement socialiste*, nos. 200–205 (July–December 15, 1908).

Committee meetings devoted almost exclusively to the Affair of the Maison des Fédérations. On January 5, Griffuelhes declared once again that the committee had to choose between him and Lévy. "He said that since Lévy had spread rumors, notably about the disappearance of certain sums, the other members of the secretariat [administrative bureau] were no longer willing to work alongside him [Lévy]." On January 19, the Executive Committee met to elect the CGT treasurer. "Brossier" reported that the meeting was "very stormy, like the preceding meetings [of the Executive Committee]." According to "Brossier's" colleague, agent "Roy," this was an understatement. "The conflict has reached an explosive stage," "Roy" reported; "all the gloves are off now." Blanchard, "inspired by Latapie," repeated his charge of collusion with "bourgeois elements," whereupon Garnery, Griffuelhes' closest friend on the Executive Committee, accused Latapie of "living off the prostitution of his mistress." Latapie replied by calling Griffuelhes a "bogus revolutionary," charging that the only "dangerous strike" he had ever participated in was the textile workers' strike at Armentières in 1903.[33] In the midst of this unedifying hullabaloo, which, as we have seen, also featured Pierre Monatte's anti-Semitic slur on Lévy, the committee somehow held elections for treasurer. Lévy defeated Théophile Sauvage, Griffuelhes' candidate, fifty-six to fifty, with thirty-three abstentions, but considering his position untenable, he then resigned.

This was not a victory for Griffuelhes. Lévy's reelection, though by a narrow margin, clearly demonstrated that Griffuelhes' old mastery of the CGT Executive Committee was at an end. That point was further underscored by the large number of abstentions; in all, only fifty committee members had chosen to stand with the general secretary in his "him or me" challenge. Commented "Brossier": "Morally [Griffuelhes' camarilla] is beaten, and many who believe in Griffuelhes' sincerity are now asking themselves if he will resign, since it was he who posed the question of confidence."[34] But Griffuelhes himself best described his situation following the January 19 confrontation. His opponents, in planting doubts and raising "delicate questions," had succeeded in creating the atmosphere that forced him "to clear out."[35]

The moral authority he considered so vital to leadership now compromised, Griffuelhes announced his resignation as CGT general secretary on February

---

33. APP, B/a 1602, notes of January 27 ["Brossier"], January 20, 1909 ["Roy"].
34. *Ibid.*, note of January 20, 1909 ["Brossier"].
35. Griffuelhes quoted in CGT, *XVII*ᵉ *Congrès national corporatif . . . Toulouse*, 132.

2, 1909.[36] Some believed that even if he stepped aside now, it was not the end, that he would be back when the furor had died down and it became evident how much he was needed. It *was* the end, however; after seven years and four months, his tenure as general secretary of the CGT, "to which I was so fiercely attached," was over. Griffuelhes would never again serve officially in the administration of the CGT.

I have suggested earlier that the standard version of Griffuelhes' fall from power requires revision. Rather than viewing Griffuelhes exclusively as a victim of Aristide Briand's intrigues, carried out by Briand's friend Jean Latapie and by Albert Lévy, it is possible to see his fall at least partly as a self-inflicted wound. Had he attempted to explain to Lévy why the CGT's books were in disarray, rather than demanding his confidence without explanation, the Affair of the Maison des Fédérations might never have developed. Had he attempted diplomacy, perhaps conceding that bookkeeping was not his strong suit rather than making the dispute with Lévy a matter of "me or him," he might have won more support from the CGT federations. But Dolléans, Julliard, and others may be correct. Perhaps Griffuelhes' nature was not to bend or make concessions; for those who believe that power stems from moral authority, to admit error or negligence is to weaken that authority.

I have also suggested, however, that the Affair was not essentially a conflict over Griffuelhes' honesty or shoddy bookkeeping. More serious, longer-term issues were at stake. For some—Guérard, Renard, and perhaps even Latapie—the struggle was a continuation of the battle for CGT leadership and control over its guiding philosophy, which began in 1899–1901 with the displacement of the reformist old guard by Griffuelhes and his Young Turks. The former had never accepted their loss of control to those they called the "anarchists," and the Affair presented an opening to attack Griffuelhes and the CGT revolutionary syndicalist leadership on "moral" grounds. This battle did not end with Griffuelhes' departure but continued into the prewar years, as a key element in the trade-union crisis of 1909–1914. It resurfaced in the wartime and postwar struggles between CGT majority and minority factions and reached a first climax in the schism of 1921–1922. No doubt it still continues.

Also at stake in the Affair was the related issue of the CGT's relationship to the socialist party, an issue not resolved by the neutrality proclaimed in the

36. Dolléans, *Histoire du mouvement ouvrier*, II, 151.

Charter of Amiens. That this issue emerged during the Affair in a way so damaging to Griffuelhes was partly his own fault. By casting his lot with the socialist-syndicalists—Lagardelle, Lafont, Morizet, and company—he was, I believe, pursuing his dream of a *parti du travail*, with the CGT serving as a catalyst in forming a genuine workers' party that employed direct action as opposed to parliamentary action to achieve a classless society. The socialist-syndicalists seemed to share that vision. By allying himself with this faction, however, Griffuelhes opened himself to serious attack. At a lower level of conflict, he exposed himself to charges of dallying with a coterie of Paris intellectuals, bourgeois, and *non-manuels,* thus violating a major tenet of the working-class code of behavior in the heroic age of French trade unionism—and one to which he had once so fiercely subscribed. At a higher level, his ties to the socialist-syndicalists, who after all constituted a left-wing faction of the SFIO, reintroduced socialist sectarianism into trade-union ranks, just as Griffuelhes' reformist enemies had done in 1899–1901 by espousing Millerandism. Georges Sorel claimed that suspicion of the motives of Griffuelhes' socialist-syndicalist friends had finally alienated him from the syndicalist movement. In a letter to Agostino Lanzillo, the Italian revolutionary syndicalist militant, Sorel wrote: "You ask why Berth and I left *Le Mouvement socialiste;* it was because of the politicians who had put themselves at the head of it in order to feather their nests within the socialist party."[37]

To sum up, Griffuelhes in 1908–1909, in the eyes of some militants, appeared to be a "Parisian," an elitist, a self-serving "labor statesman," a centralizer, a would-be "dictator"—characteristics that betrayed the spirit of revolutionary syndicalism. Whether he was all or any of those is beside the point. What matters is that he had allowed himself to *appear* to be. His "mistakes" were highlighted in a fundamental way by two of the speakers, one an opponent and the other a partisan, who joined the debate at the CGT Congress of Toulouse in 1910 that officially cleared Griffuelhes of wrongdoing in the Affair.

Jules Le Guéry, a diamond cutter, anarchist, and strong antimilitarist who opposed Griffuelhes during this time, told the delegates: "We cannot tolerate men setting themselves above organizations. We do not believe that trade-union organizations should have masters. . . . To the contrary it is [the orga-

---

37. Sorel to Agostino Lanzillo, March 28, 1910, in Francesco Germinario, "Due Lettere autobiografiche di Giorgio Sorel ad Agostino Lanzillo," *Studi Piacentini,* no. 15 (1994), 178–79.

nizations] which should set the pace and tell the leaders what direction to march in. . . . [Griffuelhes'] greatest fault was that he wanted to act alone."[38]

The second speaker was Georges Yvetot, general secretary of the CGT's Bourse du Travail Section and a one-time adversary of Griffuelhes who rallied to the general secretary in the final stages of the Affair. In his response to the "Enquete" of *Le Mouvement socialiste* in January, 1910, eight months before the Toulouse Congress, Yvetot had declared that had he and Griffuelhes not been in Corbeil Prison together at the time of the Marseille congress in 1908, "We would have gone there as adversaries. I had a number of complaints to make. There were certain facts, certain statements of the CGT general secretary, about which I wanted explanations. They concerned tactics, his conduct in certain phases of the struggle, not what he had done, with so much courage and perseverance, to give the CGT a home." Griffuelhes' biggest error, in Yvetot's opinion, was falling under the spell of "certain intellectuals [the socialist-syndicalists] who assiduously paid him court and made him believe that syndicalism began with his arrival on the scene. They spoiled him."[39]

At Toulouse, the painfully honest Yvetot rose to say: "I was an adversary of Griffuelhes, one of those who were against him [but] I admire Griffuelhes for having done what he ought never be reproached for. . . . For if you repudiate Griffuelhes, you repudiate all the comrades who have tried to build something."[40] For Yvetot, Griffuelhes' greatest legacy was the Maison des Fédérations.

Elections to replace Griffuelhes as CGT general secretary were held on February 24, 1909. In the meantime, his partisans tried to convince Griffuelhes to stand for reelection. The leatherworkers' union announced it retained full confidence in Griffuelhes and would "present him to the affiliated federations as a candidate for general secretary." If Griffuelhes was reconsidering his resignation, the leatherworkers' announcement could have been a trial balloon to find out if he could win support, but this seems unlikely. Georges Yvetot, who was in a position to know, stated that "if he had accepted, he would have been elected, [but] he did not accept." On February 24, when the Executive Committee met to choose a general secretary, Griffuelhes reaffirmed his decision to stand down.[41]

38. CGT, *XVIIe Congrès national corporatif. . . Toulouse*, 119.
39. Yvetot response to the "Enquete," 60.
40. CGT, *XVIIe Congrès national corporatif. . . Toulouse*, 104.
41. *L'Humanité*, February 19, 1909; Yvetot response to the "Enquete," 60; Brécy, *Mouvement*

In the weeks before the election, both sides—the reformist-revolutionary alliance and the pale faces—searched feverishly for candidates who could win broad support among the federations. Their selections clearly demonstrate the CGT's great disarray at this time. Griffuelhes' partisans finally agreed on Jean Nicolet, a Batiment radical of the Péricat stamp. This was not a fortunate choice; Nicolet had just retired from Batiment's executive committee, declaring "What I had, I gave; now, it's all used up." The alliance's candidate also proved unfortunate—a reluctant Louis Niel, secretary of the Montpellier Bourse du Travail and one of the architects of the CGT–Bourses du Travail merger in 1902. Once a well-known anarchist, Niel had lately gravitated to the SFIO. At the time of his selection to replace Griffuelhes, he was considering a run for a recently vacated Chamber seat in his native Hérault; he did stand for it in the spring of 1910, but lost.[42]

The election of February 24 took place in two rounds. In the first, Griffuelhes' name was entered as a candidate despite his refusal to run. The totals were Niel, 27 votes, Nicolet, 12, and Griffuelhes, 19. As might be expected, competition for votes was fierce between the two rounds. The Niel camp appears to have been especially assiduous, since the combined first round totals of Nicolet and Griffuelhes promised a victory for Nicolet on the second. On the second round, however, Niel won by the narrowest of margins, 28 votes to 27, with two abstentions and one vote for Griffuelhes.[43] The Nicolet camp immediately cried foul. Three federations changed their votes between rounds: the foodworkers' union switched from Griffuelhes to Niel, and the stokers' and typographers' unions, which backed Nicolet the first round, abstained on the second. The abstaining unions, which had the reputation of being revolutionary, "have some explaining to do," growled Benoit Broutchoux from his bailiwick in the Pas-de-Calais. But Broutchoux and others also noted Emile Dumas' persistence in voting for Griffuelhes on the second round, when the latter had clearly thrown his votes to Nicolet. The behavior of the bucherons' delegate has never been explained, but Griffuelhes enjoyed great

---

syndical, 130. Dolléans is mistaken in writing that the election occurred on March 2, 1909, (*Histoire du mouvement ouvrier,* II, 157, n. 2).

42. See Nicolet's articles in *VdP,* nos. 334 and 336, January 31–February 7 and February 28–March 7, 1909; APP, B/a 1652, Louis Niel dossier personnel, notes of February 21, 1909, May 8, 1910.

43. André Thuillier, "Quel est l'élu?" *La Révolution,* February 26, 1909. *La Révolution* was the revolutionary syndicalist daily founded by Emile Pouget on February 1, 1909; a complete breakdown of the second round voting appeared in the February 25 issue.

popularity among the timber workers and had long been friends with Dumas.[44]

The narrowness of his victory and its contested circumstances did not bode well for Louis Niel's tenure as CGT general secretary. The opposition believed the election was bought and portrayed him as a tool of the government; it quickly set out to bring him down. A police report claiming federations that had supported Griffuelhes or Nicolet were contemplating schism "to protest against an election they consider fatal to the CGT" seems exaggerated, but it does indicate the deep divisions within the confederation after the election. Survivors on the CGT administrative bureau from the Griffuelhes regime, such as Georges Yvetot, refused to work with Niel, while key figures on the CGT Executive Committee, such as Alphonse Merrheim, were openly contemptuous of him.[45] And Pouget's newspaper, *La Révolution,* kept up a steady drumfire of criticism about his administration.

Niel was in some ways his own worst enemy. Even before his election, stories began circulating, apparently with Griffuelhes' help, that Niel was in the pay of local authorities in the Hérault. This charge became a steady whispering campaign against the new general secretary. The accusation of corruption, which Griffuelhes apparently picked up from a disgruntled trade-unionist in Niel's native Montpellier, appears to have been true. Records in the Archives Nationales and the Archives Départmentales of the Hérault trace a relationship between Niel and the local chief superintendent of the Sureté going back to 1898.[46] The crucial report, however, is one from the chief superintendent dated March 23, 1905: "The secretary [of the Montpellier Bourse du Travail], M. Niel, appears to have considerably mended his ways, and I don't think, after the measure of benevolence bestowed upon him, at my

44. Thuillier, "Quel est l'élu?"; Benoit Broutchoux, "La CGT aux pieds de Viviani [minister of labor]," Pt. 2, *L'Action syndicale,* March 14, 1909; A. Mathieu [Batiment] charged that Dumas' vote for Griffuelhes cost Nicolet the election ("Lequel doit siéger?" *La Révolution,* February 27, 1909). In 1910, Griffuelhes replaced Dumas as the bucherons' delegate to the CGT Executive Committee (Jules Bornet, "Le 8ᵉ Congrès de la Fédération des Bucherons," *Le Mouvement socialiste,* no. 224 [October, 1910], 235).

45. APP, B/a 1652, Niel dossier personnel, notes of February 27, April 9, 1909; Merrheim, response to "Enquete," 296.

46. APP, B/a 1652, Niel dossier personnel, notes of February 18, April 17, 1909; *La Révolution* quotes a M. Arnal, who claimed that Niel had worked hand-in-glove with local government to domesticate the Montpellier trade unions ("Croque-syndicats: Comment Niel fit 'évoluer' la Bourse du Travail de Montpellier," February 26, 1909); AN, F7 13.603, report of Chief Superintendent Louis Eyméry of the Sureté in Montpellier to minister of interior, April 26, 1906.

suggestion, he will again try to stir up trouble in the arrondissement of Montpellier the way he did in February and March 1904." [47]

Niel's fall was only a matter of time. The occasion was a May, 1909, strike of postal workers, their fourth major walkout in three years and the second in three months. Postal workers, like other State employees, it will be recalled, were legally barred from forming unions or going on strike. In mid May, the strikers asked for CGT support in the form of a one-day general strike. Niel, however, speaking to a miners' congress in Lens (Pas-de-Calais), said the CGT was too weak to undertake such a commitment. "On the eve of the battle, at the head of the troops, you don't say 'I'm not ready,' " snorted Georges Yvetot. No doubt Niel was right. In its current state of malaise, the CGT probably was too weak to carry out a general strike, even for twenty-four hours. But the speech appears to have had a negative effect on the postal workers' strike, which ended in defeat and the firing of eight hundred postal employees. Much of the blame for this was directed at Niel. After rough handling at two Executive Committee sessions,[48] the general secretary resigned on May 26.

Such was the state of affairs within the CGT that Niel was not replaced until July 12, 1909. A major reason for the delay was that, understandably, it proved difficult to find anyone willing to stand for the post. "Things have reached such a point," reported a police spy, "that Luquet wrote last night to Griffuelhes . . . to convince him to attempt a comeback, or to get his friends to support him [Luquet]." Griffuelhes, however, was not interested in a comeback. Henri Dret, his friend on the leatherworkers' executive board, announced that, contrary to rumor, their federation would not promote Griffuelhes for general secretary. Instead, Griffuelhes had agreed to make a six weeks' propaganda tour on behalf of the federation. "Griffuelhes accepted this assignment quite simply because he needs the money," Dret said. "He claims to be broke and must either resume his old vocation of roving strike consultant [*gréviculteur*] or go back to making shoes." [49]

Following his resignation as general secretary, Griffuelhes faced the

47. AD Hérault, 194 M 23, report of Chief Superintendent Eyméry to the prefect of the Hérault Department, March 23, 1905. I wish to thank Professor J. Harvey Smith of the History Department of the University of Northern Illinois for sharing this information with me.

48. Ridley gives a concise account of the May, 1909, postal workers' strike and Niel's role in it in his *Revolutionary Syndicalism*, 118; CGT, *XVIIe Congrès national corporatif . . . Toulouse*, 234; Dolléans, *Histoire du mouvement ouvrier*, II, 163. AN, F7 13.570, "Dossier essai de la grève générale–1909," note of May 18, 1909, portrays an atmosphere of chaos among the CGT leadership.

49. APP, B/a 1603, notes of June 23 and June 14, 1909.

question that would pursue him for the rest of his life: how to make a living. Contrary to stories circulated by his enemies about the money he had taken from Maison des Fédérations funds, Griffuelhes was broke when he stepped down as CGT general secretary in February, 1909. A police spy in August, 1909, affirmed that "from the pecuniary standpoint, right now Griffuelhes is completely 'busted.'" But this same spy reported in February, 1910, that he was "suspected of skimming off 27,000 francs from the Maison des Fédérations." [50]

The long *voyage de propagande* for the FNCP helped considerably. It paid expenses, with a bit left over to support his wife, but even better, it got Griffuelhes out of Paris for six weeks, away from the capital's stifling atmosphere and intrigues. His travels from one end of the country to the other helped to reestablish contacts with provincial militants that he had somewhat neglected in recent years. And they provided the material for his book, *Voyage révolutionnaire,* published the following year. It is a somber book, punctuated only occasionally by notes of celebration, as for example, in recounting his reunion with militants in his beloved Cher. The overwhelming impression is of a profound malaise: The trade union movement had lost momentum; the national fabric he had tried to stitch together had not taken hold; unions struggled on, isolated from one another and preoccupied with purely local matters. Worst of all in his eyes, with few exceptions once proud and independent union movements had again fallen under the sway of the politicos. "The incompatibility that exists between trade-union and political activity was etched more sharply, more clearly, for me than ever before," he wrote. "Wherever electoral activity is strong, the trade-union movement is weak. . . . Issoudun, Montluçon, Limoges, Bordeaux, preoccupied as they are with politics, have [trade-union] organizations that are weak, diminished in size, powerless to create a social movement that is sustained and combative." [51]

But whatever good the "voyage révolutionnaire" may have done for Griffuelhes' spirits, it did not resolve his financial problems. Thus in August, 1909, Georges Sorel undertook to find a job for him in journalism. Sorel thought of himself as the guardian angel of destitute syndicalists—it was he who had

---

50. APP, B/a 1603, notes of August 25, 1909, February 1, 1910.

51. The Sureté's chief superintendent in Biarritz, who listened in on one of Griffuelhes' speeches during his tour, concluded that the trip's purpose was "to obtain an anarchist majority at the next [CGT] executive committee" meeting, a reference perhaps to the upcoming CGT elections for general secretary (AN, F7 13.697, note of July 6, 1909); Griffuelhes, *Voyage révolutionnaire,* 33–34, 59.

found the dying Pelloutier a sinecure in Millerand's Office du Travail in 1900. Now, acting through his friend Paul Delesalle, Sorel proposed to help out Griffuelhes; whether his offer of a post as a contributor to the republican-socialist daily, *La Petite République,* ever reached Griffuelhes is not known. The offer makes clear, however, how out of touch Sorel was with the trade-union milieu. *La Petite République* had long been considered hostile to organized labor; from 1906 until its demise at the outset of World War I, the newspaper was the mouthpiece of Aristide Briand, who had, of course, helped engineer Griffuelhes' ouster from the CGT leadership. Writing for *La Petite République* would have been the kiss of death to any possible plans Griffuelhes had for a further career in the CGT.[52]

Griffuelhes' financial horizon began to clear in September, 1909, when he was reelected secretary of the leatherworkers' federation at a salary of 250 francs a month.[53] He would hold this office for two years, by which time he had launched the revolutionary syndicalist daily, *La Bataille syndicaliste (B.S.).* Preoccupied with the stormy politics and incessant financial woes of the newspaper, he retired from the FNCP leadership in 1911, never to return.

The traumatic events of 1908–1909 that led to Griffuelhes' departure from the CGT leadership produced a qualitative change in his life and career. Although he was involved with the CGT through his membership of the Executive Committee as the timber and leather workers' delegate and, especially, through his close relationship with the new general secretary, Léon Jouhaux, Griffuelhes was increasingly devoted to journalism and to the role he sought to create for himself as an "elder statesman of labor" and adviser to the next generation of militants.

As Georges, Tintant, and Renauld remark in their biography of Léon Jouhaux, Griffuelhes' departure and his replacement by Jouhaux were "a turning of the page" in the history of the prewar CGT. The generation that came to power with Griffuelhes in 1901 now began to drift from the scene. Yvetot remained as general secretary of the CGT Bourses du Travail Section, but his longtime assistant, Paul Delesalle, had already left in the spring of 1908, to

---

52. Brecy, *Mouvement syndical,* 52 n. 1; Sorel's offer is in a letter to Delesalle of August 31, 1909, in Sorel, *Lettres à Paul Delesalle (1914–1921)* (Paris, 1947), 15; the title of this collection is misleading, since it contains four letters from before 1914, including the one cited here. The evolution of *La Petite République* is traced in Bellanger, ed., *Histoire générale de la presse française,* III, 373–74.

53. Fédération Nationale des Cuirs et Peaux, *Compte rendu du 6ᵉ Congrès national tenu à Fougères . . . septembre 1909* (Paris, 1909), 17; Griffuelhes' longtime associate, Henri Dret, was elected as his assistant.

become a publisher of labor pamphlets and a bibliographer of Sorel.[54] Emile Pouget left in February, 1909, to launch his ephemeral revolutionary syndicalist daily, *La Révolution,* precursor of Griffuelhes' own, somewhat hardier *Bataille syndicaliste.* He published the paper only from February 1 to March 28, 1909; apparently underfinanced, it also faced stiff competition from the popular *Guerre sociale* and *L'Humanité.* Its early demise and the difficulties later faced by *Bataille syndicaliste* raise doubts about whether, as Pouget and Griffuelhes believed, a market niche really existed in France for a revolutionary syndicalist daily newspaper. After it folded, Pouget devoted himself to buying and selling "collectibles." Because he had been close to some members of the Impressionist school of French painting in his younger days, Pouget had acquired a reputation as an art expert and received a few Pissarros and Manets as gifts.[55]

Griffuelhes' friend Auguste Garnery, "Garno" of the jewelry workers, now retired to the small farm at Saclas (Seine-et-Oise) where Griffuelhes would spend his last days. Griffuelhes' reformist adversaries began to depart as well. Pierre Coupat of the machinists was driven from his union's leadership by a radical upsurge in 1908; he ended his career as an undersecretary of state for technical training in the conservative Bloc National government of 1920, appointed by Alexandre Millerand. Eugène Guérard, head of the railway workers' union since 1893, also was swept out by radicals, on the eve of the great railway strike of 1910. Louis Niel, after being pushed out at the CGT, received a post as a regional rail union chief from Guérard, only to lose it when his benefactor was driven from office. From then until the war, he worked for the government as an inspector, ensuring that provincial theaters and music halls paid royalties to playwrights and tunesmiths.[56] Of the great reformist spokesmen, only Auguste Keufer, the seemingly irreplaceable boss of Livre, continued to play a role in the CGT.

Finally, the two men alleged to have been instrumental in Griffuelhes' fall, Albert Lévy and Jean Latapie, also left the CGT. Lévy departed in June, 1909, and settled in Rouen where he worked for a time as an accountant. Later he

---

54. Bernard Georges *et al., Léon Jouhaux, Cinquante ans du syndicalisme: Des Origines à 1921* (Paris, 1962), I, 98. Maitron, *Paul Delesalle,* 128–29, 150; Delesalle's "Bibliographie sorélienne" was published in the *International Review of Social History* in 1939.

55. Goustine, *Pouget: Les Matins noirs,* 272.

56. *DBMO,* XII, 249 (Garnery); XI, 272 (Coupat); XII, 342–43 (Guérard); XIV, 181–82 (Niel), and APP, B/a 1652, Niel dossier personnel, note of October 22, 1911.

managed a cabaret, then during the war, he manufactured sheets for the army. Latapie, after removal from his post as a secretary of the metalworkers' federation in 1909, entered private business as a salesman for a phonograph record company.[57]

57. *DBMO*, XIII, 387 (Lévy); police records in 1912 give evidence of Lévy's rather sad efforts to reenter the trade-union movement (APP, B/a 1604, notes of May 12 and January 18, 1912). The notice on Latapie in *DBMO* (XIII, 207) unfortunately ends his career with the Affair of the Maison des Fédérations in early 1909, but see APP, B/a 1603, note of June 24, 1909, for the additional information.

IX

Malaise (1909–1914)

If we are to face up to the challenges of the future, which are becoming more formidable, we must enlarge our vision of the field of battle. . . . We can do this only if we face up to the tasks that will raise our consciousness, and not cheapen them by disputes that are alien to the creed we have freely embraced as militants and propagandists.

—Victor Griffuelhes, *La Bataille syndicaliste*, 1913

Victor Griffuelhes' life and career changed markedly following his resignation as general secretary of the CGT. Although in the early stages of what he called his "semiretirement" he continued to play a role in CGT decision making, largely through his influence over the new general secretary, Léon Jouhaux, that role would soon diminish.[1] By 1912 or 1913, according to some observers, he was replaced as Jouhaux's éminence grise by Alphonse Merrheim; with the advent of war in 1914, Jouhaux became his own man. As his influence within the CGT bureaucracy waned, Griffuelhes sought to confront through journalism the two great issues that dominated French trade-union life immediately before the war: the "malaise" that gripped the CGT, manifested in sometimes vicious factionalism, sagging morale, declining membership, and failed strikes; and the coming of war with Germany, which forced the CGT finally to face the implications of its longstanding pledge to meet a declaration of war with a general strike.

1. Griffuelhes, "Où va-t-on?" *La Bataille syndicaliste* (*B.S.*), January 23, 1913.

Following Louis Niel's resignation as CGT general secretary on May 26, 1909, almost two months elapsed before a successor was found. The new candidate had both to enjoy the confidence of revolutionaries and to not alienate reformists, who had lately organized a Committee for Trade-Union Unity (Comité d'Union syndicaliste), led by Eugène Guérard; its aim was to rid the CGT of "anarchist syndicalism." The dilemma was eventually resolved by putting forward a "new man," a militant with revolutionary credentials but untainted by the Maison des Fédérations Affair. This providential man was Léon Jouhaux, delegate to the CGT Executive Committee from the small union of State matchworks employees. Jouhaux had been drawn to anarchism as a young man, but after a short jail term for rioting in 1901, he had not been demonstrably active in libertarian circles. At the time of his candidacy, he was serving as interim treasurer of the CGT.[2]

When Jouhaux's name was finally proposed at the end of June, 1909, he was widely regarded as a passing phenomenon, "a last-minute candidate," in the words of one police spy. "He has been put forward by Luquet and the principal members of the [Griffuelhes] faction of the CGT to serve as a stopgap secretary," the spy reported. Agent "Brossier" agreed that Jouhaux was not likely to become a permanent fixture. "Jouhaux is a swaggerer, entirely out of his depth," he snorted—not much of an advance billing for the man who would lead the CGT for the next forty years.[3]

"Brossier" was right, however, in predicting that Jouhaux's election, on July 12, 1909, would be eased by reformist abstentions. The vote was thirty-five to none with twenty abstentions. The new general secretary was seen as Griffuelhes' man. "At first, Jouhaux passed for little more than a temporary 'stand-in' for Griffuelhes, a simple agent of the former leadership." Georges Dumoulin, the radical miners' leader, put it even more bluntly; Jouhaux, he would say later, was Griffuelhes' "phonograph." Jouhaux's biographers, while not accepting Dumoulin's unflattering judgment, nonetheless agree that "Griffuelhes was largely responsible for Jouhaux's formation and provided the push that made him general secretary of the CGT."[4]

2. Weill, *Histoire du mouvement social,* 386; *DBMO*, XIII, 123 (Jouhaux); Georges *et al., Léon Jouhaux,* I, 98.

3. APP, B/a 1603, reports of "Hermann" and "Brossier," June 24, 1909.

4. *DBMO*, XIII, 123; Brécy, *Mouvement syndical,* 72 n. 2; Georges Dumoulin, *Carnets de route (Quarante anneés de vie militante)* (Lille, 1938), 9; Georges *et al., Léon Jouhaux,* I, 32 n. 4. Dolléans adds that "it was at Griffuelhes' suggestion that Jouhaux was nominated for the post of general secretary" (*Histoire du mouvement ouvrier,* II, 164).

Jouhaux's biographers attribute the basis of this relationship to a common autodidacticism and "distrust of doctrinaires and [ideological] systems," but Dolléans sees the link as more of a friendship than an ideological matchup. Whether a matter of doctrine or mere affinity, I believe the early bond between Griffuelhes and Jouhaux stemmed from a common tie to the Parisian industrial suburb of Aubervilliers. Jouhaux lived there from the 1880s to 1913, when he and his wife moved in with the Griffuelhes family; Griffuelhes' father and sister had moved from Nérac to Aubervilliers in the 1890s. His sister and her family were still living there before the war.[5]

The factionalism that marked the years 1908–1909 did not abate with Jouhaux's election but intensified, fed by renewed feuding with the SFIO and heightened internal criticism of the CGT leadership from the insurrectionalist Left. Wrote Pierre Monatte: "I don't know which, politics or insurrectionalism, has done more harm not only to the labor movement but also to the true revolutionary spirit. Both turn people away from union action." The result, according to Georges Lefranc, was "a 'crowding into the center': *the revolutionaries settled down a bit and took pains to distinguish their position from Hervéism* [insurrectionalism]; the reformists agreed to give serious consideration to the principle of direct action."[6] Lefranc's image of crowding into the center, though apt, paints a rather benign picture of the ideological shifts within the CGT during the immediate prewar era. The centrist trend he describes certainly took place, ending in a "lowering of the sights" (*rectification de tir*) or jettisoning of the CGT's social revolutionary mission by 1913. What is also certain, however, is that the process was painful, accompanied by fierce doctrinal struggles, agonizing reappraisals of positions, and demoralization— in a word, malaise.

Not surprisingly, the majority of the militants involved, including Victor Griffuelhes, viewed this malaise as a "moral crisis," thus, this cry of alarm from the former general secretary in early 1913: "Beware, comrades! A de-

---

5. Georges *et al.*, *Léon Jouhaux*, I, 32; Dolléans, *Histoire du mouvement ouvrier*, II, 164. The *DBMO* dates the Jouhauxs' move from Aubervilliers to 1913 but fails to note they shared an apartment with Griffuelhes and his wife (XIII, 123). Dolléans suggests, wrongly I believe, that the move occurred earlier (Dolléans, *Histoire du mouvement ouvrier*, II, 164).

6. Pierre Monatte, "La CGT a-t-elle rectifié son tir?" *V.O.*, 1st ser., August 5, 1913; Lefranc, *Le Mouvement syndical sous la Troisième République*, 162. Lefranc's emphasis.

plorable atmosphere reigns in the trade-union movement. . . . The syndicalist ideal has lost its force and vigor. . . . The movement is going through a crisis that could be fatal. Take heed!"[7]

Historians have tended not to share this moral assessment of the malaise. The majority, perhaps, have seen it as the painful but inevitable accompaniment to a coming of age of French trade unionism. Val Lorwin sums up this point of view: "The revolutionary syndicalist current was receding in the few years just before the war. The optimistic revolutionary expectancy of the growing European workers' movement . . . was high. But the notion of the imminence and success of the general strike could not be forever maintained. . . . A union bureaucracy was developing with vested interests in the present, not in the social revolution."[8]

Economic historians such as Jean Lhomme and Jean-Marie Flonneau, meanwhile, locate the sources of the malaise in the cost-of-living squeeze of 1910–1914. Flonneau writes that "organized as producers, workers now had to organize as consumers and take into account the cost of living and real wages as well as nominal wages." This, he believes, helped bring about a situation whereby "revolutionary syndicalism, now concerned about economic phenomena, became less epic, less utopian . . . more realistic and objective, in keeping with the new economic circumstances."[9]

Finally, although sensitive to the coming of age perspective, Edouard Dolléans sees the approach of war, the "coming storm," as primarily responsible for the malaise. After 1911, "invisible but present, the war was already there to crush them [the workers], to break their will, and destroy their spirit." While Dolléans appears to anticipate somewhat the impact of international tension, Jouhaux's biographers use the same thesis to explain the CGT leadership's growing reformism in this period. "With Jouhaux, a new generation arose: after the *passionnés* of the Griffuelhes type, in the difficult years of the prewar era opportunism would appear to be necessary to save the workers' movement,

7. Griffuelhes, "Où va-t-on?"

8. Lorwin, *French Labor Movement*, 45. This is more or less Lefranc's view also in both *Mouvement syndical sous la Troisième République* and his earlier *Histoire du mouvement syndical français* (Paris, 1937), esp. 343–44.

9. Jean-Marie Flonneau, "Crise de vie chère et mouvement syndical, 1910–1914," *Le Mouvement social*, no. 72 (November–December 1970), 80–81. Jean Lhomme estimates a 7 percent drop in workers' purchasing power in 1910–14, observing that the period, having been interrupted by the war, is too short to permit firm conclusions ("Le Pouvoir d'achat de l'ouvrier français au cours d'un siècle," *ibid.*, no. 66 [April–June, 1968], 48–49).

which was in danger from the rightist reaction in 1912–14 and the rise of nationalism."[10]

Griffuelhes' attitude about the malaise is somewhat complicated, because his analysis of it changed significantly over time. Early in the period, in late 1909, when *Le Mouvement socialiste* was conducting its inquiry into the trade-union crisis, Griffuelhes tended to dismiss the malaise as temporary confusion injected into the movement by Briand and his agents. Speaking of the "regime of worker corruption" practiced by Briand, Griffuelhes concluded the prime minister had "succeeded, through his lackeys, in sowing disarray in the revolutionary ranks; this is the origin of the current crisis of syndicalism." But he predicted that Briand would fail just as Millerand had failed before him. As time passed and the malaise persisted, however, Griffuelhes began to see that, as Dolléans has suggested, it was an error to attribute it solely to the "crisis of trade-union corruption."[11]

In 1910–1912, Griffuelhes published a series of articles in *Le Mouvement socialiste* in which he argued that the malaise afflicting the CGT stemmed from the backwardness of French capitalism.[12] Using as an example shoe manufacturing, the trade he knew best, Griffuelhes described a managerial class so "old-fashioned, dried-up, miserly, and blinkered" that it was "incapable of conceiving, much less directing, an expansion of business." Unable or unwilling to change production or sales methods, French shoe manufacturers, he charged, were losing markets at home and abroad to more innovative, aggressive competitors, principally the Americans. Griffuelhes' managerial class was almost wholly recognizable in Karl Marx's depiction of sixty years before: "The industrial bourgeoisie can rule only where modern industry shapes all property relations to suit itself, and industry can attain this force only where it has conquered the world market, for the national boundaries do not suffice for its development. But the industry of France asserts itself for the most part in the national market only by a more or less modified prohibitive [protective] system."[13]

Unless and until France achieved a stage of true industrial capitalism, Grif-

---

10. Dolléans, *Histoire du mouvement ouvrier*, II, 205; Georges *et al.*, *Léon Jouhaux*, I, 98.

11. Griffuelhes, "La Leçon du Passé"; Dolléans, *Histoire du mouvement ouvrier*, II, 165–66.

12. Griffuelhes, "L'Infériorité des capitalistes français," *Le Mouvement socialiste*, no. 226 (December, 1910); "Stagnation capitaliste," *ibid.*, no. 227 (January, 1911); and "Utopisme petit-bourgeois," *ibid.*, no. 237 (January, 1912).

13 Marx, "Die Klassenkampfe in Frankreich 1848 bis 1850," *Neue Rheinische Zeitung*, Heft I, January, 1850, pp. 15–16, quoted in Marc Linder, *European Labor Aristocracies* (Frankfurt, 1985), 215.

fuelhes continued, her labor movement would remain weak, dispersed, and unequal to its revolutionary mission. "For our part, we demand that French manufacturers become more like American manufacturers. . . . We want a country that is businesslike, active, humming, a veritable beehive of activity. . . . This will give us [workers] the kind of security and stability which, by improving our material situation, will prepare us for the struggle. . . . Our power will then be increased." This was not an entirely new theme for Griffuelhes. As far back as December, 1901, shortly after assuming the post of CGT general secretary, he had welcomed the advent of American-type trusts in France, on the grounds that the concentration of capital would force a concentration of labor and thus hasten the coming of revolution. "The truth is," Griffuelhes now wrote, "that there is a direct link between the economic development of a country and the growth of its trade-union organization; the progress of the one is inextricably tied to the growth of the other."[14]

But, Griffuelhes asked, perhaps reflecting on the criticism his theories were beginning to arouse, was there anything revolutionary in all this?[15] To begin with, the advent of real industrial capitalism in France would confront the proletariat with "new tasks" and increase its "productive power" and thus its ability and will to "conquer."[16] In the stage of industrial capitalism, "great proletarian and capitalist forces" would assemble, whose "combat" would carry the revolutionary struggle to a higher level. For this to happen, the proletariat must have in front of it "a management sure of itself and of its future." Besides, he concluded, "Isn't it in the interests of the working class, on the day when it finally seizes power, to be able to take command of an economic system which has been developed to its highest level of perfection?"

The "Final Battle" was still a long way off, with neither owners nor workers "ready for the tasks ahead," he wrote. "Workers seldom know employers who are active, audacious. On the other hand, the bosses are faced with a proletariat which is insufficiently organized," and which rarely saw where its real interests lay. Implicit in Griffuelhes' desire for a dialectic between the labor movement and an "active, audacious" capitalist class was his growing suspicion that the French working class, at its present level of development, was incapable of

---

14. Griffuelhes, "L'Infériorité des capitalistes français," 331–32; "Phénomène capitaliste," *VdP*, no. 57, December 29, 1901–January 5, 1902; "Utopisme petit-bourgeois," 33.

15. Griffuelhes later remarked on the "astonishment and surprise" that greeted his theories in trade-union circles (Griffuelhes, "Autour du Congrès fédéral du Batiment," *L'Encyclopédie du mouvement syndicaliste*, no. 4, April, 1912, p. 37).

16. Griffuelhes, "Utopisme petit-bourgeois," 33–37.

taking command of the nation's economy. Griffuelhes' doubts on this score would intensify in the coming years and would bulk large in his thinking in the postwar era when events in Russia apparently brightened revolutionary prospects in France.

By early 1913, Griffuelhes' outlook had become decidedly gloomy. An anti-Masonic campaign with strong anti-Semitic overtones was then in full swing in Paris trade-union circles. Its leading proponents, veteran militants Émile Janvion of the municipal employees' union and Emile Pataud, the notorious "Prince of Darkness" of the electricians' union, were men of some standing in the labor movement, despite recent connections to the royalist Action Française.[17] Janvion, Pataud, and their followers charged that membership in the Masons, whom they saw as the occult general staff of the Radical republic, was tantamount to "class collaboration" and thus incompatible with union membership. The campaign threatened to tear some unions apart. Griffuelhes did not himself come under attack, but his newspaper, *La Bataille syndicaliste,* did. So did his close associate, Jules Bled, secretary of the market gardeners' union, who was a veteran member of the CGT Executive Committee and an active Mason.

Shaken by the campaigns against *La Bataille syndicaliste* and Bled, Griffuelhes published a series of articles in January, 1913, calling upon militants to rise above differences and focus attention upon the trade-union tasks at hand. "What is going on?" he asked. "Pressing, complex economic, political, and social problems are piling up all around us but the only questions that seem to interest anyone are: antibureaucratism and whether or not we should allow union members to be Masons!" As for the latter issue, being a Mason was no more incompatible with union membership than being a member of the SFIO, for both were bourgeois organizations. Besides, he wrote, the CGT had always accepted that what members did outside the unions was their own business.[18]

The issue of antibureaucratism, however, had been raging within the union movement since the Affair of the Maison des Fédérations and would continue to have repercussions down to the war and beyond. The case of the critics of bureaucratism in the CGT was succinctly put by a spokesman for Seine-Métaux, the Paris branch of the metalworkers' federation. There was nothing

17. *DBMO,* XIII, 89–90 (Janvion); contacts between syndicalists and the Action Française are explored in detail in Chapters 9–11 of Mazgaj, *The Açtion Francaise and Revolutionary Syndicalism.*

18. Griffuelhes, "Où va-t-on?"

special about being a union official, he said. "You don't have to be a graduate of the [Ecole] Polytechnique to do the job; it doesn't take long to figure out what to do." What exercised the Seine-Métaux militants and other critics of the CGT bureaucracy, in addition to supposed big salaries and free travel, was the bureaucrats' sense of indispensability and seeming permanence. These charges apparently touched a raw nerve in Griffuelhes. "Men capable of intelligently filling a position are rare, extremely rare, too rare," he said loftily. "Situations may permit capable men to reveal their qualities; they never learn as they go. Allow me to say that I speak from experience." [19]

The ex-general secretary also took issue with another set of dissidents whose complaints against the CGT leadership were of even longer duration than those of the antibureaucrats. These were the activists, men like Blanchard and the provincial metalworkers who had helped bring down Griffuelhes in 1909; they felt that power in the CGT had become too centralized and that more decision making should pass to the federations and the Bourses du Travail. Griffuelhes saw this as a far more serious threat to the CGT's future than the anti-Masonic and antibureaucrat campaigns. Proposals for decentralization threatened "the very principles" on which the CGT was built, he wrote; if implemented, there would be no coordination of struggle, no "community of action." Decentralization was nothing less than a return to corporatism, the kind of craft elitism that had characterized the old CGT and whose eradication had been one of his major objectives as general secretary. "Let's not deny it, there is a turning back toward corporatism," Griffuelhes exclaimed.[20]

By the summer of 1913, however, Griffuelhes' spirits had begun to lift somewhat. From abroad came news of socialist electoral victories and of vigorous trade-union activity. And at home in France, mass agitation against the Three-Year Law was growing, a movement that for a time he thought might spark a revival of revolutionary syndicalism and forge an international movement against the threat of war.

Across Europe, socialist parties appeared to be gathering strength in 1912–1913. The elections of January–February, 1912, had made the SPD the majority party in the German Reichstag. In France, the SFIO also appeared to be

---

19. Christian Gras, "La Fédération des Métaux en 1913–1914 et l'Evolution du syndicalisme révolutionnaire français," *Le Mouvement social,* no. 77 (October–December 1971), 100; Griffuelhes, "Retour sur nous-memes," *B.S.,* January 24, 1913.

20. Griffuelhes, "Retour sur nous-memes."

gaining ground. Indeed, in the April–May, 1914, elections, it polled 1,398,000 votes and sent 103 deputies to the Chamber—its best showing of the prewar era. "In the last prewar elections, three million socialists, supported by nine million non-registered socialists, . . . sent 424 [*sic*] socialist deputies to Europe's parliaments."[21] To Victor Griffuelhes' mind, however, this surge of socialist popularity, which so frightened governments of the day, was a mixed blessing. It seemed to demonstrate that while the CGT continued to wallow in discontent, the stature it had enjoyed in French revolutionary circles since the turn of the century was passing to the socialist party. Griffuelhes harbored similar fears about the widespread demonstrations against the proposed Three-Year Law, which began in France in March, 1913.

The Three-Year Law proposed by the French government was intended to bring troop strength closer to parity with the German army—a herculean task given the great disparity between the two countries' populations. There were 65 million Germans in 1914 and 39 million French. To compensate for this, the term of military service in France would be extended from two to three years, and troops currently completing their service would be obliged to remain an extra year. The proposal aroused widespread opposition, not only because of the added imposition on thousands of French workers and peasants, but also because it seemed to presage a buildup for war.[22] A monster rally against the law took place at the Pré-St.-Gervais in Paris on March 24, 1913, with an estimated 200,000 demonstrators participating. This was the first of three rallies held at the site to protest the law; the last, on July 13, 1913, brought together 500,000 people and is said to have been the largest public gathering of the Belle Epoque. In reporting on the first one, Griffuelhes made one of the strongest antipatriotic statements of his career, in which he declared, "There is no such thing as *raison nationale* or *raison d'état*. . . . Workers should say, 'To hell with your reasons and necessities; they're not ours!' " The spirit of the antiwar rallies cheered Griffuelhes and gave him momentary hope that the agitation in France might encourage international action to stem the drift toward war.[23] Overall, the newspaper pieces he wrote during this period were

---

21. For a detailed analysis of the socialist electoral gains, see Carl Schorske, *German Social Democracy, 1905–1917* (New York, 1965), 226–35; Lefranc, *Mouvement socialiste sous la Troisième République*, 197–98; Arno Mayer, *Political Origins of the New Diplomacy, 1917–1918* (New Haven, 1959), 9–10. Mayer's count is two short; he credits the SFIO with 101 deputies in 1914, rather than its actual 103.

22. See Georges Michon, *La Préparation à la guerre, la loi de trois ans, 1910–1914* (Paris, 1935).

23. Brécy, *Mouvement syndical*, 81 n. 2; Griffuelhes, "Discuter les 3 ans, ce n'est pas l'affaire

among his most optimistic in many years. But even if enthusiastic about the outpouring of worker sentiment against the Three-Year Law, Griffuelhes perceived dangers in this new upsurge of worker activity.

The increasingly political orientation of labor struggles worried him. In August, 1912, the SFIO renewed its attempt to "subordinate" the trade unions, denouncing the CGT in the Chamber. In response, the CGT leaders defiantly published a reaffirmation of the Charter of Amiens that soon became known as the Syndicalist Encyclical.[24] Now, less than two years later, French socialists and the CGT were on better terms than at any time since the turn of the century. They had begun to work closely together during the battle against the Three-Year Law. Despite the failure of that campaign—its passage in the Chamber was secured by the votes of one-third of the socialist deputies—the supposedly temporary alliance began to look permanent. As Griffuelhes had made clear in his 1913 articles, he was willing to support CGT-SFIO cooperation only if the CGT could operate from a position of moral advantage.[25]

But despite the massive turnout for the antiwar demonstrations, Griffuelhes was far from optimistic about the moral state of organized workers as 1913 faded into 1914. To enter into a close relationship with the socialists now, when demoralization still gripped the CGT, was to risk undoing all that he and others had worked for over the past decade: an autonomous, self-sufficient trade-union organization. And any hopes of forming a new, genuinely revolutionary labor party around the CGT would be lost.

By the summer of 1914, however, these considerations took second place to concerns over the threat of war. On this score, Griffuelhes felt—or so he would later argue—that the SFIO leadership, whose influence over French workers was increasing, had rendered a great disservice by telling workers to trust their hopes for peace to the peacekeeping machinery of the Second International. That was a serious mistake, he argued, for the SPD, which dominated the International, had consistently ignored appeals to commit itself to a definite antiwar program. Yet in spite of that, "all or almost all [of the French Left]—only a handful of us thought otherwise—loudly proclaimed

---

des travailleurs," *B.S.*, March 29, 1913; "Notre Action doit créer un effort international," *B.S.*, March 21, 1913.

24. "Notre Position," *La Bataille syndicaliste,* August 20, 1912; the manifesto was signed by Jouhaux, Griffuelhes, Jules Bled, Charles Voirin of the leatherworkers, and Auguste Savoie of the foodworkers. The full text is reproduced in Dubief, ed., *Le Syndicalisme révolutionnaire,* 216–19.

25. Griffuelhes, "Pétitioner? Oui! Mais surtout développer l'action ouvrière," *B.S.*, April 6, 1913.

their belief that the Germans would honor their international obligations. Among them were some who were truly convinced and others who were not, yet their affirmations were [equally fervent]." To build hopes for peace on the belief that the German proletariat would refuse to march bordered on the criminal, because German workers were too servile and too submissive to State authority to resist the call to mobilization.[26]

These were retrospective judgments, however, rendered by Griffuelhes in 1916 in an attempt to explain why working-class resistance to the war had collapsed in August, 1914—and to explain why he had rallied to the Sacred Union (Union sacrée), which was the agreement of all political factions to support the government for the duration of the war. Did these after-the-fact assessments represent Griffuelhes' actual thinking in the summer of 1914? And, if so, did he propose an alternative to what he saw as the SFIO leaders' mistaken reliance on the Second International?

Griffuelhes' activities in the months before the war are difficult to trace. From July, 1913 to July, 1914, he was strangely silent. His collaboration on *La Bataille syndicaliste* ceased. There is no record of his participation in CGT councils or in propaganda tours, and I have been unable to locate police reports on his movements during this period. He was perhaps ill once again or had left Paris on another voyage révolutionnaire, although these possibilities seem unlikely, for it was during 1913 that Jouhaux and his wife moved in with the Griffuelhes family. I believe that Griffuelhes did remain on the scene in Paris, in daily contact with Jouhaux, and that this long silence in his state of semi retirement resulted from a mood of deep despondency. He had been buoyed by massive working-class opposition to the Three-Year Law, only to be let down when it was passed in August, 1913. *La Bataille syndicaliste* was riven by staff dissension and besieged by antibureaucrat militants who charged that the paper was merely a house organ for the CGT elite—a campaign, worse still, that was supported by his old union, the National Leatherworkers' Federation.[27] As the CGT tore itself apart in endless feuding between revolutionaries and moderates, federalists and centralists, it must have seemed to Griffuelhes that all he had worked and stood for, including the principles of revolutionary syndicalism enshrined in the Charter of Amiens, was being wrecked—with all that remained being the much-belabored Maison des Fédérations.

---

26. Griffuelhes, "Puisqu'il faut écrire," *La Feuille*, August 3, 1916.
27. Gras, "La Fédération des Métaux en 1913–1914," 109.

The news Griffuelhes received from abroad at this time—at least as passed through the filter of his newfound international "experts"—had also turned bad. During the immediate prewar years, two aging disciples of Bakunin functioned as unofficial "foreign policy consultants" to the CGT leadership: the anti-Marxists Christian Cornelissen and James Guillaume. They sat on the editorial boards of *La Bataille syndicaliste* and the theoretical organs of French revolutionary syndicalism, *L'Action directe* (1908 series) and *La Vie ouvrière* (1909–1914 series). Dumoulin later claimed that before the war, CGT leaders got their "information on German trade-union affairs" from Cornelissen, "irreconcilable enemy of all that was German." He also said that Griffuelhes was among those CGT chiefs most receptive to Cornelissen's views.[28] He claimed the nationalist wing was in the ascendancy in German social democracy, and despite denials from Jaurès and other SFIO leaders, Griffuelhes probably believed it. He was never sanguine about the chances of German cooperation in international action against the threat of war, and he remembered the rejection of his mission to Berlin in January, 1906. Thus he may well have concluded that if war came and the CGT, "more advanced than the German workers' movement," did greet mobilization with a general strike, as it had threatened, it would do so alone, and "become a victim of its own advanced state."[29]

This is the more charitable version of Griffuelhes' attitude toward the CGT's erstwhile German trade-union allies. Others stress an abiding Germanophobia or the surfacing of a latent Blanquist Jacobinism as factors in his acceptance of the Sacred Union in 1914.[30] Griffuelhes provided plenty of ammunition for those who have charged him with Germanophobia, such as his comment following the failed mission to Berlin. The Germans, he said, "aroused in me the same kind of 'admiration' one has for a smoothly turning wheel." And in 1908, he had compared German and French workers: "The German worker is frightened. He is afraid to take chances, to take part in struggles. He fears all the forces of order, authority, and hierarchy. . . . What

28. Georges Dumoulin, "Les Syndicalistes français et la Guerre," in *Le Mouvement ouvrier pendant la première guerre mondiale,* ed. Alfred Rosmer (Paris, 1936), I, 526.

29. Jean Montreuil [Georges Lefranc] ascribes this sentiment to Jouhaux, in July, 1914, "perhaps under the influence of Griffuelhes" (*Histoire du mouvement ouvrier français,* 314).

30. Montreuil [Lefranc] says that Griffuelhes' "Blanquism would seem to have reappeared" in the final days before mobilization (*ibid.,* 317). Brécy agrees, writing that Griffuelhes followed "the example of his old mentor, Edouard Vaillant," in supporting the war in August, 1914 (*Mouvement syndical,* 106 n. 2).

characterizes the French worker is his daring and independence. Nothing frightens him. He stands above all authority, respect, and hierarchy."[31]

Griffuelhes nursed a strong dislike for German trade-union leaders and perhaps for German workers as well. This view was not, however, the result of a nationalist formation, for he does not mention Alsace-Lorraine or revanche in his voluminous writings. His antipathy seems to have stemmed, rather, from his Berlin experiences in 1906. Before that, in 1901, he had praised the German unions for their attention to organization and strike funds. Nor was he consistently hostile after 1906. As late as 1911, Griffuelhes expressed admiration for German industriousness in the *Encyclopédie syndicaliste.* The question is not so much whether Griffuelhes harbored antipathy toward the Germans, but whether he allowed it to cloud his judgment. On this point, I tend to agree with Alfred Rosmer that Griffuelhes' Germanophobia "remained . . . a latent sentiment, which became dominant and dangerous only when proletarian internationalism collapsed," *i.e.,* when war came in August, 1914.[32]

Griffuelhes reappears in the CGT councils on July 25, on the eve of Jouhaux's departure for Brussels, where the general secretary would meet Carl Legien, his German counterpart, in the course of a Belgian trade-union congress. Jean-Jacques Becker describes the scene that evening at the Maison des Fédérations: "Many militants came to the Maison . . . to ask what course of action to take [regarding the war threat], proof positive that there was much confusion. Jouhaux seems to have turned to Victor Griffuelhes for advice. . . . This advice came down on the side of prudence."[33]

A Sûreté spy also reported that Jouhaux sought Griffuelhes' counsel on how to comport himself in the rendezvous with Legien: "While no longer occupying a post at the CGT, [Griffuelhes] nonetheless remains the real power in the organization," and he advised Jouhaux "to temporize and convoke the CGT executive committee at the last possible moment"—in other words, to do nothing about the war threat until he knew where the Germans stood.[34]

The subsequent meeting in Brussels between Jouhaux and Legien on July 27, 1914, is one of the most controversial events in the history of the CGT.

---

31. Repeated in Griffuelhes, "Puisqu'il faut écrire"; Griffuelhes, *Les Caractères du syndicalisme français* (Paris, 1908), 3.

32. Griffuelhes, "Une Opinion"; Griffuelhes, "Allemagne," *L'Encyclopédie syndicaliste,* no. 1, December, 1911; Rosmer, ed., *Mouvement ouvrier pendant la guerre,* I, 521.

33. Jean-Jacques Becker, *1914; Comment les français sont entrés dans la guerre* (Paris, 1977), 191.

34. AN, F7 13.348, M/9523, note of July 27, 1914.

Although I will not examine this controversy in all its ramifications here, it should be noted that Jouhaux's version, in which Legien apparently rejected any possibility of forestalling the outbreak of war, has been seriously contested. A month later, the CGT general secretary wrote that he had asked Legien, "What would be the attitude of the [German] Social Democracy in case of war?" To which Legien supposedly replied: "The German soldiers would march." Georges Dumoulin, Jouhaux's assistant who also attended the meeting, later recalled that the whole conversation had lasted five minutes—with time out for interpretation—and that "no question was asked about stopping the mobilization, or a general strike, or any other means to stop the war." One writer suggests that Jouhaux consulted with Griffuelhes upon his return from Brussels on July 27 and that the latter told him the interview confirmed his own worst suspicions: If French workers attempted to resist mobilization, they would stand alone. This would be Jouhaux's line, too, many years later, in reflecting on the charge he had done too little to resist the war. Preaching hostility toward the Germans, Griffuelhes had "perhaps led him further than he had wanted to go," write Jouhaux's biographers.[35]

Whatever transpired between the two men over the crucial question of coordinating antiwar efforts with the Germans, Griffuelhes once again disappears from the scene. Jean-Jacques Becker, who has carefully combed the record of CGT meetings in the frenetic last days of peace, gives no indication of his presence. Griffuelhes was not involved in the massive street demonstrations of July 27 against the war, nor does he seem to have been a party to the decision on July 29 to rein in the demonstrations.[36] That decision, made at the behest of Jaurès and the SFIO, gave the French foreign ministry time to try to compose its differences with the Central Powers.[37] No record exists of Griffuelhes' reaction to Jaurès' assassination on the night of July 31; perhaps he knew his name was on the "Carnet B"—the list of "principal revolutionaries of Paris and the Seine region" who were to be rounded up when war

35. Léon Jouhaux, "Le Prolétariat et la Guerre. Une des raisons de notre attitude," *B.S.*, September 26, 1914; Dumoulin, "Les Syndicalistes français et la Guerre," ed. Rosmer, I, 314. Georges *et al.*, *Léon Jouhaux*, I, 58.

36. A graphic account of this large demonstration, which turned into a pitched battle with nationalists and police, appears in a letter from Alfred Rosmer to Pierre Monatte, dated July 28, 1914, in Colette Chambelland and Jean Maitron, eds., *Syndicalisme révolutionnaire et communisme. Les Archives de Pierre Monatte, 1914–1924* (Paris, 1968), 19–20.

37. On the dominant influence of the SFIO over the CGT in the closing days of July, 1914, see Annie Kriegel, "Jaurès en juillet 1914," *Le Mouvement social*, no. 49 (October–December, 1964), 63–81.

began—and had decided to lie low. Dumoulin recalled the fear that reigned at CGT headquarters in those days. "The night we got back from Brussels, a lawyer came to the CGT executive committee to say that [Minister of War] Messimy wanted to rub out [*zigouiller*] the chiefs of the CGT and send the small fry to concentration camps. From that night on, we trembled for our skins. Nobody had to tell us to pull in our horns."[38]

There was no revolutionary general strike in France when mobilization orders were posted on August 2, 1914. Instead, *La Bataille syndicaliste* carried an editorial by the CGT secretariat declaring: "Events have overwhelmed us." On that day, Georges Dumoulin joined the first batches of mobilized reservists heading for the frontier. Around him, uniformed workers, some of them CGT militants, waved happily to relatives amid shouts of "On to Berlin!"[39]

Victor Griffuelhes left no record of his reaction to the coming of the war. Nevertheless, the balance sheet of those last frantic days before mobilization must not have surprised him greatly. He harbored grave doubts about the moral capacity of the French working class to resist the trend toward war. With no faith in the abilities of either the French government or the Socialist International to save the peace, he must have been prepared for the retreat that began with the CGT's admission of impotence on August 2 and ended with Jouhaux's emotional paean to the crusade against Kaiserism at Jaurès' funeral on August 4. In months to come, Griffuelhes would express dismay at the fulsomeness of Jouhaux's embrace of the Sacred Union in his speech of August 4. At the time, however, he appears to have kept his counsel, no less overwhelmed by events than the rest of his colleagues.[40]

---

38. Jean-Jacques Becker, *Le Carnet B* (Paris, 1973), 171; Dumoulin, *Les Syndicalistes français et la Guerre,* 10; this quotation is from Dumoulin's pamphlet, first published by the newspaper *L'Avenir internationale* in Paris in 1918, and reprinted in Vol. I of Rosmer's collection of documents, *Le Mouvement ouvrier pendant la guerre,* in 1936.

39. "La Folie Triomphe de la raison," *B.S.,* August 2, 1914; Dumoulin, "Les Syndicalistes français et la Guerre," in Rosmer, ed., I, 535–37.

40. Brécy, however, quotes Griffuelhes as saying he had been opposed to voting war credits in 1914 (*Mouvement syndical,* 106 n. 1).

X

WAR (1914–1918)

We live in such strange times! I think it will be some time before we get back to normal, if ever. I doubt that we ever will. . . . One thing is certain: one has to forget what one was yesterday.

—Griffuelhes, *La Feuille*

The outbreak of war in August, 1914, devastated the trade-union movement in France. Its membership plummeted as thousands of factories closed down to deliver up their employees for military service. A ministry of labor survey published in May–June, 1915, showed that of a sample of 27,610 factories operating in July, 1914, only 12,422 were still working in August. Of the some 1,097,000 workers employed in these establishments in July, 1914, only around 373,000 remained a month later.[1]

The labor leaders and militants who remained behind, such as Griffuelhes, who was declared unfit for service because of his tuberculosis, faced the task of preserving the CGT from total collapse. Although statistical evidence on union membership during the war years is scant—the labor ministry published no data on it from the opening of hostilities to 1919—the information available indicates a steep decline the first year, from which the confederation would begin to recover only in 1917. According to CGT figures, the number

---

1. Bulletin du ministère du travail, May–June, 1915, quoted in Paul Louis, *Le Syndicalisme français, d'Amiens à Saint-Etienne, 1906–1922* (Paris, 1924), 113. According to Maurice Labi, "In August 1914, employment [in France] fell 63 percent, of which less than half—26 percent— was accounted for by mobilized workers" (*La Grande Division des travailleurs* [Paris, 1964], 56); unfortunately, Labi gives no source for this interesting statistic.

of affiliated federations fell from forty-nine in May, 1914, to thirty-four at the end of 1915; meanwhile, the number of dues-paying members in these federations reportedly plummeted from 213,968 in 1914 (pre-August figures) to just 41,645 in 1915.[2]

The most the CGT leadership could do in this situation was to maintain some kind of presence through, for example, Griffuelhes' semiofficial daily, *La Bataille syndicaliste*. But even this was difficult. Sales of the newspaper declined by 50 percent from August to November, 1914, and in October, 1915, it folded; its slow death was recorded in police reports. What union activity remained was carried on within the federations, where new leadership slowly emerged to replace the drafted militants, local sections were reconstituted, and contact among members was resumed. The metalworkers' federation was probably the most successful of the CGT unions in this regard, due to the active leadership of Alphonse Merrheim and the relatively rapid recovery of membership as employment in metalworking, one of the critical war industries, skyrocketed.[3]

In the war's opening weeks, CGT leaders such as Victor Griffuelhes, apparently traumatized by the possibility that the French government would take advantage of the crisis to dissolve the CGT, frantically tried to convince the power structure that the labor movement was relevant to the government's war effort and should be accepted as a partner in it. To this end, Griffuelhes' shrill editorials in *La Bataille syndicaliste* in August, 1914, offered the government unsolicited advice on how to run the war economy, and the CGT leadership eagerly joined the government in its flight from Paris to Bordeaux in early September, 1914.

In the first of his wartime editorials in *La Bataille syndicaliste,* Griffuelhes expressed dismay at the state of French industry, which in his view seemed incapable of waging war or providing jobs for a growing army of unemployed. He made unflattering comparisons between the performance of French industry and its counterpart across the Rhine, continuing the polemic he had launched in the prewar years over the "inferiority" of French entrepreneurship. Now, in the crucible of war, his critique took on a new, sharp, Jacobin edge.

2. Labi, *La Grande Division des travailleurs,* 246, 248–49.

3. See APP, B/a 1605, notes of January 25, September 29, 1915; AN, F7 13.574, report of September 6, 1915; Labi found that, according to CGT records, the number of dues-paying members in the metalworkers' federation rose from only 1,083 in 1915 to 51,666 in 1917, nearly twice as many as in 1913 (27,083) (*La Grande Division des travailleurs,* 249).

Since private industry seemed unable to meet the challenges of war production and job creation, the State would have to step in.

On August 22, as a first step, he proposed that the State organize relief "to the growing number of needy persons"—the families of wage earners called into military service and the rising number of unemployed. Efforts to date, he charged, had been "scandalous" in their inefficiency; to replace the patchwork of private and municipal relief agencies, a "single fund" operated by the State was required to assure a more equitable "sharing out of the nation's resources."[4]

Two days later, Griffuelhes offered more advice to the Viviani government, this time on employment. The only means to achieve a real recovery of economic activity, he wrote, was to resume international trade, "at a standstill since the declaration of war. . . . The economic interdependence of nations is absolute and when the exchange of goods is interrupted or made uncertain, production is paralyzed. . . . When trade resumes, employment will pick up." Furthermore, the major obstacle to trade resumption was not the war, because "the freedom of the seas has been maintained [submarine warfare had not begun]." Rather, it was the government's moratorium on lines of credit for trade purposes, put into effect "to save the credit facilities from bankruptcy." A short-term solution was for the State to prime the pump by stockpiling certain goods; this, he wrote, was how the Chilean government was coping with the war-induced collapse of the world market for nitrates.[5]

On August 26, Griffuelhes again addressed the unemployment problem. Even if chances were slim for more than a "partial resumption" of production, in some industries business was or soon should be picking up. These employers were not hiring, however, because they preferred to sell off their inventories at high prices rather than increase production. The government should investigate the various industrial sectors, determine where employment opportunities existed, and use whatever pressures were necessary to see that jobs were created.[6]

As August wore on and German armies pressed closer and closer to Paris, Griffuelhes became increasingly exasperated at the government's failure to take

4. Griffuelhes, "Organisons l'assistance et la reprise du travail," *B.S.*, August 22, 1914.

5. Griffuelhes, "Un écoulement est necessaire pour la reprise du travail," *B.S.*, August 24, 1914.

6. Griffuelhes, "Pour remédier au chomage des mesures extraordinaires s'imposent," *B.S.*, August 26, 1914.

the "extraordinary measures" he believed were required. His deepest anger was reserved, however, for the nation's private sector, its bankers and industrialists, whom he found totally lacking in public spirit and patriotism. "If I were you, M. Viviani," Griffuelhes burst out, "I would have proclaimed that no one has the right to evade his responsibilities, that . . . all those not in military service must, *without exception,* . . . do their part . . . to assure the functioning of society." Draconian measures were called for: 1) banks must not be allowed to block accounts; 2) every government employee must turn over one-fifth to one-third of his salary to the State, with other wage earners giving up one-sixth to one-fifth; 3) every employer should be required to pay a profits tax of 14 centimes on the franc; and 4) stockholders should be obliged to pay a capital gains tax.[7]

As the first month of the war ended, Griffuelhes made a final proposal to revive the economy. Capital was desperately needed in most industrial sectors, and most companies either could not or would not come up with the money from their own resources. Therefore, the State had to step in. "Modern wars pose a military and a social problem. We only know how to deal with the first. The second requires measures as radical as the first [but] we have not understood that yet."[8]

By early September, however, many, including the CGT leadership, believed that time had run out. Elements of the German army were reported to be only 20 kilometers from Paris. The government, as in 1870, prepared to decamp for Bordeaux. The CGT general secretary, Léon Jouhaux, Griffuelhes, and the remaining members of the CGT Executive Committee, mindful of that awful precedent, now had to decide whether to go to Bordeaux, as some socialists in the government were urging, or remain in the capital to fight the invader, as the Communards had done.[9] In what was clearly a hasty and ill-considered decision, Jouhaux and Griffuelhes decided, without consulting the Executive Committee, that the CGT's place was in Bordeaux. On or around September 1, they accepted tickets on a special train carrying government officials to the port city. Alphonse Merrheim learned of the decision by chance

7. Griffuelhes, "Voilà des mesures!," *B.S.*, August 28, 1914.
8. Griffuelhes, "Par le Crédit Foncier on pouvait agir," *B.S.*, August 31, 1914.
9. The liaison between the CGT leaders and the government at this point was the minister of public works, Marcel Sembat, a former Blanquist and one-time heir apparent to Vaillant (Labi, *La Grande Division des travailleurs,* 53); Griffuelhes had been careful to keep open lines of communication to Sembat before the war, when the latter was a leading left-wing socialist deputy. See CGT, *Ve Congrès national corporatif . . . Amiens . . . 1906,* 136, 166.

at the *Bataille syndicaliste* offices on September 2. He was appalled by what he felt was a shocking decision, actually and symbolically. Not only had Jouhaux and Griffuelhes elected to flee Paris, leaving behind the whole CGT apparatus, but they were doing so as virtual wards of the State. Following "a row which lasted over half an hour," Merrheim forced Jouhaux to consent to a CGT Executive Committee meeting the next day, because he had learned there was more to the sudden flight than just panic. Jouhaux and perhaps Griffuelhes as well, although this is unclear, had accepted posts as "commissioners to the nation," which meant traveling about the country at government expense, stoking up patriotic fervor among the working classes.[10]

The decision to go to Bordeaux, finally accepted by the CGT Executive Committee over the objections of Merrheim and Raoul Lenoir, co-secretary of the metalworkers' federation, was a fateful step for the CGT. It launched the leadership on a course of greater and greater collaboration in the war effort, to the point where critics could argue that the confederation had become a virtual handmaiden of the Sacred Union. This policy quickly aroused opposition. In December, 1914, Pierre Monatte, the leader of the new generation of revolutionary syndicalists that had grown up around *La Vie Ouvrière,* publicly resigned from the CGT Executive Committee in protest over the leadership's refusal to support a peace conference organized by the Scandinavian socialist parties. Contemporary police reports suggest that "Griffuelhes, who, in fact, still directs the movement," was the mastermind behind the rejection of the invitation.[11]

By the second year of the war, the opposition to the CGT leadership's collaboration with the war effort, aided by the realization that the war would

10. Merrheim to Monatte, September 29, 1914, in Chambelland and Maitron, eds., *Syndicalisme révolutionnaire et communisme,* 35–36.

Merrheim wrote Monatte that "along with Jouhaux, they [Griffuelhes and François Marie, an editor of *B.S.*] had agreed to be these famous *commissaires à la nation* in government service. . . ." Later in the same letter, Merrheim refers only to Jouhaux as a commissioner, "the idea of which he himself originated . . . without consulting the [Executive Committee] even though it committed the CGT." Labi refers to Jouhaux and Griffuelhes "hoping to revive in their persons the moral role of representatives on mission of the Convention [of 1793]," but later in the same paragraph mentions only Jouhaux's service in this capacity (*La Grande Division des travailleurs,* 54).

11. See the text of Monatte's protest, "Pourquoi je démissionne du comité confédéral," which he printed himself and circulated to members of the Executive Committee, in Chambelland and Maitron, eds., *Syndicalisme révolutionnaire et communisme,* 45–49; AN, F7 13.574, note of June 11, 1915.

not be as short as predicted, had won over the metalworkers' and hatmakers' unions and—in what must have been a rebuke and a warning to Griffuelhes—the leatherworkers' federation as well.[12] In the old offices of *La Vie Ouvrière,* Merrheim gathered around him a small group of pacifist and revolutionary trade unionists and intellectuals that became the Committee for the Resumption of International Relations (CRIR) in the fall of 1915; ultimately, it formed the nucleus of a minority movement within the CGT and the socialist party that, by war's end, was large enough to challenge the prowar leadership for control.

In September, 1915, Merrheim, accompanied by Albert Bourderon, head of the coopers' union, who was an "old reformist" by his own account but a staunch opponent of the Sacred Union, attended a conference of antiwar socialists held at Zimmerwald, in Switzerland's Bernese Oberland.[13] There, in the shadow of the Alps, the French antiwar Left made its first contact with Lenin. The Russian Bolshevik leader spent some eight hours in discussion with Merrheim and Bourderon in Berne before the conference, seeking in vain their support for his strategy of "revolutionary defeatism": sabotage of the war effort on the grounds that defeat would lead to social revolution. Lenin's policy was far to the left of most Zimmerwald attendees, including his future associate, Leon Trotsky. Merrheim claimed at the CGT Congress of Lyon in 1919, after he had joined the majority camp, that Lenin had tried to convince him to call a mass strike against the war when he returned, but this does not appear to be true. During their talk before the conference, Merrheim apparently persuaded Lenin that a negotiated peace was what most participants could agree on.[14]

Merrheim and Bourderon also met at Zimmerwald with two antiwar members of the German SPD, Georg Ledebour and Adolf Hoffman. The four signed a Franco-German manifesto entitled "This War Is Not Our War," which called for an immediate negotiated peace, and also the longer "Zimmerwald Manifesto," a resolution calling upon the international working class to struggle for an immediate peace "with no annexations and no indemnities." The latter was drafted by Trotsky, who was living in Paris where he was still a militant of the Left Social Revolutionary Party, a leading member of the *Vie*

---

12. Brécy, *Mouvement syndical,* 90. The leatherworkers' secretary, Brisson, was listed by police as a "pacifist" (AN, F7 13.574, report of August 15, 1915).

13. Quoted in Louis Bouët, *La Grande Tourmente (1914–1918)* (Avignon, n.d.), 58.

14. Christian Gras, *Alfred Rosmer (1877–1964) et le Mouvement révolutionnaire international* (Paris, 1971), 161.

Ouvrière group, and editor of a series of Russian-language antiwar newspapers. Upon their return from the Zimmerwald conference, Merrheim and Bourderon launched the CRIR.[15]

Griffuelhes had watched these developments with increasing anxiety. On one hand, he could not stomach Merrheim. Their estrangement had begun in 1911–1912, when a frankly jealous Griffuelhes accused him of neglecting his trade-union work to engage in "intellectual" pursuits; his enmity did not abate during the war and extended to the CRIR group, whom he considered defeatist.[16] On the other hand, it was clear to him that Jouhaux had gone too far in his policy of collaboration with the government. What bothered Griffuelhes most was his growing realization that, for Jouhaux, collaboration was no longer a necessity forced upon the CGT by the war or even a policy dictated by dislike and fear of Germany; it had become a personal obsession. According to a police report of May 26, 1916, Griffuelhes told associates that "ever since his oration at the bier of Jaurès [on August 4, 1914], [Jouhaux] has considered himself a big shot, and has been too willing to bask in the cunning flattery of the fat cats of the Radical party." Griffuelhes believed, the spy reported, that "all his work is in peril. . . . The workers' unity so painfully achieved at the Congress of Montpellier is being undone."[17]

By 1916, Griffuelhes decided he had no choice but to break with Jouhaux. At some point in the spring of that year, Griffuelhes and his wife moved out of the flat they shared with the Jouhauxs at 44, rue de l'Avenir (20th). No doubt other factors contributed to the move in addition to Griffuelhes' belief that Jouhaux's vanity and appetite for recognition in government circles were threatening to tear apart his beloved CGT. The future looked bleak for several reasons in 1916.

In December, 1915, his old friend and mentor, Edouard Vaillant, died, broken in health and spirit by the war. The veteran Blanquist's ferocious patriotism and determination that there should be no resumption of relations with German social democracy until Germany had paid for her aggression, had helped still Griffuelhes' doubts about rallying to the Sacred Union. Now

---

15. The text of the Zimmerwald Manifesto is in *Le Mouvement ouvrier pendant la guerre,* ed. Rosmer, I, 379–82; for Trotsky's activities in Paris from 1914 to 1916, see Gras, *Alfred Rosmer,* 112–15.

16. In a police report, Griffuelhes decried the "hideous nonsense of a pacifist metalworker," an apparent reference to what he saw as the incongruity of Merrheim's pacifism and his position as secretary of a union whose members were largely engaged in supplying the war effort (AN, F7 13.574, note of November 15, 1915).

17. AN, F7 13.575, note of May 26, 1916.

that comforting voice was gone, and the political landscape was occupied by men like Aristide Briand—who had succeeded Viviani as premier in October, 1915—and Griffuelhes' greatest nemesis, Alexandre Millerand, who was back in government as minister of war. Add to this the prospect of endless slaughter raised by the half million French casualties at Verdun in 1915, and the depression that gripped Griffuelhes in late summer that year becomes all too understandable.

Another side to the break with Jouhaux reflects less well on Griffuelhes. In criticizing Jouhaux's cultivation of power in high places, he reveals a bitterness that transcends matters of principle. In fact, one suspects that Griffuelhes realized the man who had been called his "phonograph" and who had allowed Griffuelhes to continue to run the CGT through him had now finally decided to be his own boss. Jouhaux no longer needed him, and what role would Griffuelhes have in the CGT, once his influence over Jouhaux was gone? He no longer held a union office. His position as an editor of *La Bataille syndicaliste* had ceased to exist in October, 1915, and even though he had been an editor of the daily that succeeded it, *La Bataille,* this did not provide the kind of authority in CGT circles that Griffuelhes' ego and sense of proprietorship demanded.[18]

In August, 1916, Griffuelhes severed ties with *La Bataille* and joined the editorial board of *La Feuille,* a new weekly launched by the onetime anarchist publicist, Charles-Albert, now a violently anti-Marxist socialist. Charles-Albert had embraced the Sacred Union with even less reserve than Griffuelhes, but by 1916, he too had become disillusioned. *La Feuille* would seek a position somewhere "between the majority and minority" of the French Left on the issue raised so dramatically by Merrheim and the CRIR: the revival of international working-class cooperation in the cause of peace, including relations with the socialists and trade unionists of the Central Powers.[19]

Moving over to *La Feuille* was more than a break with Jouhaux and the CGT "bitter-enders," it was a break with the trade-union movement Griffuelhes had been part of since 1896 and which he had led for nearly eight years. His first article for *La Feuille* betrays a sense of bewilderment at being

18. *La Bataille,* whose editor in chief was François Marie, began publication on November 3, 1915, and appeared daily until December 31, 1920, when it was replaced by the CGT's new official daily, *Le Peuple* (Brécy, *Mouvement syndical,* 147–48, 152).

19. The newspaper was subtitled *Socialiste, syndicaliste, révolutionnaire.* For more on Charles-Albert, see Victor Méric, "Charles-Albert," *Les Hommes du jour,* no. 97, November 27, 1909, and *DBMO,* XI, 72–73 (Charles-Albert).

on the outside of the movement that had been his life. "We are marching down a road whose end we cannot see. We would like our final destination to be familiar, yet different; this is not an easy thing to accomplish. The day will come when we will have to decide who we are and what we want. It's lucky for some that this long war postpones its coming!"

It was a time for self-examination, for coming to grips with one's beliefs and locating oneself in relationship to the single inescapable fact of the time: the war. Griffuelhes felt his first duty was to examine critically his own role in the coming of the war, recognizing now that what amounted to an unqualified embrace of the Sacred Union had been a mistake: "Once we had gotten beyond those first days, that crossroads of August 4, 1914, that everyone had to face up to, it would have been useful to have taken a good look into oneself. That would have helped to clarify the situation. The inevitable errors committed as a result of our silence in that crucial moment cannot be gainsaid. There is no doubt that we did too little; perhaps we were trying to make the best of a bad situation."[20]

For the first time, in print at least, Griffuelhes attempted to explain what had motivated his actions in August, 1914. The Germans, he contended, had never been serious about their international obligations, neither the SPD nor the trade unions. They wanted to dominate everyone else and were convinced they deserved to dominate. Now, as he had come to believe that supporting the Sacred Union was an error, so he was beginning to question, if not his earlier attitude toward the Germans, at least his unwillingness until then to support negotiations with them to find ways to end the war. "Why, when facts have confirmed what I said [about the Germans], have I changed my mind? So as not to join the [patriotic] chorus! I recognize no Sacred Union." Griffuelhes was not in favor, however, of initiatives such as those undertaken by Merrheim and the CRIR. The Germans had wrecked the chances of international action by the working classes to stop the war in 1914—"Who failed to do their duty? Not us!"—and relations with them could not be resumed unless they made the first move, *i.e.,* until they admitted their culpability or at least their share of the blame. He acknowledged, "We were not exempt from errors, however," and asked if the SPD and Carl Legien's unions would make the necessary "gesture": "Do they have any intention of doing it? Perhaps a few are ready to. A half dozen maybe."[21]

If this was, as Robert Brécy has described it, a position "between the ma-

20. Griffuelhes, "Puisqu'il faut écrire."
21. *Ibid.*; Griffuelhes, "Il faut un examen de conscience," *La Feuille,* August 10, 1916.

jority and minority" on the question of peace, it was not a particularly convincing or helpful one. Although Griffuelhes' position, not surprisingly, attracted little support, in terms of his own thinking it deserves examination. Grudging though it was, his stance on resuming relations with the German labor movement, which he set forth in *La Feuille* in 1916, was a departure from the intransigence that characterized CGT majority thinking until the end of the war. It also marked a significant shift in his own attitude. At the war's outset, by all accounts he had been as violently anti-German as anyone in the French labor movement, although he was more restrained in expressing himself than some of his anarchist colleagues, including Jouhaux. Now, hesitantly and self-consciously, he was stating publicly that he favored another try at cooperation with the German working class because this was "indispensable for putting an end to wars."[22]

The "gesture" Griffuelhes hoped for from the German socialists failed to materialize—in terms he could accept, at least—in 1916 or 1917. By that time, however, a new movement had arisen that encouraged his hopes for a "real" International whose "goal would be to lay the groundwork for the elimination of the historic nation-states in favor of . . . an organization in which [the working-class peoples of Europe] would fuse their interests in a common life."[23] This was the Russian revolutionary movement, in both its March and October, 1917, incarnations.

Griffuelhes greeted the March Revolution in Russia, and especially the reemergence of the Petrograd Soviet, with great enthusiasm. Scoffing at the fears of proletarian "excesses" expressed in establishment newspapers such as *Le Temps,* he wrote, "I have no idea what the Russian workers will do next. All I know is that up to now they have done a splendid job and I hope they won't stop in midstream." His greatest fear in this regard was that the French prowar socialists, through their influence with moderate Russian socialists such as the head of the new Russian republic, Alexander Kerensky, would try to deflect the revolution from the social and economic course charted by the Petrograd Soviet to one of pure republican politics. The orthodox social-democratic argument that Russia had to pass through a "bourgeois democratic" and "capitalist" phase before it could progress to socialism left Griffuelhes as cold as it had Lenin: "Will they make a revolution in 1917 like our

---

22. Brécy, *Mouvement syndical,* 149; for Jouhaux's views on the Germans, see Jouhaux to Georges Dumoulin, December 9, 1914, in Chambelland and Maitron, eds., *Syndicalisme révolutionnaire et communisme,* 81; Griffuelhes, "Comprendra-t-on?" *La Feuille,* October 4, 1917.

23. Griffuelhes, "Comprendra-t-on?"

revolution of 1789? If they do, what will have been the use of the lessons of history and of the progress made [since then]?"[24]

Griffuelhes' hopes that the March Revolution would spark the creation of a new, genuinely international working-class movement were soon dashed. The Petrograd Soviet on March 27, 1917, appealed "to the peoples of the whole world [to] take into their own hands . . . the question of war and peace"; the appeal was taken up by socialists of the neutral countries, who called for an international conference of socialist parties, including those of both belligerent camps, in Stockholm in the spring of 1918.[25] Griffuelhes had been enthusiastic about the initiative at first. "Has the war opened eyes [sufficiently] to forge an International that will undertake truly international action? I hope so and I have begun to believe it since [reading the Stockholm appeal] yesterday," he wrote. His interest soon died, however. The Stockholm initiative collapsed as the Entente governments, backed up by the leadership of the Western socialist parties and trade unions, refused to issue passports to would-be delegates. Even worse, the March Revolution in Russia had been derailed by the "defensism" of the Kerensky government and the soviets' failure to maintain their earlier revolutionary momentum. "I no longer expect much from Kerensky or from the current soviet," he wrote in December, 1917. Griffuelhes was also disappointed that French antiwar forces failed to take advantage of what he considered a revolutionary situation—the strikes and army mutinies that had erupted earlier in May and June. "There was a moment in France when action would have been possible, at the time of the strikes this summer," he recalled.[26]

In the absence of a revolutionary upheaval in France, Griffuelhes saw the October Revolution as the potential catalyst of a Europe-wide revolution that might usher in the genuine working-class internationalism he had called for since 1916. Lenin believed a world revolution would spring from and consolidate the Russian Revolution, and even though Griffuelhes saw the latter as a success, a worldwide continuation of it seemed a doubtful proposition. In France, for example, "one sees no trace of action parallel to and concordant with [the Bolshevik Revolution]. . . . That would require moral preparation, an exercise in will power. We're not at that point yet." He lamented the failure

24. Griffuelhes, "Le Procès Hervé-Caillaux: La Révolution russe," *La Feuille*, December 13, 1917.

25. Quoted in Olga Hess Gankin and H. H. Fisher, eds., *The Bolsheviks and the World War: The Origin of the Third Internationale* (Stanford, 1940), 585–86.

26. Griffuelhes, "Comprendra-t-on?"; "Le Procès Hervé-Caillaux."

of the French revolutionary Left to take advantage of the strikes and mutinies the previous spring and summer; had that movement spread, he seemed to say, France might have made a revolution that was "parallel to and concordant with," or even anticipated, the October Revolution. That moment had passed, however, and now Lenin and the Bolsheviks must consider the possibility that their revolution would have to be "carried through on its own . . . in isolation, with all the dangers that entails." Griffuelhes said, in one of his rare references to the theorist of "scientific socialism," that Marx "should have foreseen this possibility."[27]

These are prescient comments, especially since they appear so early in the history of international communism. Griffuelhes' early skepticism about the chances of world revolution sparked by Soviet Russia never left him. He experienced the power of nationalism in the course of the world war and apparently was convinced it was greatly underestimated by the Bolshevik leaders. His fears on this score were borne out over the next three years, as was his prediction of the forced option of "socialism in one country."

It would be helpful to know more about the sources of Griffuelhes' early assessments of developments in Russia and their likely impact on the outside world. As a number of writers have pointed out, very little detailed information about the October Revolution or the new Bolshevik regime had reached France at this early date, before the schism in the SFIO in 1920 that produced the French communist party. Almost none of the works of its principal figures, even Lenin, were available in French, although some of his and Trotsky's brochures made their way into France via Germany and Switzerland in December, 1918—at least that is when French police began seizing them. There were, of course, accounts from French newspaper correspondents in Russia. We know Griffuelhes read—and distrusted—*Le Temps'* reporting from Petrograd. And there was "the first workers' rally to greet the red dawn, held at the Maison des syndiqués [*sic*], rue Granges-aux-Belles [CGT headquarters], a few days after the [October] revolution," which was described by Charles Rappaport, one of the SFIO's more orthodox Marxists and himself a veteran of the Russian social-democratic movement. In addition to Rappaport, the orators who addressed the "overflowing" and "enthusiastic" crowd included Alphonse Merrheim; Alexander Losovsky, future head of the Red International of Labor Unions (Profintern), but at the time an anti-Leninist Bolshevik exile in Paris; and Vladimir Antonov-Ovseenko, former editor of

27. Griffuelhes, "Le Procès Hervé-Caillaux."

Trotsky's antiwar journal in Paris, *Nashe Slovo*.[28] Griffuelhes probably attended this rally and others like it, in hopes of learning more about what was really happening in Bolshevik Russia.

Whatever influences shaped his thinking, it is clear that Griffuelhes emerged in 1917 a strong supporter of the Bolshevik Revolution and an admirer of Lenin. Looking back over the war period and the Sacred Union and its German equivalent, the Burgfrieden, Griffuelhes had written that "Lenin alone remained a socialist." Robert Brécy, in analyzing Griffuelhes' reaction to the October Revolution, has remarked that "there are almost no examples among syndicalists of backtracking [from Right to Left]; the case of the revolutionary syndicalist Victor Griffuelhes, who was the most prominent leader of the CGT, is quite exceptional. . . ."[29] One should not, however, draw unwarranted conclusions from Griffuelhes' reactions to the Bolshevik Revolution. As he made clear numerous times in the years that followed, his undoubted support for the revolution and his respect for the Bolsheviks stemmed from his belief that their victory in October, 1917, and subsequent establishment of a "workers' state" proved it was possible to overthrow capitalism through revolutionary action and offered encouragement to workers elsewhere to do the same. He never believed, however, that the October Revolution could or should serve as a model for revolutionary movements in other countries; he was too sensitive to Europe's varying economic, social, political, and cultural configurations and too aware of the relative economic backwardness of Russia to look for—or accept—lessons from the Bolsheviks.

Thus, despite his obvious respect for Lenin and Trotsky and his own eventual membership in the French communist party, he was never at ease with the Bolshevik concept of the party or its increasingly obvious role in directing the dictatorship of the proletariat. His pro-Bolshevik stance came from a belief—perhaps erroneous but widely shared on the French Left until at least 1920—that the new regime was centered on the soviets and thus derived from the French syndicalist blueprint for the producers' commonwealth. When he

---

28. Claude Willard, "La Connaissance de la révolution russe et de l'expérience soviétique par le mouvement ouvrier français en 1918–1919," *Cahiers d'histoire de l'Institut Maurice Thorez*, nos. 12–13 (1975), 318–30; AN, F7 13.090, note of December 28, 1918; Griffuelhes, "Le Bien-etre frère de la liberté," *La Feuille*, April 19, 1917; unpublished manuscript in the Rappaport Archives, International Institute for Social History (IISH), Amsterdam, quoted in Annie Kriegel, *Aux origines du communisme français 1914–1920* (Paris, 1964), I: *De la guerre à la révolution*, 189 n. 1.

29. Brécy quotes Griffuelhes on Lenin (*Mouvement syndical*, 106 n. 1). I have been unable to verify the quote, but it does not seem to be out of character for this period of Griffuelhes' career.

finally realized that the party was in charge, following his trip to Moscow in November, 1921, his enthusiasm waned. In sum, Griffuelhes' postwar "communism" was essentially a restatement of revolutionary syndicalist precepts he had espoused in the prewar era.

After *La Feuille* closed down in January, 1918, apparently from revenue lost because of troubles with government censors, Victor Griffuelhes disappeared from the pages of labor history for over a year and a half. He next surfaced in August, 1919, when he reviewed Sorel's *Matériaux pour une théorie du prolétariat* for the anarchist/communist newspaper—its ideological slant defies accurate description—*Le Journal du Peuple*.[30] In the interim, according to one well-placed source, Griffuelhes devoted his time to business—not the shoe business he might have dreamed about as a young journeyman bottier in the early 1890s, but *big* business. On September 26, 1920, an angry Alphonse Merrheim, now back in the CGT's majority fold, accused Griffuelhes of being a "war profiteer" in the pages of *L'Atelier,* a journal of the reformist wing of the confederation. Merrheim's acidic account is the only evidence of Griffuelhes' alleged wartime business activity:

> Griffuelhes' pride and vanity have never allowed him to forgive the CGT for being able to get along without his leadership. His "victories" as general secretary of the CGT are the defeat of May 1, 1906, and the massacre of Villeneuve-Saint-Georges [1908]. The war broke out. He became the pillar of ministries, where he begged all sorts of favors. He did better than that, our little shoemaker, he set up a metalworking firm that manufactured munitions and war matériel, of which he was one of the principal administrators. And this is the man who brings the charge of "apostasy" against militants who have tried, beset by endless difficulties, to remain true to revolutionary syndicalism.[31]

Although it has not been possible to confirm his charge from other sources, no one in the French labor movement was better placed to know such things than Alphonse Merrheim. As the most active secretary of the metalworkers' union, a large portion of whose members were engaged in war production, Merrheim had intimate knowledge of the defense industry. He also had access to useful sources of information within the government. "[Merrheim] had his

---

30. AN, F7 13.575, telegram, Paris prefect of police to Sureté, July 6, 1917; Griffuelhes, "A propos d'un livre," *Le Journal du Peuple,* August 30, 1919.

31. Alphonse Merrheim, "A la veille du [CGT] Congrès d'Orléans: La Motion d'Amiens," *L'Atelier,* September 26, 1920.

big and small entrées into the Ministry of Armaments," remarked a ranking police official. Merrheim's case is also strengthened by the lack of any attempt by Griffuelhes to refute it. It was a serious charge, delivered when Griffuelhes was making every effort to recover his lost influence in trade-union circles. If Merrheim's story was false, Griffuelhes would have had everything to gain by denying it; instead, he seemed to confirm it when he wrote, concerning his November, 1921, trip to Moscow, that he was "still in business."[32] It seems implausible that Griffuelhes could have set up such a firm and left no trace of his activities, but I have found no evidence of his alleged company either in the papers of state-owned or public-private defense contractors for 1914–1918 in the Archives Nationales or in the accessible files of private suppliers to the ministry of munitions.

Assuming that his portrayal of Griffuelhes as a "merchant of death" during the war is correct and given the hostility between the two men, Merrheim's delay in dropping his bombshell is puzzling. The context for Merrheim's charge is important, for if Griffuelhes had indeed abandoned trade unionism for a business career, he had at the same time emerged as one of Bolshevism's leading sympathizers in France. This latter aspect of Griffuelhes' evolution appears to have disturbed Merrheim most; his blast against the former general secretary followed a widely publicized, cleverly staged interview with Griffuelhes and the general staff of the pre-1914 CGT (Pouget, Yvetot, Delesalle) in which Griffuelhes declared that in the postwar CGT the mantle of revolutionary syndicalist legitimacy had passed to the minority movement. He claimed that "an atmosphere of pre-revolution" existed in France and that the CGT majority, far from demonstrating the leadership such a situation demanded, was "taking refuge in . . . dreams of collaboration with capital and the State." The interview was written up in the SFIO newspaper, *L'Humanité,* by Amédée Dunois, Griffuelhes' old friend and future comrade in the communist party.[33] Dunois was a leading member of the left-of-center bloc that had just taken control of the French Socialist Party and was pushing it toward membership in the Comintern; this group was the nucleus of the new French Communist Party (Parti communiste français—PCF) after the Congress of

32. Henri Maunoury, *Police de guerre* (Paris, 1937), 100; Griffuelhes, "L'Actualité et les Faits. Ce que personne n'a jamais dit. Huit Mois en Russie, en Esthonie, en Lettonie, en Lituanie et en Allemagne," *La Bataille,* pt. 7, June 15, 1922.

33. Dunois, "Une Conversation sur la motion d'Amiens avec l'ançien bureau confédéral." *DBMO,* XII, 109–13 (Dunois); see also Dunois' tribute to Griffuelhes in *L'Humanité,* July 5, 1922.

Tours three months later. The interview and article could not have come at a worse time for the CGT majority; appearing on the eve of the 1920 CGT congress, it emboldened the opposition already threatening Merrheim and the majority, of which he was now a leader.

Personal issues were at stake as well. As the former leader of the wartime minority within the CGT who had now made peace with Jouhaux, Merrheim was a special target for abuse from the minority at congresses and in the press, although not so much from his former friends and associates Monatte and Alfred Rosmer, who were relatively courteous in debate.[34] His real enemies were the so-called pure syndicalist and anarchosyndicalist factions within the minority, some of whose members he suspected were close to Griffuelhes and were being primed by him for their attacks on the "apostates"—himself and Georges Dumoulin, another of Griffuelhes' prewar colleagues who had moved from revolutionary syndicalism to reformism by 1918. There may also have been an element of "bad conscience" in Merrheim's attack on Griffuelhes; as Christian Gras and Annie Kriegel have suggested, Merrheim's own hands were not entirely clean as far as compromising behavior during the war is concerned.[35]

Merrheim's suspicions about Griffuelhes' links to elements within the CGT minority were correct. From around May, 1920, Griffuelhes was closely involved with leaders of its extreme Left faction, pure syndicalists like Pierre Besnard and Guillaume Verdier whose bible was the Charter of Amiens and whose stock-in-trade as minority activists, for the moment at least, was good old-fashioned Griffuelhian "boring from within" or noyautage. As Merrheim suspected, Griffuelhes was making a comeback.

34. After Merrheim's death, Monatte wrote, "He was sometimes unjust toward us [the minority], toward me; I tried not to be toward him" (*La Révolution prolétarienne*, no. 11 [November, 1925], 11–12).

35. Gras suggests that Merrheim began to soften his antiwar stand in 1915 in deference to Jouhaux and Albert Thomas, who had intervened to save him from being sent to the front (*Alfred Rosmer*, 111); Kriegel develops the thesis that out of "personal hatred for Lenin and perhaps Trotsky," Merrheim switched his allegiance, following the 1915 Zimmerwald conference, to "bourgeois pacifists" such as Aristide Briand and Joseph Caillaux (Kriegel, *Aux origines du communisme français*, I, 229).

XI

DÉNOUEMENT (1919–1922)

The atmosphere in the movement makes it impossible to breathe. . . . The men of the movement and I—we feel and understand things differently. I feel like a man from another age.

—Griffuelhes, "Ce que personne n'a jamais dit"

Victor Griffuelhes' active involvement in the trade-union movement did not end during World War I, as some scholars appear to believe. F. F. Ridley, for example, states that "Griffuelhes, [general] secretary of the CGT from 1902 [*sic*] to 1909, played no role in union affairs thereafter, though he did sympathize with the communists after the war."[1] This was not the case. The October Revolution in Russia brought Griffuelhes out of retirement and back into the trade-union movement; he emerged as a leading exponent of the thesis that the new Russian state was rooted in the workers' soviets, which, he argued, were inspired by the prewar French revolutionary syndicalist blueprint for a producers' commonwealth coordinated and managed by the unions. In February, 1920, he made this view the centerpiece of a much remarked upon speech entitled "Soviets and Unions," before a worker-student audience in Paris. Shortly thereafter, Griffuelhes began a new career as éminence grise of the emerging pure syndicalist faction of the CGT revolutionary minority, playing an important, if behind-the-scenes, part in the events that led to the breakup of the CGT in December, 1921. Concurrently, he seems to have made a last, futile bid to recapture a position of power in the French labor move-

1. Ridley, *Revolutionary Syndicalism in France*, p. 261.

ment, by seeking the patronage of Trotsky and Lenin—the purpose of his trip to Moscow in November, 1921.

"There was a moment just after the armistice," wrote Victor Griffuelhes in November, 1920, "when a revolutionary psychology was in evidence." At street level, "We lived in a genuinely revolutionary time: sudden, intensive unemployment; soldiers impatient to be demobilized; the continuation of war government in all its forms; an economic crisis that weighed more and more heavily upon the poor, who were obliged to queue up at the baker's and coal seller's. There was electricity in the air."[2]

Above street level, Griffuelhes, ever closely attuned to the moral dimension of events, also perceived an "end of an era psychology" among French political and economic leaders in 1919. Industrialists, for example, were convinced that "the war would usher in a new and transformed world," not one to their liking, certainly, but one to which they were, Griffuelhes believed, "fatalistically resigned." This resignation stemmed from a widespread but rarely acknowledged belief that the common soldier, angered and exasperated by the sacrifices of the long, bloody war, "had acquired a revolutionary outlook and that, stirred up by the events in Russia, he was prepared to use the skills gained in wartime to make a revolution." Griffuelhes' perspective was no mere left-wing fantasy; fear and pessimism were indeed widespread in business and government circles in the immediate postwar years. As late as November, 1921, the French conservative politician André Lichtenberger still believed that the war "has so profoundly overturned the conditions of life for the French bourgeoisie that it is undergoing a crisis whose gravity just cannot be exaggerated."[3]

These fears appeared to be borne out by the spectacular rise in union membership following the armistice and the aggressive strike activity it engendered. From the close of 1918 to December, 1919, the number of dues-paying members in the CGT increased from just under 499,000 to 1,136,766. "The demobilized soldiers," wrote Paul Louis, "who hoped, now that the war

---

2. Griffuelhes, "La Psychologie d'une fin de régime," *La Revue communiste,* November, 1920, 245; Griffuelhes' "Soviets and Unions" speech in Paris, February 6, 1920, quoted in Marcel Vergéat, "Soviets et Syndicats: La Conférence de Griffuelhes," *La Vie Ouvrière,* 2nd ser., February 13, 1920.

3. Griffuelhes, "La Psychologie d'une fin de régime," 245; André Lichtenberger, "Le Bourgeois," *Revue des deux mondes,* November 15, 1921, quoted in Charles S. Maier, *Recasting Bourgeois Europe* (Princeton, 1975), 39.

was over, to make a better place for themselves, flooded into the unions. . . . To many of them, who had never belonged to any kind of movement before, the union meant job security and putting the employer in his place . . . and they demanded immediate action."[4]

Not surprisingly, given the belligerent attitude of these newcomers, strike activity reached record proportions in 1919. Government figures for the year show 2,098 strikes, involving 1,160,618 strikers and resulting in 15,528,312 workdays lost; the latter figure was seven times that of 1913, the last full year of peace before the war. The most militant unions in 1919 and 1920 were the railway workers, now clearly the largest industrial union in the CGT, and the metalworkers. On January 25, 1919, the revolutionary minority in the rail union, whose total membership had risen from 154,000 in 1918 to just under 290,500 in mid 1919, demonstrated their newfound muscle within the union by successfully organizing a one-minute halt of every train in France. The metalworkers, whose union had grown from 100,000 at the close of 1918 to just over 151,000 in mid 1919 and approximately 200,000 by year's end, launched massive strikes in the Paris region in June, 1919.[5]

What seems important, however, is not the number of strikes in 1919, but their prevailing mood. For the first time since the confrontation at Villeneuve-Saint-Georges in 1908, the strikes of 1919 and, later, in 1920, went beyond the defense of jobs and purchasing power. Marcel Vergéat, an anarchosyndicalist metalworker and a leader of the CGT minority, wrote in *La Vie Ouvrière,* which had been revived by its prewar editors, principally Pierre Monatte and Alfred Rosmer, on April 30, 1919: "Sure, the workers are striking back at the arrogance and double-dealing of the bosses. But there's more to this movement than that. Already during the war, the long, hard struggle of the [antiwar] minority had begun to make headway among the masses. . . . Some of that idealism remains. Today one can safely say that better wages and working conditions, or the eight-hour day, are no longer the real objectives."[6]

Victor Griffuelhes and many within the CGT minority would have stressed

4. These are union figures presented at the CGT congresses of Lyon (1919) and Orléans (1920) (Labi, *La Grande Division des travailleurs,* 248–49); Louis, *Le Syndicalisme français,* 190.

5. Labi, *La Grande Division des travailleurs,* 304, 248; Brécy, *Mouvement syndical,* 107; Louis, *Le Syndicalisme français,* 193. On the 1919 strike wave, see *Le Mouvement social,* no. 93 (October–December, 1975), especially Bertrand Abhervé, "Les Origines de la grève des métallurgistes parisiens, juin 1919," 75–85, and Nicholas Papayanis, "Masses révolutionnaires et Directions réformistes: Les Tensions au cours des grèves métallurgistes français en 1919," 51–73.

6. Marcel Vergéat, *V.O.,* 2nd ser., June 11, 1919, quoted in Dolléans, *Histoire du mouvement ouvrier,* II, 304.

that the source of the strikers' revolutionary aspirations in 1919–1920 was more the Bolshevik Revolution than the French antiwar movement's idealism. In his "Soviets et Syndicats" theme and indeed all of his postwar activity, Griffuelhes demonstrated his belief that the Bolshevik experience was primordial in shaping a "revolutionary mentality" in France in the immediate postwar era. He was not alone. Val R. Lorwin, the dean of American historians of French labor, reached a similar conclusion: "Just as a new generation was beginning to forget the Paris Commune, the Russian Revolution added its spell. In no country did this great twentieth century myth make a deeper impression than in skeptical France; among no group a greater impression than on the workers who had never made a successful revolution of their own."[7]

The "spell" cast upon French workers was most hypnotic in 1919, and its impact was felt most deeply by those revolutionary syndicalists of the prewar era—such as Pierre Monatte, Alfred Rosmer, and Victor Griffuelhes who stood with the CGT minority against its reformist leadership—and perhaps more surprisingly, by militants who called themselves anarchosyndicalists or plain anarchists. Although it is somewhat easier to understand the revolutionary syndicalists' reasons for rallying to the Russian Revolution than those of their libertarian comrades, the phenomenon is nevertheless more complicated than Robert Wohl has proposed in his *French Communism in the Making*. According to Wohl, revolutionary syndicalism "shared with Leninism a disdain for democracy and democratic socialism, elitism, and a stress on violent revolution."[8] This view has its roots in the long-running polemical battle between the revolutionary syndicalists and their reformist adversaries in the CGT and the socialist party. Charges of elitism and a fondness for violence have been leveled against revolutionary syndicalism since at least 1904, and it is not surprising to find them surfacing in discussions of the revolutionary syndicalist–Bolshevik rapprochement in the immediate postwar era.

Careful analysis of what leading members of the pro-Bolshevik faction within revolutionary syndicalism wrote and said in 1919–1920, however, leads to somewhat different conclusions. The first is that in 1919 and less so in 1920, these militants, Griffuelhes included, tended to see the Bolsheviks as revolutionary syndicalists in Russian dress and lauded them for putting their own prewar blueprint for a new social order into practice. The relaunched *Vie*

7. Val R. Lorwin, "Labor and Economic Development in France," unpublished manuscript quoted in Gordon Wright, *France in Modern Times* (3rd ed.; New York, 1981), 371–72.
8. Robert Wohl, *French Communism in the Making, 1914–1924* (Stanford, 1966), 27.

Ouvrière, for example, abounded with articles in 1919 portraying the new communist state as based on the soviets and linking their role to the syndicalist conception of the unions as postrevolutionary coordinators of production and distribution.[9] The other conclusion to be drawn is that revolutionary syndicalists supported the Bolsheviks because, as Marcel Vergéat put it, whatever else one might think of the October Revolution, it was the long-awaited "social revolution and that's already something."[10]

The more incongruous anarchosyndicalist and anarchist fascination with Bolshevism in 1919–1920 has frequently been explained as the result of Lenin's influence, especially through his tract, *State and Revolution,* in which he elaborated his concept of the "withering away of the state." The main problem with this thesis where France is concerned is that when anarchist enthusiasm for the October Revolution was highest, almost none of Lenin's works were available in French. Alfred Rosmer recalled later that in 1919 "some copies" of the French translation of *State and Revolution* printed in Moscow found their way into France, but certainly not enough to cause the groundswell of sympathy for Bolshevism among French anarchosyndicalists and anarchists at this early stage. A more plausible explanation was offered by the anarchosyndicalist building trades' militant, Louis Bertho, alias Lepetit, in 1919: "It's clear that the Bolshevik Revolution isn't ideal from our point of view. Such as it is, however, it still merits our interest" because the Russian workers "have carried out the first attempt at social revolution the world has ever known."[11]

This was a key point, not only for anarchosyndicalists like Lepetit, but also for revolutionary syndicalists like Monatte or Griffuelhes: The Bolshevik Revolution was the long dreamed-of *social* revolution, the one that would transcend mere political democracy and usher in economic democracy. This revolution inspired Eugène Varlin and like-minded Communards in 1871, Fernand Pelloutier and his associates in the Bourse du Travail movement in the 1890s, and the revolutionary syndicalists who drafted and adopted the Charter of Amiens. As such, the October Revolution must be defended against its adversaries and, if possible, emulated within France. This point was dra-

9. See, for example, Lucien Midol, "Soviets et Syndicats," *V.O.,* July 16, 1919, and Robert Louzon, "Guesde avait-il raison?" and "Le Régime des conseils," *ibid.,* August 27, October 15, 1919; Louzon, the former Paris gasworks engineer, had loaned Griffuelhes the money to launch his controversial Maison des Fédérations project in 1907.

10. Vergéat, in the anarchist journal, *La Mêlée,* March 1, 1919, quoted in Jean Maitron, *Le Mouvement anarchiste en France: De 1914 à nos jours* (Paris, 1975), 43.

11. Alfred Rosmer, *Moscow Under Lenin* (New York, 1971), 46; Lepetit [Louis Bertho] in *Le Libertaire,* June 8, 1919, quoted in Maitron, *Le mouvement anarchiste,* II, 44.

matically underscored by Michel Kneler, another anarchosyndicalist from the building trades and a postwar disciple of Griffuelhes, who was sentenced on May 17, 1919, to six months in prison, one for each shot he fired in the air outside the Elysée Palace to protest Allied intervention in Russia.[12]

The CGT's reformist leadership also sensed that the "real objectives" of the postwar workers' movement transcended bread-and-butter issues. They were unwilling to concede, however, the minority's claim that international developments—creation of a workers' state in Russia and the westward sweep of Bolshevism—together with the ruling classes' moral bankruptcy, had produced a revolutionary situation in France. They insisted instead that greater participation by trade unions in the nation's economic decision-making machinery and a more equitable division of national wealth were called for.

The issues in the confrontation between the CGT's majority and minority between 1919 and 1921 were fundamental and had been at the heart of the confederation since its founding in 1895. The war and the Bolshevik Revolution, profound as those experiences were, only intensified debate over these fundamental issues; they had introduced little that was really new. Thus, the objectives of the French working-class struggle remained for the postwar reformists what they had been for Auguste Keufer in his July, 1904, debate with Griffuelhes: gradual improvement of the worker's lot within the framework of capitalism and the Republic. For the CGT minority, the objectives were still the same as those of the prewar revolutionary majority—and the Bolshevik Revolution reinforced rather than altered them: suppressing capitalism through workers' action (*i.e.,* "generalized" strikes and/or the general strike) and replacing it with a producers' commonwealth.

Both sides departed from prewar tradition in the means used to attain their proclaimed ends. The degree of departure on this score was much greater for revolutionaries than for reformists, and among the factions now emerging within the revolutionaries, there were also significant differences as to means. The reformists now saw the means to achieve their social-democratic ends as largely political, rather than trade-unionist, *i.e.,* close collaboration with the SFIO and pressure on parliament to secure reform legislation, but this was a change only in the sense that some reformists, such as Keufer, had now abandoned all pretense of trade-union independence, or what was known as pure syndicalism before the war.

Among the revolutionaries, the shift from the previous stance was much

12. *V.O.*, May 21, 1919.

greater—at least in the immediate aftermath of the October Revolution. In essence, it was accepting to varying degrees and for varying lengths of time the need for a vanguard political party, which further implied accepting— again, there were differences on this point—the need for a political revolution as a precondition for a successful social revolution, a notion that would have been anathema to most prewar revolutionary syndicalists. This was the real legacy of the Bolshevik Revolution to postwar French trade unionism. The *Vie Ouvrière* group of Monatte and Rosmer, whose international outlook and contacts had already set them apart from most other syndicalists in the pre-1914 period, showed the greatest sustained enthusiasm for a vanguard party. In the shorter term from 1917 to 1920, however, this enthusiasm was perhaps greater among the anarchist and anarchosyndicalist wing of the labor movement, including the new-style pure syndicalists of the CGT minority, who were fierce devotees of the Charter of Amiens. One of those was Guillaume Verdier, the radical metalworkers' leader; speaking before his union's national committee in December, 1919, he said: "I consider myself a revolutionary, but I must also say that I firmly believe that the economic revolution, which should lead to social transformation, will take years. This [economic] revolution—and I sincerely believe this—must be preceded by a political revolution whose psychological task is the seizure of power." [13]

Verdier believed the Bolsheviks had shown the way, and his view was shared by most if not all members of the pure faction until at least mid 1920. Earlier, in 1919, Verdier had told another meeting of the metalworkers' national committee: "Instead of a Jouhaux or a Merrheim, what we need is a Lenin, a Trotsky! That's what's holding us back!" [14] It would seem from these remarks that Verdier and the pure syndicalists in general saw the vanguard party as a kind of "Red Guard" whose task was to demolish the old order, then stack its arms and let the soviets set up the syndicalist commonwealth. They may also have held the same conception of the new French Communist Party, which many joined with great enthusiasm when it was founded in 1920.

Griffuelhes apparently joined forces with Verdier and the pure faction in early 1920, probably following his "Soviets et syndicats" speech on February 3 at the Salle des Sociétés Savantes in Paris. It was Griffuelhes' first public appearance since before the war, and the correspondent of *L'Information ouvrière et sociale* wrote that the evening had the "air of a comeback in the

---

13. Quoted in Donald Reid, "Guillaume Verdier et le Syndicalisme révolutionnaire aux usines de Decazeville (1917–1920)," *Annales du Midi*, no. 166 (April–June, 1984), 196.
14. *Ibid.*

making." Speaking to a packed house, a "curious mixture of students and workers," Griffuelhes stressed two main themes: The old order was passing in France; and workers, guided by the example of the Bolshevik Revolution, must face up to their responsibility to build a new order on its ruins, a nation of producers and consumers rather than citizens and governed by workers' councils rather than a parliament.[15]

There had been a "psychological moment" in 1919, said Griffuelhes, when revolution had been possible, but the moment had passed and the frightened bourgeoisie had quickly recovered its aplomb: "It is winning now and believes the danger has passed." This belief did not mean, however, that the danger had indeed passed; the situation was still revolutionary because of the State's serious financial trouble, which it was "impossible to do anything about." Austerity was not the answer because that would decrease production and consumption, thus reducing tax revenue, and the State needed all the revenue possible to service its enormous war debt. Clearly, consumption should be stimulated to relaunch industrial production and generate tax revenue, but proposals along these lines fell on deaf ears.[16]

But if the situation in France remained revolutionary and yet no revolution was forthcoming, the fault lay squarely with the working class—not so much with its leaders, although Jouhaux and the CGT majority were not up to "the challenge of the times," but with the workers themselves.[17] To Griffuelhes' mind, the main problem was not lack of a revolutionary program or strategy, but a psychological one of deep-seated mentalities. France, said the former *bottier*, was still a nation of artisans, with old-fashioned tools, methods, and ways. It needed less production for conspicuous consumption and more production for mass consumption, and it must transform itself into a nation of producers. Workers must think of themselves not as workers but as "functionaries," he stated, quickly adding that this meant taking a "functional" approach to their work. If French workers continued with their old artisan mentality, there would be no revolution, and "we will be to the world what Nice and the Cote d'Azur are to France, . . . where the women are courtesans and the men valets."

Griffuelhes then asserted that Germany was the only country that understood the need for the social philosophy of production he referred to; indeed,

---

15. R. Roure, "Une Conférence de M. Victor Griffuelhes, ançien secrétaire de la CGT," *L'Information ouvrière et sociale*, February 8, 1920.

16. Vergéat, "Soviets et Syndicats"; Roure, "Une Conférence de Griffuelhes."

17. Vergéat, "Soviets et Syndicats."

"in less than twenty years, global moral authority will be in the hands of Germany." "What about the U.S.A.?" "What about Russia?" the audience shouted. Germany was more developed than the U.S.A., Griffuelhes replied, and had the added advantage of its social philosophy of production. The Soviet Union, meanwhile, had "such an enormous effort of construction ahead of her that she cannot dream for a long time of being a dominant people." [18]

In conclusion, Griffuelhes called for all workers to unify in a concerted effort to deny the State and the capitalists the one thing that could save them from collapse—production. He then introduced an idea he had begun developing just after the war: the need to eliminate the distinctions that had so long existed between what he called "workers of the mind and workers of the hand." [19] This was not a plea for a union between workers and intellectuals, but a call for a Saint-Simonian-type common front of manual workers with technicians and engineers. Though by no means unique to Griffuelhes, the notion was a relatively new departure for him and warrants examination as to its likely sources.

First, Griffuelhes' desire to broaden the concept of "worker" to include what we would today call "mental workers" may have reflected the great enthusiasm for trade union membership shown by French civil servants immediately following the war. For example, in May, 1920, the Fédération des Fonctionnaires, representing 200,000 civil servants, joined the CGT.[20] A second influence may have been ideas emanating from the contemporary German "conciliar" or *Räte* movement. There is a striking resemblance between Griffuelhes' thought and, for example, that of Ernst Daumig, as summarized by Albert Lindemann in his book, *The 'Red Years'*:

> On the one hand [Daumig] emphasized the enormous importance of the revolution in Russia, but on the other he termed it a "fundamental error" (*Riesenfehler*) of the bolsheviks to have based their rule exclusively on the lowest ranks of the working class. He felt that it was of the utmost importance to unite the intellectual and manual workers (*Kopf- und Handarbeiter*) in the socialist *Rätesystem*. Moreover, he explicitly rejected the idea that the Russian model was one that the German

18. Roure, "Une conférence de Griffuelhes."
19. Griffuelhes first spelled out this thesis in "A propos d'un livre," *Journal du Peuple*, August 30, 1919.
20. Brécy, *Mouvement syndical*, 108.

revolutionaries should follow dogmatically, and he disassociated himself from those "confused workers and intellectuals who have made a fetish out of the Russian example."[21]

One suspects that the Rätesystem was the social philosophy of production that Griffuelhes found so impressive in Germany and that he imbibed this and his concept of uniting "workers of the mind and workers of the hand," which was very close to that of Daumig, from postwar contacts in Germany. This new view of what constitutes a worker corresponded to another Griffuelhes concern—one he had expressed earlier but posed with even greater acuity after the war: the lack of technical and managerial expertise among workers who would, in the syndicalist scheme of things, be called upon to direct and coordinate production after the revolution. Griffuelhes transmitted this concern to his new allies among the pure syndicalists ("pures" from now on), and it occupied a prominent place in their thinking on the future structure and tasks of the trade-union movement.

In February, 1921, eighteen of the pure faction's leaders signed a then-secret document that they referred to simply as "The Pact"; it was leaked to the press in June, 1922, and created a considerable scandal, as will be seen. Of the "Pactists" whose backgrounds can be traced in some detail, four played prominent roles in the postwar CGT revolutionary minority and in the schism of 1921: Guillaume Verdier, Pierre Besnard, Henri Sirolle, and Henri Totti. All were of working-class origins, born in the provinces, and they held leadership positions in the CGT's most militant unions. Besnard, Sirolle, and Totti occupied important posts in the railway workers' union, which was the CGT's largest, with 290,000 members at peak postwar strength in mid 1919, and the detonator of the massive general strike of May, 1920. Besnard, a chief porter, served as secretary of the union's key Paris branch during the strike, while Sirolle acted as liaison between the union and the CGT during the opening days of the walkout. He and Totti, a car porter and secretary of the Marseille branch of the rail union, were jailed shortly after the strike began. An electrician by profession (as was Sirolle), Verdier made his reputation during the war as the radical union leader in the Decazeville (Aveyron) steel works. After the war, he was one of the leaders of the sizeable revolutionary minority in the metalworkers' union.[22]

21. Albert Lindemann, *The 'Red Years': European Socialism Versus Bolshevism, 1919–1921* (Berkeley, 1974), 42; the author's summary is based on Daumig's book, *Der Aufbau Deutschlands und das Rätesystem* (Berlin, 1919), 8, 12, 28–29.

22. Labi, *La Grande Division des travailleurs,* 248; *DBMO,* XIX, 110–11 (Besnard); XV, 169

Compared to the leaders of the CGT reformist majority and those of the *Vie Ouvrière* or communist-syndicalist faction, the pure militants were relatively young men, averaging around thirty-five years of age in 1921, with minimal previous experience in the labor movement. Of the group, apparently only Sirolle and Totti were involved in the prewar CGT and only in the context of the 1910 railway strike.[23] The majority chiefs—general secretary Léon Jouhaux, assistant general secretary Georges Dumoulin, and metalworkers' secretary Alphonse Merrheim, for example—were around twelve years older and were prominent veterans of the Heroic Age of revolutionary syndicalism. The communist-syndicalist leaders also boasted years of service to the trade-union cause, although more as labor journalists and theoreticians than as men of action. Alfred Rosmer and Pierre Monatte had edited *La Vie Ouvrière,* the major theoretical journal of revolutionary syndicalism in the prewar period, and had revived it in 1919 as an organ to foster solidarity with the Bolshevik Revolution and create a new revolutionary labor international.

Another characteristic of the pure leaders was that, in contrast to the majority hierarchy and especially the militants of the communist-syndicalist faction, they had not served in the war or taken much part in the controversy over CGT participation in the Sacred Union that so troubled Griffuelhes. They had spent the war years, like Verdier, in the defense plants or, like Besnard, Sirolle, and Totti, on the state-run railways. For them, the CGT leadership's responsibility for the failure of the French working class to prevent the war or to stop the mass slaughter through a negotiated peace were not the burning issues they had been for the majority or for the *Vie Ouvrière* group.

The pures' involvement in the revolutionary minority of the CGT stemmed, rather, from their initially enthusiastic response to the October Revolution. Like Victor Griffuelhes, they greeted it as a vindication of the theory and practice of prewar revolutionary syndicalism and a guide and inspiration for the revolution in France that they fervently believed was possible in 1919 and 1920. A number of them joined the new French Communist Party in 1920, apparently believing that its purpose was to organize a French October Revolution. Compared to Monatte and Rosmer, however, the pures took little interest in the Bolshevik Revolution as a Russian or European phenomenon or in promoting solidarity with it, reserving their enthusiasm for the object

---

(Sirolle); XV, 242–43 (Totti); the best source on Verdier is Reid, "Guillaume Verdier et le Syndicalisme révolutionnaire."

23. *DBMO*, XV, 242–43.

lessons that could be learned from it and applied in France. When it became clear to them, as it did by early 1921, that the new Russian state was in fact a party dictatorship, the pures' reaction was to sabotage efforts to affiliate the French unions with the Comintern or the Red International of Labor Unions (Profintern); to seize control of the CGT minority's organizational structures in order to keep them out of communist hands; and to use the influence of their members who had joined the communist party to isolate the PCF from the trade-union movement.

In terms of ideological background, the pures profiled here were anarchists, at least in inspiration. Jean Maitron has pointed out, however, that none of them belonged to a traditional anarchist group, such as the Anarchist Federation. He calls the pures "anarchosyndicalists"; they were also autodidacts in the venerable tradition of French labor militants going back to Alphonse Delacour and his revolutionary bookbinders in the 1860s. Besnard, the theoretician of the group, was "the prototypical utopian," according to Monatte. "He never bothered to find out whether what he had read in his books measured up to reality." Verdier was fond of quoting Proudhon and Bakunin at CGT congresses. At the Orléans congress in 1920, for example, he must have startled some delegates by declaring that revolutionaries now had "a practical example to follow which takes its inspiration from Proudhon: It's the Russian Revolution."[24] One can only imagine how Lenin would have reacted to this revelation.

What has confused historians about the politics of the pures is the membership of Verdier and Totti—along with Griffuelhes—in the French Communist Party from early 1921 through the CGT schism (except for Griffuelhes), and the pures' subsequent battle with the communists for control of the new Unified General Confederation of Labor (CGTU). This paradoxical behavior also misled Jules Humbert-Droz, the Comintern agent for the Latin countries, and perhaps even Lenin and Trotsky, who saw the pures' membership in the party as a sign of their imminent conversion to Bolshevism.[25]

Although Griffuelhes appears to have known only one of these younger men, Henri Totti, from the prewar era, he brought a great deal to his new partnership with these novices of the labor movement. First and foremost was his considerable prestige as "the man of the Charter" of Amiens. The charter

24. Maitron, *Le Mouvement anarchiste,* II, 59; CGT, *XXIe Congrès national corporatif . . . Orléans,* 82.

25. Jules Humbert-Droz, "Syndicalistes et Communistes en France," *Bulletin communiste,* January 26, 1922.

was the bible of the pures. Said Verdier at the CGT Congress of Orléans in 1920: "We must restore the CGT to . . . what it was before the war. Maybe then we [majority and minority] will be in agreement." This devotion to orthodox revolutionary syndicalism gave the pure faction its name and set it off, not only from the communist-syndicalists and the majority but also from its erstwhile anarchist allies to the left. Not that these other factions eschewed the charter, for as Maurice Labi has remarked, "The Charter . . . was seized upon by everyone, casually and with little forethought. The communists espoused it because it was the expression of revolutionary trade unionism, the reformists because it denounced subjection to parties or sects. The anarchists made it their own [because] it seemed to define a decentralist road to proletarian revolution."[26]

None of these other factions, however, made as much of a fetish of the charter as the pures did. There was an element of incongruity in this, which did not escape the sharp eyes of Alfred Rosmer. The pures, he wrote, want to go back to the syndicalism of the prewar years, but "it is a task that is beyond them; they never lived prewar syndicalism."[27] All the more fortunate then that the pures could claim Griffuelhes as their guide and inspiration.

The pures also latched on to Griffuelhes' vision of a State on the verge of collapse under its weight of debt and therefore vulnerable to a determined workers' onslaught. Thus Verdier stated at the CGT Congress of Orléans: "I don't need to tell you what the financial situation is at the moment. . . . I challenge the government to tell us the real truth about its budget. . . . Even if they don't understand everything that is going on, the masses instinctively know . . . the powerlessness of capitalism to restore the equilibrium wrecked by the war."[28]

As long as the pures (and Griffuelhes) were under the impression that the workers' soviets, and not the Bolshevik party, were the force behind the new communist state in Russia, they continued to cite the October Revolution as a beacon of light for the revolutionary movement in France. They were convinced that events in Russia in 1917 had vindicated the tenets of prewar revolutionary syndicalism. Griffuelhes had written that although "I never knew Lenin or Trotsky . . . I have the strong impression that their stay in France

26. Griffuelhes, "La Lutte pour la nationalisation," *La Revue communiste,* no. 4, June, 1920; CGT, *XXIe Congrès national corporatif. . . Orléans,* 224; Labi, *La Grande Division des travailleurs,* 170.
27. Rosmer, *La Lutte des classes,* July 5, 1922, quoted in Gras, *Alfred Rosmer,* 242.
28. CGT, *XXIe Congrès national corporatif. . . Orléans,* 308.

imbued them with all that has been for the last twenty years the thought, the life, and the substance of the trade-union movement of this country." Thus, to his mind, the soviet system looked like a copy of the CGT table of organization. "The soviet—*i.e.*, the union—[is] in charge of production under the direction of national soviets—*i.e.*, the national federations—and under the inspiration of a grand soviet composed of delegates from the national soviets—*i.e.*, the CGT." [29]

Verdier parroted this view almost literally. In a letter of April 6, 1920, to Pierre Monatte, setting out his views on the proper course for the CGT minority, Verdier stated he favored a movement that "achieves revolution through the efforts of the unions: local unions, departmental unions, federations and CGT functioning together as organs of production and distribution and thus exercising the power of the State and the authority of the capitalist owners." [30]

Griffuelhes' plea for a union of workers of the mind and of the hand, however, seems to have made the most lasting impression on the pures. Pierre Besnard, the group's "theorist," at least in his view, proved to be this notion's most prominent advocate. Besnard was the main author of the pures' draft constitution for a new CGT *Révolutionnaire* presented on the eve of the CGT schism in December, 1921; the united front of manual and mental workers occupied a prominent position in it.

Jean Maitron is the only French labor historian who, to my knowledge, has asked what Griffuelhes hoped to gain from his alliance with the pures, with whom he appears to have had so little in common, at least in terms of shared experience. His answer is a plausible one: that the former CGT leader wanted to play éminence grise to these aspirants to leadership of a new, more radical CGT, as he had once done for Léon Jouhaux. "The man, general secretary of the CGT until 1909, was a front-rank figure and was never satisfied to be anything else. In the shadows behind Jouhaux before and at the beginning of the war, did he dream, after a trip to Moscow at the beginning of 1920 [*sic*], of playing éminence grise once again? To whose profit? All we can say for sure is that his death in July [*sic*] 1922 put an end to the dream, if dream there was." [31]

29. Griffuelhes, "A propos d'un livre."

30. Chambelland and Maitron, eds., *Syndicalisme révolutionnaire et communisme*, 275.

31. Maitron, *Le Mouvement anarchiste*, II, 65. Maitron placed Griffuelhes' Moscow trip in the early months of 1920, a year and a half before it actually occurred, and Robert Brécy writes that it took place before Griffuelhes' "Soviets et Syndicats" speech in February, 1920 (Brécy,

I believe Griffuelhes' "dream" was grander than this, even though he failed to act as forcefully on it as he might have done in earlier years. In 1921, Griffuelhes actively considered bidding for leadership of the CGT Révolutionnaire that would emerge from the schism he felt was inevitable in the old CGT; I believe this was the reason he went to Moscow in November that year. But aside from using the alliance with the pures as a springboard to a position of trade-union leadership once more, Griffuelhes probably also entered into the relationship because, after so many years out in the cold, it was good to be surrounded by militants again, especially ones who saw him as a sage and spiritual leader.

The alliance was a two-way street, however. One has the strong impression that the pures used the old man as much as he used them, particularly Besnard, who tried to add lustre to his own schemes to divide the trade-union movement—the Pact of 1921 and later, the Charter of Lyon, the statutes for the *CGT Syndicaliste Révolutionnaire* he founded in 1926—by touting Griffuelhes' patronage of them.[32]

The pures began organizing as a force within the CGT minority following the disastrous railway strike in May–June, 1920. "It wasn't in 1921 or 1922 that we first judged that syndicalism was in danger," Pierre Besnard wrote, "but in May 1920 and just after." There was a "double danger. . . . First, we felt that the working-class movement was headed for defeat [in the strike] and that no one else was going to do anything to save it. Second, . . . we were in no doubt that the effort to subordinate [syndicalism to Moscow] was already underway."[33]

It was about this time that Griffuelhes began to work with the pures as a group. On May 8, 1920, he intervened with the CGT Executive Committee

Mouvement syndical, 106 n. 2). I have considered the possibility of two Griffuelhes visits to the USSR but remain convinced, from internal evidence in Griffuelhes' account of his November, 1921, trip, that this was his first and only visit to the Russian capital.

32. Besnard says "Griffuelhes was involved" in planning the Pact: "Pourquoi y eut-il le pacte? Son histoire," *Le Journal du Peuple*, July 23, 1922. Later he claimed that the draft for the Charter of Lyon, which was "born of the necessity of defending *the independence of the trade-union movement* against the enterprises of the communist party, at the same time as the famous pact which united militants for this defense . . . in the spring of 1921," was the work of "Victor Griffuelhes, *the author of the Charter of Amiens and former secretary of the CGT*" (*L'Ethique du syndicalisme* [Paris, 1938], 127). Besnard's emphasis.

33. Besnard, "Pourquoi y eut-il le pacte?"

on behalf of Besnard and the leadership of the Paris railwaymen, calling upon the CGT to organize an all-out general strike in support of the railroad strike launched five days earlier. But, "this body, dominated by men totally opposed to any sort of action, categorically refused to accept our proposal," Besnard recalled. "The result . . . was defeat of the strike after a hopeless struggle." This was not entirely true. The CGT leadership eventually did call out other unions in support of the railwaymen, although in successive waves, not en masse as Griffuelhes had proposed. The strike was a defeat, regardless, and the workers were forced to go back without obtaining any concessions; some twenty thousand, including Besnard, were fired. The crushing of the rail strike marked the end of the immediate postwar era of labor militancy and led to a sudden, sharp decline in union membership.[34]

This episode seems to have marked the point of no return in relations between the pures and the CGT's reformist majority. Although perhaps not willing to go as far as Verdier, who believed the strike would establish "the direct power of workers', peasants', and soldiers' unions," the pures had seen the walkout as a revolutionary thrust, and their disillusionment and anger were acute.[35]

But as Besnard noted, the pures had also become concerned at this time about the threat of subordinating the French trade-union movement to the Russian Bolsheviks. He recalled that the threat first became palpable at a conference of the CGT revolutionary minority on September 25–27, 1920, on the eve of the confederation's Congress of Orléans. "Under the pretext of solidarity with the Russian Revolution," Besnard wrote, "certain individuals tried to place syndicalism under the control of a political party: the so-called communist party [Bolsheviks]." This referred to the minority group's decision to seek membership in the Comintern. A further alarm was sounded on October 3, 1920, at the close of the Orléans congress, when the minority met again and voted to create the Revolutionary Labor Committees (Comités Syndicalistes Révolutionnaires–CSRs). The pures, who later seized control of these new organizations and used them to dominate the CGT minority movement, were highly suspicious of the CSRs at the outset, Besnard claimed. "When they were formed, it appeared to us that the CSRs, both in structure

---

34. *Ibid.*; according to Labi, the CGT's total dues-paying membership dropped from 1,634,673 in the first half of 1920 to 736,800 in the second half; dues-paying membership in the railway union sank from 190,600 in the first half of 1920 to 120,714 in the second half, and to just 80,000 in 1921 (*La Grande Division des travailleurs*, 248–49).

35. Verdier quoted in Wohl, *French Communism in the Making*, 163 n. 6.

and in orientation, were designed to promote a new deviation of syndicalism rather than to return it to its correct path [*i.e.,* pre-1914 revolutionary syndicalist]." Besnard felt that the original purpose of the CSRs was to "politicize" the minority and pave the way for its takeover by pro-Bolshevik elements.[36]

In February, 1921, eighteen members of the pure faction, modestly claiming to represent revolutionary syndicalism "collectively and individually," met in secret to sign the Pact. In the manner of the American Founding Fathers, they pledged "our fortunes and our lives" to the cause of revolution. The Pact set up a secret committee within the CSR structure whose members would "practice among ourselves an effective and thorough material and moral solidarity." Signers promised to "pursue the daily struggle only along revolutionary syndicalist lines" and to shun "external influences."[37]

The Pact and its secret committee brought speedy results. Between February and June, 1921, pure militants took over many of the key posts in the CSRs. In June, they swept the elections to the CSR Central Committee, whose new executive triumvirate was composed of Besnard, a Pactist, and his close collaborators Albert Quinton and Pierre Fargue. Such control now made it possible for the pures to sabotage negotiations for the CSRs to affiliate with the Red International of Labor Unions or Profintern. Thus, the CSR delegation to the July 3–19, 1921, Profintern Congress in Moscow, where a Zinoviev proposal that a Comintern official sit on the Profintern executive for "liaison" purposes was to be debated, was loaded in favor of the pures. Seven of its nine members were pures or anarchosyndicalists, and three were Pactists. Their mission was to defeat the Zinoviev motion, which the pures and their allies saw as a smokescreen for a political, *i.e.,* Comintern, takeover of the trade-union movement. Griffuelhes served as counselor to the delegation, as a furious Alfred Rosmer wrote to Pierre Monatte: "Griffuelhes' three puppets [Pactists Jean Gaudeaux, Henri Sirolle, and Michel Kneler]—whom he escorted all the way to Berlin—are insufferable." Rosmer, who had been in Moscow since June, 1920, as a member of the Comintern Politburo and liaison with the French labor movement, fumed as the French group forced withdrawal of the Zinoviev motion.[38]

36. Besnard, "Pourquoi y eut-il le pacte?"

37. For the text of the Pact, see Chambelland and Maitron, eds., *Syndicalisme révolutionnaire et Communisme,* 277–78.

38. Larry Stuart Ceplair, "Roster of the CSRs" (typescript, Dept. of History, University of

The French delegates to the Profintern congress hurried back to Paris to attend what would be the last congress of a united CGT until 1936—the Congress of Lille from July 25–30, 1921. The main item on the agenda was a majority motion presented by Georges Dumoulin calling for exclusion of the CSRs. Although the minority was stronger at Lille than at any preceding postwar congress—a fact that Besnard and the pures took full credit for—the Dumoulin motion passed by 1,572 votes to 1,325.[39] A police spy reported on October 1, 1921, that "the tough offensive stance taken by the majority leaves no doubt about how this row will end. Schism is now certain." Another police report on November 18 stated that "on the majority side, they are putting maximum pressure on the extremists to force them to leave the CGT. Some unions have already been kicked out; other expulsions are on the way."[40]

As the police were aware, the minority was not in agreement on how to deal with the majority challenge. At several junctures, Monatte and the communist-syndicalist faction demonstrated willingness to compromise with the CGT leadership, even if it meant disbanding the CSRs, but, reported the police, "Quinton, Fargue, and Besnard, the three secretaries of the CSR central committee, have shown themselves to be favorable to a rapid departure." They were already laying plans for a new Revolutionary General Confederation of Labor, the report concluded.[41]

Victor Griffuelhes played no direct part in the skirmishing between majority and minority in the summer and autumn of 1921. Nor was he directly involved in the looming struggle between the pures and the *Vie Ouvrière* group for control of the CGT minority. He may have been involved in formulating the Pact earlier that spring; Besnard claimed he was, as did a prominent member of the rival communist-syndicalist faction, Victor Godonnèche. Shortly after the Pact was announced in June, 1922, Godonnèche wrote: "One name is missing among the signers of 'The Pact,' the name of the eminent personality and animator to whom a letter . . . read to me in Moscow was

Wisconsin-Madison, 1970); Besnard, "Pourquoi y eut-il le pacte?"; Rosmer to Monatte, July 14, 1921, quoted in Chambelland and Maitron, eds., *Syndicalisme révolutionnaire et communisme*, 291; Colette Chambelland, "Autour du premier congrès de l'Internationale syndicale rouge," *Le Mouvement social*, no. 47 (April–June, 1964), 43–44.

39. Besnard, "Pourquoi y eut-il le pacte?" At the preceding CGT Congress of Orléans, the minority had been able to muster only 602 votes on the main motion before congress (Brécy, *Mouvement syndical*, 118, 114).

40. APP, B/a 1686.

41. *Ibid.,* notes of October 18, November 13, 1921.

sent [by Pact members]. The letter could be published and also the name—
of which we are today ashamed—of the éminence grise of 'The Pact.' " [42]

Godonnèche and his comrades did not publish the incriminating letter or
release the name of the "eminent personality" who supposedly engineered the
Pact. The letter has since been published, and even though not specifically
addressed to him, it was clearly intended for the eyes of Victor Griffuelhes.
Its contents clearly demonstrate that Griffuelhes was privy to the activities of
the Pact, if not actually a silent partner to it. The letter was addressed to
Maison, a member of the Pact in Paris, and was written by two of Griffuelhes'
alleged puppets at the July, 1921, Profintern conference in Moscow, Gaudeaux
and Sirolle; twice it directs that the information it contains be communicated
to "the group and to Griffuelhes in particular." [43] For some reason, the two
Pactists apparently read the letter to fellow CSR delegation member Godonn-
nèche, who not only was not a Pact member but was a supporter of the rival
communist-syndicalist faction.

If we are to believe Pierre Besnard, Griffuelhes was also involved in drafting
statutes for a new Revolutionary General Confederation of Labor in the spring
of 1921. This draft, whose existence is the best evidence of the pures' (and
perhaps Griffuelhes') early desire to split the CGT, first surfaced at a CGT
minority conference in Paris on October 31–November 1, 1921; it was formally
presented at the minority's Paris congress on December 22–24 that year.

By his own account, Griffuelhes spent most of the last eight months of 1921
"traveling around Germany, the Baltic States detached from Russia around
two years ago, and old Russia itself." We have some knowledge of why Griffuelhes visited "old Russia," but none about his reasons for going to Germany,

42. Victor Godonnèche, "Contribution à l'histoire des C.S.R.: A propos du pacte," *V.O.*,
June 23, 1922; Godonnèche was a printing worker from Roubaix (Nord) and one of the executive
secretaries of the CSR Central Committee ousted in the pure sweep of June, 1921. He was one
of only two members of the CSR delegation to the Profintern conference in July, 1921, to support
the Zinoviev motion and was censured for it by the CSR apparatus back in Paris. See Godonn-
nèche to Monatte (Moscow), July 28, 1921, in Chambelland and Maitron, eds., *Syndicalisme
révolutionnaire et communisme*, 302–308.

43. Gaudeaux and Sirolle to Maison, August 11, 1921, in Chambelland and Maitron, eds.,
ibid., 294–95. All I have been able to learn about Maison is that he signed the Pact and that in
March, 1921, he was a member of the finance committee at CSR national headquarters in Paris.
(Ceplair, "Roster of the CSRs").

Estonia, Latvia, and Lithuania. He spent part of June shepherding Gaudeaux, Kneler, and Sirolle from Paris to Berlin on their way to the Profintern conference in Moscow, but much more of his time is unexplained. Griffuelhes speaks of spending "weeks, months" in the capitals of Germany and the Baltic States: "Paris-Berlin, Berlin-Paris, Paris-Berlin, Riga-Moscow, are familiar routes to me now! I have made the long journey from Paris to Riga several times. So many kilometers! So many hours!" [44]

Nowhere in his account does he reveal exactly what prompted these long journeys in Central and Eastern Europe from April to December, 1921, but it required him to call on French government representatives in the countries he visited—"I called on our official representatives, either for my travel needs or at their request"—and to talk to "workers, industrialists, businessmen, bankers." Griffuelhes also indicates he was not particularly proud of what he was doing. He recalled meeting an old friend in Berlin, an unidentified French leftist who had "taken part in the Russian Revolution" and who advised him to leave his current job, which "diminishes you," and rejoin the movement. Griffuelhes replied, "My occupation *is* somewhat less than attractive, I admit, but I don't seem to be able to escape the 'material' side of life." [45]

Leon Trotsky, who had a long conversation with him during his visit to Moscow, came away with the impression that Griffuelhes was employed as some kind of traveling salesman. In November, Trotsky wrote to Alfred Rosmer in Berlin and spoke of Griffuelhes' activity in "the world of commerce" and of his reluctance to "burn his bridges" in the business world without some assurance of a "leadership post in the movement." [46] What Griffuelhes was selling and for whom can only be guessed; one possibility, based on his frequent observations on rolling stock in the Baltic States and Russia, is that he may have been selling railroad equipment. Another is that Griffuelhes was still in the arms business. At this point, France was, after all, helping to build up the Baltic States as part of the cordon sanitaire directed against the USSR.

Information about what Griffuelhes did in Russia in November and why is not much better. Griffuelhes' own extensive account of his Russian trip is, to put it kindly, misleading. It gives the strong impression of a repentant

---

44. Griffuelhes, "L'Actualité et les Faits," *La Bataille*, pt. 1, May 4, 1922; pt. 2, May 11, 1922; pt. 6, June 15, 1922.

45. *Ibid.*

46. Trotsky to Alfred Rosmer, November, 1921, quoted in Pierre Broué, ed., *Léon Trotsky: Le Mouvement communiste en France (1919–1939)* (Paris, 1967), 131–32.

"sanitizing" of his immediate past so as to ingratiate himself with the "old crowd," in this case the moderates around the journal *La Bataille* that he had left behind in his last radical fling. For one thing, Griffuelhes failed to mention that he did not go to the USSR alone but traveled—at his request—with Jean Gaudeaux. To have revealed this capital fact would have given away the real reason for the Russian odyssey: to win Lenin and Trotsky's blessing for the hegemony of the pures in the new trade-union body that would emerge from the CGT's imminent breakup—and the same for himself as its head.

Instead, Griffuelhes stated that he went to Russia to "study and observe . . . the mechanisms of Russian life and thought." He approached his "study tour," as if it was "a problem about which I have no facts and about which I must learn everything if I want to bring back a useful harvest." He had two specific areas of concern, however. First, he was eager to learn for himself how the Russian people were able to endure the immense sacrifices of the world war, revolution, civil war, and then famine. "I have often asked myself how it is that the Russian people can endure . . . hardship beyond the capacity of human nature as we know it in the West? How can one explain this ability to resist? I never found out the answer and no one who had been there was ever able to enlighten me, so I decided to go to see for myself."

Griffuelhes also wanted to know more about the durability of the Russian Revolution, about its chances of "finishing its task." He felt there was little likelihood "the Revolution can be threatened from outside"; the only real menace it faced was "within Russia itself." "I will try to learn," he wrote as his train began the long journey from Riga to Moscow, "if there is such an internal opposition, if it is organized, and what degree of organization it has attained."[47]

It is doubtful that Griffuelhes' visit to the Soviet Union was a simple study tour. He makes clear, for example, that his trip was negotiated with Soviet authorities in Berlin, where the Comintern maintained its only active office outside Russia, and in Riga. Berlin was headquarters for the Western European Secretariat (W.E.S.) of the Comintern almost from its beginning. All Comintern agents who operated in western Europe used it as a base, as did agents of the Cheka, the Soviet secret police, who maintained surveillance of all foreign guests of or emissaries to the Comintern—or so one of the pure

47. Griffuelhes, "L'Actualité et les Faits," *La Bataille,* pts. 1, 2, 3, and 12, May 4, 11, 18, and July 20, 1922.

delegates to the 1921 Profintern congress claimed.[48] Although Griffuelhes informed readers of *La Bataille* that "I am the delegate of no group whatsoever; I represent only myself," there can be no doubt that his was an official visit, arranged and organized by the Comintern. Gaudeaux, his traveling companion, suggested that the Moscow trip was closely coordinated with Jules Humbert-Droz, the Comintern agent for southern Europe, and that "this enigmatic personage whom no one approaches" was well known to Griffuelhes, "who had the confidence of the 'Soviet gods.'" They were housed in the Hotel Lux, the residence in Moscow for Comintern delegates and other foreigners on official visits to the USSR.[49] But it is Griffuelhes' remarkable access to the highest officials of the Soviet government—Lenin, Trotsky, Losovsky, and Zinoviev—that really gives the lie to his story of an unofficial study tour.

The former CGT general secretary left Riga on November 7 and arrived in the Soviet capital on November 9. His interviews with the Bolshevik leaders, except for a "brief conversation" with the belligerent Zinoviev, bear all the characteristics of a Soviet charm offensive. Losovsky, general secretary of the Soviet trade-union apparatus and head of the Profintern, asked Griffuelhes to write an article for the Profintern bulletin, *L'Internationale Syndicale Rouge*. Lenin, "affable, comradely, full of humor, joy, and gaiety," chatted at length with his obviously admiring guest about "everything": France, exchange rates, rural electrification in Russia, mutual acquaintances in the French Socialist Party of yesteryear. "Only the French really understand us," remarked Lenin, prompting Griffuelhes to say, "One thing is perfectly clear about Lenin: his profound admiration for France, his interest in the lessons and examples offered by our Revolution [of 1789]." But there was a purpose behind all this charm; suddenly, Lenin asked the question that greeted Griffuelhes seemingly at every turn in Moscow: "Why don't you rejoin the movement?" When Griffuelhes replied that there really was no place for him in the movement, that it was too late for an old man like himself to start afresh, and so on, the Soviet leader dismissed these protests with a wave of his hand: "You're not here for very long, come back again for the [next Comintern] congress."[50]

48. Jean Gaudeaux, *Six Mois en Russie bolchéviste* (Paris, 1924), 19; for a full if unsympathetic account of W.E.S. activities during this period, see Branko Lazitch and Milorad Drachkovitch, *Lenin and the Comintern* (Stanford, 1972), I, 143–201.

49. Griffuelhes, "L'Actualité et les Faits," pts. 2 and 4, May 11 and 25, 1922; Gaudeaux, *Six Mois en Russie bolchéviste*, 19, 103.

50. Griffuelhes, "L'Actualité et les Faits," pts. 6 and 12, June 8, July 20, 1922. On Losovsky (real name Salomon Abramovitch Dridzo), see Georges Haupt and Jean-Jacques Marie, eds., *Les Bolchéviks par eux-memes* (Paris, 1969), 277–82. The Comintern congress to which Lenin

The purpose of the Soviet charm offensive and, coincidentally, that of Griffuelhes' visit to Moscow, becomes clear in the course of his long interview with Trotsky on November 16, the day before his visit to Lenin in the Kremlin. Indeed, I suggest that Griffuelhes' trip was arranged with Trotsky's approval; Jules Humbert-Droz, the famous "eye of Moscow," had advised him of its potential utility. Humbert-Droz apparently consulted with Griffuelhes in Berlin before his departure for Russia; he also accompanied him to the rendezvous with Trotsky and spoke alone to the former war commissar before Griffuelhes went in to see him.[51]

Griffuelhes presents the long interview—"the minutes and hours passed rapidly for both of us"—as a sort of question-and-answer session in which he had the opportunity to expound at length on the economic, political, and trade-union situation in France.[52] But there was more to the interview than this, as Trotsky reported to Alfred Rosmer: "G[riffuelhes] came here, I talked with him or rather listened to him, for an hour and a half or two: . . . I have the impression that G. wants to rejoin the ranks [of the trade-union movement] and is looking for the shortest route. He stated that his age and experience preclude for him the possibility of starting all over again at the bottom, without perspectives, connections, and a well-prepared plan."[53]

Griffuelhes was not eager to jump into the fray if it meant "increasing the already large number of revolutionary groups and heightening the already great ideological confusion" in the movement, Trotsky continued. "Rightly assuming that his past and his personal qualities guarantee him a leadership post in the movement should he rejoin it, G. clearly wants political clarity from the beginning, to establish a proper relationship with the International, so as to more easily surmount, with its authority behind him, eventual obstacles and resistance."

Trotsky professed to see no evidence of "careerism" in Griffuelhes' position: "His position is perfectly understandable and above suspicion." Thus, Rosmer should "expect an initiative from G. and, far from making it difficult, everything should be done to facilitate it. . . . But under no circumstances enter into relations with G. before he has demonstrated, on his own initiative, in an open declaration to the working class of France, that he has definitely

---

invited Griffuelhes was held a year later, from November 5 to December 5, 1922, five months after Griffuelhes' death.

51. Griffuelhes, "L'Actualité et les Faits," pt. 8, June 22, 1922.

52. *Ibid.*, pts. 8 and 9, June 22 and 29, 1922.

53. Trotsky to Rosmer, November, 1921, quoted in Broué, ed., *Léon Trotsky*, 131–33.

abandoned his commercial activity and has placed his services entirely at the disposal of the Revolution."

Trotsky seems to be saying in his letter to Rosmer that Griffuelhes had offered his services as a leader, perhaps the leader, of the minority trade-union movement in France. Trotsky further suggests that he was prepared to accept his offer since Pierre Monatte, Rosmer's close friend and the Bolsheviks' first choice for the post, refused to abandon his revolutionary syndicalist reservations about "organic" links between the unions and the vanguard party.[54]

Monatte's friends quickly concluded that Griffuelhes was being used as a club to bring Monatte into line, and that if Monatte failed to comply, the Comintern might bestow its patronage on Griffuelhes. Fritz Brupbacher, the Swiss anarchist who had sheltered Monatte in the aftermath of Villeneuve-Saint-Georges in 1908, was also in Moscow at this time and saw Trotsky shortly after Griffuelhes' interview, writing to Monatte: "Griffuelhes is in Moscow, surrounded by attentions. Trotsky is thinking of using him if you don't change your attitude." Brupbacher once again warned his friend of Trotsky's game upon his return to Zurich in January, 1922. Lapsing into German as he often did in his letters to the uncomprehending Monatte, Brupbacher said Trotsky had told him, "If Monatte doesn't want [the post], it is possible that Griffuelhes will eclipse him."[55]

Some interesting questions arise here. First, one wonders what Trotsky thought of Griffuelhes' involvement with the pure faction back in France. He must have been aware of it; Rosmer knew about it and it is unlikely he would neglect to share this information with his good friend Trotsky. But if Trotsky knew Griffuelhes was allied to the people who had prevented establishing a link between the Profintern and the Communist International, why did he indicate to Rosmer and Brupbacher his possible willingness to support Griffuelhes? A logical conclusion is that even though Trotsky was fully aware both of Griffuelhes' companions in the CGT and of what Maitron called his "dream" of returning to power in the French labor movement, he was still willing to work with him and his pure allies because, after all, they were members of the communist party while the other contenders for Soviet support within the CGT were not. If Humbert-Droz thought that PCF mem-

---

54. *Ibid.*

55. Brupbacher's first letter is quoted in Gras, *Alfred Rosmer*, 260. His second letter is quoted in Marc Vuilleumier, "La Russie en 1921–1922 et l'Internationale: Lettres de Fritz Brupbacher à Pierre Monatte," *Documents sur l'histoire du mouvement ouvrier en Suisse*, no. 1 (April, 1970), 18. I wish to thank Marc Vuilleumier for drawing my attention to this useful source.

bership was a factor favoring the pures, then perhaps it is reasonable to assume that Trotsky took the same view. The more cynical explanation favored by Rosmer and Brupbacher, however, was that Trotsky was simply stringing the old man along, hoping to pressure Monatte into joining forces with the communists. Monatte finally did so but only temporarily, joining the PCF in 1923 and leaving it definitively in 1924.[56]

The man at the center of this drama apparently believed Griffuelhes was more than a simple instrument to bring him into line. Pierre Monatte wrote that when the CGT schism was consummated at the minority congress of December, 1921, "Griffuelhes supported the men of 'The Pact'; for he had returned from Moscow and the Bolshevik leaders had told him they were in agreement with them." These lines were written in 1955, however, and Monatte's memory, dulled by years of struggle against Stalinism in the trade-union movement, possibly had lost some of its acuteness by then.[57]

One piece of evidence suggests that any influence Griffuelhes gained from his talks with the Soviet leaders was nullified by an incident that occurred at the end of his Russian visit. Jean Gaudeaux, the militant pure who accompanied Griffuelhes to Moscow, wrote that when they arrived there, he contacted the Russian wife of fellow pure Michel Kneler; Kneler and Gaudeaux had served together on the French delegation to the Profintern congress in Moscow the previous year. The woman had been denied an exit visa to join her husband in France. Gaudeaux introduced her to Griffuelhes, and she subsequently served as guide and interpreter for the two Frenchmen in Moscow. Gaudeaux wrote that he and Griffuelhes repeatedly asked Soviet authorities to grant her an exit visa, but without success. And so, "Griffuelhes and I decided to take a chance and try to smuggle the unfortunate woman out of the country in our compartment in the diplomatic railway car that had been reserved for us." All went well until the train reached the Latvian border, where a Cheka official was waiting with an order to search the compartment. The order stated that the two Frenchmen could continue once they had passed through customs and passport control but that the Russian woman was to be taken back to Moscow and imprisoned. Before leaving Russia, Griffuelhes and Gaudeaux sent appeals to Trotsky and Losovky to free Kneler's wife but to no avail.[58]

56. Wohl, *French Communism in the Making,* 344.

57. Monatte's remarks appeared in his preface to Fritz Brupbacher, *Socialisme et Liberté* (Neuchatel, 1955).

58. Gaudeaux, *Six Mois en Russie bolchéviste,* 103, 113–14, 119–20.

Griffuelhes' last impression of the USSR could not have been a favorable one, and the incident may have heightened doubts Griffuelhes already had about the character of the communist regime in Russia. On the other hand, Griffuelhes' attempt to spirit a political undesirable out of the country probably disinclined Trotsky to back Griffuelhes for the leadership of a new, revolutionary CGT. In any case, Griffuelhes returned to Paris in time to follow the debates at the CGT minority congress, which sealed the breakup of the CGT. When the minority met there December 22–24, to decide a course of action in the face of continuing expulsions of unions with CSR majorities, the pures were ready with a draft program for a new, revolutionary CGT. It was a "Griffuelhian" document, encompassing some of the themes he had developed since the end of the war: the fragility of the State; the need for a new worker's mentality, one in which the worker defined himself as a producer rather than a citizen; and especially, the need for harmony and cooperation between "workers of the brain and of the hand" to bring to the social revolution the fruits of new innovations in science and technology.[59]

The pures' program for a new CGT was shelved, however, amid last-ditch efforts to seek a compromise with the reformist majority. Victor Griffuelhes would have understood how difficult it was for even the most committed revolutionaries to abandon the "old house." Thus, on the first day of the minority congress, a delegation was sent to CGT headquarters to demand yet another special congress to try to patch things up; only a minor functionary was on hand to greet them. The congress then passed a resolution giving the majority until January 31, 1922, to call an extraordinary congress. The deadline passed and schism became a reality.[60]

The pures continued to manage the affairs of the new minority organization for the next six months. When the minority met at St.-Etienne from June 26 to July 1, 1922, to adopt statutes for the new Unified General Confederation of Labor (Confédération générale du travail unifiée—CGTU), however, the pures were driven from office. The press revealed the existence of the Pact on the eve of the congress, which was instrumental in undoing the pures' hegemony.[61] Two years later, the CGTU would be in the hands of the communists.

Victor Griffuelhes would play no role in these events. His days as an ém-

---

59. Chambelland and Maitron, eds., *Syndicalisme révolutionnaire et communisme*, 279–85.

60. Brécy, *Mouvement syndical*, 122–23.

61. Pierre Monatte, "Le Syndicalisme est-il mort à St.-Etienne?", *Clarté*, nos. 18, 21 (July 15, September 1, 1922); Rosmer, "La Petite Franc-maconnerie," *La Lutte des classes*, June 20, 1922.

inence grise were over. He returned from Moscow exhausted, and the severe cold there appears to have aggravated his tubercular condition. Sometime in the spring of 1922, he fell desperately ill. Half of the articles that comprise his account of the trip were written from his sickbed. Whatever he had worked at the last years of his life brought him very little monetary reward, because when he fell ill, Griffuelhes could not pay for hospital care and was forced to take refuge with his old friend, Garnery. Garno had left the union movement before the war and moved to a farm at Saclas (Seine-et-Oise), where he raised chickens and rabbits for the market at Les Halles.[62]

On June 29, 1922, as the delegates at St.-Etienne were completing the break-up of the CGT he had done so much to build, Griffuelhes died in this "forgotten corner of the Seine-et-Oise, far from the noise and bustle of this great Paris where he gave the best of himself." [63]

62. Griffuelhes, "L'Actualité et les Faits," pt. 4, May 25, 1922; *DBMO*, XII, 249.

63. Albin Villeval *fils*, Griffuelhes obituary, *La Bataille*, July 6, 1922; François Marie, the paper's editor, wrote that "despite all the vile rumors about Griffuelhes' brilliant situation, he died virtually penniless." This was not an exaggeration—apparently Garnery paid for his funeral, and Griffuelhes' old comrades at *La Bataille* took up a collection for his wife, Marie (Griffuelhes obituary, *La Bataille*, July 6, 1922).

CONCLUSION

The transfiguration of Victor Griffuelhes began the day after he died. At the founding congress of the CGTU in St.-Etienne on June 30, Paul Cadeau, a communist, rose to give the official eulogy of Griffuelhes and in the process, passed a discreet veil over the awkward events of the great man's final years. "This comrade whom so many believed had left our ranks," Cadeau said, "died as a militant in the cause of the Revolution."[1] Five years later, the man who had intrigued to regain his lost power by helping provoke the CGT schism had become a virtual patron saint of the French labor movement.

At the CGT Congress of 1927, Pierre Monatte claimed Griffuelhes' patronage; the communist-syndicalist enemy of 1921, who left the communist party and the CGTU in 1924, was now leader of the revolutionary syndicalist opposition in the old house. In reply, the CGT general secretary Léon Jouhaux, at one time Griffuelhes' "phonograph" and later his "neo-Millerandist" foe, rose to claim the departed hero for his own. "Just now, Monatte, you dared at this very rostrum to evoke the memory of Griffuelhes and to claim that [he] would have been on your side. Never!" Jouhaux thundered. "Griffuelhes had his own opinions and a fiery temper that his friends often took the brunt of, but he also loved the CGT and, rather than hold the opinions you ascribe to him, he would have killed himself on the altar of the CGT."[2]

Scholars, most of them as partisan in their way as were the labor militants, also began to assess Griffuelhes' place in the history of the French labor move-

1. *Compte rendu, Confédération Générale du Travail Unifiée, Ier Congrès tenu à Saint-Etienne du 25 juin au Ier juillet 1922* (Paris, 1922), 389.
2. CGT, *Compte rendu des débats du XXVe Congrès national corporatif . . . tenu à la Salle Bullier* [Paris] . . . *1927* (Paris, n.d.), 132ff.

ment during the interwar years. To this first generation of French labor historians, Griffuelhes was the greatest hero of the pre–World War I era of French trade unionism. He "symbolized a whole epoch in the history of the CGT," wrote the Marxist Paul Louis, "just as Varlin [symbolized] the era of the First International and Pelloutier the Bourse du Travail movement." For the Proudhonist Edouard Dolléans, "Victor Griffuelhes possessed the virtues of a leader. . . . During the heroic age of [French] trade unionism, the energy and authority of Griffuelhes were decisive forces." Modern historians of French labor have not departed from this early assessment as much as might have been expected; the greatest of these, Jacques Julliard, has described Griffuelhes as "the purest incarnation" of revolutionary syndicalism.[3]

The aim of this book is not to celebrate Griffuelhes, however, but to use his life and career as a vehicle for better understanding the phenomenon of revolutionary syndicalism. Thus, my analysis of his early years suggests a need for rethinking the stock profile of the revolutionary syndicalist militant. I have tested and found wanting the notion, much in vogue among recent labor and social historians, that the "de-skilling" or, more broadly, the proletarianization of artisans was the key impetus to radical trade unionism in France and elsewhere. Griffuelhes' experience, typical of many skilled workers of the period, argues for caution in applying the proletarianization thesis to the artisanat of the Belle Epoque.

First, it is not at all clear that for Griffuelhes and workers like him, the process of proletarianization, which certainly took place, was accompanied by much de-skilling. Instead, the two main elements in the process that affected skilled workers like Griffuelhes and his fellow artisan shoemakers were falling incomes and frustrated upward mobility. The latter seems to have been particularly galling to Griffuelhes, suggesting that perhaps thwarted social mobility deserves more attention as an impetus to radicalism than it has received to date.

Nor will those who have argued that revolutionary syndicalism harked back to some kind of Proudhonian utopia find much comfort in Griffuelhes, who from his maiden CGT speech in 1900 to his last articles in the 1920s argued forcefully that the artisanat and the artisan mentality were dead and deserved to be, along with France's routine-minded capitalist employers, and that the law of progress, as he understood it, dictated that the future would belong to the proletarian machine tenders. Griffuelhes' reaction to proletarianization

---

3. Louis, *Histoire du mouvement syndical,* I, 202; Dolléans, *Histoire du mouvement ouvrier,* II, 118; Jacques Julliard to author, August 5, 1987, author's files.

suggests that rather than agitating for a return to a "golden age" of artisan endeavor, many frustrated artisans may well have greeted industrialization as a form of liberation.

Given these views, it is not surprising that Victor Griffuelhes' CGT does not conform to the standard image of a revolutionary syndicalist movement built around the skilled workers of smaller, more radical unions (supposedly dominated by the militant minority composed of proletarianized artisans), rather than the "genuine" proletarians of heavy industry. The enemies of the Griffuelhian CGT promoted this image from 1904 on. Perhaps unintentionally, Bernard Moss has given it new life with his concept of the "socialism of skilled workers." This image is belied by Griffuelhes' involved and time-consuming efforts to capture for the CGT the reformist miners' federation, the largest and most cohesive trade-union organization in the early 1900s; by his attempts to organize France's vast pool of agricultural labor; and by his promotion of industrial unionism in his own leatherworkers' federation, as well as in the more substantial metal, textile, and building workers' federations. This large-scale organizing effort was carried out with at least some success under clearly revolutionary auspices, with minimal concessions to the CGT's powerful reformist minority. No other labor movement, at least in western Europe, attempted such a feat in the pre-1914 era. As critics have pointed out, however, the CGT failed to bring as many workers under its umbrella as did the British TUC or the German social democratic unions. Nevertheless, that the CGT organized as many workers as it did on a clear-cut revolutionary program—just over 340,000 in 1912—merits more respect than it has heretofore received.

But how would Victor Griffuelhes have been remembered by his followers among the rank and file during the CGT's heroic period? Some would recall him as the architect of the protests and strikes that jarred the laggard governments of the Third Republic into finally adopting measures to ease the lot of the average French worker: the ten-hour day (1904); the six-day week (1906); and the creation of a labor ministry (also 1906) to look into workers' problems. They might also have recalled, however, that Griffuelhes was never entirely at ease with campaigns to wrest reforms from the State. In fact, it was his stubborn opposition to the welfare statism of the Belle Epoque's premier labor reformers, Prime Minister René Waldeck-Rousseau and his socialist minister of commerce, Alexandre Millerand, that launched Griffuelhes' career. He liked to say—and this was a staple of his brand of revolutionary syndicalism—that "the State is not the fount of earthly happiness it thinks it is. It cannot grant this happiness, for it is not its to give. . . . Happiness is achieved and con-quered; it is not *given*." [4]

The CGT had almost ceased to function as a labor organization when Victor Griffuelhes took charge in 1901. A creature of the Paris working-class quartiers, it had few members and even less clout outside the capital. It was a virtual ward of the Allemanist faction of French socialism, lacking ideological independence and freedom of action, and because the laws that regulated trade-union activities disallowed renting property, the CGT did not even have a home of its own.

When Griffuelhes resigned as general secretary of the CGT, it had nearly a half-million adherents, most of them members not of the craft unions that had dominated the CGT in 1901, but of newly minted industrial unions. This membership was not confined to the Paris region; the CGT of 1909 boasted militants and a real presence among the farmworkers of the Midi, the coal miners of the Pas-de-Calais and the Loire Valley, and the shoe-factory workers of Brittany. It also possessed a creed and program of its own, enshrined in the Charter of Amiens coauthored and presented to the 1906 Congress of Amiens by Victor Griffuelhes. And symbolic of its newly won autonomy, the confed-eration now had its own headquarters, again thanks to Griffuelhes. In insti-tutional terms at least, Victor Griffuelhes is the founder of the modern labor movement in France.

His greatest legacy to French workers, however, may have been less tangible than the reforms and institutional initiatives listed here. In the hundreds of stump speeches he gave, the articles and brochures he wrote, and equally important, in the proletarian pride and defiance he symbolized personally, he sought to instill in the working classes the sense that as producers they were the bedrock of society, the ultimate source of all wealth and human progress and bearers of a special destiny: By emancipating themselves, they would emancipate all humankind.

4. Griffuelhes, "Le Syndicalisme révolutionnaire," in Griffuelhes and Louis Niel, *Les Ob-jectifs de nos luttes de classe* (Paris, 1910), 15. Griffuelhes' emphasis.

BIBLIOGRAPHY

Griffuelhiana

Books and Pamphlets by Griffuelhes

L'Action syndicaliste. Paris, 1908.
Les Caractères du syndicalisme français. Paris, 1908.
Un Grand Conflit social: La Grève des délaineurs de Mazamet (du 9 janvier au 7 mai 1909). Paris, 1909.
Le Syndicalisme révolutionnaire. Paris, 1909.
Voyage révolutionnaire: Impressions d'un propagandiste. Paris, n.d. [1910].

———— and Auguste Keufer. *Les Deux Méthodes syndicalistes: Réformisme et l'Action Directe.* Paris, 1905.
———— and Robert Michels, Arturo Labriola, and Boris Krichevsky. *Syndicalisme et Socialisme.* Paris, 1908.
———— and Louis Niel. *Les Objectifs de nos luttes de classe.* Paris, 1910.
———— and Emile Pouget, Paul Delesalle, and Georges Yvetot. *Syndicats et Syndicalisme.* Paris, n.d.

Articles by Griffuelhes

"Allemagne." *L'Encyclopédie syndicaliste,* No. 1, December, 1911.
"A propos de la grève générale des mineurs." *Le Mouvement socialiste,* Nos. 116–117 (1903), 555–59.
"A propos d'un livre." *Le Journal du Peuple,* August 30, 1919. Review of Georges Sorel's *Matériaux pour une théorie du prolétariat* (Paris, 1919).
"Autour du Congrès fédéral du Batiment." *L'Encyclopédie du mouvement syndicaliste,* No. 4 (April, 1912).
"Autour du Congrès socialiste tenu à Lyon les 18, 19, 20 et 21 février 1912." *L'Encyclopédie du mouvement syndicaliste,* No. 2 (1912), 17–19.

"Ayons des idées générales." *L'Encyclopédie du mouvement syndicaliste,* No. 1 (1912), 3–5.

"Basly et ses domestiques sont des menteurs sans scrupules." *L'Humanité,* January 8, 1907.

"Besoin d'agir." *La Voix du Peuple,* May 1, 1904.

"Bulletin syndical: Opinion." *Le Petit Sou,* February 3, 1901.

"100 Meetings." *La Voix du Peuple,* No. 163, November 29–December 6, 1903.

"Comprendra-t-on?" *La Feuille,* October 4, 1917.

"Dans l'attente de la manifestation d'aujourd'hui." *Le Matin,* July 30, 1908.

"Dans l'Internationale." *La Voix du Peuple,* No. 271, December 24–31, 1905; No. 272, January 1–7, 1906; No. 273, January 7–14, 1906.

"Des chiffres." *La Voix du Peuple,* October 29–November 4, 1905.

"Discuter les 3 ans, ce n'est l'affaire des travailleurs." *La Bataille syndicaliste,* March 29, 1913.

"Il faut un examen de conscience." *La Feuille,* August 10, 1916.

"L'Action ouvrière dans la Maçonnerie." *La Voix du Peuple,* May 10–17, 1908.

"L'Actualité et les Faits. Ce que personne n'a jamais dit. Huit Mois en Russie, en Esthonie, en Lettonie, en Lituanie et en Allemagne." *La Bataille,* Nos. 1–16 (1922).

"La Fédération des Cuirs et Peaux." *Le Mouvement socialiste,* No. 200 (July 15, 1908), 26–35.

"La Formation du syndicalisme français." *Le Mouvement socialiste,* No. 193 (1907), 473–77.

"La Grève des mineurs." *Le Petit Sou,* April 11, 1901.

"La Leçon du Passé." *La Vie Ouvrière,* 1st ser., No. 1 (1909).

"La Lutte pour la nationalisation." *La Revue communiste,* No. 4 (June, 1920), 357–60.

"La Politique ministérielle et le syndicalisme." *Le Mouvement socialiste,* No. 221 (1910), 338–41.

"La Psychologie d'une fin de régime." *La Revue communiste,* No. 9 (November, 1920), 245–48.

"La Revue 'L'Action Directe' (1903–1904)." *L'Encyclopédie du mouvement syndicaliste,* No. 1 (1912), 18–19.

"Le Bien-etre frère de la liberté." *La Feuille,* April 19, 1917.

"Le Congrès des bucherons." *La Voix du Peuple,* No. 83, June 15–22, 1902.

"Le Congrès syndical de Bourges." *Le Mouvement socialiste,* No. 142 (November 1, 1904).

"Le Conseil supérieur du travail." *Le Mouvement socialiste,* No. 129 (October 1, 1903), 225–44.

"Le Mouvement des ouvriers résiniers des Landes." *Le Mouvement socialiste,* No. 187 (1907), 494–506.

"Le Nouveau Millerandisme." *La Revue communiste,* No. 1 (March, 1920), 30–33.

"Le Procès Hervé-Caillaux: La Révolution russe." *La Feuille,* December 13, 1917.

"Le Propagande dans le Pas-de-Calais." *La Voix du Peuple,* No. 111, December 20–26, 1902.

"Le Soviet est la terme de la guerre." *Le Journal du Peuple,* September 9, 1919.

"Le Syndicalisme révolutionnaire," in "Les Deux Conceptions du syndicalisme: Controverse." *Le Mouvement socialiste,* No. 146 (January 1, 1905), 1–17.

"Le Valeur du mot." *La Voix du Peuple,* January 1–15, 1902.

"Les 10 Heures." *La Voix du Peuple,* No. 182, April 10–14, 1904.

"Les Huit Heures." *La Voix du Peuple,* September 17–24, 1905.

"Les Réunions." *La Voix du Peuple,* No. 116, February 1–8, 1903.

"Les Subventions du conseil municipal." *La Voix du Peuple,* No. 34, July 21–28, 1901.

"Lettre au Sénat." *La Voix du Peuple,* No. 163, November 29–December 6, 1903.

"L'Infériorité des capitalistes français." *Le Mouvement socialiste,* No. 226 (1910), 329–32.

"L'Internationale syndicale." *L'Action Directe,* 2nd ser., No. 18 (1908), 1–2.

"Manque de solidarité." *La Voix du Peuple,* November 23–30, 1902.

"Méthode de corruption." *L'Action Directe,* 1st ser., No. 2 (August, 1903), 22–28.

"Notre Action doit créer un effort international." *La Bataille syndicaliste,* March 21, 1913.

"Notre Position." *La Bataille syndicaliste,* August 20, 1912.

"Opinion," in "Enquete: La Grève générale et le socialisme." *Le Mouvement socialiste,* Nos. 137–138 (1904), 153–64.

"Organisons l'assistance et la reprise du travail." *La Bataille syndicaliste,* August 22, 1914.

"Où va-t-on?" *La Bataille syndicaliste,* January 23, 1913.

"Par le Crédit Foncier on pouvait agir." *La Bataille syndicaliste,* August 31, 1914.

"Pas de réponse." *La Voix du Peuple,* January 17–24, 1904.

"Pétitioner? Oui! Mais surtout développer l'action ouvrière." *La Bataille syndicaliste,* April 6, 1913.

"Phénomène capitaliste." *La Voix du Peuple,* 1901–1902.

"Pour remédier au chomage des mesures extraordinaires s'imposent." *La Bataille syndicaliste,* August 26, 1914.

"Production capitaliste ou sociale." *Le Journal du Peuple,* October 8, 1919.

"Puisqu'il faut écrire." *La Feuille,* August 3, 1916.

"Résultats." *La Voix du Peuple,* No. 186, May 8–15, 1904.

"Retablissons." *La Voix du Peuple,* No. 113, January 4–11, 1903.

"Retour sur nous-memes." *La Bataille syndicaliste,* January 24, 1913.

"Romantisme révolutionnaire." *L'Action Directe,* 2nd ser., No. 15 (1908).

"Stagnation capitaliste." *Le Mouvement socialiste,* No. 227 (1911), 34–36.

"Sur une délégation." *La Voix du Peuple,* February 4–11, 1906.

"Théorie en pratique." *La Voix du Peuple,* December 28, 1902–January 4, 1903.

"Trop longtemps complice!" *La Feuille,* November 8, 1917.

"Un Écoulement est necessaire pour la reprise du travail." *La Bataille syndicaliste,* August 24, 1914.

"Une Opinion." *Le Petit Sou,* January 9, 1901.

"Utopisme petit-bourgeois." *Le Mouvement socialiste,* No. 237 (1912), 30–36.

"Voilà des mesures!" *La Bataille syndicaliste,* August 28, 1914.

Biographical Materials on Griffuelhes

Archives de la Préfecture de Police, B/a 1686. "Victor Griffuelhes," in report "Au sujet de la CGT. Ses effectifs. Son Comité [confédéral]. Renseignements sur les principaux membres de ce comité." March, 1907, 17–19.

Bridgford, Jeff. "Griffuelhes, Jean Victor (1874–1922)," in *Biographical Dictionary of French Political Leaders Since 1870,* edited by David S. Bell, Douglas Johnson, and Peter Morris. New York, 1990.

Kneler, Michel. "Un Anniversaire: Victor Griffuelhes." *Bien-etre et Liberté,* July, 1946.

LeClerq, M., and E. Girod de Fléaux. *Ces Messieurs de la CGT (Profils révolutionnaires).* Paris, 1908.

Leroy, Maxime. "Griffuelhes et Merrheim." *L'Homme Réel,* No. 40 (April, 1937), 9–14.

Méric, Victor [Flax]. "Victor Griffuelhes." *Les Hommes du jour,* No. 56 (February, 1909), 2–5.

Nord, Philip G. "Griffuelhes, Victor." In Vol. 1 of *Historical Dictionary of the French Third Republic, 1870–1940,* edited by Patrick H. Hutton. Westport, Conn., 1986.

Richard, O. "Victor Griffuelhes." *Revue de l'Agénais* (Fall/Winter, 1951), 16–17.

Vandervort, Bruce. "Griffuelhes, Henri," and "Griffuelhes, Victor," in Vol. 12 of *Dictionnaire biographique du mouvement ouvrier français,* edited by Jean Maitron. Paris, 1973.

Other Primary Sources

Unpublished Government Documents

Archives Nationales, Paris (AN)

BB18 2335: Mémorandum, Procureur-Général de la République, 9 juin 1906

F7 12.493: Congrès ouvriers, 1893–1906

F7 12.496: Renseignements généraux sur le mouvement socialiste en France

F7 12.717: Milieux réactionnaires, 1906

F7 12.770: Congrès de mineurs, 1900–1909

F7 12.783: Grèves, mouvements sociaux, 1906

F7 12.867: Impérialistes [Bonapartists]

F7 12.889–90: CGT, 1901–1906

F7 12.915: Villeneuve-Saint-Georges, 1908

F7 13.090: Anarchistes

F7 13.348: Rapports quotiediens sur la CGT, 1914

F7 13.568: CGT, diverses notes

F7 13.570: Dossier essai de la grève générale, 1909

F7 13.574–75: CGT, 1914–17

F7 13.603: Congrès socialistes, 1905–14

F7 13.697: Fédération nationale des Cuirs et Peaux, 1906–14

F7 13.788: Congrès de mineurs, 1900–1914

F22 234: Grèves en 1882

Archives de la Préfecture de Police, Paris (APP)

B/a 693: Elections municipales, 1900

B/a 956: Dossier personnel Beausoleil

B/a 991: Dossier personnel Capjuzan

      Dossier personnel Besset

B/a 1028: Dossier personnel Delacour

B/a 1061: Impérialistes [Bonapartists]

B/a 1367: Grèves et coalitions: Cuirs et Peaux

B/a 1601–1606: Rapports journaliers sur la CGT, 1906–17

B/a 1608–11: Bourses du Travail

B/a 1637: Premier mai, 1906

B/a 1652: Dossier personnel Niel

B/a 1686: Mouvement social en mars, 1906

      Dossier personnel Louzon

      Au sujet de la CGT, 1907

      Scission dans la CGT, 1921–22

Archives Départmentales (AD)

Gironde (Bordeaux)

    1 M 474: Syndicats ouvriers, 1884–90

Hérault (Montpellier)

    194 M 23: Bourse du Travail, Montpellier, 1904–1906

Nord (Lille)

    M 626: Grèves de mineurs, 1906

Pas-de-Calais (Arras)

    M 1795–96: Grèves, 1902–1906

    M 2116: Mouvement syndical, Lens, 1902–1906

Archives Municipales (AM)

Aubervilliers (Seine)

    Etat Civil. Actes de mariage, 1899

Aurillac (Cantal)

    Etat Civil. Actes de naissance, 1827

Nérac (Lot-et-Garonne)

Etat Civil. Actes de mariage, 1866
Actes de naissance, 1869, 1871, 1874

French Newspapers and Periodicals

Daily Newspapers
L'Echo de Paris, 1899, 1906.
L'Echo du Nord, 1906.
Le Matin, 1906, 1908.
Le Temps, 1903, 1906, 1917.

Political Press (Anarchist, Socialist, and Communist)
Bulletin communiste, 1920–22. French-language version of international communist
   publication.
Clarté, 1924.
L'Aurore, 1900.
Les Hommes du jour, 1909
L'Humanité, 1906–1909, 1920, 1922.
Le Journal du Peuple, 1916–29. Not to be confused with anarchist daily of same title
   published in 1899.
La Lutte des classes, 1922.
Le Petit Sou, 1900–1902.
La Petite République, 1892–1906.
La Revue communiste, 1920–22.
La Revue socialiste, 1905–10.

Trade-Union, Syndicalist, and Syndicalist-Oriented Press
L'Action Directe, July, 1903, to February 9, 1905. Designated in footnotes as "1st ser."
   to avoid confusion with 1908 series of same title.
L'Action Directe, January 15, 1908, to October 3, 1908. Designated in footnotes as "2nd
   ser." to avoid confusion with 1903–1905 series of same title.
L'Action syndicale, Lens (Pas-de-Calais), 1904–10.
L'Avant-garde, April 23, 1905, to March 4, 1906.
La Bataille, February 1–15, 1921, to 1929.
La Bataille syndicaliste, April 27, 1911, to October 23, 1915.
Bulletin international du mouvement syndicaliste, 1907–14.
Le Contrat social, November, 1957.
Encyclopédie du mouvement syndicaliste, January–May, 1912.
La Feuille, August 3, 1916, to January 10, 1918.
L'Information ouvrière et sociale, March 7, 1918, to December 30, 1920.
Le Mouvement socialiste, January, 1899, to May–June, 1914.
Le Père Peinard, February 24, 1889, to April 16, 1899.
Le Reveil du Nord, Lille, 1899–1914.

La Révolution, February 1, 1909, to March 28, 1909.

La Revue syndicaliste, May 15, 1905, to January 15, 1910.

Le Travailleur du Batiment, 1908, 1910.

La Vie Ouvrière, 1st ser., October 5, 1909, to July 20, 1914. Bimonthly periodical.

La Vie Ouvrière, 2nd ser., April 30, 1919, to 1939. Weekly newspaper.

La Voix du Peuple, December 1, 1900, to August 3, 1914.

French Trade-Union and Socialist Party Congresses

Confédération générale du travail (CGT)

XIe Congrès national corporatif (V^e de la CGT) tenu à la Bourse du Travail de Paris les 10, 11, 12, 13, 14 septembre 1900. Compte rendu des travaux du Congrès. Paris, 1900.

XIIe Congrès national corporatif (XVe de la CGT) tenu à la Bourse du Travail de Lyon les 23, 24, 25, 26 et 27 septembre 1901. Compte rendu des travaux du Congrès. Lyon, 1901.

Rapport du comité confédéral pour l'exercice 1900–1901 et Rapport de La Voix du Peuple, *23–27 septembre 1901.* Paris, 1901.

XIII Congrès national corporatif, tenu à Montpellier les 22, 23, 24, 25, 26 et 27 septembre 1902 . . . . Compte rendu officiel des travaux du Congrès. Montpellier, 1902.

XIVe Congrès national corporatif (VIIIe de la Confédération) et Conférence des Bourses du Travail, tenus à Bourges du 12 au 20 septembre 1904. Compte rendu des travaux. Bourges, 1904.

XVe Congrès national corporatif (IXe de la Confédération) et Conférence des Bourses du Travail, tenus à Amiens du 8 au 16 octobre 1906. Compte rendu des travaux. Amiens, 1906.

XVIe Congrès national corporatif (X^e de la CGT) et 3e Conférence des Bourses du Travail ou Unions des Syndicats, tenus à Marseille du 5 au 12 octobre 1908. Compte rendu sténographique des travaux. Marseille, 1909.

Compte rendu de la conférence extraordinaire des Fédérations nationales et des Bourses du Travail ou Unions des Syndicats, tenue les 1er, 2 et 3 juin 1909, Paris. Paris, n.d. [1909].

XVIIe Congrès national corporatif (XIe de la Confédération) et 4e Conférence des Bourses du Travail ou Unions de Syndicats, tenus à Toulouse du 3 au 10 [11] octobre 1910. Compte rendu des travaux. Toulouse, 1911.

XXIe Congrès national corporatif (XVe de la CGT), tenu à Orléans du 27 septembre au 2 octobre 1920. Compte rendu des travaux. Villeneuve-St.-Georges, n.d.

XXIIe Congrès national corporatif (XVIe de la CGT), tenu à Lille du 25 au 30 juillet 1921. Compte rendu des travaux. Villeneuve-St.-Georges, n.d.

Compte rendu, Confédération Générale du Travail Unifiée, 1er Congrès tenu à Saint-Etienne du 25 juin au 1er juillet. Paris, 1922.

Compte rendu des débats du XXVe Congrès national corporatif (XIXe de la CGT) tenu à la Salle Bullier les 26, 27, 28 et 29 juillet 1927. Paris, n.d.

La Confédération générale du travail et le Mouvement syndical. Paris, 1925.

Fédération Nationale des Bourses du Travail

Compte rendu du 8ᵉ Congrès national. Paris, 5–8 septembre 1900. Paris, 1900.

IX Congrès national des Bourses du Travail de France et des colonies. Nice, 17, 18, 19, 20 et 21 septembre 1901. Nice, 1901.

Xᵉ Congrès national des Bourses du Travail de France et des colonies tenu à Alger les 15, 16, 17 et 18 septembre 1902. Algiers, 1902.

Congresses of CGT-Affiliated National Federations

Fédération nationale des Travailleurs de l'Industrie du Batiment. *Compte rendu du 2ᵉ Congrès national tenu à . . . St.-Etienne, les 19, 20, 21, 22 et 23 avril 1908.* Courbevoie, 1908.

Fédération nationale de la Céramique. *Compte rendu du VIᵉ Congrès (14 juillet 1906) et Iᵉʳ International (15 juillet 1906) tenus [à] Limoges.* Limoges, 1906.

Syndicat national des Travailleurs des Chemins de Fer. *Compte rendu du Xᵉ Congrès national, convoqué extraordinairement à Paris . . . 20 et 21 janvier 1899.* Paris, 1899.

———. *Compte rendu du 11ᵉ Congrès national tenu à Paris les 1er, 2 et 3 [avril] 1900.* Paris, 1900.

Fédération nationale des Cuirs et Peaux. *Compte rendu du 4ᵉ Congrès national, tenu à la Bourse du Travail de Chaumont, les 18, 19 et 20 septembre 1905.* Puteaux, 1905.

———. *Compte rendu du 5ᵉ Congrès national tenu à Limoges, les 16, 17 et 18 septembre 1907.* Paris, 1907.

———. *Compte rendu du 6ᵉ Congrès national tenu à Fougères, Maison du Peuple, les 20, 21, 22 et 23 septembre 1909.* Paris, 1909.

Fédération nationale de l'Industrie Textile. *Compte rendu du Congrès de l'Industrie Textile, tenu à Paris les 20, 21 et 22 septembre et à Lyon les 27, 28 et 29 septembre 1901.* Paris, 1901.

———. *Compte rendu du VIᵉ Congrès national ouvrier de l'Industrie Textile, tenu à Reims les 14, 15 et 16 aout 1904.* Lille, 1904.

———. *Compte rendu du 8ᵉᵐᵉ Congrès national ouvrier de l'Industrie Textile tenu à Tourcoing du 12 au 15 aout 1906.* Lille, 1906.

Fédération (nouvelle) nationale des Travailleurs du Verre. *Compte rendu du XIᵉ Congrès national (Vᵉ de la Fédération Nouvelle) tenu à Albi les 6, 7, 8, 9, et 10 septembre 1906.* Lille, 1906.

Socialists

Congrès général des organisations socialistes françaises tenu à Paris du 3 au 8 décembre 1899. Compte rendu sténographique. Paris, 1900.

Published Government Documents

Ministère du Commerce, de l'Industrie, des Postes, et des Télégraphes. Office du Travail. *Annuaire des syndicats professionnels, industriels, commerciaux et agricoles.* Paris, 1898–.

———. *Les Associations professionnelles ouvrières.* Vol. II of 4 vols. Paris, 1894–1904.

———. *Résultats statistiques du recensement des industries et professions. Dénombrement général de la Population, effectué le 24 mars 1901.* Paris, 1906.

———. *Salaires et Durée du travail dans l'industrie française.* 5 vols. Paris, 1894–1915.

———. *Statistique des grèves et des recours à la conciliation et à l'arbitrage, 1893–1914.* Paris, 1894–1915.

OTHER SECONDARY SOURCES

Reference Works

Bell, David S., Douglas Johnson, and Peter Morris, eds. *Biographical Dictionary of French Political Leaders Since 1870.* New York, 1990.

Brécy, Robert. *Le Mouvement syndical en France: Essai bibliographique.* Paris, 1963.

Compère-Morel, Adéodat C. A., ed. *Encyclopédie socialiste, syndicaliste et coopérative de l'Internationale Ouvrière.* 12 vols. Paris, 1912–21.

Hutton, Patrick H., ed. *Historical Dictionary of the French Third Republic, 1870–1940.* 2 vols. Westport, Conn., 1986.

Maitron, Jean, ed. *Dictionnaire biographique du mouvement ouvrier français.* Part 3, Vols. 10–15: *De la Commune à la Grande Guerre (1871–1914).* Part 4, Vols. 16–: *De la Première à la Seconde Guerre Mondiale.* Paris, 1964–.

Books and Pamphlets

Aftalion, Albert. *Le Développement de la fabrique et le travail à domicile dans les industries d'habillement.* Paris, 1906.

Amdur, Kathryn E. *Syndicalist Legacy: Trade Unions and Politics in Two French Cities in the Era of World War I.* Urbana, Ill., 1986.

Anderson, Eugene N. *The First Moroccan Crisis, 1904–1906.* Chicago, 1930.

Andrew, Christopher. *Théophile Delcassé and the Making of the Entente Cordiale: A Reappraisal of French Foreign Policy, 1898–1905.* New York, 1968.

Avrich, Paul. *The Russian Anarchists.* Princeton, 1967.

Bahne, Siegfried, ed. *Origines et débuts des partis communistes des pays latins.* Dordrecht, 1970. Vol. I of Bahne, *Archives de Jules Humbert-Droz.* 2 vols.

Barberet, Joseph. *Le Travail en France. Monographies professionnelles.* Vol. V of 7 vols. Paris, 1886–90.

Becker, Jean-Jacques. *Le Carnet B: Les Pouvoirs publics et l'Antimilitarisme avant la guerre de 1914.* Paris, 1973.

———. *1914: Comment les français sont entrés dans la guerre: Contribution à l'étude de l'opinion publique printemps-été 1914.* Paris, 1977.

Bellanger, Claude, ed. *Histoire générale de la presse française: De 1871 à 1940.* Vol. III of 3 vols. Paris, 1972.

Berlanstein, Lenard. *The Working People of Paris, 1871–1914.* Baltimore, 1984.

———, ed. *Rethinking Labor History.* Urbana, Ill., 1993.

Besnard, Pierre. *L'Ethique du syndicalisme.* Paris, 1938.

Bosquet, Michel [André Gorz]. *Strategy for Labor: A Radical Proposal.* Translated by Martin A. Nicolaus and Victoria Ortiz. New York, 1969.

Bouët, Louis. *La Grande Tourmente (1914–1918).* Avignon, n.d.

Branciard, Michel. *Société française et luttes de classe: 1789–1914.* Vol. I of 2 vols. Lyon, 1967.

Brécy, Robert. *La Grève générale en France.* Paris, 1969.

Broué, Pierre, ed. *Léon Trotsky: Le Mouvement communiste en France (1919–1939).* Paris, 1967.

Brown, Roger Glenn. *Fashoda Reconsidered: The Impact of Domestic Politics on French Policy in Africa, 1893–1898.* Baltimore, 1970.

Brupbacher, Fritz. *Socialisme et Liberté.* Neuchatel, 1955.

Challaye, Félicien. *Syndicalisme révolutionnaire et Syndicalisme réformiste.* Paris, 1909.

Chambelland, Colette, and Jean Maitron, eds. *Syndicalisme révolutionnaire et communisme. Les Archives de Pierre Monatte, 1914–1924.* Paris, 1968.

Coornaert, Emile. *Les Compagnonnages de France.* Paris, 1966.

Crook, Wilfrid Harris. *The General Strike: A Study of Labor's Tragic Weapon in Theory and Practice.* Chapel Hill, N.C., 1931.

Dangerfield, George. *The Strange Death of Liberal England, 1910–1914.* 4th ed. New York, 1961.

Deffontaines, Pierre. *Les Hommes et leurs travaux dans les pays de la moyenne Garonne (Agénais, Bas-Quercy).* Lille, 1932.

Dolléans, Edouard. *Histoire du mouvement ouvrier: 1871–1936.* Vol. II of 2 vols. Paris, 1939.

Dommanget, Maurice. *La Chevalerie du travail française, 1893–1911.* Paris, 1967.

———. *Edouard Vaillant, un grand socialiste, 1840–1915.* Paris, 1956.

———. *Histoire du premier mai.* Paris, 1972.

Dret, Henri. *La Chaussure.* Paris, 1927.

Dubief, Henri, ed. *Le Syndicalisme révolutionnaire. Textes choisis.* Paris, 1969.

Dumoulin, Georges. *Carnets de route (Quarante années de vie militante).* Lille, n.d. [1938].

———. *Les Syndicalistes français et la Guerre.* Paris, 1918.

Duveau, Georges. *La Vie ouvrière en France sous le Second Empire.* 7th ed. Paris, 1946.

Farrar, Marjorie Millbank. *Principled Pragmatist: The Political Career of Alexandre Millerand.* Oxford, 1990.

Gankin, Olga Hess, and H. H. Fisher. *The Bolsheviks and the World War: The Origin of the Third Internationale.* Stanford, 1940.

Gaudeaux, Jean. *Six Mois en Russie bolchéviste. Documents inédits.* Paris, 1924.

Geary, Dick, ed. *Labour and Socialist Movements in Europe Before 1914.* Oxford, 1989.

Georges, Bernard, Denise Tintant, and Marie-Anne Renauld. *Léon Jouhaux, Cinquante ans du syndicalisme: Des Origines à 1921.* Vol. I of 2 vols. Paris, 1962.

Goldberg, Harvey. *The Life of Jean Jaurès.* Madison, Wisc., 1962.

Goustine, Christian de. *Pouget: Les Matins noirs du syndicalisme.* Paris, 1972.

Gras, Christian. *Alfred Rosmer (1877–1964) et le Mouvement révolutionnaire internationale.* Paris, 1971.

Guillaume, Pierre. *La Population de Bordeaux au XIXe siècle: Essai d'histoire sociale.* Paris, 1972.

Hagnauer, Roger. *L'Actualité de la Charte d'Amiens.* Paris, 1956.

Halévy, Daniel. *Essais sur le mouvement ouvrier en France.* Paris, 1901.

Hampson, Norman. *A Social History of the French Revolution.* Toronto, 1966.

Haupt, Georges, ed. *Bureau socialiste international, comptes rendus des réunions, manifestes et circulaires (1900–1907).* Vol. I of 2 vols. Paris, 1969.

Haupt, Georges, and Jean-Jacques Marie, eds. *Les Bolchéviks par eux-memes.* Paris, 1969.

Howorth, Jolyon. *Edouard Vaillant: La Création de l'unité socialiste en France: La Politique de l'action totale.* Paris, 1982.

Jellinek, Frank. *The Paris Commune of 1871.* 2nd ed. New York, 1965.

Jennings, Jeremy R. *Georges Sorel: The Character and Development of His Thought.* New York, 1985.

———. *Syndicalism in France: A Study of Ideas.* New York, 1990.

Joll, James. *The Second International, 1889–1914.* New York, 1966.

Julliard, Jacques. *Clemenceau briseur de grèves: L'Affaire de Draveil Villeneuve-Saint-Georges 1908.* Paris, 1965.

———. *Fernand Pelloutier et les origines du syndicalisme d'action directe.* Paris, 1971.

Kaplan, Steven Laurence, and Cynthia J. Koepp, eds. *Work in France: Representations, Meaning, Organization, and Practice.* Ithaca, N.Y., 1986.

Kriegel, Annie. *Aux origines du communisme français 1914–1920: Une Contribution à l'histoire du mouvement ouvrier français.* Vol. I of 2 vols. Paris, 1964.

Kriegel, Annie, and Jean-Jacques Becker. *1914: La Guerre et le mouvement ouvrier français.* Paris, 1964.

Kuczynski, Jürgen. *A Short History of Labour Conditions in France, 1700 to the Present Day.* London, 1946.

Labi, Maurice. *La Grande Division des travailleurs, première scission de la C.G.T., 1914–1921.* Paris, 1964.

Lazitch, Branko, and Milorad M. Drachkovitch, eds. *Lenin and the Comintern.* Vol. I of 2 vols. Stanford, 1972.

Lefranc, Georges. *Histoire du mouvement syndical français.* Paris, 1937.

———. *Le Mouvement socialiste sous la Troisième République (1875–1940).* Paris, 1963.

———. *Le Mouvement syndical sous la Troisième République.* Paris, 1967.

Lequin, Yves. *Les Ouvriers de la région lyonnaise (1848–1914).* 2 vols. Lyon, 1977.

Leroy, Maxime. *La Coutume ouvrière, syndicats, Bourses du Travail, Fédérations professionnelles, coopératives. Doctrines et institutions.* 2 vols. Paris, 1913.

Lindemann, Albert S. *The 'Red Years': European Socialism Versus Bolshevism, 1919–1921.* Berkeley, 1974.

Linder, Marc. *European Labor Aristocracies: Trade Unionism, the Hierarchy of Skill, and the Stratification of the Manual Working Class Before the First World War.* Frankfurt, 1985.

Lorwin, Lewis Levitski. *The Labor Movement in France.* New York, 1912.

Lorwin, Val R. *The French Labor Movement.* Cambridge, Mass., 1954.

Louis, Paul. *Histoire du mouvement syndical en France: De 1789 à 1918.* Vol. I of 2 vols. Paris, 1947.

————. *Le Syndicalisme français d'Amiens à Saint-Étienne (1906–1922).* Paris, 1924.

Maier, Charles S. *Recasting Bourgeois Europe: Stabilization in France, Germany, and Italy in the Decade After World War I.* Princeton, 1975.

Maitron, Jean. *Le Mouvement anarchiste en France: De 1914 à nos jours.* Vol. II of 2 vols. Paris, 1975.

————. *Le Syndicalisme révolutionnaire: Paul Delesalle.* Paris, 1952.

Maitron, Jean, ed. *1906: Le Congrès de la Charte d'Amiens: 9ᵉ Congrès de la C.G.T.— 8–14 octobre 1906.* Paris, 1983.

Marty-Rollan, Eugène-Jules. *Comment fut elaboré de la Charte d'Amiens.* Paris, 1933.

Maunoury, Henry. *Police de guerre.* Paris, 1937.

May, André. *Les Origines du syndicalisme révolutionnaire: Evolution des tendances du mouvement ouvrier (1871–1906).* Paris, 1913.

Mayer, Arno J. *Political Origins of the New Diplomacy, 1917–1918.* New Haven, 1959.

Mazgaj, Paul. *The Action Française and Revolutionary Syndicalism.* Chapel Hill, N.C., 1979.

Michon, Georges. *La Préparation à la guerre, la loi de trois ans, 1910–1914.* Paris, 1935.

Milner, Susan. *The Dilemmas of Internationalism: French Syndicalism and the International Labour Movement, 1900–1914.* Oxford, 1990.

Mitchell, Allan. *The Divided Path: The German Influence on Social Reform in France After 1870.* Chapel Hill, N.C., 1991.

Mitchell, Barbara. *The Practical Revolutionaries: A New Interpretation of the French Anarchosyndicalists.* Westport, Conn., 1987.

Monatte, Pierre. *Trois Scissions syndicales.* Paris, 1958.

Montgomery, David. *The Fall of the House of Labor: The Workplace, the State, and American Labor Activism, 1865–1925.* Cambridge, Engl., 1987.

Montreuil, Jean [Georges Lefranc]. *Histoire du mouvement ouvrier en France: Des origines à nos jours.* Paris, 1946.

Moss, Bernard H. *The Origins of the French Labor Movement, 1830–1914: The Socialism of Skilled Workers.* Berkeley, 1976.

Noland, Aaron. *The Founding of the French Socialist Party (1893–1905).* Cambridge, Mass., 1956.

Oved, Georges. *La Gauche française et le Nationalisme marocain, 1905–1955.* Vol. I of 2 vols. Paris, 1984.

Papayanis, Nicholas. *Alphonse Merrheim: The Emergence of Reformism in Syndicalism, 1871–1925.* Dordrecht, 1985.

Pelling, Henry. *A History of British Trade Unionism.* Harmondsworth, Engl., 1963.

Pelloutier, Fernand. *Histoire des Bourses du Travail: Origine–Institutions–Avenir.* Paris, 1902.

Pelloutier, Fernand, and Maurice Pelloutier. *La Vie ouvrière en France.* Paris, 1900.

Pipkin, Charles W. *Social Politics and Modern Democracies.* Vol. II of 2 vols. New York, 1931.

Rancière, Jacques. *La Nuit des prolétaires.* Paris, 1981.

Reddy, William M. *The Rise of Market Culture: The Textile Trade and French Society, 1750–1900.* Cambridge, Engl., 1984.

Reinach, Joseph. *Histoire de l'Affaire Dreyfus.* 7 vols. Paris, 1901.

Ridley, F. F. *Revolutionary Syndicalism in France: The Direct Action of Its Time.* Cambridge, Engl., 1970.

Rosmer, Alfred. *Moscow Under Lenin.* Translated by Ian H. Birchall. New York, 1971.

———, ed. *Le Mouvement ouvrier pendant la première guerre mondiale.* Vol. I: *De l'Union sacrée à Zimmerwald.* Paris, 1936. Vol. II: *De Zimmerwald à la Révolution russe.* Paris, 1959.

Rudé, George. *The Crowd in History, 1730–1848.* New York, 1964.

Schorske, Carl. *German Social Democracy, 1905–1917: The Development of the Great Schism.* New York, 1965.

Scott, Joan Wallach. *The Glassworkers of Carmaux: French Craftsmen and Political Action in a Nineteenth Century City.* Cambridge, Mass., 1974.

Seilhac, Léon de. *Syndicats ouvriers, Fédérations, Bourses du Travail.* Paris, 1902.

Séverac, Jean-Baptiste. *Le Mouvement syndical.* Vol. IV of A.C.A. Compère-Morel, ed., *Encyclopédie socialiste, syndicaliste et coopérative de l'Internationale Ouvrière.* Paris, 1913.

Shorter, Edward, and Charles Tilly. *Strikes in France, 1830–1968.* Cambridge, Engl., 1974.

Sieburg, Heinz-Otto. *Die Grubenkatastrophe von Courrières 1906: Ein Beitrag zur Sozialgeschichte der 3. Republik und zum deutsch-franzosischen Verhaltnis an der Jahrhundertwende.* Wiesbaden, 1967.

Sorel, Georges. *Lettres à Paul Delesalle (1914–1921).* Paris, 1947.

Sorlin, Pierre. *Waldeck-Rousseau.* Paris, 1966.

Stearns, Peter N. *Revolutionary Syndicalism and French Labor: A Cause Without Rebels.* New Brunswick, N.J., 1971.

Sternhell, Zeev. *La Droite révolutionnaire, 1885–1914: Les Origines françaises du fascisme.* Paris, 1978.

———. *Neither Right nor Left: Fascist Ideology in France.* Translated by David Maisel. Berkeley, 1986.

Stone, Judith F. *The Search for Social Peace: Reform Legislation in France, 1890–1914.* Albany, N.Y., 1985.

Terrail, Gabriel [Mermeix]. *Le Syndicalisme contre le Socialisme: Origine et développement de la Confédération générale du travail.* Paris, 1907.

Thompson, E. P. *The Making of the English Working Class.* London, 1963.

Watson, David Robin. *Georges Clemenceau, A Political Biography.* New York, 1976.

Weill, Georges. *Histoire du mouvement social en France, 1852–1910.* 2nd ed. Paris, 1911.

Willard, Claude. *Le Mouvement socialiste en France (1893–1905): Les Guesdistes.* Paris, 1965.

Williams, Gwynn. *Artisans & Sans-Culottes: Popular Movements in France and England During the French Revolution.* New York, 1967.

Wohl, Robert. *French Communism in the Making, 1914–1924.* Stanford, 1966.

Wormser, Georges. *La République de Clemenceau.* Paris, 1961.

Wright, Gordon. *France in Modern Times: From the Enlightenment to the Present.* 3rd ed. New York, 1981.

Essays in Collections

Dumoulin, Georges. "Les Syndicalistes français et la Guerre." In *Le Mouvement ouvrier pendant la première guerre mondiale: De l'Union sacrée à Zimmerwald,* edited by Alfred Rosmer. Vol. I of 2 vols. Paris, 1936.

Geary, Dick. "Socialism and the German Labour Movement Before 1914." In *Labour and Socialist Movements in Europe Before 1914,* edited by Dick Geary. Oxford, 1989.

Green, Nancy L. "The Contradictions of Acculturation: Immigrant Oratories and Yiddish Union Sections in Paris Before World War I." In *The Jews in Modern France,* edited by Frances Malino and Bernard Wasserstein. Hanover and London, 1985.

Kriegel, Annie. "Vie et Mort de la Ire Internationale." In *Le Pain et les Roses: Jalons pour une histoire du socialisme,* edited by Annie Kriegel. Paris, 1968.

Moissonnier, Maurice. "Le Syndicalisme français à l'heure du Congrès d'Amiens." In *1906: Le Congrès de la Charte d'Amiens,* edited by Jean Maitron. Paris, 1983.

Rancière, Jacques. "The Myth of the Artisan: Critical Reflections on a Category of Social History." In *Work in France: Representations, Meaning, Organization, and Practice,* edited by Steven Lawrence Kaplan and Cynthia J. Koepp. Ithaca, N.Y., 1986.

Raymond, Justinien. "Un Tragique Épisode du mouvement ouvrier à Cluses (Haute Savoie) en 1904." In *Mélanges d'histoire sociale offerts à Jean Maitron.* Paris, 1976.

Watson, David Robin. "The Nationalist Movement in Paris, 1900–1906." In *The Right in France, 1890–1919,* edited by David Shapiro. London, 1962.

Willard, Germaine. "La Charte d'Amiens et les rapports entre syndicats et partis politiques." In *1906: Le Congrès de la Charte d'Amiens,* edited by Jean Maitron. Paris, 1983.

Winock, Michel. "Robert Michels et la démocratie allemaniste." In *Mélanges d'histoire sociale offerts à Jean Maitron.* Paris, 1976.

Periodical and Newspaper Articles

Abhervé, Bertrand. "Les Origines de la grève des métallurgistes parisiens, juin 1919." *Le Mouvement social,* No. 93 (1975), 75–85.

Ader, Paul. "La Crise viticole et la Classe ouvrière." *Le Mouvement socialiste,* No. 193 (1907), 434–47.

Airelle, Georges. "Les Evénements de Raon-L'Etape." *Le Mouvement socialiste,* No. 194 (January 15, 1908), 14–33.

Basly, Emile. "Au pilori." *Le Reveil du Nord,* December 8, 1906.

Becker, Jean-Jacques, and Annie Kriegel. "Les Inscrits au 'Carnet B.'" *Le Mouvement social,* No. 65 (1968), 109–21.

Besnard, Pierre. "Pourquoi y eut-il le pacte? Son histoire." *Le Journal du Peuple,* July 23, 1922.

Bouvier, Jean. "Mouvement ouvrier et conjunctures économiques." *Le Mouvement social,* No. 48 (1964), 1–30.

Briquet, Raoul. "La Grève générale des mineurs." *Le Mouvement socialiste,* No. 114 (1903), 171–92.

Chambelland, Colette. "Autour du premier congrès de l'Internationale syndicale rouge." *Le Mouvement social,* No. 47 (1964), 31–44.

Delesalle, Paul. "Le Congrès [de Bourges] et l'Opinion ouvrière." *Le Mouvement socialiste,* No. 142 (1904), 72–75.

Dret, Henri. "Enquete ouvrière sur la crise de l'apprentissage: Les Cuirs et Peaux." *Le Mouvement socialiste,* No. 197 (1908), 246–52.

Dumoulin, Georges. "La Fédération des mineurs." *Le Mouvement socialiste,* No. 203 (October 15, 1908), 242–57.

Dunois, Amédée. "Une Conversation sur la motion d'Amiens avec l'ançien bureau confédéral." *L'Humanité,* September 23, 1920.

Fink, Leon. "'Intellectuals' vs. 'Workers': Academic Requirements and the Creation of Labor History." *American Historical Review,* XCVI (April, 1991), 395–421.

Flonneau, Jean-Marie. "Crise de vie chère et mouvement syndical, 1910–1914." *Le Mouvement social,* No. 72 (1970), 49–81.

Gabion, Marius. "Les Grèves du Nord." *Le Temps,* October 14, 16, 1903.

Germinario, Francesco. "Due Lettere autobiografiche di Giorgio Sorel ad Agostino Lanzillo." *Studi Piacentini,* No. 15 (1994), 171–84.

Gras, Christian. "La Fédération des Métaux en 1913–1914 et l'évolution du syndicalisme révolutionnaire français." *Le Mouvement social,* No. 77 (1971), 85–111.

Guérard, Eugène. "Les Conseils du travail." *La Voix du Peuple,* December 23–30, 1900.

Howorth, Jolyon. "French Workers and German Workers: The Impossibility of Internationalism, 1900–1914." *European History Quarterly,* XV (1985), 71–97.

Humbert-Droz, Jules. "Syndicalistes et Communistes en France." *Bulletin communiste,* January 26, 1922.

"In Memoriam: Maxime Leroy." *Le Contrat social,* I (1957), 279.

Jouhaux, Léon. "Le Prolétariat et la Guerre. Une des raisons de notre attitude." *La Bataille syndicaliste,* September 26, 1914.

Julliard, Jacques. "Jeune et Vieux Syndicat chez les mineurs du Pas-de-Calais (à travers les papiers de Pierre Monatte)." *Le Mouvement social,* No. 47 (1964), 7–30.

————. "Fernand Pelloutier." *Le Mouvement social,* No. 75 (1971), 1–19.

Keufer, Auguste. "Le Syndicalisme réformiste." *Le Mouvement socialiste,* No. 146 (January 1, 1905).

Kriegel, Annie. "Jaurès en juillet 1914." *Le Mouvement social,* No. 49 (1964), 63–81.

Levy, Albert. "Syndicalisme et Anticléricalisme." *Le Mouvement socialiste,* Nos. 189–90 (August 15–September 15, 1907), 166–69.

Lhomme, Jean. "Le Pouvoir d'achat de l'ouvrier français au cours d'un siècle." *Le Mouvement social,* No. 66 (1968), 48–63.

Longuet, Jean. "Alliance communiste révolutionnaire." *L'Encyclopédie du mouvement syndicaliste,* No. 1 (January, 1912), III.

Louzon, Robert. "La Faillite du Dreyfusisme ou le Triomphe du parti juif." *Le Mouvement socialiste,* No. 176 (July, 1906), 193–99.

Maitron, Jean. "La Personnalité du militant ouvrier français dans la seconde moitié du XIXe siècle." *Le Mouvement social,* No. 33 (1961), 67–86.

————. "Le Groupe des étudiants E.S.R.I. (1892–1902): Contribution à la connaissance des origines du syndicalisme révolutionnaire." *Le Mouvement social,* No. 46 (1964), 3–26.

Marty-Rollan, Eugène-Jules. "Exposé historique sur la Charte d'Amiens." *La Voix du Peuple,* n.s., No. 158, November 1933, 854–61.

Merrheim, Alphonse. Response to the "Enquete" on "La Crise syndicaliste." *Le Mouvement socialiste,* No. 126 (November–December, 1909), 295.

Michels, Robert. "La Grève générale des mineurs de la Ruhr." *Le Mouvement socialiste,* No. 152 (April 1, 1905), 481–89.

————. "Le Congrès syndical de Cologne." *Le Mouvement socialiste,* No. 158 (July 1, 1905), 313–21.

Monatte, Pierre. "Alphonse Merrheim." *La Révolution prolétarienne,* No. 11 (1925), 11–12.

————. "Souvenirs [sur le Congrès d'Amiens]." *L'Actualité d'Histoire,* No. 16 (1956), 6–19.

————. "Le Syndicalisme est-il mort à Saint-Etienne?" *Clarté,* Nos. 18, 21 (July 15, September 1, 1922), 399–415; 468–71.

Papayanis, Nicholas. "Alphonse Merrheim and the Strike of Hennebont: The Struggle for the Eight-Hour Day in France." *International Review of Social History,* XVI (1971), 159–83.

————. "Masses révolutionnaires et Directions réformistes: Les Tensions au cours des grèves métallurgistes français en 1919." *Le Mouvement social,* No. 93 (1975), 51–73.

Pouget, Emile. "L'Etranglement de grèves." *La Voix du Peuple,* No. 16, January 6, March 17–24, 1901.

Ratreau, Jules. "La Grève du Creusot." *L'Echo de Paris,* September 29, 1899.

Reid, Donald. "Guillaume Verdier et le Syndicalisme révolutionnaire aux usines de Decazeville (1917–1920)." *Annales du Midi,* No. 166 (1984), 171–98.

Renauld, M.-A. "Documents: Mémoires de Léon Jouhaux." *Le Mouvement social,* No. 47 (1964), 81–109.

Rosmer, Alfred. "Le Petite Franc-maconnerie." *La Lutte des classes,* No. 4 (June 20, 1922), 7–8.

Rougérie, Jacques. "L'A.I.T. et le Mouvement ouvrier à Paris pendant les événements de 1870–1871." *International Review of Social History,* XVII, Parts 1–2 (1972), 3–103.

Roure, R. "Une Conférence de M. Victor Griffuelhes, ançien secrétaire de la CGT." *L'Information ouvrière et sociale,* February 8, 1920.

Seilhac, Léon de. "Les Grèves dans l'Industrie Textile—dans le Nord (en 1903)." *La Quinzaine,* September 16, 1904, 264–65.

Silberner, Edmund. "Anti-Jewish Trends in French Revolutionary Syndicalism." *Jewish Social Studies,* XV (1953), 195–202.

Spitzer, Alan B. "Anarchy and Culture: Fernand Pelloutier and the Dilemma of Revolutionary Syndicalism." *International Review of Social History,* VIII (1963), 379–88.

Trempé, Rolande. "Le Réformisme des mineurs français à la fin du XIXᵉ siècle." *Le Mouvement social,* No. 65 (1968), 93–107.

Umbreit, Paul. "Des faits!" *La Revue syndicaliste,* November 15, 1905.

Vergéat, Marcel. "Soviets et Syndicats: La Conférence de Griffuelhes." *La Vie Ouvrière,* 2nd ser., February 13, 1920.

Vuilleumier, Marc. "La Russie en 1921–1922 et l'Internationale: Lettres de Fritz Brupbacher à Pierre Monatte." *Documents sur l'histoire du mouvement ouvrier en Suisse,* No. 1 (April, 1970).

———. "Notes sur James Guillaume, historien de la Première Internationale et ses rapports avec Max Nettlau et Jean Jaurès." *Cahiers Vilfredo Pareto,* VII–VIII (1965), 81–109.

———. "Quelques documents sur les conférences de Jaurès en Suisse (1907)." *Bulletin de la Société d'Etudes Jaurésiennes,* No. 18, pt. 2 (1965).

Willard, Claude. "La Connaissance de la révolution russe et de l'expérience soviétique par le mouvement ouvrier français en 1918–1919." *Cahiers d'histoire de l'Institut Maurice Thorez,* Nos. 12–13 (1975), 318–30.

Yvetot, Georges. Response to the "Enquete on "La Crise syndicaliste." *Le Mouvement socialiste,* No. 217 (January, 1910).

Theses and Unpublished Manuscripts

Besançon, Alain. "Le Mouvement syndical des mineurs du Nord et du Pas-de-Calais (1884–1914)." Diplome d'études supérieures, Université de Paris, 1954.

Binstock, Allan. "The Shoemakers of Fougères: A Study of the Development of the

Shoe Industry in the City of Fougères (Brittany, Department of the Ille-et-Vilaine)." Ph.D. dissertation, University of Wisconsin-Madison, 1972.

Blume, Daniel. "Recherches sur le syndicalisme ouvrier dans le Batiment à Paris (1892–1906)." Diplome d'études supérieures, Université de Paris, 1957.

Ceplair, Larry Stuart. "Roster of the CSRs." Typescript, Department of History, University of Wisconsin-Madison, 1970. Photocopy.

Marchal, Arlette. "Le Mouvement blanquiste (1871–1905)." Diplome d'études supérieures, Université de Paris, 1949.

McMechan, William Edgar. "The Building Trades of France, 1907–1914: An Exploration of Revolutionary Syndicalism." Ph.D. dissertation, University of Wisconsin-Madison, 1975.

Nord, Philip G. "Victor Griffuelhes and the Development of the CGT, 1901–1909." M.A. essay, Columbia University, 1976.

Poujade, Maurice. "Les Allemanistes à Paris (1890–1905)." Diplome d'études supérieures, Université de Paris, 1958.

Vandervort, Bruce. "The Early Political Career of Pierre Laval (1883–1927)." M.A. thesis, University of Cincinnati, 1966.

INDEX